IBERIAN AND LATIN AMERICAN STUDIES

Golden Age Drama in Contemporary Spain

Series Editors
Professor David George (Swansea University)
Professor Paul Garner (University of Leeds)

Editorial Board
David Frier (University of Leeds)
Lisa Shaw (University of Liverpool)
Gareth Walters (Swansea University)
Rob Stone (Swansea University)
David Gies (University of Virginia)
Catherine Davies (University of Nottingham)
Richard Cleminson (University of Leeds)

IBERIAN AND LATIN AMERICAN STUDIES

Golden Age Drama in Contemporary Spain

The Comedia *on Page, Stage and Screen*

DUNCAN WHEELER

UNIVERSITY OF WALES PRESS
CARDIFF
2012

© Duncan Wheeler, 2012

All rights reserved. No part of this book may be reproduced in any material form (including photocopying or storing it in any medium by electronic means and whether or not transiently or incidentally to some other use of this publication) without the written permission of the copyright owner except in accordance with the provisions of the Copyright, Designs and Patents Act 1988. Applications for the copyright owner's written permission to reproduce any part of this publication should be addressed to The University of Wales Press, 10 Columbus Walk, Brigantine Place, Cardiff CF10 4UP.

www.uwp.co.uk

British Library CIP
A catalogue record for this book is available from the British Library.

ISBN   978–0–7083–2474–5 (paperback)
          978–0–7083–2473–8 (hardback)
e-ISBN 978–0–7083–2475–2

The right of Duncan Wheeler to be identified as author of this work has been asserted in accordance with sections 77, 78 and 79 of the Copyright, Designs and Patents Act 1988.

Typeset by Columns Design XML Limited, Reading
Printed by CPI Antony Rowe, Chippenham, Wiltshire

Contents

Series Editors' Foreword	vii
List of Illustrations	ix
Translations of Play Titles	xi
List of Abbreviations	xv
Acknowledgements	xvii
Introduction	1
Chapter 1: The performance history of Golden Age drama in Spain (1939–2009)	17
Chapter 2: An (early) modern classic: *Fuente Ovejuna* in contemporary Spain	75
Chapter 3: Resurrecting lost traditions? Calderón's wife-murder plays and the CNTC	105
Chapter 4: Cinema and Golden Age drama: the *comedia* goes to the movies	135
Chapter 5: Locating Spanish classical drama in (inter)national contexts: Almagro, the CNTC and the RSC	189
Conclusion	217
Notes	221
Works Cited	245
Index	285

Series Editors' Foreword

Over recent decades the traditional 'languages and literatures' model in Spanish departments in universities in the United Kingdom has been superceded by a contextual, interdisciplinary and 'area studies' approach to the study of the culture, history, society and politics of the Hispanic and Lusophone worlds – categories that extend far beyond the confines of the Iberian Peninsula, not only in Latin America but also to Spanish-speaking and Lusophone Africa.

In response to these dynamic trends in research priorities and curriculum development, this series is designed to present both disciplinary and interdisciplinary research within the general field of Iberian and Latin American Studies, particularly studies that explore all aspects of cultural production (inter alia literature, film, music, dance, sport) in Spanish, Portuguese, Basque, Catalan, Galician and indigenous languages of Latin America. The series also aims to publish research in the History and Politics of the Hispanic and Lusophone worlds, at the level of both the region and the nation-state, as well as on Cultural Studies that explore the shifting terrains of gender, sexual, racial and postcolonial identities in those same regions.

List of Illustrations

Front Cover:	Still from film of *La dama boba* (Manuel Iborra, 2006). Courtesy of DeA Planeta.	
Figure 1:	Photograph of *Marta la piadosa* (dir. Alberto González Vergel, 1975), Teatro Español. Courtesy of the Museo Nacional del Teatro, Almagro.	44
Figure 2:	Photograph by Ros Ribas of *El vergonzoso en palacio* (dir. Adolfo Marsillach, 1989), CNTC. Courtesy of the CNTC.	59
Figure 3:	Photograph by Agustín Espinel of *Los balcones de Madrid* (dir. Ángel Gutiérrez, 2007), Teatro de Cámara Chejov. Courtesy of the Teatro de Cámara Chejov.	71
Figure 4:	Sketch for *Fuente Ovejuna* (1965) by José Caballero. Courtesy of the Museo Nacional del Teatro, Almagro.	91
Figure 5:	Photograph of *Fuente Ovejuna* (dir. Emilio Hernández, 1999), CAT. Courtesy of the CAT.	96
Figure 6:	Photograph by Ros Ribas of *El médico de su honra* (dir. Adolfo Marsillach, 1986), CNTC. Courtesy of the CNTC.	110
Figure 7:	Photograph by Chicho of *El pintor de su deshonra* (dir. Eduardo Vasco, 2008), CNTC. Courtesy of the CNTC.	127
Figure 8:	Photograph by Chicho of *El pintor de su deshonra* (dir. Eduardo Vasco, 2008), CNTC. Courtesy of the CNTC.	128
Figure 9:	Still from film of *El alcalde de Zalamea* (José G. Maesso, 1954). Courtesy of Video Mercury.	150
Figure 10:	Still from film of *El príncipe encadenado* [*The Prince in Chains*] (Luis Lucia, 1960). Courtesy of Video Mercury.	155
Figure 11:	Backstage still from *La dama boba* (Manuel Iborra, 2006). Courtesy of DeA Planeta.	180
Figure 12:	Photograph by Ros Ribas of *La vida es sueño* (dir. Calixto Bieito, 2000), CNTC and Teatre Romea. Courtesy of the CNTC.	203
Figure 13:	Photograph by Nicolas Trémouilhe of Pavón Theatre. Courtesy of Nicolas Trémouilhe.	206

Translations of Play Titles

A secreto agravio, secreta venganza [*Secret Vengeance for Secret Offense*]
Abre el ojo [*Open your Eye*]
Absalón [*Absalom*]
El acero de Madrid [*The Steel-Water of Madrid*]
El alcalde de Zalamea [*The Mayor of Zalamea*]
Amar después de la muerte [*Love After Death*]
Antes que todo es mi dama [*My Lady First of All*]
El anzuelo de Fenisa [*Fenisa's Bait*]
Ardor con ardor se apaga [*Ardour Extinguishes Ardour*]
El arrogante español [*The Arrogant Spaniard*]
Arte nuevo de hacer comedias [*New Art of Making Plays*]
Asalto a una ciudad [*Assault on a City*]
El astrólogo fingido [*The Fake Astrologer*]
Bajarse al moro [*Going Down to Marrakesh*]
Los balcones de Madrid [*The Balconies of Madrid*]
La bella aurora [*The Fair Aurora*]
La bella malmaridada [*The Mismarried Beauty*]
Las bizarrías de Belisa [*The Gallantries of Belisa*]
El burlador de Sevilla [*The Trickster of Seville*]
El caballero de milagro [*The Knight of the Miracle*]
El caballero de Olmedo [*The Knight from Olmedo*]
Calderón enamorado [*Calderón in Love*]
Casa con dos puertas mala es de guardar [*A House with Two Doors is Difficult to Guard*]
El casamiento engañoso [*The Deceitful Marriage*]
Castelvines y Monteses [*The Capulets and Montagues*]
El castigo sin venganza [*Punishment without Revenge*]
Céfiro agreste de olímpicos embates [*A Zephry Toughened by Olympic Battle*]
La cena del rey Baltasar [*Belshazzar's Feast*]
La cisma de Inglaterra [*The Schism in England*]
Los comendadores de Córdoba [*The Knight Commanders of Córdoba*]
Con quien vengo, vengo [*I Will Come with Whoever Comes with Me*]
El condenado por desconfiado [*Damned for Despair*]
La cueva de Salamanca [*The Salamanca Cave*]
La dama de Alejandría [*The Lady from Alexandria*]

La dama boba [*Lady Nitwit*]
La dama duende [*The Phantom Lady*]
La dama del Olivar [*The Lady of the Olive Grove*]
Dar tiempo al tiempo [*Give Time the Time It Takes*]
¿De cuándo acá nos vino? [*When did this Befall us?*]
Desde Toledo a Madrid [*From Toledo to Madrid*]
El desdén con el desdén [*Disdain with Disdain*]
La desdichada Estefanía [*Unfortunate Stephanie*]
El despertar a quien duerme [*To Wake he who Sleeps*]
La devoción de la cruz [*Devotion to the Cross*]
La discreta enamorada [*The Clever Girl in Love*]
Don Gil de las calzas verdes [*Don Gil of the Green Breeches*]
Ello dirá [*That Will Tell*]
Los embustes de Celauro [*Celauro's Tricks*]
Los encantos de la culpa [*The Sorceries of Sin*]
La Estrella de Sevilla [*The Star of Seville*]
Farsa del triunfo del Sacramental [*The Farce of the Sacramental Triumph*]
Las ferias de Madrid [*The Fairs of Madrid*]
La fianza satisfecha [*A Bond Honoured*]
La fiera, el rayo y la piedra [*The Fierce, the Ray and the Rock*]
Fiesta barroca [*Baroque Festivities*]
Fuente Ovejuna [*The Sheep Well*]
La fuerza lastimosa [*The Pitiful Force*]
El galán fantasma [*The Phantom Suitor*]
El gran mercado del mundo [*The Great Market of the World*]
El gran teatro del mundo [*The Great Theatre of the World*]
Los guanches de Tenerife y conquista de Canarias [*The Guanches from Tenerife and the Conquest of the Canary Islands*]
La hidalga del valle [*The Noblewoman of the Valley*]
El hijo pródigo [*The Prodigal Son*]
La hija del aire [*The Daughter of the Air*]
El honroso atrevimiento [*The Honourable Audacity*]
El hospital de los locos [*The Madman's Hospital*]
El jardín de Falerina [*Falerina's Garden*]
El José de las mujeres [*The Female Joseph*]
El lindo don Diego [*The Handsome Don Diego*]
Los locos de Valencia [*Madness in Valencia*]
Lope de Vega a capa y espada [*A Cloak and Dagger Lope de Vega*]
El maestro de danzar [*The Dancing Master*]
El mágico prodigioso [*The Prodigious Magician*]
La malcasada [*The Unhappy Bride*]
Las manos blancas no ofenden [*White Hands do not Offend*]
Mañanas de abril y mayo [*April and May Mornings*]

Marta la piadosa [*Pious Martha*]
El mayor hechizo, amor [*Love, the Greatest Enchantment*]
El médico de su honra [*The Physician of his Honour*]
El mejor alcalde, el rey [*The Best Mayor, the King*]
Mejor está que estaba [*Tis Better Than it Was*]
El mejor mozo de España [*The Best Boy in Spain*]
El monstruo de los jardines [*The Monster of the Gardens*]
La moza de cántaro [*The Girl with a Pitcher*]
La mujer por fuerza [*Woman against her Will*]
No hay burlas con el amor [*Love is No Laughing Matter*]
No hay burlas con Calderón [*Calderón is No Laughing Matter*]
No son todos ruiseñores [*They're Not All Nightingales*]
La noche de San Juan [*St John's Eve*]
La noche toledana [*The Toledan Night*]
El nuevo mundo [*The New World*]
Pastores de Belén [*The Shepherds of Bethlehem*]
Peribáñez y el Comendador de Ocaña [*Peribáñez and the Commander of Ocaña*]
El perro del hortelano [*The Dog in the Manger*]
El pintor de su deshonra [*The Painter of his Dishonour*]
El pleito matrimonial del cuerpo y el alma [*Matrimonial Dispute Between the Body and Soul*]
Por la puente, Juana [*Take the Bridge, Juana*]
Porfiar hasta morir [*Persistence until Death*]
El príncipe constante [*The Constant Prince*]
La prudencia en la mujer [*Prudence in Women*]
La prudente venganza [*Prudent Vengeance*]
El retablo de las maravillas [*The Marvellous Puppet Show*]
El rufián castrucho [*Castrucho, the Hustler*]
Sainetes [*Short Comic Urban Plays*]
El secreto a voces [*The Noisy Secret*]
Sentido del deber [*Sense of Duty*]
Los siete infantes de Lara [*The Seven Princes of Lara*]
Tragicomedia de don Duardos [*The Tragicomic Tale of don Duardos*]
La vengadora de las mujeres [*The Avenger of Her Sex*]
La venganza de Tamar [*Tamar's Vengeance*]
La verdad sospechosa [*The Suspect Truth*]
El vergonzoso en palacio [*The Bashful Man in the Palace*]
La vida es sueño [*Life is a Dream*]
El villano en su rincón [*The Peasant in his Corner*]
La villana de Getafe [*The Peasant Woman from Getafe*]
La viuda valenciana [*The Valencian Widow*]
La zapatera prodigiosa [*The Shoemaker's Wonderful Wife*]

List of Abbreviations

Institutions and Organisations

ADE – Asociación de Directores de Escena [Association of Stage Directors]
AHGBI – Association of Hispanists of Great Britain and Ireland
AHRC – Arts and Humanities Research Council
BFI – British Film Institute
CAT – Centro Andaluz de Teatro [Andalusian Theatre Centre]
CDN – Centro Dramático Nacional [National Centre for Dramatic Arts]
CDT – Centro de Documentación Teatral [Theatrical Documentation Centre]
CIFESA – Compañía Industrial Film Española [Industrial Company of Spanish Film]
CiU – Convergència i Unió [Convergence and Union]
CNNTE – Centro Nacional de Nuevas Tendencias Escénicas [National Centre for New Stage Tendencies]
CNTC – Compañía Nacional de Teatro Clásico [National Classical Theatre Company]
ETC – Escuela de Teatro Clásico [Classical Theatre School]
INAEM – Instituto Nacional de las Artes Escénicas y de la Música [National Institute of Stage Arts and Music]
MLA – Modern Language Association
NO-DO – Noticiario y Documentales [News Service and Documentaries]
PP – Partido Popular [People's Party]
PSOE – Partido Socialista Obrero Español [Spanish Socialist Workers' Party]
RESAD – Real Escuela Superior de Arte Dramático [Royal Higher School of Dramatic Arts]
RSC – Royal Shakespeare Company
RNE – Radio Nacional de España [Spanish National Radio]
RTVE – Radio Televisión Española [Spanish Television and Radio]
SEU – Sindicato Español Universitario [Spanish University Union]
TEC – Teatro Español de Cámara [Spanish Chamber Theatre]
TEI – Teatro Español Independiente [Spanish Independent Theatre]
TEU – Teatro Español Universitario [Spanish University Theatre]

TNC – Teatre Nacional de Catalunya [National Theatre of Catalonia]
UCD – Unión de Centro Democrático [Union of the Democratic Centre]

Publications

ALEC – *Anales de la literatura española contemporánea* [Annals of Contemporary Spanish Literature]
B.Com. – *Bulletin of the Comediantes*
BHS – *Bulletin of Hispanic Studies*
BOE – *Boletín Oficial del Estado* [Official State Bulletin]
HR – *Hispanic Review*
PA – *Primer Acto*

Acknowledgements

There is an element of compromise in almost every book: it is often harder to decide what to leave out than what to include. This is equally true of the acknowledgements and, if I were to include everyone who had contributed to this work, it could have easily run to the length of a chapter. Conscious as I am, however, that it may well be the first – and, in some cases, only – part of the book to which some readers may turn, the recognition of some specific debts of gratitude is in order. Firstly, I would like to thank Sarah Lewis, Siân Chapman, Richard Thomson, Catrin Harries and Dafydd Jones at the University of Wales Press for their commitment to the book and their professionalism in aiding its passage into published form.

This monograph is largely the result of my postgraduate research during which I was the beneficiary of various grants and scholarships which funded my studies and allowed me to spend often extended periods of time in Spain. I am, therefore, forever indebted to the following institutions and funds: the AHRC; the European Scatcherd Scholarship; the Sir George Labouchere Fund for Spanish Studies; the Hargreaves–Mawdsley Fund for Spanish Studies at Wolfson College, University of Oxford; and the Instituto de Valencia de Don Juan, Madrid. Jonathan Thacker first encouraged me to embark on this project when I was a final year undergraduate. I am proud and fortunate to now be able to call him my friend, colleague and mentor; my admiration for his human and academic qualities has only increased over the intervening years, and I could not have asked for a better or more supportive supervisor.

Ever since the days of sixth-form college, I have been blessed at every stage of my academic development in that I have met individuals who have simultaneously enriched my life and appreciation of Spanish culture. It was quite a clash of personalities and egos when I first met Charlotte in Mrs T's 'A' Level class but we have shared so much over the intervening years; she has never let me down, and means more to me now than she ever has. As an undergraduate, Dave provided just the right kind of bad company as we discovered Oxford and then Madrid together; I am privileged to retain arguably the world's most illustrious – and definitely the most rock and roll – taxman since Cervantes as my unfailing partner in crime. My many visits to Spain during my doctoral years would not have been anywhere near as fun if it were not for the frequent company of Betlem who may long ago have stopped being my teacher but from whom I never stop learning. Gemma can only speak a few choice sentences in Spanish but she deserves a special mention in this section for her constant companionship in our travels over the years; long may they continue.

In my years at Oxford, I received constructive feedback, comments and advice on multiple drafts of what would ultimately result in this book. I would like to express my particular gratitude to Robin Fiddian, Tyler Fisher, Nigel Griffin, Kathleen Jeffs, Dominic Moran, Xon de Ros, Eric Southworth, Colin Thompson, Barbara Whitfield and Edwin Williamson. In terms of an external and timely critical eye, this book has been enriched in many respects by Maria Delgado's constructive and supportive feedback. The conversion of a thesis into a book took place following my appointment at the University of Leeds which has proved to be an extremely personable, supportive and stimulating environment in which to work and write. I am grateful and, if truth be told, somewhat mystified by the faith that Stephanie Dennison, David Frier, Paul Garner and Ángel Smith placed in me from the outset. I was fortunate enough to join the department at the same time as Gregorio Alonso and Mila López-Peláez Casellas, both exemplary colleagues and friends, whilst Stuart Green has not only become an ideal drinking partner in Madrid and Leeds but also a great sounding board for my ideas on Spanish theatre and cinema. I am also very grateful to the Leverhulme Trust for awarding me an Early Career Fellowship which has allowed me the luxury of being able to dedicate my time almost exclusively to research for two years between 2010 and 2012.

I have carried out research in a number of different libraries and archives in the UK and Spain where I have generally been greeted with gracious and efficient service. I am grateful to the staff of the Archivo General de la Administración, Alcalá; Biblioteca Nacional, Madrid; Brotherton Library, Leeds; Bodleian, Oxford; BFI, London; British Library, London; Centro de Documentación Teatral, Madrid; Filmoteca, Madrid (especially to my friends Margarita Lobo and Trinidad del Río); Fundación Juan March, Madrid; and the Taylorian, Oxford. My thanks also extend to all of the institutions and individuals who granted me permission to reproduce photographic images, especially Nicolas who not only took a great picture of the Pavón theatre but, more importantly, honoured me in asking me to be best man at his wedding. I also benefited immensely from conversations with practitioners to whom I am grateful for taking the time out of their invariably demanding schedules. I would like to take this opportunity to wish Silvia Abascal, whose image graces the front cover, a full and speedy recovery from her recent health problems.

Space precludes me from individually thanking all of those friends who have made the completion of this project, with its multiple trips to cinemas, theatres, archives – and the lunches and dinners these necessitate – less of a job than an enjoyable vocation. I know it may be an anachronistic and self-centred indulgence on my part but I find the memories of these experiences inscribed in print far more meaningful and satisfying than any photograph on Facebook. The final words must, however, belong to my parents. For Steve who endeavoured to show me there was a world to be discovered beyond Birmingham and, more recently, took the time to read and correct the many typos throughout the manuscript. To Wilma who always ensured that the *mala educación* I received at school was more than compensated for at home, and who unconditionally encouraged me to do whatever I wanted to do in life and would have accepted whatever path I might have chosen.

Introduction

As Melveena McKendrick notes, '[u]nder the auspices of Lope de Vega, Spain's commercial theatre became probably the most successful theatre ever in terms of the number of plays written and the number of people, proportionate to population of course, who flocked to see them' (1989, p. 72). Nevertheless, the legacy of this remarkably popular and prolific national drama, collectively known as the *comedia*, is somewhat less impressive; Calderón de la Barca, Lope and Tirso de Molina are now relatively minor players – certainly in comparison to Shakespeare – largely unknown outside the Iberian peninsula beyond specialist circles. This relegation is clearly not unrelated to the relative (mis)fortunes of the British and Spanish empires, but how have the three main Golden Age dramatists fared in their homeland during the modern era? This is the principal question that this book seeks to answer.

Raymond Williams has convincingly argued that '[d]rama is always so central an element of the life of a society that a change in its methods cannot be isolated from much wider changes' (2002, p. 416). This statement is, I will suggest, as applicable to transitions in the performance and reception of classical texts in contemporary settings as it is to the staging of living playwrights. As a result, my research is aimed not only at *comedia* specialists but also at those with an interest in the culture and politics of modern-day Spain that, for the purposes of this study, I have defined as beginning with Franco's victory in the Civil War. The defeat of the Republican forces marks a clear rupture in Spanish history and a seventy-year period, a lifetime, allows me to move beyond the anecdotal and accidental while not being so broad that it precludes detailed historical and aesthetic analyses.

An underlying belief in an active dialogue between past and present serves to bring my work under the general rubric of reception studies as advanced by theorists such as Hans Robert Jauss and Wolfgang Iser. In an overview of their critical principles, Robert C. Holub observes how '[a]n interpretation of a text could no longer be undertaken by placing it in its historical context; rather, the history of its very interpretation was considered an integral part of our ability to understand it' (1985, p. 159). In other words, plays by Calderón, Lope and Tirso mean different things in 2009 than they did in 1939.

The task I have set myself is therefore to track and explain at least some of these changes through the study of Golden Age drama on the page, stage and screen. This is the first study of its kind in any language but this does not thereby imply that it has emerged in a vacuum or that there are no antecedents. It is therefore incumbent upon me to situate the work within the existing field of scholarship before moving onto a justification of my methodological approach alongside a discussion of the specific challenges and opportunities it raises.

The textual bias: performance criticism and *comedia* studies

As José María Ruano de la Haza notes, there is 'a long, distinguished and well established critical tradition (. . .) determined to treat Golden Age drama as dramatic poetry, rather than poetic drama' (1996, p. 15). This is in contrast to Shakespeare studies where, in spite of initial resistance and trepidation, 'a huge concourse of scholars and critics have been seriously concerned with what is usually known as "the study of Shakespeare's plays in performance"' (Brown, 2003, p. 18). Hence, for example, editions of plays tend to contain references to stage history and specific productions, while it is also now standard practice to include at least one article on screen adaptations in edited collections of critical essays (Cartmell, 1999, p. 29).

No such paradigm shift has occurred in the study of early modern Spanish drama, although some tentative attempts have been made to extend the heuristic parameters beyond pure textual exegesis so as to incorporate the study of historical, modern-day and hypothetical performances into critical readings. I am particularly indebted to the work of Susan Fischer, who has done much to develop a vocabulary for analysing performances of Golden Age drama; her detailed and well-informed case studies, recently collated in one volume (2009), are an invaluable resource to which I will frequently direct the reader for more information on individual productions.

In recent years, the emergence of a specialist journal, *Comedia Performance*, has provided a hospitable forum for work of this kind. Nevertheless, concerns raised by Jonathan Thacker in the first issue over literary scholars' timidity and conservatism remain valid five years down the line: '[m]ost critics line up on the shore, curious and feeling slightly guilty, but unwilling to cast off the security-blanket of text-based study, traditional or modern' (2004, p. 145). This reluctance and unease has been even more pronounced in Spain as a result of specific sociohistorical factors.

Under Franco, literary criticism was generally limited to what it had been in the nineteenth-century, namely philological study (López, Talens and Villanueva, 1994, p. ix). It is still the case that drama and theatre studies are either completely absent or inadequately addressed at *bachillerato* level (Vieites, 2009). Universities in Spain have rarely contained drama departments although a theatre chair was established in Murcia in 1969,[1] and José A. Sánchez, the chair of art history at the University of Castilla-La Mancha at the time of writing, works largely on theatre. In general, however, a lack of communication and tradition has clearly affected the way in which the *comedia* has been taught and studied: 'se hace difícil un enfoque en profundidad y con sentido de realidad de lo que puede y debe ser la enseñanza del teatro en la universidad' [it makes it difficult to focus in a serious and realistic fashion on what the teaching of theatre at university level could and should entail] (Quintana, 1999, p. 319).[2]

The overhaul of the higher education system by the PSOE in 1985 theoretically created a more hospitable climate for literary theory and non-philological approaches (Lewis, 1994, p. 171) yet both performance and cultural studies remain in their infancy (Smith, 1998, p. 6).[3] Furthermore, as Eduardo Pérez-Rasilla has lamented:

> El teatro no constituye lo que en el argot académico se denomina 'área BOE', pese a los denodados esfuerzos de algunos profesores cuyos estudios se relacionan con el teatro. Es decir, no se considera el fenómeno teatral como merecedor de la asignación de un área de conocimiento – investigación y docencia – en la universidad española. (2008, p. 15)
>
> [In spite of the valiant efforts made by some teachers whose research is related to theatre, it still does not constitute what is referred to in academic lingo as 'tenure track'. In other words, the theatrical experience is not considered to warrant an independent field of knowledge in terms of teaching and research within the Spanish university system.]

As this critic intimates, there have nevertheless been some lone voices in the wilderness that have sought to take performance seriously and/or improve relations between the page and stage. For example, as early as 1956, Ángel Valbuena Prat made frequent allusion to specific productions in his discussion of different *comedias* in *Historia del teatro español*. Seventeen years later, Juan Antonio García Barquero, a veteran of independent theatre, wrote the first study dedicated exclusively to the modern-day performance of Golden Age drama. This was an attempt to improve communication between *comedia* specialists, practitioners and spectators in the hope of resurrecting seventeenth-century plays for the contemporary stage: 'este libro va dirigido a un público potencial, que está ahí, disperso, pero que podría mañana congregarse de nuevo ante un escenario' [this book is directed to a potential audience that is dispersed out there somewhere, but that could congregate once again in front of a stage in the near future] (1973, p. 11). The analysis is undertaken in a rather superficial and laborious manner but the underlying motives are commendable nevertheless.

César Oliva, who has held the theatre chair in Murcia since 1988, provided the first detailed and sophisticated study of the national drama from a theatrical standpoint in *Corral de Almagro: una propuesta sin resolver* (1977). He begins with an overview of how *comedias* were staged in the sixteenth and seventeenth centuries, before moving onto a discussion of their performance in the modern period. This analysis is accompanied by a remarkably prescient plea for the *corral* to be reopened. From 1978 onwards, the small Manchegan town would bring academics and theatre practitioners together in a series of *Jornadas* [research days] dedicated to Golden Age drama that would pave the way for the international festival of which the reconstructed *corral* would prove one of the star attractions. Thirty-one years later, these annual meetings continue to take place. In addition, the *Jornadas* in Almeria that adopt a similar approach celebrated their twenty-fifth anniversary in 2008.

This longevity and continuity could easily be construed as a sign of both cultural normalization and a reconciliation of theorists and practitioners. There is an element of truth in this diagnosis but, unfortunately, these ostensibly novel initiatives have not been altogether successful. Francisco Ruiz Ramón noted a complete lack of complicity and communication between the theatrical and academic fraternities in Almagro in 1978 (1988, pp. 9–10), and there has not been a dramatic improvement in relations since. When, for example, Adolfo Marsillach took charge of the nascent CNTC in 1986, he clearly saw university scholars not as colleagues but as rivals to be outclassed. A sense of mutual hostility and suspicion would later be encapsulated in the director's proud boast, 'preferíamos que se escandilizase Domingo Ynduráin a que bostezara un estudiante' [we would prefer Domingo Ynduráin to be scandalized than for a student to yawn] (2002, p. 465).

Both sides have undoubtedly become more diplomatic over time but, on visiting Almagro in 2008, I was disheartened to discover that the conference and the festival now operate as almost completely independent entities that happen to coincide. Hence, for example, the archive held in the theatre museum ignores its potentially captive audience by denying access to readers because the librarians are too busy running an exhibition for the festival. Similarly, very few of the academic papers addressed performance and, beyond the opening ceremony and two specific sessions in which platitudes were exchanged, theatre practitioners were conspicuous by their absence.[4]

A similar apartheid system also underpins performance texts that have been published to coincide with specific productions. These print editions tend to be very attractively designed and often contain essays by both academics and practitioners that have in many cases been highly informative. Nevertheless, the two camps tend not to venture beyond certain parameters with the former concerned with historical and philological questions and the latter almost exclusively preoccupied by theatrical and cultural matters.

This mutual lack of interest is both a symptom and cause of performance generally not being taken seriously within the Spanish university system. On the rare occasion when theatrical matters are taken into consideration, it is almost inevitably from the perspective of the sixteenth or seventeenth century (Pérez-Rasilla 2008, pp. 16–17). There are undoubtedly culturally specific reasons that underpin this absence but, as we have seen, the international academic community has also been reluctant to settle this methodological deficit. Consequently, performance studies remains conspicuously absent from Golden Age scholarship despite the fact that 'it is patently absurd and perverse to attempt to judge *comedias* on the basis of the written text alone' (McGaha, 1991, p. 91).

Applying performance studies to the research and teaching of Golden Age drama

Peter Hall, the founder of the RSC, argues that studying plays purely as literature is the equivalent of 'studying music without having heard a note of it – or being unable to "hear" the music of a score as you read it' (2000, p. 10). The ostensible permanence and immutability of the text in contrast to performance can, nevertheless, result in an exclusively literary based approach appearing to be more stable and 'objective'. In the words of Martin Esslin:

> Because the only portion of the dramatic event that leaves a permanent residue for posterity is usually the written record ... the text has been regarded by critics and scholars as the essential element of drama. Indeed it has often become synonymous with the whole of drama, something akin to the 'Platonic idea' of the play, with the performance only, at best, an imperfect realisation of that metaphysical entity. (1987, p. 79)

As he proceeds to note, however, words by no means 'represent the "Platonic code" of the spectacle, but are merely an important ingredient that may or may not be the ultimate determinant of its meaning for the spectators of a given performance' (1987, p. 81). In fact, as W. B. Worthen observes, the analogy with music may not in fact go far enough because it implies that performance is encoded in print, and thereby fails to take account of the performativity – the ability to create as well as recreate meaning – of theatrical performance: 'The dramatic script seems at once (like the *blueprint*, the *score*, and *software*) to imply a process of doing, to be instrumental to performance, even while the conduct of that performance is likely outside the instructions' (2010, p. 20).

In the analysis of performance scripts, the use of the term 'faithful' to refer to a lack of overt philological intervention on the part of the adaptor may be a useful analytical descriptor – and one which I will deploy on numerous occasions – but its ontological status ought to remain within parentheses. Even the ostensible stability of the printed word is a misnomer in reference to early modern drama; as I will discuss in more detail in chapter five, different modes of transmission ensure indeterminacy in many editorial choices. Furthermore, modern readers and theatregoers arrive at a text or performance with their own horizon of expectations. Even if we were somehow able to read exactly the play Lope wrote, or see it as it was performed in a seventeenth-century *corral*, we would not *see* or *read* the same play as Lope's contemporaries; there is always a 'hermeneutical bridge' to be built (Ganelin, 1991, p. 36). As Patrice Pavis notes:

> The change in context of utterance goes hand in hand with a renewed concretization of the dramatic text; a two-way relationship is established between the dramatic text and the Social Context. With every new *mise en scène*, the text is placed in a situation of enunciation according to the new Social Context of its reception, which allows or facilitates a new analysis of the text and so on, *ad infinitum* . . . Philology and literary criticism use words to explain texts, whereas *mise en scène* uses stage actions to 'question' the dramatic text. (1992, pp. 30–1)

It is thus clear that the historical contingency of reception functions as a challenge to the notion of the play text as a stable object, or authorial intention as the privileged ground for interpretation. Hence, modern reworkings are not a priori aberrations and ought not to be judged according to some chimerical standard of authenticity. As Fischer remarks:

> All performances of classical theatre of the early modern period, whether that means Shakespeare, Molière or Lope, are in some sense 'foreign' with respect to the author's original 'intentions'; to read or perform any of these playwrights today . . . is always to be involved in a kind of translation. (2009, p. 220)

A number of caveats are, nevertheless, in order. The danger of such an approach is that it demystifies the holy text only to then deify the performance. The academy's propensity to privilege the written word to the detriment of all other considerations has been a justifiable source of consternation amongst theatre practitioners. Equally dogmatic and parochial, however, is the despotic attitude adopted by some involved in staging the classics that places artistic freedom and a modernizing impulse as absolute rights immune to criticism. As with any translation process, there are clearly better and worse examples. While these cannot be adequately judged without reference to the word, neither can they be assessed according to a strictly philological criterion. In Worthen's eminently sensible appraisal,

> to understand 'performance studies' through a simple opposition between text and performance is to remain captive to the spectral disciplines of the past. Both texts and performances are materially unstable registers of signification, producing 'meaning' intertextually in ways that deconstruct notions of intention, fidelity, authority, present meaning. At the same time, texts and performances retain the gesture of such semiosis, and discussions of both text and performance remain haunted by the desire for authorization. (2004, pp. 19–20)

Many *comedia* scholars have begun to accept that performance cannot be judged solely in terms of the play text. However, in order to adopt a genuinely theatrical mode of criticism, we must go a step further and recognize that performance holds the potential to generate meanings that, without their aid, we would not have been able to 'negotiate' through the play text. This is not, of course, to say that this will occur in every instance and we must retain the critical right to denounce productions that are theatrically deficient and/or offer no new insights into the plays on which they are ostensibly based. Throughout this book, I apply the basic criterion that an important hallmark of a dramatic representation of a *comedia* that resurrects a seventeenth-century play for a modern-day audience is if, after seeing a performance, I am unable to read the play text in the same way that I had previously.

Even those academics predisposed to accept the theoretical worth of performance may be deterred from pursuing it as a serious avenue of research due to methodological reservations. In general, colleagues are able to verify the sources of textual exegesis with relative ease but this process is complicated in relation to stage performances. As a result, there is an increased onus on the performance historian and analyst to be rigorous in their scholarly practices. Nevertheless, even the most well-informed critic will be unable to record everything they see and hear; attendance at multiple performances is likely to sharpen appraisals but they will never be exhaustive.

An additional challenge is how to describe the experience of live drama when 'the uniqueness of an event is not in its materiality but in its interactivity' (Schechner, 2002, p. 23). Although the theatrical environment tends to place us in close physical proximity to our fellow theatregoers, we are inevitable only ever in possession of a partial and subjective perception of the collective experience. Thus, 'we share the signal but not its reception':

In this sense performance analysis and history are always partial and forms of fiction, just as biography is: the imposition of a perception that is external to individual perception. Thus the job of the performance history is to understand and give meaning to the event through social and aesthetic analysis, not to be the sum of the audience's experiences. (Kennedy, 2006, p. 337)

The challenge therefore is not to flee the subjective prism but rather to register its presence and acknowledge the constitutive effect it will inevitably exercise over our judgements. Nevertheless, an element of subjectivity is inherent in every critical inquiry; it is simply that this is explicitly manifested in performance studies and exacerbated by a perceived lack of accountability. The difference between performance studies and other fields of inquiry is, therefore, a question of degree rather than kind; the subjective element is blatant rather than latent. There is, therefore, no methodological justification for its traditional exclusion from the academy. Furthermore, its presence not only supplies an indispensable heuristic lens but also has the potential to provide valuable pedagogical tools. These could be applied to meet the challenge outlined nearly twenty years ago by Peter W. Evans to resurrect what he refers to as 'mummified texts' for future generations:

> We must take this simultaneously marvellous and conventional, consistent and contradictory, challenging and subservient literature out of its moribund academic contexts – and the uninhabited wastes to which the Philistines would condemn it – and into the hearts and minds of anyone unenthusiastic about spending an entire university career adjusting the volume of sound and fury flooding out of those over-heated headphones. (1990a, p. viii)

At least in the UK, this challenge has not been met. It may appear that an increasingly consumer-based culture has led to the felling of many Golden Age courses and posts yet the continued cachet and popularity of, say, the Greeks and Tudors demonstrates that antiquity does not have to equate to anachronism. The issue of contemporary relevance emerges largely from perception and visibility; rather than bemoaning our collective misfortunes, it is incumbent upon *comedia* scholars to increase marketability without sacrificing quality. I believe that a performance-based approach provides an important tool for this undertaking. As Elaine Showalter notes, '[i]ntellectually as well as pedagogically, exploring the connections and contradictions of page and stage is part of the most up-to-date thinking in the field' and 'of all teaching techniques, performance can be the most active and student-catered, and can lead to engaged intellectual discovery of the text' (2003, pp. 80, 87).

A book on teaching the *comedia* published by the MLA in 2006 appears to recognize this worth and contains numerous essays that address the importance of performance in different pedagogical environments.⁵ In my own classes, undergraduates have responded enthusiastically to the study of plays on stage and screen. This has been the case both at the University of Oxford – where Calderón's *El médico de su honra* continues to be a set text for all first years reading Spanish – and at the University of Leeds where students' only encounter with the *comedia* will currently take place in the optional final year module on theories and practices of adaptation in contemporary Spain.

To refuse to take modern-day productions seriously or to test out plays and theories in performance unnecessarily forecloses an important field of inquiry and source of knowledge; it is equivalent to staging a play without reading anything about the work, its author and the period in which it was written. The study of the *comedia* on page, stage and screen will not provide a holistic panacea that will dispel all our doubts on a given play or dramatist; in reality, it is likely to raise at least as many questions as it will solve. Neither should it seek to displace more traditional modes of critical enquiry. It will, however, provide a considerable heuristic and pedagogical aid.

Performance and Golden Age dogma

Beyond its (in)conspicuous absence, nothing that I have stated thus far in my advocacy of a performance-based approach has been specific to *comedia* studies and would be equally applicable to many theatrical traditions from the past. In this section, I want to suggest some ways in which an appreciation of seventeenth-century plays as dramatic works produced for the stage could potentially intervene in wider debates on Spain's national classical theatre.

In an article published in 2006, Matthew Stroud offers an overview of 'generalisations about Golden Age drama widely accepted in the past and now subject to question' that leads him to the following conclusion: 'the monolithic definition of the *comedia* simply cannot hold' (p. 291). He attributes this shift away from dogma and towards pluralism to a series of new critical approaches among which this North American academic singles out theory as the most important (p. 286).

In practice, this hypothesis is very credible; theory has clearly facilitated a transition beyond 'the search for and establishment of totalizing, regularizing, authoritative generalizatons that would tell one how to read all *comedias*' (p. 287). However, whether this is because theory is inherently the most effective antidote to grand overarching narratives or whether it has simply been the most frequently applied is more open to contention. I would like to suggest that the study of plays on the stage and screen at least has the potential to perform this task in an equally if not more convincing and effective manner.

Let us take, for example, one of the totemic myths of twentieth-century Hispanism in which A. A. Parker claims that 'Spanish dramatic plots are constructed on the principle of poetic justice' (1957, p. 7), and that individual psychology is neither a priority nor an end in itself.[6] Thomas Austin O'Connor has suggested that the theory that the *comedia* only contains stock characters has held sway for so long because most critics are textually bound (2000, p. 6). Nobody would claim that the absence of stage directions in the printed play texts suggests that they were non-existent in the *corrales*; is it not, therefore, reasonable to presume that a similar process of reconstruction needs to be applied at the level of characterization? The question of whether and how this reconstruction process has been applied in different productions is a question to which I will return throughout the book.

Nevertheless, the monolithic theory that I believe performance studies is best equipped to challenge and which could deliver the most profitable results is one advanced in Spain during the 1970s by José Antonio Maravall and José María Díez Borque. In a series of studies, they advance the thesis that the *comedia* was a form of mass propaganda that sought to immobilize the progressive currents of social change that had swept across Spain during the Renaissance. According to this interpretation, the *comedia* universalized the interests of a particular class so that they appeared to be to everyone's advantage. In the prologue to Díez Borque's most influential book, *Sociología de la comedia española*, Maravall summarizes their stance in the following terms:

> Él y yo estamos completamente de acuerdo en hacer depender la amplia campaña propagandística a que se entrega la comedia, de un objetivo socio-político muy específico: la captación de voluntades en amplias masas de individuos a favor del sistema, paralizando el proceso de transformación que la onda expansiva del siglo XVI había suscitado. (1976, p. 15)

> [He and I are in complete agreement in attributing the widespread propaganda campaign – in whose service the *comedia* placed itself – to a very concrete sociopolitical objective: the conversion of large masses of individuals to favour the system, thereby halting the process of transformation that the expansive wave of the sixteenth century had set in motion.]

Both authors marshal decontextualized fragments of information to make reductive and totalizing claims about Golden Age drama in its entirety. Hence, for example, Díez Borque states that '[e]n la comedia se produce una evasión de la realidad, proponiendo una ideología gratificadora y conservadora, tendente a mantener los grandes ideales patrocinados por la aristocracia' [in the *comedia*, there is an evasion of reality that proposes a conservative and anodyne ideology designed to maintain the grand ideals promoted by the aristocracy] (1976, p. 359). As I have discussed in more detail elsewhere (Wheeler, 2012a), these interpretations have been highly influential but have nevertheless been subject to a number of serious critiques. It is not my intention to reproduce these counter-arguments here but what I do want to do is rehearse a theory of how viewing the *comedia* from a performance-based perspective automatically undermines this influential school of thought.

Both critics scan play texts as if they were historical documents in search of ideologically salient scenarios or quotations to support their theories. They assume that fictional constructs reflect the beliefs of the playwright, fail to take sufficient account of dramatic context, and do not allow for the possibility of multiple interpretations. As Thacker notes, an approach of this kind is inherently flawed because:

> The *comedia*, we must constantly remind ourselves (especially when we see relatively few performances), is a play which makes us feel. A particular speech should not automatically be taken at face value, its content interpreted through the lens of some 'reality' or 'truth'. This content can be undermined or modified by its form, or the contexts of its delivery, for example whether it is delivered as a whisper or with an accompanying wink. (1999, p. 27)

By not taking such considerations into account, the propaganda model effectively bypasses the *comedia*'s artistic and dramatic possibilities. Hence, for example, Díez Borque assumes that the message/meaning (on his model, the two terms are completely interchangeable) of a play can be derived from the denouement alone. In line with his argument that the *comedia* is completely analogous to the use of the *disfraz* [disguise] in festive settings (1986), he dismisses any ostensibly subversive content from within the body of the text as either an exception or compensation. For example, the fact that parental authority is overridden by love so that a woman always marries the man she loves is construed as a form of wish-fulfilment that will distract female spectators from prosaic reality in which they are subject to strict parental control (1976, pp. 94–5).

As a result, it proves impossible to offer any evidence from within the body of the play text to undermine his belief in 'el cáracter conformista de la comedia y el repudio de toda actividad crítica, también en esos momentos en que el autor, en apariencia, se sitúa contracorriente' [the conformist nature of the *comedia* and the aversion, even in those moments when the author is ostensibly opposing the system, to any form of critical activity] (1976, p. 103). If the play has an explicitly conservative message, it reflects the playwright's vision while any ostensibly radical or dissident view is nothing more than a licensed dalliance with subversion that will ultimately be contained so as to strengthen rather than diminish the play's reactionary content. In a similar vein, Maravall assumes that a play's denouement and restoration unambiguously convey a conservative and evasive message:

> Cada uno acepta y es feliz en su puesto: por lo menos así se da a entender en el teatro. Sólo quedan explosiones episódicas y ejemplarizantes, de carácter justiciero, contra el que se ha salido de las obligaciones de su papel. (Tales explosiones, lejos de quebrantar el sistema, son un apoyo, en la medida en que prometen a todos que cualquier desorden encontrará su castigo y la restitución consiguiente). Todo esto en el teatro, claro está, precisamente porque en la sociedad amenazaba otra cosa. (1972, p. 114)
>
> [Everyone accepts and is happy with their social position: at least, this is what the theatre makes us think. There are only the occasional ruptures, designed to convey a moral message presented from the perspective of justice, and used against those who have shirked the duties their role entails. (Ruptures of this kind, far from shaking the system's foundations, are a support in that they suggest to everyone that transgressions of any kind will be punished and recompensed accordingly). It is clear that this was the case in the theatre because threats of a very different kind were prevalent in everyday life.]

Both critics homogenize audience response and thereby remove much of the contingency that is inherent to theatrical performance. This results in an internally consistent yet unconvincing model of how the *comedia* affected audiences. They are only able to bypass the threat of subjectivity because they refuse to accept that 'el término "espectador" es sólo una abreviatura para lo que es en realidad una variedad de diferentes actos de participación en y respuesta a aquel espectáculo' [the term 'spectator' is merely shorthand for what is, in reality, a broad range of participatory models and responses to the given theatrical event] (Connor, 2000, p. 8). This deterministic model of cultural consumption often leads even those critics who are sympathetic to their ideas to question their more monolithic claims. Hence, for example, John Beverley critiques what he terms 'an essentially behaviorist model of cultural interpellation':

> I would find the best critiques of Maravall not so much in Golden-Age studies as in Media studies. Any media critic worth his or her salt would say, 'hey, there is a reception dimension that is missing in Maravall. Texts can be rewritten by their audiences.' If we take seriously Maravall's very fruitful idea that the Baroque is a form of mass culture, then we need to pay attention to the question of reception. (2008, pp. 153–4)

I think it is clear that the application of performance studies at an early stage would, in all probability, have dispelled these theories long ago. However, their content is less interesting than their mere existence and the effect they have had. It is difficult to think of a Spanish writer from the last century who has had more influence on the performance and reception of Golden Age drama than Maravall. Within Spain itself, his impact has transcended academia and, as we will see, the image of seventeenth-century playwrights as state lackeys is firmly entrenched in a wide range of discursive contexts.

This raises a number of questions that this book will seek to address. What was the sociohistorical context in which these theories were advanced and how do they relate to earlier interpretations? If these theoretical readings and theatrical practice are as inimical as I have suggested, how and why have Maravall and Díez Borque proved to be so resilient in a country that has a high-profile company dedicated to staging classical drama? It is, I would suggest, only through the detailed study of the *comedia* on the page, stage and screen that we will be in a position to answer these questions and have a better understanding of what Ignacio Arellano has termed the 'tópicos sempiternos que se resisten a desaparecer' [the perennial clichés that refuse to disappear] (2004, p. 77).

Tracing a performance history of Lope, Calderón and Tirso on the Spanish page, stage and screen (1939–2009)

Unlike most of the previous work done in the field, I frame my analyses of individual performances within concrete sociocultural contexts. I also aim to counteract what I consider to be the disproportionate attention paid to the CNTC's output at the expense of earlier and contemporaneous productions; this tendency has, in my opinion, created a distorted image of *comedia* performance in Spain among the international scholarly community. The book consists of five chapters that could theoretically be read in isolation; they are, nevertheless, designed to have a cumulative effect so as to provide the first monograph on the performance and reception of Spain's national classical drama.

In the first, I offer an overview of the history of Golden Age plays on the contemporary Spanish stage. This is an updated and expanded version of an article that originally appeared in the *Bulletin of the Comediantes* (Wheeler, 2008a). Although I often focus on specific productions, my interest is primarily in identifying some general trends in the staging of the *comedia* and relating them to broader social and historical changes rather than in the kind of detailed aesthetic analysis that I provide in subsequent chapters. This is, by some margin, the longest of the five studies; it is the first detailed historical overview of how and why Calderón, Lope and Tirso have been performed in modern-day Spain, and is thereby designed to ground the rest of the book.

I then move onto a case study that focuses on *Fuente Ovejuna*. By 1939, this play had accrued very specific connotations as a result of its performance prior to and during the Civil War. It is therefore necessary to begin with some 'pre-history' before moving on to examine productions staged between 1939 and 2009. Through the application of Jonathan Bate's concepts of 'aspectuality' and 'performativity', I will suggest that the stage history of Lope's most (in)famous play eludes the delineation of precise meanings which has been the hallmark of much textual exegesis. This *comedia* is unique, I will argue, not only because it has been staged almost continuously throughout the period but also because there is a genuine performance tradition.

In the third chapter, I question whether the CNTC emerged from a vacuum or whether it was heir to previous initiatives and traditions. I then examine the challenges of establishing a performance tradition in relation to the reception of their debut production: *El médico de su honra* (1986). This is followed by a detailed analysis of a production staged twenty-two years later of *El pintor de su deshonra*. A comparison of the two wife-murder plays in performance provides scope for an in-depth study of changing perceptions to the gender politics of baroque theatre in addition to a detailed appraisal of the achievements and limitation of the first major Spanish company of the modern era to be dedicated to the staging of the national classics.

The fourth chapter focuses on film adaptations. As Tom Conley notes, 'since the end of the nineteenth century Spain has remained a nation nourished on celluloid' (1998, p. xi). This cultural ubiquity makes cinema the modern-day equivalent of the *comedia*, and also ensures that screen versions have the potential to reach a far wider demographic than the vast majority of stage productions. As a result, any study of the reception of Golden Age drama would be incomplete if it did not at least take cinema into account. In addition, there are copies available of all the cinematic adaptations made after 1939. This permits a detailed aesthetic overview that is simply not possible in relation to the stage due to the general absence of extant theatrical recordings from the 1940s or 1950s.

The final chapter locates the performance of Golden Age drama in national and international contexts. I begin with an analysis of the reception of the RSC's Golden Age season in Madrid that questions what, if anything, Spanish practitioners might be able to learn from this foreign institution. I then use co-productions between the CNTC and theatres from the autonomous regions as a springboard to discuss why *comedia* performance is so heavily concentrated in Madrid. In the final section, I examine how discourse surrounding the Almagro Festival tends to be framed almost exclusively in reference to more established foreign institutions, and consider whether or not this has benefited or hindered Golden Age drama on the contemporary stage.

Enrique García Santo-Tomás and Pérez-Rasilla have observed in recent articles that *comedia* studies and practice have, in some respects, reached an intellectual and creative cul-de-sac (2001, 2008). They argue that a detailed overview of performance and reception could serve to open new communication routes. To what extent the content and impact of this book will be able to fulfil this promise remains to be seen but it should, I hope, be of interest to practitioners and scholars alike. In terms of the former, I have sought to encourage them to engage with predecessors and position their labours within a tradition, however fragmentary, of *comedia* performance. As for the latter, I have included extensive bibliographical material throughout in the hope that individual readers may pursue and develop any number of areas that I am only able to mention in passing. Overall, my optimistic intent is to unite the two contingents through the establishment and consolidation of a suitable methodological and empirical framework conducive to the discussion and performance of Golden Age drama in the twenty-first century.

Chapter One

The performance history of Golden Age drama in Spain (1939–2009)

Following Franco's victory in 1939, the legacy of the Civil War was felt in all aspects of Spanish life; the performance of Golden Age drama was no exception. Commentators have, traditionally, tended to direct more attention towards theatre produced by the Republicans than the Nationalists during the conflict. This is mainly because the former were more inventive in their theatrical endeavours and also because Madrid and Barcelona, the principal loci of theatrical activity, remained Republican strongholds until near the end of the war (Oliva, 2002a, p. 118). However, Golden Age works were performed by both sides. On the Republican front, Cervantes proved particularly popular; Alberti staged *Numancia,* and there were various productions of the *entremeses* [short plays] adapted to fit the contemporary context. There were also representations of Lope's *Fuente Ovejuna.*[1]

While Republican forces looked to adapt Golden Age works to fit the needs of the present, Nationalist forces saw the need for the present to be rooted in the past. Franco had already taken to comparing himself to the great Castilian rulers of the past, and as early as February 1938 he had adopted the imperial crown and shield of Charles V as the arms of state (Preston, 1995, p. 324). It was felt that Spain had lost its way and had, in many respects, ceased to be 'Spanish' since the seventeenth century.[2] Golden Age authors were seen to represent an eternal Spain that the Nationalist side would reawaken. It is from this conception that José María Salaverría's daydream emerges:

> Yo imagino a Garcilaso de la Vega ciñéndose apresuradamente la espada para correr a ponerse a las órdenes de Franco, como hiciera otrora con la persona del emperador Carlos V . . . En cuanto a Cervantes, sin duda posible se vendría con nosotros, y aunque con la mano estropeada, pediría un

puesto entre nuestros soldados, porque él se enorgullecía, más que de nada, de haber sido un soldado leal ... Tampoco vacilaría mucho Lope de Vega, aquel que se embarcó de voluntario en la Gran Armada; ni menos aún Calderón de la Barca, que fue soldado en Flandes y conservó siempre en su larga vida una nostálgica veneración por la gente militar. (1938)

[I can imagine Garcilaso de la Vega hurriedly sheathing his sword so that he could run and place himself under Franco's orders, as he once did for the Emperor Charles V ... As for Cervantes, there can be no doubt that he would be with us. Even with his limp hand, he would ask for a post among our soldiers because he was proud, above all else, of having been a brave soldier ... Neither would Lope de Vega, who once volunteered for the Great Armada, take much convincing; even quicker off the mark would be Calderón de la Barca who was a soldier in Flanders and retained throughout his life a nostalgic veneration for those in the military.]

According to this conception, Republican productions of Golden Age works were perversions of their author's intentions. However, it was only at the beginning of 1938 when Dionisio Ridruejo, nicknamed 'the Spanish Goebbels', took charge of press and propaganda for the Nationalist side, that dramatic art began to perform an important function in consolidating ideology (Payne, 1961, p. 181). He encouraged the staging of *autos sacramentales* [Corpus Christi plays] and, on 1 June, the Ministry of Interior announced a special literary prize for the best production (Schwartz, 1969, p. 201). The eventual winner, *El casamiento engañoso* by Falangist Gonzalo Torrente Ballester, explicitly linked the past and present as an *argumentador* [disputant] emerges to deliver a statement of intent:

Cuando Calderón ofrecía a la Hostia festejada el homenaje de su pompa poética, el tejido conceptual de sus figuraciones era el mismo que empujara a nuestros soldados a pelear en Breda y a nuestros diplomáticos a suscribir melancólicamente los protocolos del tratado de Westfalia. El poeta que escribió este Auto quiere igualmente, festejar la divina presencia ofreciendo, con menos poesía y ornato, pero con idéntico fervor, representado también en alegorías, el pensamiento que ha conducido hasta hace muy escasos días a nuestros soldados a mucho más dura pelea. (1941, pp. 8–9)

[When Calderón paid homage to the Host with his poetic grandeur, the conceptual basis of his figurations was the same as that which spurred on our soldiers in Breda, and our diplomats with melancholy resignation to abide by the protocols of the Westfalia Treaty. The poet who wrote this Corpus Christi Play also wants to celebrate the divine presence with an offering of equal conviction, albeit with lesser poetic art and decoration, depicting through allegory those very same beliefs that, until very recently, led our soldiers to fight a much tougher battle.]

Considering the key role Catholicism was to perform in forging national identity, the attractions of the *autos sacramentales* were clear; they also lent themselves to the kind of spectacular outdoor productions that were already very popular in Mussolini's Italy.³ Hence, for example, Luis Escobar directed an elaborate version of Valdivielso's *El hospital de los locos* in the square outside Segovia Cathedral on 28 July 1938 that was also aired on the very recently created Spanish national radio (Munsó Cabús, 1988, p. 34).⁴ In addition to the main actors, the production featured one hundred and fifty extras draped in cloaks and hoods, and had lavish sets designed by José Caballero, an ex-member of La Barraca. Though the Republicans were inspired by the kind of social engagement advocated by García Lorca's troupe, Nationalist productions benefited from the technical expertise of many of its veterans.

A new Golden Age? Forging a Francoist national identity (1939–50)

Up until the day that Nationalist forces occupied Madrid, a version of *El alcalde de Zalamea* staged by Manuel González's company was playing at the Teatro Español (García-Alegre Sánchez, 1981, p. 2), but it would not be long before those on the victorious side offered their version of the classics to the capital. The cultural policy of the early Franco regime would seek inspiration in Spain's glorious past that, it was hoped, would arm the nation against dangerous foreign influences and provide a moral and political model for the present. There was an implicit belief, not evident in such force since the Golden Age, that the health of language and empire were inextricably linked (Brown, 1942, p. 65).

Though all genres would be represented over the coming years, it is not surprising that initially the focus was on the kind of works that had been championed through the Civil War. When Franco entered Madrid on 19 May 1939, Escobar, as head of the Falange's National Theatre, was put in charge of staging the first theatrical celebrations of the Nationalist victory. Later in the year, Escobar and his company were asked to stage a spectacular performance to celebrate the *Día de la Victoria* [Victory Day] (18 July). Beginning on 23 July, he offered a series of open-air performances of Calderón's *La cena del rey Baltasar* in the Retiro Park. According to *Ya*, this 'acontecimiento teatral, desborda en realidad el limitado marco del espectáculo público para adquirir categoría de servicio nacional' [theatrical event transcends the restricted domain of a public spectacle so as to acquire the status of national service] (1939), and an advertisement printed in *Arriba* on 27 July announced an extra two performances due to the high demand for tickets. Despite the occasional patriotic work, generally staged by the Falange, and performances of works by the martyred Nationalist playwright Pedro Muñoz Seca (executed by Republican forces), the plays on offer in Madrid in 1939 did not, however, radically differ from those that had been performed prior to Franco's victory (García Ruiz, 1997a, p. 530).

Theatre was never manipulated by the regime to the same extent as some other media, most noticeably cinema, in the forging of a new national identity (Higginbotham, 1988, p. 8). The ideological role of the stage was, in the post-Civil War years, performed largely by Golden Age drama and the regime would exert its authority and influence on the theatrical world primarily through its exclusion of undesirable elements. On 15 July 1939, the official state censor was established. The classics did not have to be submitted for authorization although any changes to the play text as well as the specific staging (e.g. costumes and sets) did require the censor's approval.[5] Implicit in this procedure was the belief that the classics in themselves were ideologically sound but that they could nevertheless be corrupted by deviant productions.[6]

Although in 1939 Escobar staged *autos sacramentales* at the Teatro María Guerrero, and Felipe Lluch[7] staged *comedias* and *entremeses* at the Español, both buildings remained in private hands. It was in 1940 that the state acquired these venues and they became the National Theatres.[8] From the outset, seventeenth-century drama was an important part of both theatres' programmes and they remained loyal to the classics for many years. Between 1939 and 1950, 15.1 per cent (23 out of 152 productions) and 10.6 per cent (13 out of 122 productions) of output, at the Español and María Guerrero respectively, was based on Golden Age plays (Serrano, 2003, p. 1339).[9] These figures, in isolation, diminish the role these plays performed in the theatrical, cultural and ideological panorama of the time as the classics were often reserved for the most high-profile performances and always generated heavy press coverage. This, along with the fact that productions of seventeenth-century plays were relatively immune to the censor, helped foster the impression that Golden Age drama was the regime's *niño mimado* [golden boy].

It is perhaps too easy both to overstate the ideological role of the National Theatres and to use this as grounds for understating their artistic achievements. As Francisco Linares notes, they were under the auspices of National Education rather than the Propaganda Ministry (1996, p. 212), and this is reflected in their output. Both theatres undoubtedly exalted nationalist values but they also provided one of the few alternatives to the commercial theatre and allowed a level of professionalism that was conspicuously absent from the Spanish stage at the time. Traditionally, the leading actor had taken the role of director in theatrical productions and the National Theatres were among the first to have a genuine director figure who coordinated all aspects of the production.[10] They collaborated with an illustrious group of set designers and costume designers (e.g. Sigfrido Burmann, Emilio Burgos, Víctor Cortezo, José Caballero and

Vicente Viudes), many of whom had worked abroad and/or in the past with Alberti, Rivas Cherif and/or García Lorca.[11]

The extra financial resources that the theatres had at their disposal, combined with more time for rehearsals than was habitual in most private companies, allowed the Español and María Guerrero to maintain a standard of production that was unparalleled in the admittedly bleak theatrical landscape of the post-Civil War period. Most obviously, they were able to dispense with the *apuntador* [prompter], a ubiquitous presence on the Spanish stage at the time.[12] Even in this period of economic hardship, huge amounts of money were invested in these state theatres, which were also exempt from taxation.[13]

Performances outside Madrid and/or by private and independent companies were rare but not unknown. Ricardo Calvo and Enrique Borrás, two renowned actors with their own companies, were famed for their grandiloquent renditions of Calderón's verse. The Compañía Ricardo Calvo staged, for example, a version of *La vida es sueño* at the Coliseum in Madrid from 1–3 and 6–8 March 1940 (García-Alegre Sánchez, 1981, p. 6). Enrique Rambal was also famed for his emotionally wrought productions which toured extensively. From 1942 onwards, the Español Company travelled to Barcelona where it often staged classics as part of its repertoire; *La dama duende* was included in its first season there (Gallén, 1985, p. 45). Also in the Catalan capital, the Teatro de Arte de Marta Grau y Arturo Carbonell performed an eclectic range of Spanish classics including Lope's *La discreta enamorada* and Calderón's *El gran teatro del mundo* throughout the 1940s, although the plays were normally staged for one night only.[14]

Beyond the National Theatres, the other principal outlet for Golden Age drama in the period was the TEU. This movement, which would come to encompass companies from across the country, began in Madrid when Modesto Higueras was asked by the SEU to create a National TEU.[15] The company debuted at the Español with Tirso's *La mujer por fuerza*; the play was performed alongside an act from a Thornton Wilder play (Higueras, 1965, p. 67). In its choice of dramatic works, the TEUs were even more geared towards the performance of the classics than the National Theatres.

Higueras had worked alongside Lorca, and the TEUs were clearly inspired by La Barraca and Misiones Pedagógicas although they lacked the social conscience of these groups. In Antonio Zapatero Vicente's memorable if reductive phrase, 'el TEU es La Barraca pasada por la doctrina del Imperio' [the TEU is La Barraca filtered through the doctrine of empire] (1999, p. 201). According to Eduardo Pérez-Rasilla:

> En principio los TEUs se orientan hacia la representación de los clásicos españoles del Siglo de Oro. Los universitarios parecen echar de menos la presencia de estos textos en los escenarios comerciales u opinan que falta calidad en sus montajes. Por las noticias de que disponemos, parece que

estos trabajos se orientaron hacia una puesta en escena digna, que cuidara lo que tradicionalmente se ha denominado propiedad escénica, pero rara vez debieron de plantearse otros objetivos, aunque éstos justifican ya una labor teatral. (1999, pp. 37–8)

[In theory, the TEUs were orientated towards the staging of the Spanish classics from the Golden Age. University students appear to have missed the presence of these texts on the commercial stage, or to have felt that productions were lacking in quality. From the information available to us, it appears that their efforts were orientated towards quality performance that took care of what has traditionally been termed stage propriety. Their aspirations may have stopped there, but were sufficient in themselves to justify their theatrical endeavours.]

By the end of 1939, the classics were being performed by the TEU Barcelona. In October 1939, a fifteenth-century *auto* and Cervantes's *La cueva de Salamanca* were staged; Lope's *La dama boba* was performed in 1940, and Tirso de Molina's *Don Gil de las calzas verdes* in 1941 (Aznar Soler, 1999, pp. 112–13). All over the country, TEUs emerged to offer exemplary (according to the standards of the time) versions of 'universal' texts. Performances were often given in the presence of illustrious guests and served an important sociopolitical function. For example, in 1941 the TEU Sevilla performed Schiller's *Mary Stuart* along with excerpts from *La vida es sueño* in honour of their visitors from the Nazi Women's Movement.[16] When Franco visited the city in May 1943, the TEU staged Calderón's *El gran teatro del mundo* and *Los encantos de la culpa* as part of an evening of entertainment prepared in his honour (Bajo Martínez, 1999, p. 224).

On a smaller scale, the Sección Femenina [Women's Section] was also responsible for staging *comedias*. Within the movement's official school, there was a small theatre where dramatic works could be performed. Although a surprisingly eclectic range of works was staged, special emphasis was placed on Golden Age drama that was used for both dramatic and pedagogical purposes. For example, Mercedes Fórmica, one of the movement's early leaders, staged a number of works by Lope, Tirso and Calderón for children and adolescents (Suárez Fernández, 1993, pp. 138, 345). In many cases, the Sección Femenina did not have a suitable theatrical space and teachers would simply choose dramatic works from a prescribed list, heavily loaded towards the national classics, that they would make adolescents recite out loud (Noval Clemente, 1999, pp. 151–3).

More generally, the civilizing function of the classics was reflected in education policy. As early as 1938, the Nationalist side had supported special pedagogical editions of play texts including *El alcalde de Zalamea, El príncipe constante* and *El condenado por desconfiado* (Valls, 1983, pp. 124–5). Subsequently, in a talk delivered at the Seventh Week of National Education, Gabriel Orizana asked the following rhetorical question:

'¿Dónde podría verse expuesto con más galanura el amor conyugal, base de la familia, que en el lindísimo diálogo entre Casilda y Peribáñez?' [Where can one see marital love expressed as the bedrock of the family with more finesse than in the lovely exchange between Casilda and Peribáñez?] (1940, p. 111).

On 2 November 1941, the Ministry of Education created a centre of studies on Lope de Vega with the aim of increasing awareness and knowledge of the life and works of a figure often referred to as the national phoenix through the filter of Nationalist ideology. *Peribáñez y el Comendador de Ocaña* and *Fuente Ovejuna* were the plays taught most, and they were seen to embody national values. The former was thought to be of special use in educating girls as Casilda provided a model of the ideal Spanish wife. Nevertheless, as Fernando Valls argues, '[s]obre Lope de Vega llovaron en la posguerra gran cantidad de tópicos, su vida y su obra fueron completamente mitificados y su obra, en comparación, poco estudiada' [There was a deluge of clichés about Lope de Vega in the post-war period. His life and works were completely mythologized; in comparison, the work itself was studied very little] (1983, p. 151). This is borne out in the recollections of Rafael Pérez Sierra who would, in years to come, play a vital role in the revitalization of *comedia* performance:

> En los estudios de mi bachillerato, antiquísimo, aprendíamos grandes listas de obras y no leíamos ninguna; entonces decíamos de nuestro repertorio que era el más abundante de todos los repertorios. Mencionar el número exagerado y equivocado de obras de Lope era como sentir orgullo de esa 'armada invencible', que no fue tan invencible. Podíamos con todos. ¿Qué era Shakespeare con sus treinta y siete únicas obras? (1994, p. 261)

> [In my studies for the very old-school bachillerato, we learnt huge lists of works but without reading any; in those days, we said that our repertory was the the most abundant of all repertoires. To mention an exaggerated and incorrect number of works by Lope was equivalent to feeling proud of that 'invincible armada' that was not quite so invincible. We could take on anyone. What was Shakespeare with his thirty-seven plays?]

It was, however, Calderón who was the most regularly staged of all the Golden Age playwrights; at the Instituto de Teatro [Theatre Institute] in Barcelona, for example, the conservative Guillem Díaz-Plaja focussed student performance almost exclusively on the Castilian classics and, between 1940 and 1949, Calderón was the most performed of all playwrights with the students staging five of his dramatic works (Graells, 1990, p. 93). Across the peninsular, Luciano García Lorenzo and Manuel Muñoz Carabantes have calculated nineteen productions of his plays between 1939 and 1949. As they argue, this prominence was most likely a consequence of the potential many of his works had to be reappropriated in tune with the political climate of the time: 'Posiblemente se consideró que la gravedad de sus dramas y la elevación teológica de sus autos cuadraban más con la austeridad del momento que el carácter lírico o festivo de muchas obras de Lope' [It is possible that the seriousness of his dramatic works and the theological weight of his Corpus Christi plays provided a better fit for the austerity of the time than the lyrical and festive nature of many of Lope's plays] (2000, p. 423). As early as 1941, Ángel Valbuena Prat advanced a similar argument, albeit from a very different perspective: 'Calderón es un poeta esencialmente católico. Por esto en la nueva y cada vez más extensa catolicidad se halla un motivo más para la vuelta a Calderón' [Calderón is essentially a Catholic poet. In the context of an increasingly widespread Catholicism, we have an additional reason for us to return to Calderón] (1941, p. 47).

In addition to the ideologically informed choice of repertoire, the approach to the staging of the classics was also the result of assumptions that had huge political ramifications. Golden Age drama was construed as universally good art that contained 'universal' truths. The challenge facing the theatre practitioner was not to adapt the work to the needs of the present but to facilitate access to the genius of the past.

Cayetano Luca de Tena (director of the Español 1942–52 and 1962–4), Lluch's young assistant, took charge of the National Theatre following his former boss's premature death. Luca de Tena has directed more *comedias* than any other Spanish director in the modern age and has summarized his approach in the following terms:

> Si se hace una obra de Lope hay que atenerse a lo que él escribió, porque el teatro es producto de una sociedad concreta, con unos problemas concretos y una forma y un fondo específicos. Es un documento histórico, como la pintura o la novela, y a nadie se le ocurre ponerse a retocar *Las Meninas*, por ejemplo. Sólo debe eliminarse, aligerarse, aquello que por el paso del tiempo no se entienda. (cited in Santa-Cruz, 1993, p. 72)

> [If one stages a Lope play, attention must be paid to what he wrote; the theatre is a product of a given society with concrete problems and a specific content and form. It is a historical document akin to paintings or novels and, to cite just one example, it would not occur to anyone to give *Las Meninas* a makeover. The only changes should involve excising or making intelligible that which has been made obscure by the passage of time.]

It might seem that this claim was contradicted by his costly stage sets which were often greeted with applause the moment the curtain opened. However, Luca de Tena argued that such techniques could help bring out the essence of the play. In his 1941 production *of La dama duende*, there were revolving platforms on which characters would enter and exit at the beginning and end of every scene; the director claimed in the programme his wish to 'hacer patente, por medio de una escenografía adecuada, el ritmo gracioso y suave que su autor le infundiera al escribirla en 1629 en pleno Madrid de Felipe IV' [to make clear, via a suitable stage design, the comic and light rhythm with which the author infused his play on writing it in 1629 in the midst of Philip IV's Madrid] (Teatro Español, 1941). He also argued that elaborate staging made the works more accessible and that this did not constitute any betrayal of the play text: 'Si nuestros clásicos no acumularon más recursos escenográficos en sus representaciones, era sencillamente porque aún no se habían inventado' [If our classics did not amass more scenic devices, it was simply because they had yet to be invented].[17] He asserted that the fact audiences need help in understanding the classics as a lamentable, but undeniable, truth. The only alternative was to cut, or make significant changes to, the playwright's text and this was tantamount to blasphemy. For someone who was seemingly so enamoured of Golden Age playwrights, he showed remarkably little faith in their ability to communicate with the modern-day spectator:

> Todo el secreto de la representación de estos autores, que llamamos nuestros clásicos, estriba en la velocidad y lógica de las mutaciones escénicas. Lo que no se puede hacer es aburrir previamente, con intervalos repetidos, a un espectador que – generalmente – no se siente demasiado interesado por lo que ocurre. Los que asisten a estas representaciones tienen ya motivos de sobra para considerarlas soporíferas. (1953a, p. 46)
>
> [The whole secret of performing those authors we refer to as our classics lies in the speed and logic of the scene changes. What one cannot do is bore a spectator who – generally speaking – has little interest in what is going on with repeated pauses. Those who attend these performances already have reasons aplenty to consider them soporific.]

This does raise the question of why, if he felt that the classics had such an effect on the audience, he insisted on staging them. However, emerging as he did from a culture in which the moral and pedagogical value of the classics was accepted without reflection, he never poses this question.[18] Though he accepted that plays emerged, like Velázquez's *Las Meninas*, from a given historical moment, he took for granted that they contained universal values and were, as such, timeless. There is clearly a political correlative to such a conception; if the classics are universal and inalterable, then there are universal values; hence materialist and Marxist interpretations of history can be dismissed in favour of more elevated and spiritual values.

This conception of the classics underpins reviews written in this period. Newspaper critics were remarkably homogenous in their approach and style; reviews took the format of a couple of lines eulogizing a playwright supported by a comment from an expert, usually Marcelino Menéndez y Pelayo or Karl Vossler, followed by a brief description of the literary version prepared for the stage (the closer it is perceived to be to the play text, the better the review) and then some references to the staging and an account of how enthralled the audience was.[19] These reviews performed an important role in forging what Jochen Heymann has referred to as 'comunidad virtual' [virtual community] that encompassed a wider demographic than the minority urban audience who were the almost exclusive clientele of most theatres (1998, pp. 132, 140). From a practical perspective, a good or bad review from Alfredo Marquerie in the pages of *ABC* would determine whether a production was a success or failure (Marsillach, 2002, p. 221).[20]

Similarly, the censors at the time had to write in their reports a comment on the literary and theatrical worth of the works they received; when they were theatrical versions of Spanish classics, of all the files I have viewed from the 1940s and 1950s, they are unconditionally positive. It is nevertheless interesting to note that most productions of Golden Age plays were only authorized for spectators over the ages of sixteen or eighteen.[21] It is not clear whether these classifications suggest a conscious or unconscious concern that national drama was not as innocuous as the official view purported it to be or whether, more simply, the formal environment in which the classics were generally staged was not considered as suitable for minors.

It is within this context that we must understand the production and reception of Lope's *Peribáñez* directed by Luca de Tena that opened the 1942–3 season at the Español. The appeal of the play at a time when the 'essence of the Spanish character was usually seen as being embodied in the virtues of the Spanish small-holding peasantry of Castile' is clear (Richards, 1996, p. 163). As we have seen in relation to education policy, rural dramas such as *Fuente Ovejuna*, *El villano en su rincón* and *El alcalde de Zalamea* were considered to be exemplary, and they were frequently staged. Hence, for example, when RCA Española released a 'greatest hits' of the Golden Age titled *Teatro clásico español* (available for consultation at the Biblioteca Nacional), it opened with the exchange between Casilda and her husband on the merits of marriage.

Nicolás González Ruiz's version is generally faithful to Lope's text,[22] although it is has been abridged and some lines have been changed to facilitate audience understanding and retain propriety.[23] The musical score was provided by Manuel Parada de la Puente who collaborated with Luca de Tena on most of his productions. *Peribáñez* gave him ample scope to demonstrate his talents with the inclusion, for example, of what was seen to be authentic and traditional folkloric music for the wedding scene.[24]

Tomás Borrás was very unusual in expressing reservations; he rigorously applies the fidelity criterion to argue that the sumptuous set was too dominant and acted to the detriment of Lope's verse (1942). Nevertheless, other critics were unanimous in praising Spain, its national playwright and the creative team at the Español. For example, a representative review from

ABC praised the expert depiction of '[d]os ejemplares magníficos de una raza, que ni se da ni se vende, porque son ejemplares sus actos y la recia conducta que observaron en su vida' [two magnificent examples of their race that are incorruptible and true to themselves through the exemplarity of their acts and the righteous conduct of their day-to-day living] (Rodenas, 1942).

The years of development? The *comedia* as exemplary theatre (1950–63)

In the 1950s, the staging of Golden Age plays came to represent more of a cultural than a patriotic rite, and there was a general move away from the more overt nationalism of the previous decade. Indicative of this fact is that in 1951 the National Theatres ceased to be under the jurisdiction of the Ministry of National Education and became the responsibility of the newly created Ministry of Information and Tourism. It is also reflected in the choice of repertoire. Although the most emblematic works (*Fuente Ovejuna, El alcalde de Zalamea, La vida es sueño*) continued to be performed, there was an increased preference for comedies (*Don Gil de las calzas verdes, La discreta enamorada, El acero de Madrid, La dama duende*, etc.).

The National Theatres and the TEUs remained loyal to the classics though they gradually became more adventurous in their repertoires and more open to foreign playwrights as the decade progressed. Most private theatre impresarios avoided Spanish seventeenth-century drama as they had little faith in its commercial viability. Jacinto Benavente criticized this attitude, and claimed that it was a national duty to represent more Golden Age drama and that, if performed well, these works could generate significant revenue (1949).

As we have seen, there were nevertheless a select number of private commercial companies, generally run by ageing but much-loved actor/ directors that occasionally dabbled with the classics. In 1951, the Compañía Borrás-Guitart staged a special one-off performance of *El alcalde de Zalamea* starring Borrás and Calvo 'con motivo de haber sido nombrados hijos predilectos de Madrid' [in honour of them being named favourite sons of Madrid] (*ABC*, 1951).[25] Until very near his death in 1956, Rambal ran a company that alternated classics, both Spanish and foreign, with more modern fare although he claimed that his repertoire made little commercial sense: 'Ya sé que con esas obras suelo perder el dinero que gano con las otras, pero no me importa. En ese contrapeso hallo una de mis más íntimas satisfacciones' [I know that I tend to lose the money with these works that I earn with the others, but it does not bother me. I find one of my most innermost pleasures in this balance] (cited in Marquerie, 1956).[26]

Given this context, it is perhaps surprising that the mid 1950s constituted a veritable boom in *comedia* performance; the 1953–4 season marked the first significant increase since the end of the Civil War in the number of productions outside Madrid, and also by private companies. This pattern would be repeated in the following two seasons (Muñoz Carabantes, 1992, p. 187). Both increases were largely due to José Tamayo and the precedent he set. Tamayo was probably the most important person working with the classics in the 1950s. He claims that, inspired by the achievements of the National Theatres, he was determined to take quality theatre beyond the capital (1953). In 1941, he had created the Grupo de Teatro Universitario 'Lope de Vega' in Granada which later became a private company, simply named Lope de Vega. It was his very successful productions of *Peribáñez* and *La cena del rey Baltasar* in different South American countries that really established his name and throughout the 1950s his company toured Spain incessantly. From 1954 onwards, he combined this activity with directing the Español where he managed to install his own company and negotiate the tightrope of public and private investment in nimble fashion (Checa, 2003).[27]

The results may have been fairly old fashioned and conservative in their approach but their popularity among audiences cannot be denied. Mary Carrillo, who was for a long time the company's leading lady, claims in her memoirs that Tamayo's success was due to a mixture of business acumen and artistic sensibility:

> Empezó a conseguir importantes subvenciones del estado sin las cuales era imposible representar comedias y dramas del Siglo de Oro. Tuvo la inteligencia y sagacidad de rodearse de los mejores actores de su época y juntar a los mejores artistas. De los primeros, recibía opiniones y consejos que él pagaba con largueza y de los artistas (como decoradores, pintores, autores, traductores, etc.) extrajo lo mejor. Era un artista de artistas y un empresario modélico. (2001, p. 133)

> [He began to receive important subsidies from the state, without which it was impossible to stage Golden Age dramas and comedies. He had the intelligence and foresight to surround himself with the best actors of the time and to bring together the best creative team. From the former, he would receive opinions and advice that he rewarded generously, and he got the best out of the artists (in their capacities as set designers, painters, writers, translators). He knew how to use artists artistically, and he was an exemplary businessman.]

Although the company included actors of the calibre and fame of Carrillo and a young Francisco Rabal, it was Tamayo himself who provided the real market value. As Marquerie argues, this was because his name became something of a brand and assurance of quality:

A la consigna 'es un film de Paramount' sucedió la de 'es un espectáculo Tamayo' y aunque, lo que él hizo recibió el mote de 'teatroscope' y no le faltaron ni enemigos ni envidiosos, Tamayo siguió adelante y además estrenó unas obras estupendas, españolas y extranjeras, clásicas y actuales, que de otro modo no se habrían presentado nunca en nuestros escenarios y a las que sirvió de cebo lícito y legítimo esa espectacularidad que tanto le censuraron algunos. (1969, p. 174).

[In a manner akin to the logo 'a film from Paramount', there appeared 'a theatrical production from Tamayo'. Although he was not lacking in enemies or jealous competitors, and he was dismissed with the moniker 'theatrescope', Tamayo kept going. Furthermore, he managed to stage some excellent works from both Spain and abroad, combining classics with modern-day plays, which could not otherwise have been performed on our stages; this in itself legitimized the spectacular style, which was often so heavily criticized, as a justifiable means of enticing the general public.]

As the decade progressed, more people outside Madrid came to have access to classic plays as an increasing number of productions began to tour. In the early 1950s the tradition of national TEU competitions began. Golden Age works were often entered, and were occasionally taken to international festivals. The Barcelona TEU, for example, won the National Competition for University Drama with Lope's *La dama boba*, and their version of *El castigo sin venganza* was also very well received at international festivals in Saarbrücken and Parma (Pérez de Olaguer, 1999a, p. 57).

It was also in this decade that the famous Festivales de España began. These events which took place all over Spain would feature a range of public and private theatre companies presenting their works in large outdoor settings. Hence, for example, in May 1953 the people of Seville had the opportunity to see subsidized performances of three comedies in the Parque de María Luisa: Tirso's *Don Gil*, Lope's *La discreta enamorada* and Calderón's *La dama duende*. One of the slogans of the Festival was 'Llevar la cultura a las plazas de todos los pueblos' [Taking culture to every village square], and it is clear that this project constituted 'toda una maniobra paternalista de la dictadura franquista' [a genuinely paternalistic manoeuvre by the Francoist dictatorship] (Santa-Cruz, 1995, p. 192). Nevertheless it is also likely that such productions provided a welcome relief from the drudge of everyday existence and attracted a wider cross section of social classes than would be found in the National Theatres.[28]

Especially at the beginning of the decade, discussion of the Spanish classics was still used as a thinly veiled pretext for national exaltation: 'Familiarizarse con el teatro de Shakespeare es buena cosa, pero lo es mejor conocer, comprender y admirar a Lope, a Calderón, a Tirso de Molina, a Moreto y tantos autores españoles, fuente y cuna del teatro universal' [It is a good thing to familiarize yourself with Shakespeare's theatre but it is even better to get to know, to understand and to admire Lope, Calderón, Tirso de Molina, Moreto and so many Spanish authors who have provided the bedrock and cradle of universal theatre] (Alcalá, 1952). As N. de la Ruiz observed, critics were also complimentary to audiences attending such works: 'el público que asistía a una obra clásica era juzgado culto y el mismo de asistir a un estreno "raro" era tildado de "sediento de emociones inconfesables", "snob", "afrancesado", etc. . . ') [the audience that attended a classical play were considered to be cultured whilst those who attended a 'strange' premiere were branded as 'gasping for inadmissible emotions', 'snobbish', 'Frenchified', etc. . .] (1971, p. 23)

Spanish classical drama also continued, throughout the decade, to represent an exemplary kind of theatre well suited to important ceremonial occasions. In the summer of 1953, Tamayo took his spectacular production of *La cena del rey Baltasar* to Rome, and it became the first dramatic work ever to be performed in the Vatican. In addition to the presence of the pope, important Spanish dignitaries, including the director general of cinema and theatre, were present at the auspicious occasion.[29] When, in May 1954, an original seventeenth-century *corral* was reopened in Almagro, it was attended by most of the major reviewers from the capital and important local and national dignitaries (Espinosa, 1997, p. 49). To cite another example, the University of Salamanca invited three professional companies to perform *Don Gil de las calzas verdes*, *La discreta enamorada* and *La vida es sueño* in celebration of the university's seven hundredth birthday (Pérez Bowie, 1999, p. 148).

Though national exaltation remained the dominant tone, there was an increasing openness to foreign works and productions. Although it occurred less frequently than in the Republican period, foreign companies did begin to perform again in Spain; in 1950, for example, the Comédie Française visited Madrid.[30] Equally, with the appearance of specialist theatre magazines, *Teatro* and later *PA*,[31] writers and practitioners who had travelled abroad began to discuss the superiority of foreign theatre, especially English and German, in terms of writing, production and receptive audiences. In reference to the classics, this was manifested in envious references to Shakespeare performance (Ferrers, 1953). The fetishization of the English theatrical experience and an almost pathological case of Shakespeare envy have characterized Spanish discourse on Golden Age drama to this day.

While reviews of performances from this period are generally positive, with the exception of the *autos sacramentales*, productions of Golden Age drama ceased to be as immune to criticism as they once had been.[32] Two charges were constantly levelled against productions: the unreflective recourse to spectacle (Calvo, 1952; Sánchez, 1957), and the inability of the actors to recite verse (Ayllón, 1952; Díaz Cañabate, 1952). Both criticisms were indicative of the fact that, despite there being a large number of *comedias* being staged, there was no investigation of how they ought to be performed. It is incredible, when one considers how many works were staged at the Español, that no training schemes or discussion forums were ever established. The end result was that every actor had a different way of reciting verse, usually learnt from observing others, and the productions had a default setting whereby they used lavish settings to entice audiences. As Muñoz Carabantes notes:

> Un cierto acartonamiento pareció hacerse inevitable con el tiempo. Y esta rutina en vez de combatirse mediante el análisis del sentido de las obras (qué ideas o valores de cualquier índole podían éstas aportar a la España de 1950–1960), se intentó obviar a través de la hipertrofia escenográfica. (1992, p. 115)
>
> [A certain staidness seems to have become inevitable over time. Instead of combating this routinism through the detailed analysis of the plays' meaning (what kind of ideas or values could they offer to the Spain of the 1950s), they tried to circumvent the problem through scenographic overload.]

Until the mid 1950s, Golden Age plays continued to perform an important role in the repertoires of Tamayo's troupe, the National Theatres, the TEUs and some private companies. The classics often attracted generous subsidies and this, in part, accounted for their continued performance. However, as the decade approached its end, there was an increasing interest in contemporary and foreign playwrights. This transition is hardly surprising when one takes into account the move towards social and economic modernization, and European integration, actively pursued by the regime from the mid 1950s onwards. Thus, for better or worse, Golden Age drama was performed less and less. As the Peruvian Nobel prize winning novelist Mario Vargas Llosa has recently recalled of the year he spent in the Spanish capital:

> Una de mis ilusiones, en 1958, cuando obtuve la beca Javier Prado para hacer el doctorado en la Complutense, en Madrid, fue que en España vería por fin, en un escenario y no en los libros, como debe verse el teatro, obras de Calderón, de Lope, de Tirso de Molina y otros dramaturgos del gran siglo de la literatura en lengua española. Pero en los años 58 y 59, en Madrid, la única obra clásica que pude ver fue *La dama boba*, de Lope, montado por Ricardo Blume ¡un joven actor y director peruano! (2007, p. 33)
>
> [One of the things that excited me in 1958 when I received the Javier Prado scholarship to study for my doctorate in Madrid Complutense was that I would, in Spain, at last be able to see plays by Calderón, Lope, Tirso de Molina and other great dramatists from the great century of literature written in the Spanish language. I would be able to see them not in books but on the stage, where theatre ought to seen. But the only classical play on

offer in Madrid during the 1958–9 season was Lope's *Lady Nitwit* staged by Ricardo Blume, a young Peruvian actor and director!]

This is not, however, to say that the *comedia* was completely absent from the Spanish stage. In 1955, the Barcelona TEU of Philosophy and Literature performed a version of *El burlador de Sevilla* which featured modern-day clothes and music (Ciurans, 2009, pp. 141–2). This was an early precursor to a small number of very important productions in the late 1950s and early 1960s. At the beginning of 1958, Adolfo Marsillach's company staged a very popular version of one of Lope's lighter comedies, *Los locos de Valencia*, at the Teatro Lara in Madrid; Marsillach, who also directed the production, was rewarded for his efforts with the National Prize for Theatre.

On a smaller scale, but arguably more important in terms of influence, an independent theatre company called Dido staged a version of Lope's risqué *La viuda valenciana*. The project began modestly but according to director Ángel Fernández Montesinos, 'tuvo tal éxito que pasó al Teatro Reina Victoria en temporada comercial, caso totalmente infrecuente' [it was so successful that, in a very unusual transfer, it went on to be staged at the Queen Victoria Theatre as part of its commercial season] (2008, p. 49). Most reviews of this production were positive although critics often took the opportunity to lament the fact that Golden Age drama now had to rely predominantly on the Teatro de Cámara [Chamber Theatre] (Álvaro, 1961, pp. 271–4). Traditionally, it had been possible for more radical works to be performed in these spaces because there was a category that allowed the censor to permit works by these groups to be staged solely in specific locations. In this case, if we look at the censorship file for *La viuda valenciana*, we can see that this perhaps led Dido to be more ambitious in the cuts and edits that they made to the text than previous productions had been. Josefina Sánchez-Pedrero, writing on their collective behalf, notes that the company had originally staged the play in a faithful version in 1955, but that editing the text further would reap additional benefits:

> Plenamente convencidas de la necesidad de divulgar el teatro clásico haciéndolo llegar al espectador actual por medio de adecuadas adaptaciones que resalten su vigencia, el teatro experimental que dirijo va a iniciar una serie de representaciones de aquella naturaleza con una de las joyas del teatro de Lope: *La viuda valenciana*.[33]

> [Convinced as we are of the need to disseminate classical theatre, facilitating access to the modern-day spectator by means of suitable changes that highlight its relevance, the experimental theatre company that I direct will initiate a series of performances of this kind with one of the jewels of Lope's theatre: *The Valencian Widow*.]

Perhaps inspired by the success of *Los locos de Valencia* and *La viuda valenciana*,[34] José Luis Alonso – a young director who had previously voiced his desire to stage a version of Calderón's *El hijo pródigo* in the modern day with jazz music (Hormigón, 1991, p. 164) – staged a version of Lope's *El anzuelo de Fenisa* in 1961 at the María Guerrero. From the pages of *PA*, José Monleón applauded the production that he thought boded well for the upcoming centenary of the playwright's birth:

> En el María Guerrero se aplaudió con justificado entusiasmo. ¡Qué dimensión popular, viva y suficiente, la del lenguaje! Pienso que este cuarto centenario deberíamos aprovecharlo para devolverle a Lope, en nuestros escenarios, su vitalidad y lozanía, tan a menudo ignorada para los que todo reducen a un ¡Viva a Cartagena! (1961)

> [At the María Guerrero, it was applauded with justified enthusiasm. It was incredible how popular, alive and effective the language was! I think that we ought to take advantage of this fourth centenary to reimbue Lope with his vibrancy on stage; a vitality so frequently ignored by those who want to reduce everything to 'Long Live Cartagena!']

This vogue for Lope's lighter comedies, many written when he was a young man and featuring lively and proactive female characters, was not unrelated to wider social changes. The Francoist regime had traditionally sought to ensure that social encounters and relations between the sexes had been subject to a series of codified rules and gendered hierarchies that set Spain apart from the rest of Europe.[35] Nevertheless, as Giuliana Di Febo notes:

> A finales de los años cincuenta, el crecimiento económico, el éxodo rural y la difusión de modelos de emancipación, debidos también a la expansión del turismo y los medios de comunicación, traen consigo una separación creciente entre la norma y los comportamientos sociales. (2003, pp. 41–2)

> [At the end of the 1950s, economic growth, the rural exodus, and the diffusion of libertarian models largely as a result of the tourist and media booms led to an increasingly wide gulf between prescribed conduct and actual social behaviour.]

Women took on a more public role in an increasingly capitalist society in which they now performed an important role as consumers and agents of change (Agustín Puerta, 1998). Even ostensibly conservative magazines such as those produced by the Sección Femenina presented 'a new ambivalent femininity which combined both the traditional and the modern' (Coca Hernando, 1998, p. 13).[36] An oscillation between activity and passivity in female characters alongside the clash or tension between official mores and individual actions is the hallmark of much Golden Age comedy.[37] These continuities and parallels are, for example, one reason why Gustavo Tambascio's 2005 production of *La discreta enamorada*, set in and around the Chicote bar of the 1950s where actress Ava Gardner, bullfighter Luis Miguel Domínguín and singer Sara Montiel were regulars, was so entertaining and well executed.

Perhaps as a result of individual productions being successful, the state once again attempted to resurrect public interest in the *comedia* in the early 1960s. Los Títeres, Teatro Nacional de Juventudes [The Puppets, National Youth Theatre], operating under the auspices of the Sección Femenina, began to stage adaptations of classic texts. In their first two seasons, they staged Tirso's *Don Gil de las calzas verdes*, Lope's *El acero de Madrid* and *Pastores de Belén*, and Calderón's *El pleito matrimonial del cuerpo y el alma* for teenagers.[38] It was, however, the 1962–3 season, coinciding with the anniversary of Lope's birth, which constituted the regime's most systematic engagement with a seventeenth-century dramatist while also marking the final point in which official channels would dedicate energy to the staging of the classics. It is worth detailing the activities surrounding this year as they illuminate the limitations of the approach to the classics of the time while also helping to explain the future trajectory of Golden Age drama on the Spanish stage.

Considering that the tricentenary of Lope's death in 1935 had been celebrated so effusively by the Second Republic, there was arguably a conscious or unconscious desire to better these earlier commemorations.[39] In preparation, the compulsory subject for all students studying for university entry course was *Lope de Vega y su tiempo: Estudio especial de 'El villano en su rincón'* (Ruiz-Fornells, 1963, p. 563). Luca de Tena, who had been dismissed from the Español in the 1950s as a result of his living with an unmarried woman, returned to the helm. He clearly believed that Lope ought to outlive these celebrations: 'Entiende el Ministerio de Información y Turismo – y yo comparto plenamente este punto de vista – que el Teatro Español debe destinarse a la representación sistemática de los autores españoles llamados "clásicos"' [The Ministry of Information and Tourism believes – and I am in complete agreement – that the Teatro Español ought to dedicate itself to the continual performance of those Spanish authors known as 'the classics'] (1962). As will later become evident, this hope was both premature and optimistic. Muñoz Carabantes has calculated that, of the seventy-four productions of Lope's works staged between September 1955 and August 1969, exactly half of them took place in the year of the fourth centenary (1992, p. 240).

In line with the mood of the time, the repertoire was largely based around lesser-known comedies with strong female roles (e.g. *El perro del hortelano, La malcasada, El caballero de milagro, La bella malmaridada, Por la puente, Juana*). As a result, mainstream audiences were often exposed to a more risqué and picaresque side of the *comedia* than they had been accustomed to. Take, for example, *La bella malmaridada* in which Alfredo Landa appeared in a *comedia* which anticipates the Iberian comedy films that would make him a household name in the late 1960s. In the play, Leonardo's voracious sexual appetite leads him to compulsively pursue extra-marital sexual adventures yet when he suspects his wife, Casandra, of having an affair, he wants to have her killed. The censor wrote of this play that it was '[m]oralmente, sin peligro' [morally harmless] but then adds a rather cryptic disclaimer: 'Por tratarse de una obra clásica, los conceptos, frases y situaciones a los que se pudiera hacer algún reparo desde el punto de vista normal, no tienen ninguna importancia' [There are concepts, phrases and situations which would normally occasion some doubts but, as we are dealing with a classical play, these are of no importance]. In theory, major productions of this kind ought to have broadened public opinion on Lope. However, Spaniards were still bombarded with an image of the national phoenix as a source of pride. This was reflected in many productions that were often rendered through vast spectacles and/or in a light folkloric guise.

Even before the official 1962–3 season had begun, a new version of *El nuevo mundo* was staged at the Español; its opening night was the so-called *Día de la Hispanidad* [*Hispanic Day*]. Elsewhere in Madrid, Luca de Tena directed at the Alcázar theatre a new play with an old title: Alfonso Paso's *El mejor mozo de España*. The production, featuring over sixty actors, depicted a day in the life of a young and hot-blooded Lope, in the style of one of his *comedias* with cameo appearances from many famous contemporaries: Cervantes, Quevedo and Góngora.[40] The María Guerrero also provided a temporary home for two prestigious student productions: *El acero de Madrid* by the Sección Femenina TEU and *El mejor alcalde, el rey* by the TEU from the faculty of medicine (Peláez Martín, 1996, p. 96).

Over the course of the year, Tamayo offered a typically grandiose reposition of *Fuente Ovejuna* that then toured extensively, as did many of the National Theatre productions. *El perro del hortelano* was, for example, performed alongside Moreto's *El lindo don Diego* as part of the Cuenca Festival which the programme claimed was 'destinado a elevar el nivel cultural de un pueblo sustentado sobre la paz, la serenidad y la alegría' [designed to raise the cultural level of a population sustained by peace, serenity and happiness] (Ministerio de Información y Turismo, 1963). Local towns also staged and/or housed performances of Lope plays that related to their geographical environs; *Fuente Ovejuna* was performed in Fuente Ovejuna, *El cabellero de Olmedo* in Olmedo,[41] and *Los guanches de Tenerife y conquista de Canarías* in Santa Cruz de Tenerife (Álvaro, 1963, p. 24).

There were also a number of student productions staged across the country. One of the most memorable of these nearly did not take place at all. The TEU Zaragoza, attracted by the play's light and frivolous vaudeville feel, decided to stage *La noche toledana* at the Teatro Principal. However, the SEU failed to pay the owner of the theatre to rent the space and the event only went ahead when the actors and director took to personally selling tickets in a venture that ultimately became a huge success as a gala performance that attracted both celebrities and dignitaries.[42]

Despite this burst of activity, the fourth centenary celebrations were disappointing in that they did not constitute an engagement with, or an investigation of, Lope's work. According to Monleón, the only exception to this was a version of *Porfiar hasta morir*, performed alongside Lorca's *La zapatera prodigiosa* by a company from Uruguay (1980, pp. 253–4). The vast majority of productions relied on spectacle to hide their failure to genuinely engage with the text. Private companies did not generally stage Lope's works – now the almost exclusive preserve of official and state subsidized theatres – and there were no additional activities beyond the performances themselves.

By the end of the year, Monleón had become disillusioned with the celebrations and felt that most productions had simply tried to emulate Marsillach's comic style in *Los locos de Valencia* without any panache, intellectual penetration or consideration of what Lope could mean to a contemporary audience (1962). He was not alone in lamenting the generic homogeneity in the representation of Lope's plays in the early 1960s. Ricardo Domènech noted how:

> Antes que nada, debo confesarle al lector que en un año escaso he visto – calculo a ojo – unas veinte obras de Lope. Como, por lo general, los criterios selectivos que han presidido dichas representaciones dejaban mucho que desear, el resultado es que casi todas estas piezas nos ofrecían la imagen de un Lope desenfadado y superficial, que es, claro está, el Lope que hoy menos nos importa. (1963, p. 54)

> [First of all, I should admit to the reader that in barely a year I would hazard a guess that I have seen around twenty plays by Lope. As, in general, the criteria that have guided these performances have left much to be desired, almost all of these pieces have offered us the image of a superficial, free and easy Lope; suffice to say, this is the Lope who is of least relevance to us today.]

With self-congratulatory performances of this kind, it is perhaps not surprising that more adventurous theatre practitioners and audiences began to look elsewhere for their dramatic sustenance. As modern foreign dramatists came to be staged with increasing regularity, the image of the national classics was not helped by conservative critics' tendency to use the *comedia* as a rallying call for their reactionary attitudes towards the theatre and the world in general. Hence, for example, Blas Piñar proved as intransigent in matters of cultural taste as he was in politics,[43] and wrote an essay in *ABC* that praised Lope and Tamayo's production of *Fuente Ovejuna* for unconditionally glorifying the institutions of marriage and social order (1962). This tendency resulted in a pervasive yet false dichotomy between tradition and innovation in artistic sensibility that was often construed as a reliable indicator of political affiliation. The aesthetic and ideological straitjacketing that took place from both ends of the political spectrum would have an increasingly decisive and detrimental effect on how the classics would be staged over the coming years.

Waiting underground: the wilderness years (1964–75)

A reduction in the level of state support and an increased cynicism on the part of many theatre practitioners and audiences meant that, for the first time in the post-Civil War period, Golden Age drama had to consistently justify its existence on the stage. It was no longer thought to be of a priori value. In many respects, patterns established in the late 1950s and early 1960s prior to Lope's fourth centenary were a rehearsal for what would take place between 1964 and the end of the dictatorship. While the majority distanced themselves from the *comedia*, those that remained engaged in its performance often fought against Luca de Tena's archaeological approach to examine how the classics had to be adapted so as to address the needs of the present rather than merely resurrect the past. This resulted in a number of innovative and intelligent productions that constituted a paradigm shift in performance style and established an important precedent. I will begin by sketching the general decline in the staging of seventeenth-century Spanish drama before examining the alternative, albeit minority, discourse that emerged in this period.

The classics were performed less and less as the 1960s progressed. Only 2.4 per cent of works programmed in Madrid between 1960 and 1969 were from the Golden Age and the fact that, in terms of number of performances, this percentage was reduced to 1.8 is indicative of their lack of success (Cuesta Martínez, 1988, pp. 130–1). There was an increased eclecticism in the programming at the National Theatres and, as such, Spanish classical drama no longer had a guaranteed sanctuary. In this period, Tamayo also began to turn his attention primarily to foreign works. Furthermore, tensions between the SEU and the TEUs alongside an increased politicization in universities meant that the TEUs gradually morphed into independent theatre as the 1960s progressed and generally turned away from the classics to more contemporary fare (Oliva, 1980, p. 2). The fact that no Calderón plays were staged at all during 1964 is symptomatic of this wider trend.

In 1966, the Español made one last systematic attempt to resurrect Calderón by inviting a series of high-profile directors (Luca de Tena, Huberto Pérez de la Ossa, Tamayo, Alonso) to stage his works. However, there was no overall directive or objective; the productions could thus have no hope of generating a cumulative effect beyond their individual merits. In general, ticket prices rose throughout the decade confirming the theatre as a primarily elite and minority pastime (Muñoz Carabantes, 1992, p. 202). Nevertheless, the National Theatres attempted to entice a younger and more educated audience by introducing subsidized tickets; students only paid half price and all tickets were reduced by fifty per cent on Mondays and Thursdays. Unfortunately, this did little to help the now ailing theatre whose productions of the Spanish classics proved particularly vulnerable; versions of Shakespeare's works were, for example, far more commercially successful than those by Lope (Pérez Cabrera, 1984, pp. 174–5).

In a similar attempt to encourage a more heterogeneous demographic to watch Golden Age drama, the regime launched the National Theatre Campaign. The first season in 1968 featured productions of *La vida es sueño* and *El castigo sin venganza* as well as Alarcón's *La verdad sospechosa*. Works by Brecht and Valle-Inclán were also included, but some commentators still felt that too much attention was paid to established playwrights, most notably the classics, at the expense of living dramatists (Olmo, 1968). The second campaign in 1969 included Marsillach's production of *Los locos de Valencia* with the Grupo de Teatro 70, and a version of *Fuente Ovejuna* directed by José Osuna with the Compañía Dramática Española (Peláez Martín, 1996, p. 100). By the fourth campaign, however, no Golden Age works were included at all, and the scheme itself was abolished in 1973.

On seeing Marsillach's production of Lope's *Los siete infantes de Lara* in 1967, even the minister of tourism and information, Manuel Fraga, lamented in his diary, 'es indudable que ya no sabemos declamar el verso, y que la sensibilidad actual obligue a seleccionar mucho los clásicos que se repongan' [the fact that we no longer know how to recite verse is beyond doubt, and the modern-day sensibility requires us to be very selective about which of the classics we choose to revive] (1980, p. 157). The *comedia* was seen to be increasingly irrelevant to the concerns of modern-day Spaniards, and a lack of familiarity on the part of the majority of practitioners meant that it was difficult to stage the classics effectively. Indicative of this fact is their virtual absence from the Madrid stage in the theatrical year 1969–70. This season marked the culmination of years of experimental and underground work that was eventually allowed to break into the mainstream. Hence, in the Español, various works by Valle-Inclán and foreign dramatists were staged. In contrast, the only Lope play staged in Madrid was a student production of Lope's *Castelvines y Monteses*; no Calderón play was staged, and Tirso was represented solely by Miguel Narros's *El condenado por desconfiado* (Cornago Bernal, 1997). There were occasional productions in the early 1970s, but I have not been able to find any record of Calderón or Lope being staged in either 1973–4 or 1974–5.

There were various heavily politicized versions of Cervantes's *entremeses* staged in the early 1970s, a political legacy largely derived from the versions staged in the Civil War, and there was a feeling among many that Cervantes was a free thinker as opposed to Lope and Calderón, state lackeys par excellence (Trías, 1968). The overall impression was therefore that Golden Age drama had been superseded by works with more contemporary relevance that had been marginalized by the official culture of the regime (of which the *comedia* had been a prime example). According to this view, the classics were construed as the antithesis of the present, both politically and aesthetically.

On seeing an English production of Lope's *La fianza satisfecha* adapted by angry young man John Osborne, a radical figure venerated in Spanish theatrical circles, Alberti Adell would comment on the irony that in his native land, 'Lope tiene hoy mala prensa: Quien hace más de treinta años "pertenecía al Pueblo", ha venido a identificarse poco menos que con un representante del carcamalismo, de las "derechas" de nuestras letras' [Lope has bad press these days. The man who more than thirty years ago 'belonged to the people' has come to be identified as nothing less than the archetypal decrepit figure that embodies the 'right' of our literary tradition] (1967). An alternative view nevertheless argued that the classics could speak to the needs of the present if only their performance was given due thought and consideration. Throughout the 1960s, the writers of *PA* almost always expressed their admiration for the *comedia* while lamenting the level of performance and engagement supplied by apolitical productions that relied on tried and tested theatrical formulas: 'El problema no está en los "clásicos", sino en nuestro teatro contemporáneo. En nuestra medrosidad polémica. En nuestra falta de audacia. En esa especie de gris solemnidad que cubre el vacío conceptual e ideológico de tantos y tantos abigarrados espectáculos' [The problem does not lie with the 'classics' but rather in our contemporary theatre. In our fear of controversy; in our lack of audacity; in that form of stilted solemnity that attempts to conceal the ideological and conceptual vacuity of so many productions of all different kinds] (Monleón, 1966, p. 51). José María de Quinto adopted a similar logic in his theatre columns in *Ínsula* where he spoke of how 'eran y continúan siendo más modernos nuestros clásicos que quienes en la actualidad tratan de llevarlos a la escena' [our classics were and continue to be more modern than those who try and stage them in the present day] (1965).[44] In opposition to the dominant discourse, these writers thought that the classics were the victims rather than the beneficiaries of their official patronage.[45]

From a practical perspective, a select number of key productions of Golden Age plays took place during the 1965–75 period, and many echoed the belief that the classics were not mere archaeological artefacts. Although most ostensibly progressive independent theatre practitioners simply dismissed national classical drama, a select number chose to critically interrogate the texts and their relevance to a modern-day audience. In the vein of Dido's *La viuda valenciana*, many of these emerged from the Teatros de Cámara where, according to Paloma Cuesta Martínez's calculations, the percentage of Golden Age works rose to 6.9 (high in relative although not absolute terms) (1988, p. 234).

In 1967, for example, Juan Antonio Hormigón directed a heavily politicized Marxist version of *La dama del Olivar* for the Teatro de Cámara de Zaragoza. The production shied away from any elaborate staging, relying instead on Tirso's words and distancing effects such as humorous interludes, and songs and posters that announced the beginning of each scene with a series of socio-economic reflections. Fernando Herrero, on seeing the production, remarked, '[s]in duda alguna es éste el espectáculo de alcance político y social más directo que he visto en España' [without a shadow of a doubt, this is the most politically and socially charged production that I have seen in Spain] (1968, p. 71).

Hormigón claims, in a text originally written in 1967, that 'no estamos ante una mente monolítica, cuadriculada e inflexible; panegírica del boato y loor de la monarquía absoluta, como fueron con frecuencia sus contemporáneos Lope y Calderón' [we are not faced here with a monolithic mind, boxed in and inflexible, eulogizing the ostentation and grandeur of an absolutist monarchy, as was so often the case with his contemporaries, Lope and Calderón] (2002b, p. 471).[46] The fact that most of the more radical and innovative productions of Golden Age plays staged in this period were based on Tirso's works suggests that Hormigón was probably not alone in a contention that was, in all likelihood, not so much the result of close textual analysis as of the fact that the regime had traditionally invested far more energy into presenting Lope and Calderón as the playwrights who most perfectly embodied their vision of the national spirit.

During this period, there was also the occasional student production. In 1968, for example, the TEU Murcia, always a hotbed of theatrical activity, staged a version of Calderón's *El astrólogo fingido*.[47] The most infamous student production of the time was Alberto Castilla's heavily politicized version of *Fuente Ovejuna* set in the present day. Neither the timing nor the choice of work was coincidental.[48] By 1965, Spanish universities were increasingly in conflict with the regime as they became a hotbed of anti-Francoism. Castilla notes how 'la preparación de *Fuenteovejuna* era un hecho teatral vivo, absolutamente integrado en nuestra realidad cotidiana, un montaje repleto de impresionantes significados en relación con los acontecimientos político-sociales que nos había tocado vivir' [the preparation of *The Sheep Well* was a theatrical undertaking full of life, intimately connected to our everyday reality in a production hugely relevant to the sociopolitical events that we were living through at the time] (1992, p. 44).

The play won the first prize at Nancy and was greeted with enthusiasm at a number of European festivals.[49] In Spain, however, it was banned and its success abroad was something of a pyrrhic victory. As Jesús Rubio Jiménez and Patricia Almárcegui note:

> A su vuelta, debido a las críticas en la prensa francesa – *Espirit, Le Monde* (Paris), *Il Giorno* (Milán) y *L'Unità* (Roma), entre otros diarios –, a las huelgas y manifestaciones universitarios madrileños de oposición al régimen y a la versión ofrecida de *Fuenteovejuna* el TEU Nacional es disuelto. Alberto Castilla decide no mucho después marcharse de España. (1999, p. 80)

> [On its return, as a result of the reviews in the French press – *Espirit, Le Monde* (Paris), *Il Giorno* (Milan) and *L'Unità* (Rome), and other newspapers –, strikes and university demonstrations held in Madrid in opposition to the regime, alongside the adaptation of *The Sheep Well*, the national student theatre is dissolved. Alberto Castilla decides not long afterwards to leave Spain.]

A rejection of the traditional archaeological approach was also evident in more mainstream ventures. There had always been occasional television productions of Golden Age plays, primarily in the theatre slot Estudio 1, but the *comedia* received a greater prominence in a parallel slot entitled Teatro de siempre. From 1967, it featured a series of productions filmed in the Almagro *corral*. Despite the historical interest of the site, the avowed aim of these productions was not historical reproduction; according to the programme makers the performances 'no pretenden, ni pueden pretender ser simplemente arqueológicas' [they do not attempt, neither could they attempt, to be merely archaeological] (cited in Peláez Martín, 1997, p. 22). These recordings were, as will be discussed in chapter four, hugely successful, yet in a familiar pattern the project soon dwindled away; from 1971 until the inauguration of the Jornadas de Almagro, some seven years later, hardly any Golden Age plays were staged in the *corral*.

The director of the nascent National Theatre in Barcelona, Ricard Salvat, was also an advocate of staging Golden Age drama. In 1971, he staged *El caballero de Olmedo*, and claimed that it ought to be a priority to develop a classical repertoire: 'Creo que hasta que no logremos esto haremos el ridículo internacionalmente' [Until we achieve this, I think we will be an international laughing stock] (cited in Pérez de Olaguer, 1971, p. 7). Throughout the 1960s and early 1970s, the Español had a number of younger artistic directors (Narros, Marsillach, Alonso, Alberto González Vergel).[50] A lack of continuity undoubtedly had a detrimental effect in that it prevented the development of a house style that could have potentially provided a new model for the performance of the national classics. There were, nevertheless, an impressive number of individual productions that moved beyond Luca de Tena's traditional archaeological approach to offer a new vision of both official theatre and the classics

Narros was, for example, a staunch defender of Golden Age drama and sought to redefine traditions that had been established in the Español. In 1966, he had courted controversy by staging *El burlador de Sevilla* in place of Zorrilla's *Don Juan Tenorio* that, for years, had been the only play that was performed every year at the National Theatre.[51] A year later, he staged an adventurous version of Antonio and Manuel Machado's adaptation of Tirso's *El condenando por desconfiado* featuring music by Tomás Marcos and cinematographic inserts by Jorge Grau.[52] One advantage of the *comedia* now having to justify its presence on the contemporary Spanish stage was that some directors began to think more carefully and precisely than the previous generation had done about how and why these works ought to be staged. Narros argued that classics should not be updated to make them relevant to the everyday but rather that practitioners should look for works that could connect with the modern-day spectator:

> El tema es lo más difícil de encontrar y lo que debe tener una importancia primordial. Debe darse con una situación o unos personajes que tengan alguna conexión con nuestra época, esto es imprescindible ... Yo lo que pretendo por encima de todo es que los personajes que salen a escena parezcan seres vivos, personas de hoy día. No tienen ningún valor como estatuas arqueológicas. (cited in Hernández, 1968, p. 44)

> [The most difficult thing to find is the subject-matter, and this should be of paramount importance. It is necessary for us to unearth a situation or a series of characters that have some connection to the present-day, that is vital ... And what I prioritize above all else is making the on-stage characters seem like real flesh and blood human beings with relevance to today. They have no value as archaeological statues.]

Vergel, who began his theatrical career in TEU Murcia, proved particularly adept at facing this challenge. On taking charge of the Español, he responded as follows to a question about his main priorities for the theatre:

> En primer lugar, a revisar a nuestros autores clásicos, desde el tiempo en que vivo, 1970 ... fiel a las constantes y esencias humanas de los españoles del siglo XVII y a los condicionamientos económicos, sociales, estéticos y políticos de la sociedad actual. Ni la fidelidad absoluta a estos autores, ni la traición a ultranza, como en algún caso se ha hecho. (cited in Salvador, 2008, p. 173)

> [Firstly, to revitalize our classical authors from today's perspective, that is to say 1970 ... being true to the continuities and human essences inherent to Spaniards of the seventeenth century alongside the economic, social,

aesthetic and political conditions of the present day. Neither absolute fidelity to these authors nor the complete desecration that has taken place on occasion.]

He personally went on to direct two innovative and exciting productions of the *comedia* that shatter many of the preconceptions that we may have about theatre under the dictatorship and, more specifically, theatre at the Español. In 1971, he staged a version of *La Estrella de Sevilla*, starring a young Marisa Paredes in her first lead role (Francia, 1993, p. 65), which featured electronic music and focussed on the abuse of power and humanized the king so as to demystify his divine presence. Vergel also wrote in the programme about how he saw in the play a 'concepto brechtiano de la tragedia optimista' [Brechtian concept of optimistic tragedy] (Teatro Español, 1971).

This production was merely a precursor to his 1973–4 version of *Marta la piadosa* as a rock musical that would later be screened by TVE over Christmas 1975. This production, complete with a giant bed on which the various couples could simulate sexual acts, was a cultural phenomenon that ran for over one hundred performances and found Tirso a new audience among young people. Given the historical context, it is easy to see the appeal of a play text rich in cynical and pithy remarks on false piety, which positively contrasts youthful sexual exuberance with an anachronistic paternal figure more concerned with reputation than morality. The play thereby performed both functions that Northrop Frye associates with comedy: 'It may emphasize the birth of an ideal society as you like it, or the tawdriness of the sham society which is the way of the world' (1992, p. 77). As such, the production did not shy away from controversy and, in the programme, Vergel wrote:

> Convertir la obra de Tirso en un musical rock no es, ni mucho menos, un capricho o una arbitrariedad de director, sino un firme propósito de esclarecer y aproximar a nuestro tiempo lo que de parábola o cuento moral tiene el, por muchas razones, fabuloso texto original. (Teatro Español, 1973)

> [Turning Tirso's play into a rock musical is by no means a whim or a capricious directorial choice; it arises instead from the firm conviction of illuminating and bringing closer to our time those aspects of the fabulous original text that can, for many reasons, be read as a parable or moral tale.]

Jaime Campany adapted the version and defended his new vision of Tirso's work in the following terms: 'El "rock" de hoy es la mojiganga de ayer. Representar *Marta la piadosa* como fue representado en el siglo XVII no sería hacer teatro. El teatro es algo vivo y palpitante. Es lo opuesto a la arqueología.' [Today's rock is the musical farce of yore. To stage *Pious Martha* as it was staged in the seventeenth century would not be theatre.

Theatre is something that is vibrant and alive. It is the antithesis of archaeology] (cited in Laborda, 1973). What is perhaps surprising is that the production was greeted with virtually unanimous praise, even from the more conservative elements of the critical establishment.

Figure 1 Photographs of *Marta la piadosa* (dir. Alberto González Vergel, 1975), Teatro Español

One reviewer prefaced his judgement with the admission that he was generally an advocate of not making any changes to the play text and that he went to the theatre with deep reservations. Nevertheless, because the creative team 'se alian fidelidad a la esencia e imaginación' [combine fidelity to the play's essence with imagination], the modifications did not prevent him from acknowledging that 'el resultado artístico sea de primera calidad' [the artistic product is first class] (Aragonés, 1973). Marqueríe wrote that 'la verdad es que revitalizar a los clásicos con humor y desenfado no sólo no es recusable, sino altamente plausible. Vayan a ver *Marta la piadosa* en su versión 1973–4, que lo pasarán de un modo fenomenal' [The truth is that revitalizing the classics with humour and irreverence should not be subject to censure, but ought rather to be encouraged. Go and see the 1973–4 version of *Pious Martha*, you will have a great time] (1973). M. Díez Crespo went as far as stating that 'estoy seguro de que Tirso de

Molina lo habría pasado "bomba". Entre otras razones, porque él sabe que para haber podido entrar entre los clásicos, tuvo que romper con muchas cosas de su tiempo que se consideraban "intocables"' [I am sure that Tirso de Molina would have had a 'whale of a time'. Among other reasons, because he knew that in order to rub shoulders with the classics, he had to break many of the ostensibly 'untouchable' conventions of his time] (1973).

While previously it had been conceded that changes to the play text could be justified in order to avoid confusion, and even that it might be appropriate to make omissions, this was the first time that notions of fidelity had been interrogated so deeply. Hence, by the time of Franco's death, a surprisingly eclectic range of artists and critics had accepted that theatrical worth and truth could not be judged solely in terms of the play text or the original performance.

Negotiating the past through the present: the *comedia* and Spanish democracy (1975–86)

Between 1975 and 1986, the two views of Golden Age drama outlined in the previous section continued but, as the new decade dawned, the previously marginal views gained credence within both political and theatrical circles. Nevertheless, in the years immediately following the dictatorship, there were very few productions of seventeenth-century Spanish plays. This was no doubt due to the political situation of the time and was not aided by the fact that a devastating fire at the Español destroyed the stage and a large part of the auditorium; the theatre was not to reopen until 1980.

One notable exception was Tamayo's 1976 version of *La vida es sueño* at the Teatro de las Bellas Artes. During his career the director and impresario had staged the work on numerous occasions, and his various productions function as a social barometer for the times. In the 1950s, he had performed it for the Corpus celebrations held in Charles V's palace at the Alhambra as a clear exaltation of the Spanish genius. Then, in 1968, his new version had been one of the successes of the First Campaign, taking theatre about the country. Now, in 1976, he presented the play as a work of social progress.[53] Critics were divided on whether the production worked or not but even its detractors praised its spirit of adventure.[54]

In 1977, the Ministry of Information and Tourism was changed to the Ministry of Culture and Welfare, and government censorship was abolished not long afterwards. In theory, this ought to have presented a positive climate for the theatre, but the commercial stages were dominated by *destape* [unveiling] works that revelled in the superficial liberties afforded by the incipient democracy while the remnants of independent theatre focussed on the changing political climate, although the speed of change meant that plays constantly seemed to lag behind the reality of the country (Oliva, 2002a, p. 226).[55] Practitioners claimed that the theatre was in crisis, lacked the infrastructure and resources to aid professional and artistic development, and had been deserted by the politicians.[56]

At this juncture, the revitalization of the classics was not considered a priority and, perhaps understandably, the majority of works written and set in the past that were staged in the 1975–81 period had been prohibited under the dictatorship (Vilches de Frutos, 1999, p. 80). Furthermore, as Francisco Nieva noted, many uncritically rejected Golden Age dramatists in the light of recent sociohistorical developments: 'A fuerza de hablar mal de nuestros clásicos, con tal de singularizarse y pasar por progresistas – puesto que era el teatro de Imperio y su propaganda – hemos llegado a olvidarnos de su parte más positiva' [Badmouthing our classics so as to stand apart and give the impression of being progressive – given that it was the theatre of the Empire and its propaganda – we have forgotten their more positive aspects] (cited in Laborda, 1977). There remained, however, a dedicated minority who saw the value of the classics and felt that, through their reappropriation, a development in dramatic praxis could occur. Rafael Pérez Sierra notes how:

> Circulaba entonces la peregrina idea de que el teatro de Lope y de Calderón había disfrutado de trato especial favorable durante aquel largo período de nuestra historia que todos queríamos olvidar, y en cualquier caso, se podría pensar que era demasiado cómodo ponerse a oír aquellas voces lejanas, cuando era tiempo de arreglar y cambiar tantas cosas. Algunos, en cambio, pensamos que había que colocar a los clásicos en el lugar que ocupaban en los países que nos llevaban alguna delantera en vitalidad teatral y que precisamente haciendo eso andábamos el buen camino hacia nuestra revitalización. (1997, p. 49)

> [The somewhat strange idea that Lope and Calderón's theatre had enjoyed favourable treatment during that long period of our history which we all wanted to forget was common currency at the time; in any case, one could have thought that it was all too easy to listen to those far-off voices when it was time to remedy and change so many things. There were, however, those of us who believed that we had to position the classics where they were placed in those countries that were ahead of us in terms of theatrical dynamism, and that this would provide a steady route towards our own revitalization.]

It was with this in mind that Pérez Sierra organized the first Jornadas de Teatro Clásico in Almagro in 1978, which became an important forum for the discussion and performance of Golden Age plays.[57] A widespread hostility to the classics at home might, however, explain why two former exiles supplied much of the theatrical action. José (Pepe) Estruch accompanied students from Spain's most prestigious acting school, RESAD, to perform Lope de Rueda's *Medora* while Rafael Alberti penned a version of Lope's *El despertar a quien duerme* to be staged by the Compañía José Luis Pellicena.[58]

Hence we can see how the two discourses identified in the dictatorship's final decade continued into the incipient democracy. In a period when those commenting on cultural matters were almost universally rejecting the old regime, most chose to adopt one of two positions as regards the classics: either they were politically suspect and not that interesting, or they needed to be rescued from perversions undertaken by those previously in power. There are clear similarities between the second approach and the one adopted by the victors of the Civil War in the late 1930s and early 1940s.

These two viewpoints were reflected in most appraisals of Golden Age drama until the early 1980s. Hence, for example, while playwright Antonio Gala claimed that the *comedia* was repetitive, conservative and characterized by 'la entrega del autor a su público en vez de a su pueblo' [the author's adhesion to his public rather than his people] (cited in Pérez Fernández, 1978), Miguel Bayón was equally as damning and general in his critique of the performance of seventeenth-century plays as:

> un tipo de teatro del que el franquismo, infectado de retórica vana e hipócrita, abusó al máximo. Festivales de España, Estudios 1 en TVE, montajes en los Teatros Nacionales, giras más o menos auspiciados por los figurones de la época: todo eso, y más, se abatió sobre el espectador de tiempos pretéritos y, por supuesto, también sobre los pobres clásicos, que no tenían culpa alguna. (1983, p. 93).

> [a type of theatre that Francoism, infected with vain and hypocritical rhetoric, abused to the hilt. Festivals of Spain, Studio 1 on Spanish State Television, productions in the National Theatres, tours generally endorsed by the bigwigs of the age: all this, and more, subjected the viewer to an overdose of pastness that also weighed down on the innocent victims that were our poor classics.]

Though there are grains of truth in this latter conception, the problem is that such a wholesale rejection is reductive and dismisses everything that was staged during the dictatorship period. As we have seen, there were many adventurous and engaging productions in the late 1960s and early 1970s, and even more overtly ideological pieces such as those directed by Luca de Tena in the 1940s had their positive aspects.

It does seem that there has been an unfortunate *pacto de olvido* [pact of forgetting] between Golden Age theatre practitioners that refuses to look to the past where there are references for present-day projects.[59] As such, there is a performative aspect to the lack of performance tradition; because everyone asserts that there is no tradition, any possible tradition ceases to exist. This is a tendency that has persisted to the present day; political parties uncritically reject their predecessor's cultural activities, the novelty of new initiatives is foregrounded, and reviewers consistently embrace any Golden Age production they enjoy as being almost exclusively without precedent.

In the late 1970s, the UCD government began to invest more money and energy in theatre and this was reflected in new projects such as the CDN and the revitalization of the RESAD that provided new fora for Golden Age works to be performed.[60] Almagro grew in terms of both popularity and prestige. Queen Sofia attended Narros's production of *La dama boba* in 1979; Fernando Fernán-Gómez premiered his version of *El alcalde de Zalamea* in the same year although neither he nor the public and critics were particularly enthralled by the production.[61]

Also in this period, Manuel Canseco set an important precedent by establishing a company dedicated exclusively to the staging of Golden Age classics. This cooperative was particularly impressive in that it did not receive state funding. Although it went under a number of guises (Comedia de la Pacheca; Compañía Titular de su Real Coliseo Carlos III), there was a level of continuity unparalleled in recent Spanish history. Canseco always worked alongside dramaturge Juan Antonio Castro and a core ensemble who were then supplemented with guest actors for specific productions. Through their extended residencies in El Escorial and nationwide tours, they developed an impressive and eclectic repertoire. In 1979, for example, they performed Calderón's *Casa con dos puertas mala es de guardar* and *La cisma de Inglaterra* alongside works by Lope and Torres Naharro.[62]

The fact that a Calderón play was chosen to reopen the Español in 1980 was proof of Golden Age drama's renewed respectability, although the results could hardly have been more disastrous. La Compañía de Aurora Bautista presented a little known work, *El José de las mujeres*, retitled *La dama de Alejandría* on 16 April in the presence of the king and queen. The performance, described by one critic as 'una vergonzosa función de estreno en la que se han batido todas las marcas del rídiculo oficial' [a shameful debut production that has set a new benchmark in terms of state-endorsed ridiculousness] (Pérez Coterillo, 1980, p. 13), was a total catastrophe and many critics demanded explanations from the Ministry of Culture and Madrid City Council (Morales y Marín, 1995, pp. 109–10).

With the third centenary of Calderón's death in 1981, there were a number of high-profile productions. Alonso's production of *El galán fantasma* was the first real success at the reopened Español. Tamayo, with the aid of a choir and a classical ballet company, staged a typically elaborate version of *La cena del rey Baltasar*. The production was popular with audiences but critics once again disagreed about whether this kind of approach still had a place in modern Spain or whether it was simply outmoded. José Luis Gómez directed a version of *La vida es sueño* that, when Marsillach came to direct the CNTC, would be one of the few productions that he would admit acted as a precedent and influence (Marsillach, 2002, p. 442). *El gran teatro del mundo* was also staged.

The year's most significant production was arguably Lluis Pasqual's *La hija del aire* starring Ana Belén.[63] In an attempt to make the play accessible to modern audiences, the director asked Francisco Ruiz Ramón to make cuts in the text, and he also tried to make the work more contemporary by contrasting modern-day sets with period costume. The production was generally well received, and its positive reception paved the way for Pasqual to be appointed director of the CDN in 1983 (Delgado, 2003, p. 133). Both *La hija del aire* and *La vida es sueño* were commercial successes; they were, respectively, the second and third highest grossing plays staged in public theatres during the season (Fernández Torres, 1983, p. 79).[64]

However, despite some high-profile productions, there was little on offer that would convert Calderón's detractors and there was not enough to satisfy his supporters. Ángel Fernández Santos, in an article titled 'Ayuno Calderoniano' [Calderonian Fast], summarizes the year in the following terms: 'Un total de cinco espectáculos para seguir prácticamente en el mismo estado de ignorancia sobre Calderón con que empezamos este "año suyo" por excelencia' [A total of five productions enabling us to remain in the same state of ignorance with which we begun 'his year' par excellence] (1982, p. 7).[65] In his newspaper columns, Francisco Umbral consistently made snide remarks about the playwright and those who sought to resurrect him; 'hasta ahora, quien mejor ha montado el auto sacramental del centenario ha sido Tejero' [up to now, the best Corpus Christi play of the centenary year has been staged by Tejero] (1982, p. 187). Bruce W. Wardropper has been even more scathing about academic events ostensibly held to commemorate the centenary but, in his view, designed merely as a pretext to invite prestigious scholars with precious little specialist knowledge: 'Once again, Calderón's drama has become a rallying point for a national piety based on ignorance' (1982, p. 8).[66]

It was with the ascension of the PSOE to power in 1982 that the theatrical climate of the country would change definitively; from the outset, it was clear that Golden Age drama would perform an important role in this transformation. In a special report on the theatre, the party laid out its priorities that focussed heavily on the revival of Spanish classical drama:

> La dramaturgia clásica española es una de las principales riquezas de nuestro patrimonio cultural. Dramaturgia que no se limita a los grandes autores del Siglo de Oro. Desgraciadamente, a diferencia de otros aspectos de nuestro patrimonio histórico-artístico, la desatención de la sociedad española, de sus instituciones, universidades, escuelas, Ministerio, etc., raya en la indigencia. Nuestros clásicos se conocen más en Berlín y Moscú que en Alicante o Zamora. En casi todos los países civilizados, existe una compañía,

al menos, especializada en la tarea de asegurar la continuidad de la tradición clásica en los escenarios. (Comisión de Teatro del PSOE, 1983, p. 10)

[Classical Spanish drama constitutes one of the principal riches of our cultural heritage. This drama is not the unique preserve of the great authors of the Golden Age. Unfortunately, in contrast to other aspects of our artistic and historical heritage, the lack of attention paid to it by Spanish society, its institutions, universities, schools, Ministry etc, verges on the negligent. Our classics are better known in Berlin and Moscow than they are in Alicante or Zamora. In almost every civilized nation, there is at least one company dedicated to assuring the on-stage continuity of the classical tradition.]

This desire was also shared by many theatrical practitioners (ADE, 1983), and the clear connotation was that if Spain wanted to be, and to express to the outside world an image of being, a civilized nation, it needed to take care of its classics. It is with this agenda in mind, for example, that the state provided generous funding for Narros to stage a version of *El castigo sin venganza* that would, on the eve of Spain's entry into the EU, showcase an elaborate baroque set for the 'Europalia 85' festival in Brussels.[67] The production was not, however, well received and prior to the inauguration of the CNTC in 1986, very few productions reached a high level of proficiency.[68]

The debate about how and whether the classics ought to be performed alongside their fraught relationship with national identity was frequently negotiated within productions themselves. This trend began in 1981 with the staging of Alberto Miralles's *Céfiro agreste de olímpicos embates*. The play, widely and inaccurately described as 'anti-calderoniana' [anti-Calderonian] (Álvaro, 1982, p. 64), tells the story of an independent theatre company. The ostensibly radical collective has been given a generous subsidy to perform an *auto sacramental* much to the chagrin of many of its members, one of whom memorably describes Calderón as '¡El Pemán de la contrarreforma! [The Pemán of the Counter Reformation] (Miralles, 1981, p. 27).[69]

Rather than a performance of an *auto*, the play depicts the group struggling to come to terms with the text. Miralles, a veteran of 1960s radical avant-garde theatre, ridicules the fictional actors at least as much as he does Calderón. The text does not suggest an antipathy towards the baroque playwright but rather objects to the unreflective way in which subsidies are designated to 'great' dead authors without any thought for why or how the plays ought to be performed. The director/playwright expresses these feelings unequivocally in the theatrical programme:

Respetar a nuestros mayores es una consigna noble. Pero en España las consignas son excluyentes: o fe o tranca; o rojo o azul; o centenario muerto o... ¿o qué? Porque a fuerza de matar a los vivos con el puñal del desprecio y el olvido, ya apenas quedan oponentes. (Centro Cultural de la Villa, 1981)

[Respect your elders is a noble motto. But, in Spain, mottos are exclusive: either the church or a big stick; either communist or royal; either a centenary for a dead man or . . . or what? Because, having killed those who are living with the dagger of scorn and wilful amnesia, there are hardly any opponents left.]

In 1983, José Sanchís Sinisterra attempted to negotiate some kind of middle ground between these polarities with *Absalón*. The play pairs a liberal version of a Calderón text, heavily inspired by Freud and Kafka, with songs specifically written for the production. This ambitious venture that attempted to interrogate Spain's tumultuous relationship with its Jewish past opened to mixed reviews.[70]

Two years later, Hormigón returned to the *comedia* with a new version of Lope's *La vengadora de las mujeres*. This was one of the most high-profile productions of the period; it opened in Almagro before moving on to the Teatro Lara in Madrid and touring Spain for three months (Hormigón, 1986, p. 34). Before the main play begins, there is a prologue where the actors don their costumes and discuss whether it is valid to stage the classics in the late twentieth century:[71]

1. – Mira, los clásicos no le interesan a nadie. Están muertos. Huelen a naftalina, a tumba, a códice, a cueva, a cadáver, a museo, a pozo, a Universidad, a Academia, a cultura . . . sobre todo a cultura. ¡Son un asco!
5. – Respira, tío, que te vas a ahogar.
2. – Eso dicen siempre los ignorantes disfrazados de modernos.
6. – Ahora postmodernos.
3. – Pues a mí, *La vida de Eduardo II*, me moló cantiduvi.
4. – Es de un extranjero.
3. – ¡Ah, será por eso!
1. – ¡Pero los españoles . . . son inaguantables! ¡Y además están en verso! Ahora nadie habla en verso. (Hormigón, 1986, pp. 37–8)

[1. – Look, the classics don't interest anyone. They are dead. Mothballs, tombs, manuscripts, caves, museums, sediment, universities, Royal Academies, culture . . . above all else culture; that is what they smell of. They make my flesh crawl.
5. – Calm down, mate, you're going to have a heart attack.
2.– That is what those who disguise their ignorance with a false veneer of modernity always say.
6. – Postmodernity these days.
3. – Well I liked *Edward II*. It was super-cool.
4 – It is by a foreigner.
3. – Aha, that explains that one.
1 – But the Spanish ones . . . they are unbearable. Furthermore, they are in verse! Nobody speaks in verse these days.]

The adaptation is largely in prose but its content is generally faithful to a seventeenth-century play that shatters the preconceptions some audiences may have about Golden Age comedy through, for example, its inclusion of an openly homosexual servant. Hormigón adopts a playful approach to these incongruities through the device of a fictional spectator who repeatedly interrupts the onstage action. Following Laura's claim that books have taught her how badly women are treated by men, and that she does not therefore want a husband, the following objection is voiced:

> Espectador de oscuro. – Ustedes se burlan de nuestros clásicos, de nuestra gloria nacional, para ponerlos al servicio de sus ideas. ¡Manipuladores! ¡Teatreros! (p. 59)
>
> [Spectator in the dark. – You lot mock our classics, our national glory, in order to serve your ideas. You manipulators! Luvvies!]

Lope's play ends with a conventional marriage and the integration of the reformed *esquiva* [woman not interested in romance] into the institution of heterosexual marriage; at this point Hormigón introduces a new element into proceedings by having the actress who plays Laura ask the audience a presumably rhetorical question: '¿Pero creen ustedes que Laura necesitaría hoy la misma solución?' [But do you think Laura would have to find a similar solution today?] (1986, p. 131).

Also in 1985, the CNNTE – a new initiative established by the PSOE – staged Ángel Facio's *No hay burlas con Calderón*. The production weaves together various excerpts from the Golden Age dramatist's texts to yield a parody of the *comedias de enredo* [intrigue plays] performed in the style of a French vaudeville. This self-conscious interrogation of Spanish classical drama even extended beyond the stage with the inclusion in the programme of quotations from different experts discussing the merits (or lack thereof) of Calderón's output (CDN, 1985).[72]

A late entry into this subgenre was then provided in 1986 with José Ricardo Morales's play *Ardor con ardor se apaga*. The play by a veteran of La Barraca, recently returned from exile in Chile, set in Almagro and featuring a seventeenth-century character called Padre Franco, examines how predetermined notions of national identity have impinged on artistic and political freedom.[73] Morales suggests that this archetypal Spanish mythical figure was in fact a *morisco* but that Tirso had no choice but to sentimentalize and hispanify the character given the historical context in which he wrote. In the play, Don Juan attacks the seventeenth-century playwright for this action: 'la españolada es, para mí, esa violencia tremendista que practicamos reiteradamente los españoles, con saña extremada y contra nosotros mismos' [as far as I am concerned, the quintessential Spanish tale is of this exaggerated violence that we Spaniards repeatedly carry out with extreme cruelty and against ourselves] (Morales, 2002, p. 343).

There is, undoubtedly, a narrow line between reflecting and replicating confusion. While these metatheatrical experiments are positive in that they imply a serious engagement with the question of how the past ought to be negotiated through the present, they all too often fell victim to the same traps that beset anyone attempting to perform Golden Age drama in this period. Hence, for example, *No hay burlas* inspired José Ramón Díaz-Sande to argue in his review that, '[s]e impone cada vez más la necesidad de poner en marcha una Compañía Estable especializada en teatro en verso' [the need for us to create a stable company that specializes in theatre in verse is becoming increasingly apparent] (1985, p. 7). Problems with verse were symptomatic of a broader lack of rudimentary skills and expertise when it came to the performance of classical texts. José María Rodríguez Méndez has even claimed that a Lope play had to be suspended around this time because the actors were unable to recite verse and 'there did not seem to be a director who could teach them Castilian metrics' (1990, p. 108).

In general, the years 1982 to 1986 showcased a series of well-meaning, but ultimately doomed productions of classic texts; they often lacked theatrical flair and drifted into being little more than costumed recitations of the text. Such was the case, for example, with Higueras's outdoor production of *La prudencia en la mujer* in 1982, part of the state-subsidized Summer Theatre Campaign, designed to celebrate the fourth centenary of Tirso's birth. No attempt was made to make the text accessible to a modern-day audience and the performance was also hampered by bad acoustics that meant that many of those in attendance could not hear the actors (Torralaba, 1982). Even when productions gained positive reviews, such as José Caride's *El caballero de milagro*, they generally struggled to find an audience if they were not presented as part of an official programme or celebration (*Deia*, 1983). Many of the productions that arrived at Almagro demonstrated a lack of cohesion in direction and the actors' use of verse often betrayed a lack of training or engagement with the text.

It was clear that if the national classics were to be revitalized, more needed to be done. The time was ripe: the Socialists were investing far more money in theatre than previous administrations,[74] they had already shown how they construed Golden Age drama as an important part of Spain's cultural patrimony, and it had been a long time since the official theatres had systematically programmed Lope, Calderón or Tirso.[75] At the 1985 Almagro Festival, José Manuel Garrido asked Adolfo Marsillach if he would like to direct a new national company dedicated to staging classical theatre.[76] His acceptance would definitively change both the performance and reception of the *comedia* in its homeland.

The reinstitutionalization of the Golden Age: the *comedia* as sanctioned culture (1986–2004)

Between 1986 and 1996 Spanish theatre in general became more institutionalized and subject to clearly defined policies that created a new kind of audience interested in cultural kudos. The CNTC, as the most commercially successful and arguably most reliable of the new official state theatres, was both a product and cause of this new direction. I will begin by offering a potted history of its first ten years before moving on to a discussion of how and why its existence and output affected the wider panorama of *comedia* performance.

Unlike many other European countries, Spain did not have an uninterrupted tradition of performing its classics; it was this cultural belatedness that gave the CNTC its *raison d'être* while also denying it a stable performance tradition from which to emerge. As Marsillach observes, '[l]os clásicos forman parte de nuestro patrimonio y uno no desprecia el patrimonio como no tira el reloj del abuelito a la basura. Lo que ocurre – y aquí es donde empiezan las complicaciones – es que los patrimonios no se inventan, sino que se heredan' [the classics form part of our heritage and, in the same way that we would not throw our beloved grandfather's watch in the garbage, we should not disregard our heritage. The thing is – and this is where complications begin to arise – heritage is inherited rather than created] (2002, p. 455). This lack of tradition meant that it would have been virtually impossible to try and perform the *comedia* in a seventeenth-century performance style. Even if it had been possible, Marsillach – clearly inspired by Peter Brook's notion of 'the Deadly Theatre'[77] – shunned this kind of production: 'cuando el estilo deja de ser una aventura para convertirse en una seguridad, pierde de inmediato todos sus encantos. (El estilo "Comedie [*sic*] Française," por ejemplo, no me interesa en absoluto.)' [a style loses all of its charms when it ceases to be an adventure to become a security blanket. (The 'Comédie Française' style, for example, does not interest me in the least.)] (CNTC, 1996, p. 13).

In order that the Company was more than just an outlet for Golden Age works, it initially tried to use stable casts and creative personnel with the aim of developing a house style. This, it was hoped, would avoid the kind of pitfalls that the Español had, for example, encountered in the 1950s. Marsillach had two key collaborators: Carlos Cytrynowski as set designer and Pérez Sierra as literary advisor. The decision was made to alternate better known with lesser known works, and dramas with comedies. Hence the choice of the first two productions: Calderón's *El médico de su honra* and Lope's *Los locos de Valencia*.

Whenever Marsillach approached a new work, he did not look for an archaeological reconstruction of the original staging but, instead, he and

Cytrynowski tried to imagine what the play might have meant in the original setting and then attempted to update the play by finding an equivalent meaning for modern-day audiences (Marsillach, 2002, p. 464). Hence, for example, *El médico* focussed not on an idiosyncratic honour code functioning at a particular sociohistorical moment but on the alienating effect that social conventions and obligations place on the individual and their relationships with others. The director, though affirming his right to establish his own 'style', was not looking to radically change the play text to accommodate a modern-day spectator: 'El acercamiento a los clásicos no debe realizarse a través de falsas moderneces, sino buscando lo que en ellos hay de contemporáneo.' [The classics should not be brought closer to us by imposing fallacious modernizations, but rather by searching for the contemporary elements contained within them] (cited in *Deia*, 1987).

Marsillach always maintained that most theatre practitioners opposed the creation of the CNTC (2002, p. 460), and *El médico* was subject to severe criticism which, as will be discussed in chapter three, was excessive and not always constructive. Equally cumbersome, however, was the director's tendency to interpret any criticism as a critique of his general approach, and his refusal to enter into any serious debate on the relative merits of different productions. Throughout his time as director, he defined his company in opposition to two positions: Spanish academics who advocate 'la inmaculada virginidad de los textos' [the immaculate virginity of the texts] (Marsillach, 2002, p. 457), and the traditional didactic staging of the plays that, in his opinion, had blighted previous productions. The director, and he was not alone in this tendency in 1980s Spain, often appeared to ground the CNTC's identity in a rejection of the past rather than an engagement with the present.

Marsillach had a predilection for presenting himself as the *enfant terrible* of *comedia* performance who fought against those practitioners and critics immersed in 'el eterno y aburridísimo debate de por qué se le ha cambiado una coma' [the eternal and incredibly boring debate over why a comma has been changed] (cited in Piña, 1994). However, his approach to the classics was not as novel or revolutionary as he often wanted to suggest. It had been advocated by *PA* in the 1960s, had been applied in productions such as *Marta la piadosa*, and had been supported by academics at their meetings in Almagro. Furthermore, 'the immaculate virginity of the texts' had been defiled more forcefully by other companies in recent years than by any CNTC production.

The principal defence that Marsillach always fielded against his opponents was the fact that the company was popular with the public, including young people: 'hemos conseguido un público habitual y sobre todo que los jóvenes le hayan perdido el miedo, que no el respeto, a los grandes textos.' [we have managed to secure a loyal audience especially amongst young people who have lost their fear, but not their respect, towards the classics] (cited in Gil, 1993). However, it is precisely this relationship with this 'loyal audience' that constitutes the strongest objection to the CNTC. During the 1980s, in the words of César Oliva, 'la nueva política que partía de un estabilizado concepto de democracia, tan anhelado por los españoles, necesitaba el adorno de un florecimiento cultural que embelleciera los logros del desarrollo económico y las finanzas.' [the new policy arose from the consolidated notion of democracy, so keenly sought by Spaniards, which required a flourishing of cultural activity that would compliment and dignify achievements made in the economic spheres] (1994b, p. 46). This led to a changing theatrical climate where fewer new playwrights were staged and more attention was focussed on a series of high-profile and culturally prestigious productions. Theatre became more of a minority activity as, despite the investment in the sector by the Socialist government, the number of spectators decreased from eleven million in 1983 to just five in 1990 (Ragué-Arias, 1996, p. 114). Arguably, audiences did not watch the classics to engage with a seventeenth-century text in the present but rather to immerse themselves in officially sanctioned culture.[78]

This acquiescence in prescribed theatre has, according to Enrique García Santo-Tomás, created a truly *deadly* theatre as:

> podríamos afirmar que los montajes de la CNTC han divulgado un Lope que ha jugado un papel 'positivamente' arqueológico, de reliquia intocable, ingrediente indispensable de una cotización cultural que ha incluido, por ejemplo, acontecimientos como el ballet, la ópera o la música clásica. (2000a, p. 391)
>
> [we could say that the CNTC's productions have disseminated a vision of Lope that performs a 'positively' archaeological role, equivalent to the untouchable relic, an indispensable ingredient in a cultural capital that has, for example, encompassed events such as ballet, opera and classical music.]

This climate has created an audience that often greets the CNTC's productions with, to borrow the words of one reviewer, 'el respetuoso silencio, con la aburrida disciplina del que abre la boca para tragarse el cocido cultural – ésta para Lope, ésta para Calderón, está para Tirso.' [a respectful silence, with the resigned discipline of s/he who opens their mouth to swallow down their cultural stew – this one for Lope, this one for Calderón, this one for Tirso] (Sagarra, 1993). Despite Marsillach's claim to the contrary – 'Yo jamás quise crear una institución, sino provocar una búsqueda. Hay que vivir el teatro peligrosamente.' [I never wanted to create an institution but rather to initiate a search. The theatre has to be lived dangerously] (CNTC, 1991) – between 1986 and 1996, the company had the hallmarks of a successful institution: it had a loyal audience and its output guaranteed a basic level of proficiency that almost always ensured professionalism but only intermittently innovation or engagement.

Many attempts to gain stability through house actors and training courses fell by the wayside. The ETC, established by Pérez Sierra while acting as interim director of the company in 1989 during Marsillach's tenure as head of INAEM, only lasted a couple of years. Nevertheless, in overall terms, the standard of performance and direction improved drastically during the first ten years; there was a move towards greater overall cohesion, and the company staged a series of Golden Age plays that, in terms of both consistency and professionalism, are unparalleled in recent Spanish history.

Many of the best productions were those directed by Marsillach himself. In *Los locos de Valencia*, he offered a very spirited and enjoyable version of Lope's play. Although the acting and direction occasionally lacked finesse and expertise, it is difficult not to be seduced by this exuberant vision of an anarchic play text with which the director was clearly familiar. The infectious onstage energy derived not from elaborate or costly production values but instead from vibrant colours and set design, and music combined with highly kinetic performances. Marsillach imbued the production with a typical sense of irreverence. At the end, paella was brought on stage to celebrate the marriage as ribbons were dropped from the ceiling and the onstage wedding guests carried sparklers. There were times, however, where the director's penchant for ostentatious transgression was, to my mind, gratuitous. While the play clearly ridicules authority figures who are at least as mad as the asylum inmates, dressing one of them as a member of the Guardia Civil is an overly base and obvious means to try and secure a cheap laugh from a complicit audience.

The potential displayed in this early production was honed in most of Marsillach's subsequent productions. *Antes que todo es mi dama* (1987), the CNTC's first genuine success with the public and critics, presented a 1930s film crew preparing a screen version of Calderón's work.[79] The production used its generous budget judiciously to produce a lavish spectacle that complemented, rather than eclipsed, the dramatic content of the play; and the metatheatrical elements helped to bring out Calderón's playful approach to truth and reality. *Fuente Ovejuna* (1993) was a brave albeit flawed experiment that broke down the fourth wall.[80] The modernist *mise en scène* contains anachronistic features such as lit fire torches to suggest a futuristic world with modern forms of torture and oppression in the throes of primeval regression to a barbarous world of ritual, violence and sacrifice. In 1994, when Marsillach revived *El médico de su honra* with a new cast alongside an expertly paced version of Tirso's *Don Gil de las calzas verdes*, the company's progress and rudimentary professionalism were beyond question.

The CNTC's greatest single triumph was probably Alonso's very sober version of *El alcalde de Zalamea* (1988) that focussed attention on Isabel's anguish at being raped.⁸¹ As in *Fuente Ovejuna*, the sets and costumes were, in Susan Fischer's words, deliberately and self-consciously 'derrualized' thereby avoiding a simplistic idealization of village life that had been the hallmark of many productions under the dictatorship (2009, p. 65). Honour was again not presented as an anachronistic code and was instead construed as a correlative to human rights and dignities. Even Eduardo Haro Tecglen, the company's harshest press critic, was impressed by the emotion impact of the production (1988), whose starkness contrasted with the spectacular and ostentatious *mise en scène* that was more characteristic of the company.

As Oliver Ford Davies has noted in reference to Shakespeare, '[t]he gap between helping the audience to understand the play and signaling a concept that overwhelms the action is a narrow one' (2007, p. 81). The CNTC often hovered over this dividing line but it was clearly crossed in Marsillach's *El vergonzoso en palacio* (1989).⁸² So long and elaborate was this extravaganza that it required two interval breaks. It appeared to emulate the aesthetics of a Broadway musical minus the music: there were choreographed dance sequences, a synchronized display of characters brandishing umbrellas and, perhaps most incongruously of all, actors dressed as polar bears and tigers. Beyond any inherent misgivings, this spectacular style is also problematic because it establishes a dangerous precedent in that audiences, practitioners and policy makers come to expect, and demand, this kind of staging. To cite just one example, Alicia Sánchez has told me that the organizers of the Festival de Otoño were annoyed on seeing *Las bizarrías de Belisa*, a production she codirected with John Strasberg, because the expense was not showcased on stage through an extravagant *mise en scène* and had, instead, been invested in training and extensive rehearsals.⁸³

Many other productions were, to use the words of María Delgado, 'stolid stagings' that 'on the whole failed to revitalise or revise the classical canon for the contemporary age' (2003, pp. 18–19). Narros's *El caballero de Olmedo* (1990) and José Luis Castro's *El acero de Madrid* (1995) were fairly typical examples of this style; they had sumptuous production values, were reasonably well acted and were based on judicious versions, but lacked theatrical flair and any real sense of adventure or discovery to the extent that they were often boring and tedious.

There can be no doubt that the company has irrecoverably changed the way that Golden Age drama has come to be performed, but its appropriation for cultural exhibition echoes the use of the plays as a form of exemplary theatre in the 1950s. This tendency was most explicit in the *Fiesta barroca* staged in 1992 to celebrate Madrid being European City of Culture. The production, directed by Narros, consisted of a collection of *autos sacramentales*, *entremeses* and *mojigangas* that, from 6 to 13 July, was performed between the Catedral de la Almudena del Palacio Real and the Plaza Mayor. This spectacle, reminiscent of Tamayo's extravaganzas, featured eighty actors,

Figure 2   Photograph by Ros Ribas of *El vergonzoso en palacio* (dir. Adolfo Marsillach, 1989), CNTC

thirty-five dancers and two hundred extras. It was also controversial at the time for using a sizeable amount of the city's cultural budget (López Sancho, 1992).

On a wider scale, the company has ensured that Golden Age drama is respectable and prestigious, and this has benefited other activities and productions. As will be discussed in chapter five, the Almagro Festival's profile expanded over this ten-year period, in terms of both numbers of visitors and productions, to the extent that it became both a tourist attraction and a source of national pride in the international arena. Even as the economic crisis of the early 1990s hit, the government continued to provide generous support for *comedia* performance.[84]

However, beyond this culturally prestigious showcase theatre, how has the CNTC affected the role of Golden Age drama in Spanish theatre in general? The existence of a stable company dedicated to the classics could either act as an obstacle or an aid to other companies staging these works; a national company can create a fashion for staging a particular kind of work or remove the obligation. In order to see both how the CNTC has affected the activities of other companies, and also to try and gauge the role of Golden Age drama on the Spanish stage in the late twentieth and early twenty-first centuries, I have prepared a list of the number of productions of works by Lope, Calderón and Tirso alongside figures from two other universal classical dramatists (Shakespeare and Molière), and two more recent canonical Spanish dramatists (Valle-Inclán and Lorca). Though the CNTC tours, it is a Madrid-based company and I was also interested to see whether interest in the Golden Age has spread beyond its traditional home in the capital; thus, I have put in brackets the number of productions by companies based in the Comunidad de Madrid:[85]

Year	Lope	Calderón	Tirso	Molière	S'peare	Lorca	V.-Inclán
1984–5	5 (3)	3 (2)	1 (1)	6 (3)	0 (0)	10 (5)	2 (1)
1985–6	3 (3)	5 (2)	0 (0)	5 (0)	7 (3)	15 (4)	13 (4)
1986–7	4 (3)	3 (3)	0 (0)	3 (1)	5 (2)	23 (6)	5 (1)
1987–8	2 (1)	7 (3)	1 (1)	4 (1)	9 (3)	7 (3)	10 (6)
1988–9	4 (4)	4 (4)	3 (2)	6 (1)	7 (2)	11.5 (5.5)	3 (0)
1989–90	2 (2)	4 (3)	3 (1)	4 (0)	6 (1)	9 (2)	5 (1)
1990–1	5 (4)	5 (3)	0 (0)	4 (1)	4 (1)	7 (2)	3 (2)
1991–2	6 (4)	3 (3)	0 (0)	3 (0)	5 (0)	8 (1)	3 (2)
1992–3	1 (1)	5.5 (2)	1.5 (0)	9 (0)	8 (4)	10 (1)	3.5 (1)
1993–4	4.5 (2.5)	7 (3)	1 (1)	11 (2)	10 (1)	10.5 (1.5)	4 (0)
1994–5	5 (4.5)	3 (3)	3 (0)	11.5 (3)	16.5 (4)	15 (5)	6.5 (2)
1995–6	3 (2)	3.5 (2.5)	1 (1)	11.5 (2.5)	19 (7)	13 (5)	6 (5)
1997	3.5 (3)	5.5 (2)	1 (1)	5 (1)	15.5 (8)	6 (2)	3 (0)
1998	4 (1)	6 (5)	0 (0)	2 (1)	13 (8)	35.5 (13)	6 (2)
1999	6 (3.5)	8 (4)	1.5 (1)	5 (4)	23.5 (4)	15.5 (3.5)	6 (0.5)
2000	4.5 (1)	19 (13)	1 (0)	9 (1)	14.5 (4)	12.5 (2)	3.5 (0)
2001	6 (1)	4 (1)	2 (2)	5.5 (1.5)	16 (3)	10 (7)	1 (1)
2002	5 (2)	5 (1)	1 (0)	8 (4)	29 (2)	7 (2)	3 (1)
2003	9 (7)	5 (4)	5 (2)	6.5 (0.5)	29.5 (10.5)	10.5 (1)	1 (0)
2004	9 (3)	6 (2)	3.5 (0)	8 (2)	32 (7)	22.5 (3)	1 (1)
2005	5.5 (2)	6.5 (2)	0 (0)	1 (0)	21 (3)	11 (4)	4 (2)
2006	5 (2)	4 (2)	3 (2)	2 (1)	13 (2)	7 (3)	2 (2)
2007	5 (2)	4 (2)	1 (0)	3 (0)	12 (3)	3 (1)	2 (0)
2008	11 (5)	6 (4)	5 (3)	3 (1)	17 (6)	7 (4)	3 (3)
2009	14.5 (7)	4 (2)	0 (0)	10 (3.5)	25 (9)	15 (2.5)	5 (2)
TOTAL MADRID (%)	132.5 (73.5) 55.5	136 (77.5) 57.0	38.5 (18) 46.8	146 (35) 24.0	357.5 (97.5) 27.3	301.5 (89) 29.5	104.5 (39.5) 37.8

This table shows that, despite the efforts of the CNTC, Golden Age drama still does not have as prominent a presence in theatres as one would expect. Tirso is quite clearly far less popular than Calderón or Lope, who are roughly equal in terms of productions with Calderón's very slight lead mainly due to the nineteen productions staged in 2000 for the fourth centenary of his birth.[86] Shakespeare's unique role in the world canon arguably makes him an unfair point of comparison but it is still striking that there have been more productions of his works than of the three chief proponents of Golden Age drama combined.

The fact that between 1984 and 2008 more Molière productions have been staged than any Golden Age playwright is frankly astounding. When one takes into account the number of works written by Lorca or Valle-Inclán in comparison to Lope or Calderón, it also becomes clear how the former two playwrights, described by Oliva as 'buques-insignia del nuevo régimen' [iconic flagships of the new regime] (1994a, p. 172), have far more canonical status in Spain than either of their seventeenth-century counterparts.[87] The other interesting feature is how dominant Madrid based companies are in the production of Golden Age playwrights compared to the other dramatists. This is partly understandable in that these writers were illustrious *madrileños* but, as will be discussed in chapter five, it also suggests how, for many Spaniards, seventeenth-century drama is mainly the preserve of a centralist state that may, as a paternalistic gesture, occasionally tour its products. Shakespeare and Molière, as foreign playwrights, can be, and have been, translated into any of the autonomous languages,[88] and performing Lorca in Castilian does not have the same political connotations as staging Lope or Calderón might sometimes have.[89]

Even prior to the existence of the CNTC, a number of private companies staged Golden Age plays.[90] In recent years, this sector has consolidated its interest and expertise in staging classical drama. Nevertheless, the fact that the Valladolid-based company Teatro Corsario received heavy criticism, similar in kind to the fictional objections voiced in *Céfiro agreste*, when they opted to stage their first Spanish classic with Calderón's *El gran teatro del mundo* (1990) reveals the limits of the CNTC's public relations exercise.[91] These vociferous complaints did not deter the troupe from continuing along this path. Under Fernando Urdiales's assured direction, the company has subsequently toured some very popular versions of both lesser and well-known *comedias* including such titles as Lope's *Asalto a una ciudad*, Calderón's *El mayor hechizo, amor* and Tirso's *Don Gil de las calzas verdes*.

Zampanò, which exclusively stages classical works, was formed in 1980 out of the ashes of the TEC and the TEI both run under the guidance of Narros and William Layton.[92] In 1998, the company was awarded the Teatro Agora prize by the Almagro Festival for their production of *El secreto a voces* that completed a trilogy of Calderón's works following previous productions of *La vida es sueño* and *Con quien vengo, vengo*. Micomicón, founded in 1991 by four ex-members of the ETC, uses classic works as a platform from which to explore contemporary issues. In *Mudarra*, for example, they analysed modern-day Spain using verses by Lope and Juan de la Cueva.

The Teatro de Hoy, directed by González Vergel, in the late 1980s and early 1990s, specialized in staging infrequently performed Golden Age plays. In 1988, their version of *El príncipe constante* was premiered at Mérida in front of three thousand people and was later televised by TVE2,[93] as was their subsequent production of *Porfiar hasta morir*. In 1992, González Vergel returned to his hybrid of music and classical drama with a jazz version of Lope's *La malcasada*; though successful, this was sadly the company's last foray into Golden Age drama (Morales y Marín, 2008, pp. 119–20, 129).

Subsequently, the Compañía Noviembre has been assiduous in its dedication to largely unknown Lope plays. This venture, the brainchild of playwright Yolanda Pallín and director Eduardo Vasco, alternated modern-day plays, a contemporary aesthetic and classical theatre. Over the company's ten-year existence (1995–2005), they staged *La bella aurora, No son todos ruiseñores* and *La fuerza lastimosa*.[94] The latter production was particularly impressive. Deceptively bare staging was augmented by an expert use of lighting and dissonant music to deliver a consistently engaging version of a complex drama that unfolds in multiple environs and offers a perceptive interrogation of the interstices of power, honour and sexuality.

Many performances by these private groups have been increasingly proficient in recent years and, although it is impossible to quantify with any precision, the CNTC is, in part, responsible for this improvement. It has provided an important reference point and, for example, the fact that its actors place more emphasis on the content of their speech than in exact methods of declamation has clearly had an effect on other productions: actors now seem less corseted or intimidated by verse, and generally therefore inhabit their roles with greater credibility than they did twenty years ago. More practically, the increased respectability of the classics has optimized the possibility for funding, and has also increased the opportunities for companies to perform in festivals. Unfortunately, however, as the table demonstrates, beyond the efforts of a few groups, this increased respectability has not translated into a wider interest in the Golden Age and a few isolated productions, however good they may be, does not constitute a performance tradition.

In hindsight, it is clear that the mid 1990s represented a Golden Age in *comedia* performance: the CNTC celebrated its tenth anniversary and the Almagro Festival went from strength to strength while, as will be discussed in chapter four, Pilar Miró's critically acclaimed film adaptation of *El perro del hortelano* triumphed at the box office. Unfortunately, the period between

1996 and 2004 was to retain many of the negative elements of the legitimization of the *comedia* but without the same level of consistency or commitment. It would also demonstrate how vulnerable Spanish cultural projects are to shifts in political mood.

In 1995, a change in the direction at the INAEM led to the replacement of most of those involved in the running of the Almagro Festival (Peláez Martín, 1997, p. 90). Then, with the ascension of the PP to power in 1996, Marsillach left the CNTC. As would become increasingly evident over the coming years, the Spanish predilection for complete overhaul in all areas with the changes in government constitutes an overt politicization of culture and is an obstacle to the consolidation of stable companies.

Marsillach claims that he only discovered about his dismissal in the press and he was extremely bitter at what he saw as a conspiracy by three former colleagues (Tomás Marcos, Pérez Sierra and Luciano García Lorenzo): 'Agradezco vivamente a estos tres íntimos amigos su actitud, que viene a demostrar de nuevo la forma de comportarse de cierto sector de la derecha más torpe y menos educada de nuestro país.' [I effusively thank these three close friends for their attitude, which once again demonstrates the type of conduct exercised by our country's most clumsy and ill-mannered right-wingers] (cited in Torres, 1996). The CNTC's outgoing director was particularly offended by the new legislator's choice of successor:

> No será igual si quien dirige es una persona de la literatura. Este será un local en el que se invitará a directores y escenógrafos ... Rafael Pérez Sierra no puede darle un estilo teatral a una compañía puesto que él no lo tiene ... No habrá una compañía: habrá compañía por espectáculo. Aquí hay algo sangrante. Que yo salga de esta compañía se puede entender, pero que salpique a todo mi equipo de colaboradores, eso duele. (cited in Pascual, 1996)
>
> [It won't be the same if the director comes from the literary world. It will be a place where they invite directors and set designers ... Given that he does not have it himself, Rafael Pérez Sierra cannot provide a company with theatrical style ... There will not be a company: there will be a different company every production. There is something bloody and cruel about all of this. One can understand that I have to leave this company but that this extends to my team of collaborators; that hurts.]

In fact, Marsillach's prognostications were to prove to be correct as his successor's tenure lacked direction and there were constant interventions by politicians who wanted to use the theatre as an arena for their own political manoeuvrings. In 1997, the subdirector of INAEM, the dramatist Eduardo Galán, offered the directorship of the company to Calixto Bieito, and Pérez Sierra only retained his post due to the personal intervention of Marcos, former director of INAEM, and the Minister of Culture Esperanza Aguirre (Torres, 1999a).

The first work staged was Tirso's *La venganza de Tamar* directed by José Carlos Plaza. This relatively unknown and potentially fascinating – albeit challenging – play by Tirso was rendered in an excessively literal and unimaginative manner while the inclusion of a very explicit and gratuitous rape scene veered dangerously close to pornography. Later productions such as Miró's *El anzuelo de Fenisa* (1997) and Denis Rafter's *No hay burlas con el amor* (1998) were pleasing on the eye but did nothing to develop a performance style and supplied little evidence of any form of critical dialogue with the play texts. The former was privately intended by the current director of the CNTC as a posthumous tribute to Alonso who had recently committed suicide, and with whom he had begun his theatrical career as an assistant on his 1961 production of Lope's comedy at the María Guerrero.[95] Sentiment aside, the production was particularly disappointing considering that it reunited Peréz Sierra, Miró and costume designer Pedro Moreno, following their highly successful collaboration on *El perro del hortelano*.

Peréz Sierra subsequently resigned in 1999 citing political interference in his planning of the upcoming centenary celebrations of Calderón's birth. He had invited two internationally renowned directors, Jorge Lavelli and Ariel García Valdés, to direct *La hija del aire* and *El mágico prodigioso* respectively, but was told that he could not contract Lavelli because the amount that had been agreed with the Argentine director exceeded limits imposed by the ministry. Pérez Sierra claims, however, that this was merely a convenient excuse: 'En resumen, que esa contratación fue el pretexto para que un director como yo, que no quería que en un teatro público se privatizase, empezaba a ser molesto.' [To sum up, this contractual agreement was the basis on which an artistic director such as myself, who does not want a public theatre to be privatized, started to become a nuisance] (cited in Muez, 2000). Marsillach did not waste any time in diagnosing the situation: 'Un director decente dimite a la primera presión política y un gestor sumiso aguanta hasta que el presupuesto le hunde.' [A decent director would resign at the first hint of political pressure, while a submissive bureaucrat puts up with it until they are sunk by their own budget] (cited in Oliva, 2005, p. 212). Nevertheless, most other members of the profession were supportive and saw his resignation as symptomatic of a wider problem in Spanish theatre. Núria Espert, for example, spoke of how, 'España va a lograr el triste récord de ser el país de Europa donde estará más desacredito dirigir un teatro público, porque equivaldrá a ser un lacayo de poder.' [Spain is going to achieve the unenviable record of being the European country where occupying the directorship of a public theatre is most discredited for it will be equivalent to being a lackey to those in power] (cited in Torres, 1999b).

As an ostensibly interim solution, the academic Andrés Amorós replaced Pérez Sierra. Within a year, Amorós left the company to become director of INAEM and he was replaced at the CNTC by one of his associate directors, José Luis Alonso de Santos. In theory, this appointment boded well. Alonso de Santos had a strong track record in theatre: beginning his career in the independent sector during the 1960s, he had in 1971 staged a collage of Calderón's *autos sacramentales* prior to becoming a household name in the 1980s with his epochal play *Bajarse al moro*.[96] Unfortunately, however, his tenure proved to be remarkably lacklustre and uneventful; the most dramatic event to take place was the company being evicted from its home in Madrid (the Teatro de la Comedia) due to complaints made by unions about the structural safety of the building (EFE, 2002).

2000 marked the fourth centenary of Calderón's birth and was the source of a high-profile celebration that included various exhibitions, international congresses and an increased number of performances.[97] I have found records of nineteen productions of his works in the centenary year; this is a large increase on the number of works staged to celebrate the centenary of his death and is indicative of the new role that Calderón performed in Spain's cultural landscape. However, as was made clear by the centenary of Lope's birth, the number of productions is not always an index of engagement with a playwright's work. Nevertheless, there were a number of potentially interesting productions in his honour. Narros staged a version of *Mañanas de abril y mayo*, a play that had not been performed since 1927. Zampanó staged a new play entitled *Calderón enamorado*, based on a text cowritten by the academic José María Ruano de la Haza, that, in the fashion of *Shakespeare in Love*, depicted don Pedro's youthful amorous escapades by engaging with various of his texts. La Bicicleta staged a lively children's version of *El galán fantasma* and the students of RESAD performed *El monstruo de los jardines* that featured a young actress in the role of a cross-dressing Achilles, thereby making the lesbian subtext of the play text more explicit.

In 2000, for the first time, the CNTC's programming was very conservative in its repertoire, which included three Calderón plays that they had staged before (*La dama duende*, *La vida es sueño* and *El alcalde de Zalamea*) albeit with different directors.[98] Considering the sheer volume of Golden Age plays, the choice of three emblematic titles reflects an attitude of celebration and exaltation rather than investigation and discovery. Amorós justified this choice by appealing to the need to reach out to a younger generation: 'A mí me pareció que en este momento del centenario y dirigiéndonos a los jóvenes hemos de replantearnos este año la vigencia escénica de Calderón' [It seemed me that at the time of the centenary, and with young people in mind, Calderón's theatrical relevance ought once again to be foremost in our minds] (cited in Doménech, 2000, p. 80). In all fairness, the works were directed by three of the most adventurous and theatrically engaged practitioners to have worked with the CNTC: Alonso de Santos and his two associate directors, Bieito and Sergi Belbel.

Furthermore, two of these productions were joint initiatives with Catalan-based companies. As will be discussed in chapter five, Belbel's *El alcalde de Zalamea* marked the first time that the TNC had performed a Spanish classic in Castilian,[99] while Bieito's *La vida es sueño* was a coproduction with the Teatre Romea in Barcelona. The best of the three, to my mind at least, was however Alonso de Santos's production of *La dama duende*, which focussed on the protofeminist sentiments expressed in the play and attempted to engage with a young audience and displace a more austere image of Calderón.[100] Nevertheless, the overall quality of productions was disappointing and it is difficult to dispute the following claim made by Evangelina Rodríguez Cuadros:

> El centenario del año 2000 ha hecho del dramaturgo una parte de nuestro *patrimonio nacional*, un escritor del canon, precisamente en los tiempos en que el canon empieza a cuestionarse. Pero también un clásico de biblioteca, sin interés, al parecer, al margen del tiempo que lo creó. (2002, p. 10)

> [The 2000 centenary had made the dramatist part of our *national heritage*, a canonical author just at the time when the very notion of the canon is being questioned. But, also, a classical author whose home is in the library and it appears of historical interest alone.]

This impression is bolstered by the realization that more Calderón was staged in 2000 than in the following three years combined.

At the turn of the century, the trend for programming titles already staged by the company continued with Narros's *El burlador de Sevilla* (2003),[101] and José Pascual's *El caballero de Olmedo* (2003). Many productions attempted to provide elegant versions of works that eschewed the darker, or more complex, aspects of the text. One potentially fascinating exception was Alonso de Santos's production of *Peribáñez*, based on a version by José María Díez Borque. This old favourite from the 1940s has hardly ever been performed in recent times.[102] Pérez Sierra has claimed that the widespread rejection of this play was symptomatic of the left's persistent and uncritical rejection of Lope's *oeuvre*. Alonso de Santos picked up on this concern and felt that it was a moral duty to stage a play which he believes to be first rate despite its (in)conspicuous absence from the contemporary Spanish stage (CNTC, 2006b, DVD). Considering the negative spectre of the play's folkloric performance history, its direct and/or indirect influence was surprising. The production, while uplifting and engaging, simplistically contrasted an idealized peasant with his lascivious overlord. The Comendador is presented as little more than a one-dimensional monster and there is no interrogation of how Peribáñez killing the nobleman and his own wife's cousin, Inés, might affect him or his marriage.[103] This was clearly a backward step from the demystification of the rural idyll that had taken place in previous productions.

Despite this clear artistic decline, the CNTC's public remained loyal and its performances continued to play to near capacity houses.[104] By 2003, the Almagro Festival had also reached something of a nadir; there were eighteen fewer companies and thirty-nine fewer performances than there had been the previous year. Only one international company was present, and although, following the injection of public money, Narros's *El burlador de Sevilla* was performed at the Festival, there had been many doubts about whether the CNTC would go to Almagro, as they had done every year of their existence up until then (L.B., 2003). There was something of an improvement in 2004 where there were schemes directed at encouraging young people to classical theatre and the opening of the Theatre Museum by the king and queen, alongside the minister of culture, Pilar del Castillo, raised its profile. Nevertheless attendance had reduced from 35,124 in 2000 to 30,886 in 2004 (Lanza, 2005).

Given this rather bleak panorama, it is not surprising that critics become increasingly negative about Spanish directors' ability to stage the classics. When, in 2004, the RSC brought their season of Golden Age works to Madrid, reviewers from national newspapers used this British achievement as a pretext to attack Spanish theatre practitioners. Miguel Ayanz spoke of the 'orgullo que la Royal Shakespeare le dedique un ciclo a nuestros clásicos (aunque sonroja que tengan que venir a descubrírnoslos)' [pride that the RSC has dedicated a season to our classics albeit with the embarrassment that they had to bring them here for us to discover them] (2004), while Almudena Guzmán noted how '[g]racias a la Royal Shakespeare Company, el teatro Español volvió a sus orígenes y se convirtió por una noche en un corral de comedias donde el espíritu de Lope, tantas y tantas veces encarcelado por sus compatriotas, recobró su libertad perdida' [thanks to the RSC, the Español returned to its origins and became a *corral de comedias* for one night, where Lope's spirit – so frequently imprisoned by his compatriots – recovered its lost freedom] (2004). By the turn of the century, the expectations invested in the CNTC as a panacea for the performance of Golden Age drama were, at best, curtailed and, at worst, completely dashed.

Comedia performance comes of age? Golden Age drama in the twenty-first century

The return to power of the PSOE in 2004 brought renewed optimism among most theatre practitioners, and those involved in the performance of classical drama were no exception.[105] It is too early to know whether this indicates a new era in *comedia* performance, but the initial impression is that while the CNTC and Almagro are recovering, they are gradually, and perhaps prematurely, moving away from the seventeenth-century classics. More generally, Golden Age drama seems to retain its cultural cachet but is nevertheless still not successfully integrated into Spanish life.

An early success which was cause for optimism was provided by a co-production between the Teatro Español and the Teatro San Martín (Buenos Aires) of *La hija del aire*, directed by Jorge Lavelli, which vindicated Pérez Sierra's faith in the project. Blanca Portillo, one of Spain's most respected stage actresses, took on the roles of mother and son, Semíramis and Ninias, in a gothic production based solely on the darker second part of the play. The performance virtually reinvented the Español as a theatrical space; mirrors filled the stage and there was a giant wooden construction from which characters emerged and in which musicians were encased in glass cubicles. This was a phenomenally bleak and sinister performance in which even the *gracioso* [fool], Chato, provided no light relief.[106]

Not surprisingly, a new government meant that the CNTC had a new director: thirty-five-year-old Vasco. This was an apparently judicious appointment. From early on in his career, the director has shown a predilection for the *comedia*. In 1993, he staged Calderón's *Dar tiempo al tiempo* at the Teatro Cervantes in Alcalá de Henares and, as we have seen, this interest really came to the fore in his Compañía Noviembre. He has introduced some radical changes and he has, for example, pursued a policy previously mooted by Alonso de Santos (Moral, 2001, p. 29), and extended the programming with more eclectic works from other periods, such as Gil Vicente's *Tragicomedia de don Duardos* and Ramón de la Cruz's *Sainetes*, playing alongside the Company's more traditional fare.

This widening of horizons has, nevertheless, been counterbalanced by a drastic increase in productivity that has reaped a number of additional advantages. There are currently two permanent troupes in operation allowing one to perform in the Spanish capital and the other to be constantly on tour. In specific relation to *comedia* performance, Vasco has also honoured his promise to offer a more eclectic programme: 'El caso es que hay textos y textos, no todo es *La vida es sueño*.' [The thing is that there are endless texts, it's not just *Life is a Dream*] (cited in Martín Bermúdez, 2005, p. 101). The general emphasis has been on works that have rarely, if ever, been staged in recent years: *Amar después de la muerte, La noche de San Juan, Las manos blancas no ofenden, El pintor de su deshonra, ¿De cuándo acá nos vino?*

In terms of performance style, the prevailing aesthetic has been characterized by an unprecedented sobriety. From a practical perspective, this allows more of the company's budget – currently standing at ten million euros (EFE, 2009a)[107] – to be set aside for touring both nationally and internationally. It is also, however, an aesthetic choice designed to combat the tendency for spectacle that was dominant in the 1990s and that Vasco attributes to the fact that 'existía una desconfianza hacia los textos y hacia su valor' [there was a certain lack of confidence as regards the texts and their value]. In contrast, his approach is based on 'otorgándole el primer plano al actor y al aspecto emocional' [foregrounding the actor and the emotional dimension] (cited in Sánchez Jiménez, 2006, pp. 504–5). Many productions have been located in precise spatiotemporal settings with, for example, *El castigo sin venganza* staged in Mussollini's Italy,[108] and attention has often been lavished on precise details. Lorenzo Caprile, the current designer of choice, tends to supply heavily stylized variations on period costume while Vasco's own background in sound design has resulted in music being increasingly prominent.

This is clearly the first time that the CNTC has been brave enough to lay the *comedia* bare; more open to debate is how well these naked performances withstand close scrutiny. This is a question to which I will return in more detail in chapter three where I will suggest that Vasco has been unable to establish the identity that he initially sought for the company; there is still a concerning lack of consistency and, for some reason, they seem to be far more adept at performing comedies than dramas.

On a more positive note, the Joven Compañía [Young Company] made its debut in 2007 with a highly enjoyable version of *Las bizarrías de Belisa*, set in a 1930s cabaret bar complete with a grand piano, and directed by Vasco himself. The youthful cast, draped in elegant and flattering attire, was very adroit at rendering the narrative's mounting hysteria without lapsing into caricature, while Eva Rufo's commanding stage presence as Belisa marked her out as a star of the future, as was recognized in her subsequent promotion to the adult company in a production of Lope's *¿De cuándo acá nos vino?*

The first cycle has now been completed with the initial intake having performed two Lope plays: *Las bizarrías de Belisa* and *La noche de San Juan*. The second venture, based on a version by Pallín and directed by Helena Pimenta, was sadly far less successful. In theory, this was an inspired vehicle for young actors as it is one of the few Golden Age plays to contain no older characters and Lope's verse is overflowing with adolescent revelry. However, while the actors recited their lines with technical skill and they began with an ostensibly uplifting festive song, there was little sense of exuberance and debauchery and the lack of an ensemble dynamic suggested that *Las bizarrías* may have been carried by Rufo.[109]

The desire to invest in future generations has also been reflected by encouraging teenagers to attend the theatre. Vasco has continued the CNTC's practice of publishing educational guides to accompany productions, and there has been an active and sustained effort since 2004 to liaise with schools: teachers are, for example, now being requested to hold an introductory class prior to their students attending the theatre. They are often present and create a unique atmosphere in the Pavón on Thursdays when the theatre has its 'día del espectador' [audience day] and further reduces its relatively cheap ticket prices (currently eighteen euros) by 50 per cent. In the academic year 2007–8, over 1,200 secondary students attended productions by the CNTC in the capital (Villena, 2008b), a figure that may help to explain why the theatre's occupancy is so high.

There were over a thousand applications to join this new company (Torres, 2007); a cynical explanation would be that this says at least as much about the number of unemployed young actors and the advantages of working in a national company as it does about *comedia* performance. However, this interest among at least some actors does seem to be genuine, as is indicated by their increased presence in other productions. The Compañía José Estruch has, over recent years, operated an Aula de Teatro Clásico [Classroom of Classical Theatre] as part of RESAD; they have staged a number of Golden Age plays including *Castelvines y Monteses* (2004) and *El arrogante español* (2006).[110] Murcia has retained its traditional interest in dramatic art and performance at their ESAD. Having performed *Don Gil* and *Fuente Ovejuna* in previous years, in 2007 they staged a warmly received version of Calderón's *No hay burlas con el amor* that toured internationally.[111] Ángel Gutiérrez, a veteran Spanish director who received his training in Russia in the late 1940s and 1950s, has also returned to *Los balcones de Madrid*, a play he had originally staged in the mid 1980s. This reposition staged at the intimate Teatro de Cámara Chejov in the Spanish capital in 2008 featured a young cast who engaged with Tirso's verse and narrative in an energetic and intelligent manner.

Since Emilio Hernández was appointed director in 2005, the Almagro Festival has followed the CNTC's pattern of rehabilitation and widening of horizons beyond Golden Age drama. Considering the centenary of the *Quijote*, it was no surprise that the 2005 edition was high profile and dominated by Cervantes. The 2006 Festival continued this upward trend and featured a wide variety of activities. There was, for example, the inauguration of the Centro para la Interpretación de los Clásicos de Almagro [The Almagro Centre for Classical Performance] where representatives of theatrical companies from all over the world met to exchange ideas (Torres, 2005). Although the *comedia* may not have dominated the programme as it once had, this was again largely compensated for by an increase in productivity.[112]

Any apparent marginalization was, however, reversed in 2008. During my ten-day residence in La Mancha, I was able to watch ten works by Lope, Calderón and Tirso. Quantity was not, however, matched by quality and, as I will discuss in chapter five, what should have been the source of celebration

Figure 3 Photograph by Agustín Espinel of *Los balcones de Madrid* (dir. Ángel Gutiérrez, 2007), Teatro de Cámara Chejov

raised some serious concerns about the state and status of *comedia* performance. More positively, this recent return to seventeenth-century Spanish dramatists was symptomatic of a bumper year for Golden Age drama. In addition to Almagro, there is an ever-increasing number of festivals (Cáceres, Alcalá, El Escorial etc.) that provide a temporary home for productions and these proved particularly rich pickings in 2008, at least in terms of quantity. For example, the third festival of classical theatre in Olmedo held between 18 and 27 July featured ten productions, eight of which were of Lope or Calderón.[113]

Furthermore, the Teatres de la Generalitat in Valencia marked the debut of the revamped Teatro Rialto in December 2008 with a production of Lope's *La viuda valenciana*. This high-profile production, which adopted a highly enjoyable carnival aesthetic, constituted their first ever foray into Golden Age drama. The production featured a cast of actors from the region, and the last two lines of the performance were delivered in Valencian in homage to the play's setting. In the same year, La Compañía del Siglo de Oro de la Comunidad de Madrid also performed *La vida es sueño* throughout Spain. The director, Juan Carlos Pérez de la Fuente, claims that *The Matrix* was inspired by Calderón's play; he in turn takes inspiration from modern film aesthetics (Montero, 2008). Personally, I found the anachronistic costuming in which there was no continuity between characters or scenes troubling, along with the acting style that rendered Segismundo's mental torture in rather melodramatic fashion. It cannot be denied, however, that the very appreciative audience with whom I watched the production not only did not appear to share my misgivings but were entranced throughout; it was also reportedly well received when performed in Berlin (EFE, 2008c).

The cinematic dimension of the play was once again brought to the fore in a revival of Pasolini's *Calderón* that interpolates extracts from *La vida es sueño* into its examination of a bourgeois family living in Madrid, looking back to the Civil War.[114] This revival of a play, which received its Spanish debut in 1988 by the Compañía CNNTE at the Sala Olimpia in Madrid in a production directed by Guillermo Heras,[115] took place from 13 to 15 February 2009 at the Centro Cultural Moncloa in Madrid under the direction of Ainhoa Amestoy as part of a cycle dedicated to the Italian film director's theatrical work.

When I interviewed Hernández in the summer of 2008, he made it clear that he wanted to take the Almagro Festival in a new direction. Although he accepted that it was unlikely to happen in practice, he expressed his personal desire to expand the parameters of what the public considers to be a classic by, for example, staging Valle-Inclán. Nevertheless, the 2009 edition of the Almagro Festival was dedicated to commemorating the *Arte nuevo*, and the *comedia* was once again well represented, together with public events such as a recitation of Lope's dramatic treatise by a hip-hop group.[116] In a similar vein, students from RESAD performed a thirty-minute show entitled *Lope de Vega a capa y espada* under the direction of Iñaki Arano six times on the steps of the Biblioteca Nacional [National Library] on 19 September as part of the pan-European white night initiative.[117]

In an appropriate cultural setting, Golden Age drama continues to have remarkable success. Virtually all the productions at the last five editions of the Almagro Festival have played to full houses and, in August 2007, I made the mistake of trying to buy a ticket on the night for an outdoor performance of *Casa con dos puertas mala es de guardar* held at the Jardines del Galileo as part of the Veranos de la Villa festivities organised by Madrid City Council. I was told that all 390 tickets for each performance had sold out in advance for almost every night of the play's eight-week run. The director, Canseco, replicated this success the following year at the same venue with another Calderón comedy: *No hay burlas con el amor*. In 2007, the Teatro Pavón, temporary home to the CNTC, sold 74.37% of its tickets while the figures for equivalent Madrid theatres such as the María Guerrero and the Español were significantly lower: 48.38 per cent and 46.49 per cent, respectively. In percentage terms, the Pavón had the highest occupancy of any theatre in Madrid which offered more than one hundred and fifty functions. The company was also very successful elsewhere in Spain, for example selling 19,672 tickets for *Don Gil* over thirty performances in Barcelona (CDT, 2008).

Popularity for one-off or prestigious events has never, however, been too problematic for Spanish seventeenth-century drama; its principal difficulty has been to engage audiences that are not just interested in receiving a quick cultural fix. Although the panorama is undoubtedly more conducive to the successful staging of national classical drama in 2009 than it was in 2004, it would be both premature and facile to herald the arrival of a new Golden Age of *comedia* performance.

Conclusion

There is an element of arbitrariness in all attempts at chronological division. Nevertheless, in broad terms, I believe that four main periods can be detected in the performance of Golden Age drama between 1939 and 2006. From the end of the Civil War to 1950, seventeenth-century plays were used to fulfil what Bernardo Antonio González has termed 'la doble función ceremonial-ideológica' [the twin functions of ceremony and ideology] (1993, p. 66) in an attempt to project a national identity in keeping with the philosophy of the dictatorship. From 1950 to 1963, the ceremonial role came to be increasingly prominent and the *comedia* became more of a form of exemplary entertainment than a medium for proselytizing. Between 1963 and 1978, the *comedia* was largely ignored by official channels, and deemed irrelevant by the counter-culture. However, this general lack of interest did not prevent various inventive and progressive stagings of the *comedia* from taking place. Innovations and developments made in this period would prepare the ground for the reintegration of the *comedia* into Spanish cultural life in the following years. From 1978 to the present day there has been a gradual reinstitutionalization of Golden Age drama whereby the *comedia* has once again taken on an important ceremonial role.

Spain has a tradition of performing the *comedia* but this has not translated into a performance tradition. While individual productions have been able to engage with the needs and preoccupations of audiences, this has been the exception rather than the rule. The CNTC has radically improved the performance level of Golden Age drama but the company has definite limitations and there has been no project capable of harnessing the lessons learnt by the tradition of performance. A definite hindrance in this regard has been the frequent desire to begin afresh and the concomitant reluctance to admit precedents or to engage with past productions; a phenomenon clearly not unrelated to the intimate relationships of dependency between political and cultural institutions.

Chapter Two

An (early) modern classic: *Fuente Ovejuna* in contemporary Spain

In *The Genius of Shakespeare* (1997), Jonathan Bate considers whether it is a matter of chance or destiny that the Bard is considered the world genius of literature. He concludes that the truth lies somewhere in between:

> The apotheosis of Shakespeare was and was not a matter of historical contingency. It was a contingency insofar as it happened to be Shakespeare, not Lope. But it was a necessity because the chosen one had to be a particular kind of genius and could therefore only have been Lope or Shakespeare. (1997, p. 340)

This is the case, Bate argues, because the Spanish playwright is the only other dramatist to have the necessary prerequisites for genius: aspectuality and performativity. The former concept refers to the principle that there are qualities in these works that may ostensibly be mutually exclusive but can nevertheless both be identified, albeit not simultaneously; thus, an 'either/or' dichotomy is replaced by a 'both/and' binary (1997, pp. 314–15). It is not that there is a single truth inherent in the work that the critic can identify; the work is polyvalent to the extent that it can ground heterogeneous interpretations. In relation to Lope or Shakespeare, notions such as revolutionary or conservative are therefore better understood as adverbs, forms of processing information, than adjectives, consubstantial qualities that invariable attach themselves to a play. As an illustrative example, Bate observes: 'Both the Hal aspect (call it the rule of providence) and the Falstaff aspect (call it the rule of the body) are truths of the *Henry* plays, but you cannot see them both at one and the same time' (1997, p. 328).

Performativity, meanwhile, refers to the principle that the truth of a play is to be found in the performance itself. Its genius is not to be found through reference to external determinants such as style, matter, or wisdom: 'It is the process of Shakespeare [or Lope], that which is performed by the performance. As with the later Wittgenstein, the working through does not *lead to a conclusion*, it *performs the point*' (1997, p. 336). Hence, on this reading, a successful staging of a politically contentious Lope play would, for example, not so much refer to revolutionary and/or conservative ideas as it would enact these ideologies on stage through performance.

It is no coincidence that Bate proceeds to single out *Fuente Ovejuna* as possessing both aspectuality and performativity (1997, p. 339).[1] The fact that it is one of the relatively few Golden Age plays to have been translated into readily available modern editions in English is symptomatic of the fact that, in the modern era, it is Lope's best known and most regularly performed play both in Spain and internationally.[2] Furthermore, this (in)famous *comedia*'s standing has largely been forged because it has been read and performed from radically divergent political standpoints. In Joan-Antón Benach's memorable phrase, '*Fuente Ovejuna* es como una gran ramera, presta a los servicios más variopintos' [*Fuente Ovejuna* is like a great whore, predisposed to deliver the most esoteric of services] (2005).

In this chapter, I will track how the play has been performed and received in modern-day Spain, paying particular attention to how specific interpretations and productions relate to Bate's concepts of aspectuality and performativity. In order to facilitate the comparison of often radically different stagings, I have decided to focus my attention on the performance (or absence) of three specific moments in the play: the central wedding scene, Laurencia's speech and the denouement.

As Paul Julian Smith notes in his attack on the kind of literary criticism based on textual exegesis, which had traditionally predominated in Hispanic studies, 'there can be no direct engagement with Golden Age writing: access can only be made through an extensive growth of commentary, which must also be the object of analysis' (1988, p. 5). This is particularly true of *Fuente Ovejuna* which, to borrow a characteristically acerbic phrase from Adolfo Marsillach, is 'un Lope pasto de directores, intérpretes, versionistas, conferenciantes, sabios, académicos, forasteros, jubilados y otros ciudadanos de mal pasar y dudoso porvenir' [a Lope play of rich sustenance for directors, actors, adaptors, conference speakers, wise men, members of the Academy, foreigners, pensioners and other citizens with a murky past and doubtful future] (2002, p. 523). The sheer number of productions precludes a detailed analysis of them all. What I will provide, however, is a general overview of changing trends which will buttress the detailed analyses of productions from the Republican, dictatorial and democratic periods.

The rediscovery of *Fuente Ovejuna*

As Paul E. Larson has recently noted, '*Fuente Ovejuna* has not always been considered a great work, and the development of Lope's play as a masterpiece questions the very concept of how a "masterpiece" is produced, identified and invented' (2001, p. 282). This is a timely reminder for 'la necesidad de entender la construcción de todo canon en un sentido polisistémico y como consecuencia de un devenir histórico' [the need to understand the construction of every canon from a polysystemic perspective and as a consequence of its particular historical trajectory] (Pozuelo and Aradra Sánchez, 2000, p. 121). In this case, *Fuente Ovejuna*'s 'fame in literary and academic circles as Lope's most important play is clearly linked to the ebb and flow of the political tides that have swept across this century' (Larson, 2001, p. 268).

The play, let us remind ourselves, is the fictional retelling of a real-life historical event where the inhabitants of the eponymous town rose up against, and murdered, their overlord. In Lope's work, the revolt is a consequence of the abuses they suffer at the hands of Comendador Fernán Gómez; among other offences, he interrupts a wedding to abduct the bride, Laurencia, and imprisons Frondoso, the groom. When the former returns, she propels the villagers into action by questioning their masculinity and accusing her father and local mayor, Esteban, of being unable to protect her. Alongside Jacinta, another victim of the lascivious overlord and his men, Laurencia also raises a female squadron.

Following many years in the wilderness, the *comedia* was translated into French in 1822, then into German in 1845. Beyond this philological interest, the country where it first sparked the interest of practitioners was Russia. An 1876 performance was a resounding success and inspired calls for uprisings in the street; subsequently, in the early twentieth century, it became a symbol of the workers' struggle as the uprising was staged as an exemplary and inspirational model to follow (Kirschner, 1977a, pp. 257–9).

By the beginning of the twentieth century, Spanish intellectuals became interested in the classics in so far as they represented what the country had lost and the values that were conspicuously absent from their own period (García Santo-Tomás, 2000a, p. 323). Considering how closely *Fuente Ovejuna* would later be identified with questions of Spanish national identity, it is ironic that its revival would take place far beyond the borders of the Iberian peninsula. Despite its presence on foreign stages, there is no record of the play being performed in Spain during the nineteenth century (Gagen, 1993, p. 5). Equally, as Donald McGrady has noted (1993, p. 23), any mention of Lope's play is conspicuously absent from the historian Rafael Ramírez de Arellano's detailed study of the historical uprising (1901).

This discrepancy prompted Marcelino Menéndez y Pelayo to comment that '[t]al popularidad no sorprende, porque se trata de una de las obras más admirables de Lope, por raro capricho de la suerte, no sea de las más conocidas en España [*sic.*]' [popularity of this kind should not surprise us because we are dealing with one of Lope's admirable plays that, were it not for the whimsy of fortune, would be among the best known in Spain] (1925, pp. 194–5). The philologist attempts to reclaim the play and refute any revolutionary dimension: 'este drama, tan profundamente democrático, es también profundamente monárquico. Ambas ideas vivían juntas en el pueblo español; y en Lope, su poeta, su intérprete, tenían que ser inseparables' [this fundamentally democratic drama is also fundamentally monarchical. Both ideas coexisted among the Spanish people; and in Lope – their poet, their voice – they must be inseparable] (p. 201).

Menéndez y Pelayo provided the heuristic model for future interpretations of the play from both ends of the political spectrum. Firstly, he made Lope, *Fuente Ovejuna* and the essence of the Spanish national character virtually synonymous. Secondly, he equated the play's meaning with Lope's intention and assumed that this could be accessed in a direct and reliable manner. The effect of these presuppositions was that *Fuente Ovejuna* came to be equivalent to a positive abstract quality such as goodness, justice or Spanishness: everybody claimed it as their own albeit in radically different guises. This helps to explain why, as Teresa J. Kirschner notes, virtually all of the critical attention paid to the play both in Spain and abroad in the early decades of its rediscovery focussed on its ideological content (1977b, p. 452).

Given the precedent set in Russia where productions either eliminated the Catholic Monarchs or presented them in a negative light, thereby highlighting the righteousness and violence of popular rebellion, it is not surprising that the play was initially adopted by leftist elements. In a work completed in 1923, and first published in 1928, Juan Díaz del Moral notes how among 'el proletariado moderno ha logrado el drama de Lope de Vega singular fortuna' [Lope de Vega's drama has achieved an unprecedented popularity among the modern-day proletariat]. This largely self-taught historian with a strong Marxist bent praises the work because 'se propone en primer término constituir un capítulo de la historia del proletariado' [first and foremost, it constitutues a chapter in the proletariat's history] (1973, pp. 58–9), and cites it as evidence of an unchanging revolutionary spirit among the Cordovan peasantry.

On a wider scale, news of the Soviet performances became increasingly important in Spain following the proclamation of the Second Republic, as the left hoped that Golden Age drama could restore a lost sense of community (Holguín, 2002, p. 86). From 1936 to 1939, *Fuente Ovejuna* was the most frequently staged of all Lope's plays (García Santo-Tomás, 2000a,

p. 345). The most important and emblematic production from this period was delivered by Federico García Lorca's theatrical troupe, La Barraca.³ In a formulation that is equally applicable to Lope's play, Willhem Hortmann has argued:

> For the political potential of Shakespeare's plays to be realised, three things must come together: a political or social situation crying out for critical comment, a director and ensemble willing, able (and also ruthless enough) to use the plays for this purpose; and audiences alive to the sociopolitical climate and therefore primed to catch allusions. (2002, pp. 213–14)

These preconditions were ably satisfied through Lorca and Eduardo Ugarte's version of the play with La Barraca; it was a heavily politicized adaptation that, as in many Russian versions, removed the secondary action involving Ferdinand and Isabella, while offering a direct paean to the inhabitants of Fuente Ovejuna. The Comendador was dressed as a local cacique, while the townspeople wore modern-day peasant clothing.⁴ Until this day, the Second Republic and Lorca in particular continue to function as privileged repositories of retrospective fantasies about a mythical cultural and ideological landscape that does not necessarily correspond to historical reality. As a result, it has been largely forgotten that La Barraca were deceptive in their presentation of *Fuente Ovejuna*. When he spoke about his approach to adapting the classics, Lorca claims that his versions are always faithful to Lope's play texts:

> No he refundido, sino que he cortado, lo que es muy distinto. Las obras maestras no pueden refundirse. Es un pecado que yo jamás me hubiera atrevido a cometer. No es posible quitarles escenas, cuadros, ni nada que sea esencial a su trama ni a su idea. (1974, p. 953)
>
> [I have not adapted the play, but I have abridged it which is very different. Masterpieces cannot be adapted. It is a sin that I would never dare to commit. It is not possible to excise incidents, scenes or anything that is essential to the plot or the underlying intention.]

However, in this case, this approach was clearly not adopted; *Fuente Ovejuna* was the Golden Age play to which Lorca enacted the most changes (Oliva, 2008, p. 42) eliminating 714 versos from the 2,453 of Lope's play text (Huerta, 1987, p. 481). As Peter Brook notes, 'if one has a knife in one hand, one needs a stethoscope in the other' (1990, p. 92). I would not go as far as Victor Dixon who claims that '[t]o adapt can only immeasurably impoverish the work Lope wrote' (1989, p. 7) but, as multiple studies have demonstrated,⁵ it is evident that the play's two actions are carefully entwined both aesthetically and politically. The scenes with Ferdinand and Isabella simply cannot be excised without radically altering the play text. Although Lorca clearly had the right to adapt the work for his own purposes, his claims for authenticity and what Jonathan Miller has referred to as the phantom of 'some sort of quantum of intrinsic meaning' are hardly original or convincing (1986, p. 20). They can only be defended by appealing, as Menéndez y Pelayo had done for a different purpose, to a notion of national and individual spirit or soul that is sufficiently abstract and elastic to bypass historical investigation and raise itself into the realm of metaphysics.[6]

Despite these theoretical misgivings, it was undoubtedly a manifestation of political savvy and theatrical instinct to rework the play for a 1930s public who, by all accounts, seem to have been thrilled and energized by classical theatre in a way that few other twentieth-century audiences have been. According to Luis Sáenz de la Calzada, *Fuente Ovejuna* was, alongside Cervantes' *entremeses*, the most frequently performed and popular work in the company's repertoire (1976, p. 75).

The wedding scene was particularly popular and, on one occasion, the troupe even performed it independently from the rest of the play (1976, p. 71). Unlike in the majority of *comedias*, it occurs during rather than after the main action and is therefore afforded an unusual prominence (Strother, 1999, p. 32); Lorca exploited this characteristic to deliver a 'verdadera fiesta' [genuine party]:

> Ahora bien, una boda en escena no era cosa que Federico dejara irse así como así, sino que la aprovechaba para sacar de ella lo más hondo, lo más popular, digamos lo más paleolítico que una boda rural puede tener en sus entrañas, si por acaso las bodas tienen entrañas. (Sáenz de la Calzada, 1976, p. 70)

> [Now, an onstage wedding was not something that Federico was going to leave be; he was, rather, going to extract from it that which was most profound, most popular. In other words, all that is most primeval in the entrails of a rural wedding on the presumption, that is, that weddings have entrails.]

Another highlight was provided by Laurencia's harangue against the male villagers. The inclusion of the word 'maricones' [queers] (not used by respectable women at the time) invariable provoked a shocked response from audiences. Sáenz de la Calzada claims, however, that at the end of her speech, the actress Carmen Galán would invariably receive a round of applause and the actors would have to pause before recommencing the play (1976, p. 67).

In the struggle for Lope's spirit and legacy, the left may have taken their initial strategic positions with little resistance but, by the centenary of the playwright's death, a counter-attack was in preparation. Objections were raised about staging *Fuente Ovejuna* as it had been in Russia (Tamayo, 1935), and Margarita Xirgu and Enrique Borrás's production became the object of harsh criticism by the Nationalist press which claimed the production was informed by political rather than aesthetic considerations (Kirschner, 1977a, p. 261). In a more proactive vein:

> A review of Falangist publications in 1935 shows that Lope de Vega was raised to the rank of a symbol of fascist theatre. As with the Escorial, the theatre of Lope symbolised that 'eternal Spanish theatre' from which, by virtues of its essential Spanishness, the new theatre should take its inspiration. (Wahnón, 1996, p. 198)

Lope on the battlefield

Given the prior contention over the performance and reception of *Fuente Ovejuna*, it is hardly surprising that it soon became an ideologically charged prize to be fought over. La Barraca continued to perform during the Civil War albeit without their founder. In 1937, the troupe had to pass by fresh corpses in order to stage *Fuente Ovejuna* alongside Cervantes' *El retablo de las maravillas* in Gajanejos. Sáenz de la Calzada recalls that they were treated well by Spanish soldiers fighting for the Republic due to their political message while members of the International Brigade were excited to have the opportunity to see a production that had been staged by Lorca (1976, p. 161).[7]

Later, and in a more conventional setting, Manuel González directed a version of the play that was promoted in the news as 'antifascismo del siglo XVII' [anti-fascism from the seventeenth century]. This production was one of only ten plays to have more than a hundred performances in Madrid during 1938 (Collado, 1989, pp. 307–8). Beyond the stage, Republican teachers were also trained to teach the play to the next generation: 'Una obra "de masas", "típicamente antifascista", que los niños deben estudiar, representar y ver es *Fuente Ovejuna*, en la que se puede apreciar "una profunda repulsa a la opresión capitalista"' [A 'characteristically anti-fascist' play 'belonging to the masses' that the children should study, stage and see is *The Sheep Well*, in which they will be able to appreciate a 'profound aversion to capitalist oppression'] (Mayordomo, 1993, p. 79).

The Nationalist counter-attack continued on the page. Kessel Schwartz has examined how the writers of the breakaway Seville *ABC* talked incessantly about the grandeur of Lope and his desecration at the hands of Marxist provocateurs who, according to one editorial, were using the play to make villagers commit the worst kind of atrocities (1969, p. 185). In 1938, Calle Iturrino published a book dedicated exclusively to *Fuente Ovejuna* and its misappropriation. He comments on 'lo mucho que ha influido en la crisis político-social de España la crisis de nuestra poesía' [how the crisis in our poetry has impacted greatly on Spain's sociopolitical crisis] (1938,

p. 117), and suggests how the phoenix could help rectify this crisis: 'Su obra es la prueba inequívoca de la "unidad nacional", lograda ya en su tiempo, y no puesta en duda ni negada por ninguno de sus contemporáneas' [His play is the unequivocal proof of "national unity", already attained at the time and not placed in doubt or refuted by any of his contemporaries] (p. 42).

This same drive for unification that sought to suture both geographical and temporal distances was also manifested on stage, albeit with modest means. Over Christmas 1938, some young men from the nascent SEU performed the play in Cadiz. José María Pemán adopted a deliberately bellicose tone in his partisan review:

> Un *Fuenteovejuna* navideño donde el teatro nacional nacía entre pajas humildes. Pero todo él surcado por una enorme racha de decisión, de valor. Se ha representado *Fuenteovejuna* como se asalta una trinchera. Su 'provisionalidad' era hermana gemela de la de nuestros alféreces. (1939, p. 1)
>
> [A Christmas version of *The Sheep Well* where the national theatre was born amid humble hay. It was, nevertheless, ploughed with a great surge of determination and valor. *The Sheep Well* was staged as if it were a trench attack. Its 'provisionality' was the twin brother of our lieutenants in battle.]

As he goes on to say, '[r]epresentar *Fuenteovejuna* es un poco como ganarle una posición al enemigo' [performing *The Sheep Well* is a bit like winning a position from the enemy] (p. 1). The Nationalist side proceeded to win many more positions and, ultimately, the Civil War; the question to which we must now turn is how effectively and decisively they won Lope and his play.

Fuente Ovejuna in *España, una, grande y libre*

The 'rescue' of the besieged *Fuente Ovejuna* had been undertaken by the Falange, the military and parafascist wing of Franco's government. Although they were undoubtedly reacting to Republican and Soviet productions of Lope's play, its status also benefited from having been singled out for attention by Menéndez y Pelayo who was adopted by the Nationalist side and '[e]levado a la categoría de arquetipo intelectual del Nuevo Estado' [elevated to the category of the archetypal intellectual of the New State] (Santoveña Setién, 1994, p. 203). Furthermore, the play's narrative arc was particularly well suited to the Falange's political and aesthetic interests. In an attempt to outline the main tenets of fascist ideology, Roger Griffin notes how it:

fuses the hierarchic elements of *ancien régime* absolutism with the democratic dynamic of revolutionary liberalism and socialism. It promotes the vision of a new state, a new leadership, a new political and economic order born of a revolutionary movement (and not a mere 'party') arising from within the people itself. (1996, p. 16)

The appropriateness of the form and content of *Fuente Ovejuna* to an aesthetic and political agenda of this kind is self-evident. Through a righteous popular uprising forged against a bogus and corrupt form of government, the Falangists aimed to cleanse the country of malevolent intermediaries such as Marxists or caciques, thereby reinvigorating and reuniting true Spaniards in a harmonious brotherhood homologous to a macro *Fuente Ovejuna*. This birth of the nation and national culture was seen to occur in Castile under the reign of Ferdinand and Isabella, which represented 'the Reconquest and myth of unification under Catholicism and to the spiritual foundations of Spanish imperialism and conquest' (Herzberger, 1995, p. 24).

This conception can clearly be linked to Benedict Anderson's now ubiquitous formulation of the nation as 'an imagined political community' (1991, pp. 5–6). *Fuente Ovejuna* was unusual in being able to offer two highly valued national icons: Lope de Vega and the Catholic Monarchs. The latter's yoked arrows appeared on the insignia of the Falange, whose propaganda had, from an early stage, differed from most European fascist groups by virtue of its emphasis on religion (Payne, 1961, p. 127). Their presence also served to appeal to the Church, thereby ensuring Lope's work a prominent role in education and prolonging the play's canonical status beyond the wane of Falangist power and influence.[8]

Any modern production of *Fuente Ovejuna* must, by necessity, negotiate at least three historical periods: the occurrence of the historical incident on which it is based, the recreation of these events by Lope de Vega and, finally, the moment of its recreation on stage. In theory, additional historical referents might be introduced depending on when and where the modern-day production is set. This latter consideration was bypassed in this period as productions prided themselves on philological fidelity, period costumes and a spurious historical accuracy.[9]

Furthermore, there was an attempt to efface time lapses by submerging both the Early Modern period and the present under the banner of Spanish national identity and historical destiny. This process was exacerbated in relation to *Fuente Ovejuna* because there was rarely any acknowledgement that Lope used fictional devices to tell a story based on an historical event rather than simply relaying facts; in other words, historical and poetic truths are assumed to be synonymous.[10] The Golden Age also becomes a monolithic prism through which to view a long period of history. Expositions of the time rarely if ever acknowledged that, although the seventeenth century was culturally rich, it also coincided with what John Elliott has termed 'an iron age of political and economic disaster' (1989, p. 285). In fact, the psychic and material conditions of the seventeenth century proved to be a closer fit to the post-war years of autarky, 'beset with problems of self-understanding and self-esteem' (Loureiro, 2003: 65), than Spain's earlier imperial phase. In Elliott's words:

> Like other societies, Castile had created an image of itself and of its past, which had helped to shape its expectations and its goals. The disappointments and reverses of the late sixteenth and early seventeenth centuries created a crisis of confidence, because they implied that Castile was falling short of the goals – essentially military and religious – which it had set itself. The failure was then set into the context of *declinación*. (1989, p. 252)

As in Francoist discourse, the answer to this decline was thought to lie in a reawakened Golden Age rather than in radical change (1989, p. 100). This accounts for the 'verdadero culto' [genuine cult] of Ferdinand and Isabella in the early seventeenth century (Pring-Mill, 1962, p. 28). As William R. Blue notes, '[t]he Catholic Monarchs became the mythic symbol of all that had been right with Spain' (1991, p. 301). Lope clearly adapts a poetic rather than historical view of their characters and their relationship with vassals (Caba, 2008, p. 17; Ostlund, 1997, p. 11), and plays such as *Fuente Ovejuna* 'betray a powerful nostalgia for a more personal form of rule, for a time when kings were more actively involved in the processes of justice' (McKendrick, 2000a, pp. 36–7).

This idealization is also extended to a peasant class that, despite or perhaps because of their harsh material conditions, were eulogized in both periods and held up as the solutions to the nation's ills. In the seventeenth century, as in the 1940s, these idylls would have been enacted on stage primarily for an urban audience perhaps also nostalgic on the individual level for a rural life that many of them or their parents would have left behind (Jones, 1971). Although it would not have been articulated in these terms, *Fuente Ovejuna* was an obvious choice for performance in the early post-war period. Lope had written it in a society proposing many of the same solutions for similar problems and crises; its plot was remarkably amenable to the aesthetics of the Falange; and a definite Spanish version of the play was needed to finally dispel the spectre of 'anti-Spanish' versions.

Fuente Ovejuna at the Español

Modesto Higueras toured a version of the play with the Grupo de Teatro Ambulante Lope de Rueda (Teatro Móvil de la Falange) in the early 1940s. It was based on a version by Ernesto Giménez Caballero that is so close to the printed version that the performance script held in the CDT consists of a typed copy of Lope's play text with minor changes indicated by handwritten amendments.[11] These are very minor and are generally introduced to facilitate understanding (e.g. basquiñas [traditional overskirt] is replaced by faldas [skirt]), with the most significant change being Frondoso's final speech being split and delivered by the Maestre and Esteban instead. A note at the end also indicates that these closing lines should be followed by a rendition of the Falangist anthem, *Cara al sol.*

Fuente Ovejuna's major post-war debut took place, however, at the Español, where it opened the 1944–5 season.[12] This production, also based on Giménez Caballero's version, albeit with a few additional cuts,[13] was directed by Cayetano Luca de Tena; it also featured lavish stage sets by Sigfrido Burmann and included a large number of extras for crowd scenes. In what follows, I will argue that it had a blatant fascist subtext.[14] This is not to suggest that it was a fascist production per se but I think it is demonstrable that it went further than any other Spanish *comedia* performance I have encountered in its flirtation with totalitarian aesthetics and politics.

Although Burmann, a German by birth, had provided stage designs for 'anti-Spanish' productions during the Second Republic (Beckers, 1992, p. 211), he had allied himself with the Nationalists in the Civil War. In 1938, he wrote enthusiastically about 'politically correct' productions of *Fuente Ovejuna* and *Peribáñez* that had taken place in the fatherland (Schwartz, 1969, p. 187). The former was the most frequently staged play by Lope in Nazi Germany and a production that opened in Hamburg was clearly envisaged as the Third Reich's official contribution to Lope's centenary celebrations (Gagen, 1993, p. 6).[15] Giménez Caballero, a personal friend of Goebbels and 'the major literary exponent of fascist thought in Spain' (Labanyi, 1989, p. 36), was invited to attend an official reception. In the presence of various Spanish and German dignitaries, he suggested the parallels between Iberian and Germanic histories and destinies. In a subsequent speech, he went on to highlight 'que Lope afirmaba el principio del caudillaje ('Führerprinzip') y que su obra *Fuenteovejuna* representaba a su vez "el primer drama del socialismo nacional"' [Lope advocated the principle of the strong leader (Führerprinzip) and his play, *The Sheep Well*, constitutes 'the first drama of national socialism'] (Seliger, 1984, p. 400).

The extant records and stills suggest that a similar approach was in operation at the recently baptized Spanish National Theatre.[16] This was clearly a flagship production. There were seven different sets (Beckers, 1992, p. 211), while a horizontal bridge and vertical castle at the back of the stage were placed at perpendicular angles so as to give the image of a cross. The set design and directorial style were characterized by geometrical symmetry and precise choreography. As in La Barraca's version, the successful execution of Laurencia and Frondoso's wedding was considered paramount. On this occasion, it was staged below the bridge as befits the villagers' social status (Luca de Tena, 1953a, p. 46), and Manuel Parada de la Puente provided specially commissioned music for scenes that employed a vast number of extras to offer a perfectly synchronized mass spectacle of *castizo* [traditional] village life.[17]

Following her abduction by the Comendador, Laurencia made her return along the bridge where she was raised above the male town council before lowering herself to their level for her speech (1953a, p. 46). As noted, in line with the prevailing aesthetic and ideological norms of the time, Giménez Caballero's version is generally very faithful to Lope's original. Nevertheless, the sexual content of the play text is minimized with, for example, Laurencia's speech being altered so that she says 'maritones' [pansies] rather than 'maricones'. A contemporary audience would have had no problems understanding the latter word – the usual justification for altering Lope's sacred text – and its removal is surely indicative of a sense of sexual propriety and also a concern about the inclusion of a linguistic term deemed inappropriate for a Spanish heroine. Even with this change in place, it is tempting to speculate over what effect Laurencia's words might have had on an audience. Francisco Ruiz Ramón has observed that it is remarkable and unprecedented for a woman who appears to have been raped to be given a voice and centre stage in a seventeenth-century play (1997, p. 77). Given that official discourses of the 1940s were predicated on strictly demarcated and hierarchical gender roles,[18] the mere presence of this vitriolic admonition in the context of a National Theatre is no less remarkable.

Predictably, the reinstatement of the play's original denouement was afforded pride of place. Ferdinand and Isabella were positioned on the bridge and thereby looked down on all the characters so as to highlight their absolute authority (Luca de Tena, 1953a, p. 46). Audiences were directed towards the political significance of these scenes in the theatre programme, which stated:

> Finalmente hemos restablecido la integridad del texto – mutilado o deformado cien veces por sectarismos políticos – tratando a ser fieles a lo que Lope de Vega quiso indudablemente componer: un himno a la unidad española en las personas de sus creadores, los Católicos Reyes Don Fernando y Doña Isabel. (Teatro Español, 1944)

> [We have, at last, re-established the text – mutilated or deformed a hundred times as a result of political sectarianism – in its entirety, in an attempt to be true to what Lope de Vega undoubtedly set out to compose: a hymn to the unity of Spain through those personages who created it, the Catholic Monarchs, Ferdinand and Isabella.]

Elsewhere, in the first issue of a journal produced by young university students, Giménez Caballero discusses this latest production in much the same terms as he had used nearly ten years earlier in Germany. In an extended subsection, entitled 'Exaltación del Rey como símbolo caudillal' [Exaltation of the King as a symbol of the strong leader], he writes:

> Lope de Vega fué [*sic.*] el propagandista poético y máximo que tuvo la Monarquía Absoluta Caudillal en España ... 'Dios', 'Rey', 'Honor', he aquí el trinomio espiritual de la 'Comedia Española', creada por Lope: como reflejo del Estado universo o imperial de España en el mundo. (1944, pp. 6–7)

> [Lope de Vega was the greatest poetic propagandist that the strong rule of the absolute monarchy had in Spain ... 'God', 'The King', 'Honour'; these constituted the holy trinity of the Spanish 'comedia' created by Lope as a reflection of Spain's universal and imperial standing in the world.]

The vociferous and didactic nature of the extensive written commentary on the play's ending and meaning was indicative of an anger still felt about earlier productions, yet the continued insistence in both critical and performative contexts also implies an unease or anxiety about the play's potential actuality, and is perhaps indicative of an unconscious fear that Lope's message was not as transparent or unequivocal as it was consistently maintained to be. This insecurity was reflected in the anger of a censor at the dress rehearsal who objected to the presence of an onstage sickle that he understood to be a communist symbol; Luca de Tena tried to assuage his anger by explaining that it was a symbol of the *pueblo* but was only successful when the Falangist David Jato came to his aid (cited in Santa-Cruz, 1993, p. 72).

Susan Bennett notes that audiences help produce the meaning of a performance and it is therefore necessary to formulate 'reception as a politically implicated act' (1997, p. 86). Nevertheless, they are never completely free. Just as the academic critic's appraisal is mediated by previous commentaries, so too is the audience by their environment and the field of relations that surround a production: 'In the circumstance of the theatre visit, the spectator takes on his/her role(s) before the performance per se begins' (p. 125). The Español was, in the 1940s, a meeting place for an elite audience who, in this case, had been bombarded with messages in a variety of media on the importance and significance of what they were about to see. While, given the theatrical expertise of those involved, there is no reason to believe that the production was not worthy of merit, these were neither necessary nor sufficient conditions for the production's successful runs (it was revived in 1947), a set of unanimously ecstatic reviews (e.g. Cueva, 1944; Marquerie, 1944b),[19] nor for it being staged in the presence and in honour of Eva Perón during her visit to Spain in 1947 (Burmann, 2009, p. 121). The tantalising, albeit unanswerable, question is whether Melveena McKendrick's view of the play's inherent performativity and actuality would retain its credence in this most proscriptive of theatrical environments:

> What has gone before is not superseded by what comes after; nothing is left behind, everything feeds into and becomes part of the final product. Anyone who has seen a performance of *Fuenteovejuna*, with its monarchistic ending, can testify to the abiding revolutionary spirit of that play. (2000a, pp. 173–4)

A perennial classic? (1950–98)

Fuente Ovejuna is one of the very rare *comedias* to have never left the Spanish stage and to have survived various changes in political and cultural moods. In the 1950s it was also performed primarily outside Madrid, often to rural audiences who were not generally accustomed to watching Golden Age drama.[20] There are, I believe, a number of explanations for the play's success in such environments. Firstly, it is a relatively easy *comedia* for audiences to follow: it is short;[21] its fame meant that it was the Lope play that actors and spectators were most likely to be familiar with; and, at least in performances of this period, there are clearly distinguishable heroes and villains. Secondly, it has a number of set pieces that lend themselves to the kind of folkloric displays that were well suited to both the prevailing ideology and large outdoor spaces. And, thirdly, its ostensible social and political message continued to resonate. It remained an antidote to previous desecration at the hands of the *rojos*, and the Catholic Monarchs continued to be officially endorsed icons with a strong grip on the popular imagination.[22]

José Tamayo's reputation had largely been forged with *Peribáñez*, and *Fuente Ovejuna* was an obvious choice for him to stage. In 1956, he directed a major production in the town itself, featuring one hundred and fifty extras. It also starred two of the most famous actors of the day, Manuel Dicenta and Aurora Bautista.[23] Not surprisingly, these ingredients guaranteed extensive press coverage with all the major critics attending the performance in Fuente Ovejuna alongside the Director General of Cinema and Theatre. One reviewer, who began by praising the 'villa blanca, limpia y empinada' [pure, clean and elevated village] and its pretty young girls, noted how Nicolás González Ruiz had simplified and modernized the text before moving on to the following analysis of the performance and its rapt audience:

> Como espectáculo, lo más logrado es la escena de la boda, con bailes y cantares interpretados por chicas y chicos cordobeses: ellas, creo, de la Sección Femenina. Hay también una aparición del comendador a caballo

verdaderamente teatral. El público entra en seguida en la pieza; cada vez que el comendador aparece se oye decir: '¡Ese es el malo!', y como es malo se aplaude su defenestración. (Torrente, 1956)

[As a live performance, the highlight is the wedding scene complete with dances and songs performed by Cordovan boys and girls: the latter, I believe, from the Sección Femenina. There is also the genuinely theatrical appearance of the commander on horseback. The audience is engaged from the outset; every time the commander appears, you hear them say: 'There's the villain' and, as he is the villain, his defenestration is met with applause.]

As with the classics, the recuperation of popular music and dances was a trend with origins in the Second Republic that was subsequently co-opted under Francoism with a largely predetermined political agenda:

Fue prioritario por su eficacia en la finalidad propagandística del arte, ya que a través de él la Sección Femenina pudo transmitir el nacional-catolicismo justamente a las mujeres, los agentes más eficaces en la labor ideologizadora, con una penetración social casi absoluta. (Pérez Zalduondo, 2001, p. 94)

[It was prioritized due to its efficiency in relation to art's propagandistic ends. Through the Sección Femenina, it was able to transmit National-Catholicism specifically to women, the most efficient promulgators of ideology. As a result, its infiltration of the social sphere was nearly ubiquitous.]

Furthermore, this appropriation of different regional dances also constituted what Jo Labanyi has characterized as 'a particularly interesting attempt at defusing the separatist implications of regional culture by incorporating it into a popular vision celebrating "national essences"' (1989, p. 41). Hence, while Tamayo's spectacle was not overtly political in the manner of earlier productions, it was nevertheless complicit in an ideological agenda that was far from neutral.[24] This was also the case with the production directed in the town itself by José Osuna, which was the subject of a special report by the official Spanish newsreel service, NO-DO projected in cinemas before the commencement of the main feature.[25]

It is proof that the times were however changing, that when Tamayo resurrected the work in 1962, as part of the centenary celebrations of Lope's birth, it received a lukewarm reception. The traditional and conservative Marqueríe gave it a positive review as he spoke of the various ovations that Tamayo received at the première in the Español; even he, however, noted that a number of young people in the audience tried to heckle the director (1962). The majority of reviewers were less positive and criticized the actors' complete inability to recite verse and the production's general approach, which was seen to be the relic of a bygone age.[26]

There were, however, a number of productions of the play in the 1960s that began to engage with an alternative performance and political tradition. At the beginning of the decade, La Pipironda, a theatre group led by Ángel Carmona, and including playwright José María Rodríguez Méndez, performed a very liberal version of the play alongside Cervantes's *entremeses*. This modest project, aimed at working-class audiences in the poorer areas of Barcelona (predominantly Castilian-speaking immigrants from other parts of Spain), was a small-scale precursor to the TEI. Their performances, generally including songs, dances, discussions and workshops on popular theatre, were normally free and tended to take place in community centres, bars or in the open air (Thompson, 2007, pp. 45–6).

In 1963, the first meeting on the state of university theatre was held in Murcia. It was decided that there ought to be a return to the ideals of the Second Republic, more specifically La Barraca, and that they needed to try and rectify the middle-class domination of their current audiences (Oliva, 1999, pp. 20–1). In 1964, Alberto Castilla took Cervantes's *El retablo de las maravillas* to the Nancy Festival in France (Pérez Rasilla, 1999, p. 50), and then, as noted in chapter one, he returned there in 1965 with a heavily politicized version of *Fuente Ovejuna*.

According to the director, they were aware of Russian productions, but it was Lorca's version that they chose to follow, ending as it does with the villagers resisting torture (1992, p. 51). Castilla also sought to eulogize a simple and just form of Spanish traditionalism that was seen to have its roots in the *pueblo*. Although this is not too far removed from the logic underpinning Tamayo or Luca de Tena's versions, its exposition was radically different. Music was employed in the wedding scene, for example, but in an anachronistic fashion so as to distance the audience and make them think about the relationship between past and present (p. 53). In terms of performance style, Castilla claims he was trying to move away from the histrionics that were a staple of most Spanish productions. He notes, for example, how Laurencia's monologue was habitually used as a showcase for the lead actress to shine, but that he made sure it was understated (p. 54).

With Franco's death, the analytical frame whereby the presence or absence of the Catholic Monarchs indicated the political affiliation of the production had suddenly disappeared. Unlike *Peribáñez* and *El villano en su rincón*, Lope's other famous peasant honour dramas, *Fuente Ovejuna* was able to outlive the dictator on the Spanish theatrical stage. Its canonical status was also assured by a high-profile television adaptation directed by Mario Camus and a musical version for the Teatro de la Zarzuela in 1981.[27] Beyond its intrinsic merits, this process of (un)natural selection is predicated on a number of factors. The play's contested legacy and actuality fascinate practitioners and have often made it one of the most 'politically correct' *comedias*, if not the most. Its cause has also been aided by the possibility it

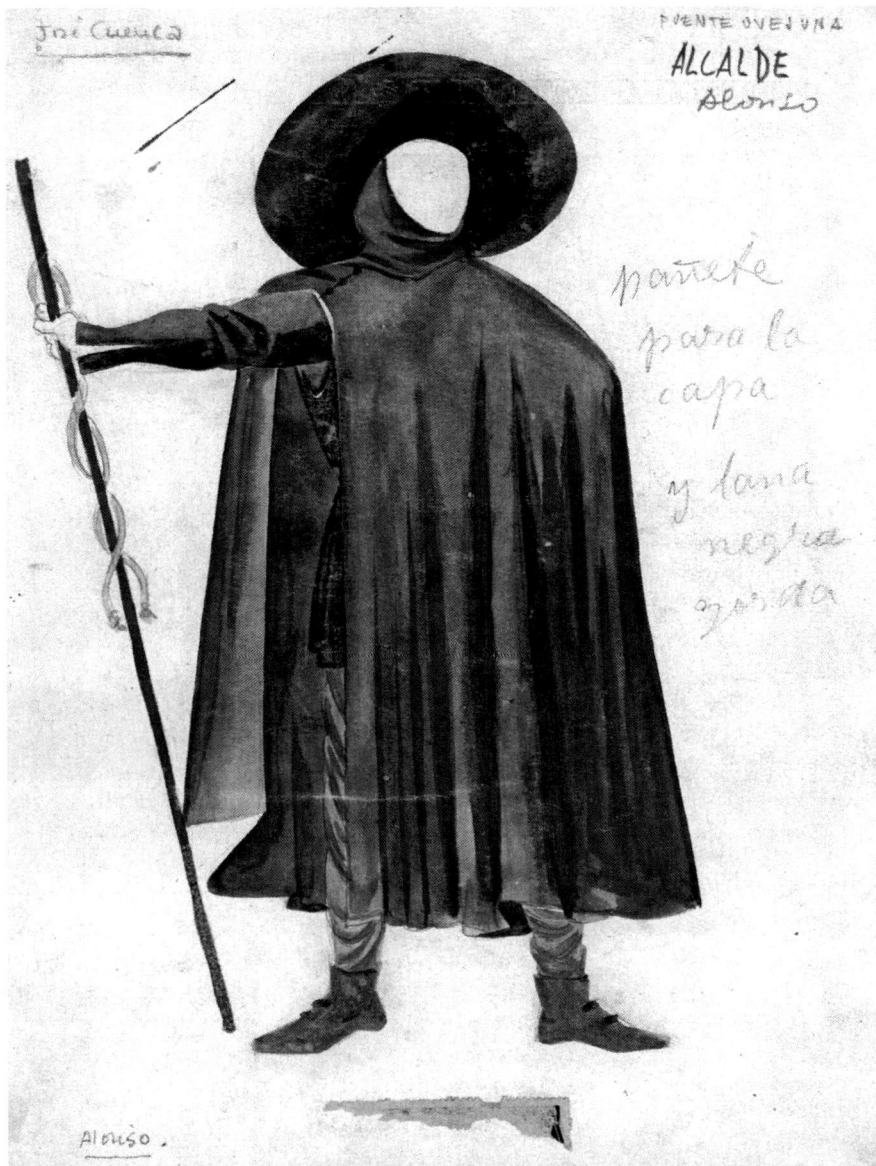

Figure 4   Sketch for *Fuente Ovejuna* (1965) by José Caballero

offers to deconstruct one of the chief Francoist icons through the Catholic Monarchs,[28] and its amenability to being interpreted as a universal call for basic human rights.

Fuente Ovejuna made its post-Franco debut during 1978 in a version directed by Vicente Sainz de la Peña and starring María Paz Ballesteros. Laurencia, who now uttered the once taboo 'maricones', was raped on stage and there was full frontal nudity. In this respect, it marked an arguably unfortunate precedent: the heroine's sexual violation is taken as a given and exploited in an opportunistic manner to disrobe a young actress.[29] This tendency is rarely criticized in a post-dictatorship culture that has increasingly negated the possibility that sexual permissiveness can in itself be a sexist practice. The denouement was retained but changes were made. While most of the villagers claim that they want to be placed under the jurisdiction of the Catholic Monarchs, Frondoso and Mengo object and exit the stage through the auditorium in an abrupt and violent manner. According to contemporary reviews, the production was lacking in almost every respect: verse was badly recited, it lacked any overall direction and was theatrically inept.[30]

Another trend that would develop over the coming years was the tendency to pinpoint the Comendador's sexual depravity through, for example, draping him in black leather costumes. This was the case, for example, in José Osuna's 1984 production that visualized his threat to Jacinta that 'del bagaje /del exército has de ser' [you will form part of the army's booty] (2001, vv. 1269–70). We see the soldiers rip her clothes off onstage and she is then tied with her arms outstretched on a giant wheel in a crucifixion pose. The actress convulses naked while the character is violated and humiliated as she is wheeled offstage with phallic spears attacking her.

This is, however, relatively tame in comparison to a version of the play based on the German filmmaker Rainer Werner Fassbinder's adaptation, directed for the stage by Rafael Bermúdez in 1992.[31] The Catholic Monarchs are complicit with the Comendador and force the villagers into choosing between submission and subversion; Laurencia at least temporarily chooses the latter and enjoys sadomasochistic sexual relations with her overlord. The play ends with the villagers killing their oppressors and eating them as part of a stew. Although the production was performed to sell-out audiences in Geneva, it was not selected for the Festival de Otoño in 1992, the year when Madrid was named City of Culture (Monleón, 1992).

In that year Spanish audiences were, however, able to see the CNTC's production which, according to set designer Carlos Cytrynowski, was designed as an antidote to 'ese universo "típico" lleno de "color local"' [that 'typical' universe full of 'local colour'] (cited in CNTC, 2006b, p. 132). This aim was certainly realized in a set design that resembled the dystopian universe of a science-fiction film replete with wire fences, metallic ramps, cubic structures and leather-clad protagonists. Characters enter and exit the stage on a metal passageway that passes through the auditorium. This invasion of the audience's public space alongside ubiquitous low lighting and the sound of deafening whistles yields what Susan Fischer has termed 'a dramatic interrogation of multiple carnivals of terror' (2009, p. 93).

In spite of manifest differences, two common characteristics can be attributed to many productions of the early democratic period. Firstly, there was a move away from the idealization of rural life. This was often manifested through a focus on the brutality committed against and by the villagers that placed a greater emphasis on the ritualistic and sexual aspects of violence. Secondly, the scenes with Ferdinand and Isabella were generally retained but their mythic status was deconstructed and they were often ridiculed and/or had their motives interrogated. Interestingly, these were among the very same themes and approaches that were being rehearsed in academic studies around the same time.[32]

Fuente Ovejuna at the CAT

Emilio Hernández directs an all-female cast in this turn of the century co-production between the Jerusalem-based Teatro Al-Kasaba and CAT. The heavily edited version of the text, by Ana Rossetti, is complimented by a riotous soundtrack provided by Bishara Khilly and Paco Aguilera and choreography by the dancer Ana María Bueno, '[para] mostrar la fiesta de una victoria de las libertades sobre el poder tiránico' [in order to show the celebration of the victory of freedom over tyrannical power] (cited in Tamayo, 1998).

The project arose from the director's interest in Spain's Arabic roots and his experiences in Palestine where he spent time teaching actors and touring refugee camps.[33] Hernández knew that he wanted to direct a collaborative project with CAT – of which he was artistic director at the time – and the Palestinian theatre company with a focus on the oppression suffered in that land. He was also keen to work with actresses from Palestine as he claims that they were more accomplished than their male counterparts.

Given its politically charged narrative and strong female characters, *Fuente Ovejuna* was, perhaps, an obvious choice. The director was also persuaded by his discovery of a nineteenth-century Arabic translation of the play. In her heavily updated version of the text often rendered in prose, Rossetti includes dialogue in Arabic; the content of these phrases is, however, always clarified and contextualized by having another character paraphrase or repeat them in Spanish.

The production shows little or no interest in even speculating over authorial intention or in engaging with Golden Age poetics, focussing instead on those elements of the plot that are considered relevant, and the dramatic tension inherent in some of its scenarios. The scenes with

Ferdinand and Isabella are, for example, removed. No apology is made for the fact that the playwright is at the service of the performance rather than vice versa. In line with Hernández's preference, there are only actresses on stage (seven Spaniards and five Palestinians) and the production engages in what Philip Auslander has defined as 'postmodern theatrical practice' through its use of gender crossing and intercultural casting (2004, p. 102). The director notes in the programme:

> En las guerras de finales del Siglo XX, el sexo de la mujer enemigo se ha convertido en un nuevo campo de batalla, una forma de dar el golpe de gracia al adversario sin riesgo de balas, bombas o minas. Un último exponente de la sublimación de la virilidad de lo militar, de su prepotencia y su impunidad al amparo de las armas. (cited in CAT, 2004)

> [In the wars of the late twentieth century, a woman's sex has become a new battleground, a means of delivering a *coup de grâce* against the enemy without running the risk of bullets, bombs or mines. The latest expression of the virile sublimation of military activity, of its arrogance and of its impunity under the protection of arms.]

This iconoclastic statement is symptomatic of the production's marketing that seemed desperate to focus on its modern and transgressive elements; the image used on promotional material, for example, resembles the poster for the cult urban French film *La Haine* (Mathieu Kassovitz, 1995). 'A woman's sex' is hardly 'a new battleground' and is registered in many *comedias* (e.g. Calderón's *Amar después de la muerte*) where, as Hernández has himself elsewhere noted, women are often 'mostradas como víctimas del abuso machista y despótico' [shown as victims of macho and despotic abuse] (2002, p. 19).[34]

Fortunately, in performance, *Fuente Ovejuna* is far more complex and sensitive as it interrogates the audience's relationship with women who suffer, but also perpetrate, violence in a visceral and intelligent manner. Although the set is not realistic, and there are no concrete geographical markers, it is clearly meant to resemble a camp in Palestine. There is dark ominous lighting, the Comendador wears a similar black leather costume and whistles are also blown. In general, the *mise en scène* resembles a more minimalist version of Marsillach's production, and it also undergoes the process Keir Elam has characterized as the attempt 'to transform architectural fixity as far as possible into dynamic proxemic informality' (1980, p. 63). Hernández's production has, however, far more impact, largely as a result of the kinetic onstage dynamism and activity which, as will be discussed, relate to events happening in the real world and bestow the production with a sense of genuine political commitment.

The actresses enter one by one, each holding a bag, and introduce themselves to the audience with their real names and say where they are from. A wire fence physically separates them from their public, yet complicity between stage and auditorium is central to the production's success. The women proceed to sing about Fuente Ovejuna and it is immediately evident that their vocal dexterity far exceeds what one is accustomed to hearing in Spanish theatre. A character then reads from a paper of the Comendador's taking of the village by force in 1478 (an obvious interpolation by Rossetti) and that he committed so many outrages the village decided to rebel. As she recounts the story, the others beat drums to an increasingly furious rhythm. This cacophony of regimented arms and deafening noise reaches a climax as the narrator furiously screws up the paper and the principal action is synaesthetically propelled into motion.

The rhythm and tone of the drums and music help determine the mood throughout. While they are played in a soothing and non-threatening manner as Mengo expounds his theories on love, they then become louder, faster and more ominous as the Comendador interrupts this harmonious scene to make his first appearance. This is complemented in visual terms as the villagers throw themselves to the floor where they remain rigidly still as they are regaled with stories of military triumphs and receive scraps of food that are condescendingly flung down to their presumably starving mouths.

A similar, albeit intensified, aesthetic dynamic is in operation during the wedding scenes which are lit, as is most of the production, in simple blue light and benefit from the actresses' tight control over their bodies that is equally suited to frenetic kinetic activity as it is to comatose rigidity. Laurencia appears in a white wedding dress and stands centre stage as confetti is dropped on her from above while the drums pound a festive beat and the villagers sing. This idyll is shattered as the Comendador reappears. Frondoso tries to escape but is caught and assaulted; he is then left hanging on the metal fence.

The bride's reappearance is handled in a sensitive and effective manner. Earlier in the production, Jacinta had hardly been able to articulate her words when she returned to the village, and now Laurencia begins her monologue calmly but gradually becomes more animated. As she speaks, Frondoso remains in view to the audience as he is left hanging on the fence as a martyred visual icon. The villagers all have long wooden sticks, and as her harangue reaches its crescendo, they begin to beat them in a synchronized manner. This becomes a battle cry as their voices become louder and louder and they move with the demeanour of a highly disciplined military unit towards the Comendador who is now on stage.

Their former oppressor is now trapped between them and the fence. Facing the audience, he begs for mercy and begins to climb but is impaled from behind by the sticks which all strike simultaneously, thereby emphasizing the collective aspect of the execution. Although the audience morally

Figure 5 Photograph of *Fuente Ovejuna* (dir. Emilio Hernández, 1999), CAT

applauds their actions, this is the only production I have seen that makes the inhabitants of the town sufficiently ferocious that they also inspire genuine fear.

As noted, Ferdinand and Isabella do not appear and the play ends with the villagers resisting torture. It is perhaps unfortunate that, while being assaulted, they are tied to the fence blindfolded and topless. Although there is a case for suggesting that this is a means of suggesting how sexuality is used as a weapon against women in warfare, I am not convinced that specularizing this means of oppression is the most ethical or effective form of condemnation.[35]

Their response on being pardoned is far more interesting: after chanting 'vivan muchos años' [may they live many years] in animalesque fashion, they begin to break down the fence that provided a physical barrier between them and their public. The drums roll and initiate an extended dance sequence that incorporates the curtain call. The dissolution of the fourth wall and modes of direct address – alongside the conflation of biographical and fictional identities – allow us to profitably apply some conclusions drawn by Bridget Escolme as regards common representational strategies underpinning some recent Shakespeare productions that contain characters who talk to the audience:

All produce meaning around a struggle between socially conferred identity and the effect of subjectivity. All depend for their impact upon figures who appear to exist both in the theatre and in the dramatic fiction. They 'talk to the audience' in the theatre from the perspective of a fiction in which their human subjectivities are unstable and worked for, just as their relationship with the audience are. (2005, p. 150)

These figures are both the product and cause of a theatrical approach she defines as 'performing human', an alternative theatrical strategy to the conventions of stage naturalism capable, in her view, 'of rendering the post-modern spectator vulnerable to the questions of subjectivity and agency embedded in these plays' (p. 152). In the case of *Fuente Ovejuna*, Hernández's production raises fundamental and unsettling questions about the psychological and aesthetic effects of closure.

Most audience members will, presumably, sympathize with the plight of their onstage counterparts, but the anger, unpredictability and agency that it unleashes is also liable to occasion genuine unease. There is a visceral thrill to this production's denouement that, I would suggest, is the result of both fear and admiration. One is impressed about the villagers' achievements but, equally, we are scared about them breaking down the fence and emerging from their enclosed compound into 'our' world. Racda Ghazaleh, the deputy director of Al-Kasaba, has argued that this aspect of the play and the production had particular relevance for women living in Palestine:

> Las doce actrices se convierten aquí en un único narrador, suman toda su energía y eso es lo más interesante de la obra ... Cuando hay problemas, la sociedad necesita que la mujer sea fuerte, luche y tome decisiones, pero cuando todo ha pasado quieren que vuelva a casa. Contra eso estamos luchando en la calle y en el teatro. (cited in Molina, 1999)[36]
>
> [The twelve actresses here form a single narrator; they combine all their energy and this is what is most interesting about the production ... When there are problems, society requires women to be strong, to fight and to take decisions, but when everything has calmed down, men want them to go back home. It is this that we are fighting against in the street and in the theatre.]

This staging revealed (at least to this spectator) the complex and often contradictory emotions provoked by justifiable and righteous outbreaks of violence by subaltern groups who are oppressed on the grounds of their race, gender and/or class. In the manner of an amputee who only becomes conscious of a limb once it has been removed, the absence of the traditional ending made me appreciate some of the psychological and theatrical reasons underpinning the restoration of order in Lope's play text. By presenting an onstage reality that, following conflicts in the Balkans and the Middle East, resembles a world that is familiar, albeit through the media, we are able to feel the fear occasioned by the breakdown of traditional hierarchies and the desire for some semblance of order. These heady emotions suddenly make Lope's ambivalence over ostensibly irreconcilable drives towards revolution and order appear both logical and human(e).

The production inspired an equally fervent emotional response in other spectators as the preconditions for communicating the political aspect of Lope's play text were once again in place. On the night I attended, the audience was visibly more engaged in the onstage action than I have seen at any other *comedia* performance in Spain. As a result of the deliberate conflation of the actresses and their roles, it was not clear whether their extended standing ovation was directed towards the former's performances or the latter's actions. The critical response was also enthusiastic. Gonzalo Pérez de Olaguer wrote of a performance in Barcelona, for example, that it was 'uno de los mejores espectáculos presentados aquí en los últimos años' [one of the best productions to be staged here in recent years] (1999b).[37] After touring Spain, Hernández took the production to New York but, perhaps unsurprisingly, he was unsuccessful in his attempts to perform it in Palestine.[38]

The repoliticization of *Fuente Ovejuna* (1999–2008)

With eight documented productions between 1999 and 2008, *Fuente Ovejuna* was more frequently staged that at any time in its history. This is not altogether surprising. Firstly, its fame and legacy makes it a popular choice for amateur and student groups who have been increasingly active. Secondly, Spanish politics have become increasingly polarized at the beginning of the twenty-first century as there has been a renegotiation of the *pacto de olvido* that had tacitly underpinned mainstream Spanish politics since the transition. This came to the fore with the passing of the Law of Historical Memory, first proposed by the PSOE in 2004, published in 2006 and approved by congress in 2007; as Georgina Blakeley notes, this new legislation 'is a product of this new and tense political environment in which the PSOE has had to rely on its left-wing and nationalist allies in the face of hostile opposition from the PP' (2008, pp. 323–4).

This climate has been readily discernible in many productions which have been politicized to an extent not seen since the 1960s. What has changed, however, is that the liberal factions of Spanish society now appear to have the monopoly on the play and its meaning.[39] This is largely a result of the political allegiances of most Spanish cultural practitioners but it is also because the left have more to gain from re-engaging with the play's performance tradition. Their opponents may not want to condemn Francoism outright, but neither do they generally want to directly associate themselves with it. A number of productions have, for example, self-consciously sought to make the play's performance history part of the theatrical experience.

Hence in 1999, for example, Achiperre Coop. Teatro staged their version of the play titled *Fuente Ovejuna 1476–1999*. This production, based on an adaptation by Michel Van Loo and directed by Carlos Herans, is something of an anomaly: an updated version of a *comedia* by a Belgian dramaturge influenced by Brecht and Marx and aimed at teenagers. Set in an occupied factory in the midst of strike action, Lope's drama provides the means by which four fictional workers articulate their thoughts. The polyvalence of *Fuente Ovejuna* is suggested by the way in which each of the workers interprets it differently and in accordance with their own preoccupations and experiences. Clara, who has been studying the play at the Universidad Popular [Workers' University], uses it to explain the Marxist doctrine that she believes holds the key to her co-workers' emancipation. In contrast, Isabel and Pedro, who only have vague recollections from school, gradually recall the plot as they identify with different narrative strands: the central love story and the popular uprising respectively. The action switches between their commentary and the acting out of individual scenes. This short production (barely over an hour) ends with a discussion about Lope's inclusion of Ferdinand and Isabella.

A similar approach would be advanced ten years later by Samarkanda Teatro in *Chrónica de Fuente Ovejuna* under the direction of the well-respected veteran, José Carlos Plaza.[40] This relatively modest production is the antithesis of Francoist productions for it seeks to disperse rather than condense historical time. *Fuente Ovejuna* is theatrically unstitched and the audience's knowledge (or lack thereof) of the play text and its stage history are woven into the very fabric of the theatrical action. Hence, for example, the performance opens with a number of actors struggling to perform the scene where the Catholic Monarchs ostensibly restore order. The apparent lack of professionalism on display does not bode well but, fortunately, it soon becomes evident that this is a staged rehearsal. The performance comes full circle at the end as the house lights are raised after the torture scenes, which are shown on rather than off stage. The onstage director says that this is where Lorca's version ends and they debate whether their version should follow this example or remain faithful to Lope's play text.

A more traditional staging of the play was undertaken by the TNC in 2005, which nevertheless engaged with aspects of the play that have often been sidelined; as J. B. Hall reminds us, 60 per cent of the verses are written in *redondillas* and this underlies the importance of love in the play (1985, pp. 75–6).[41] One of the most detrimental effects of a lack of a continuous performance tradition in Spain is that both actors and audiences have lost their sensitivity to verse as a semiotic device. As early as 1940, Karl Vossler lamented this breakdown in communication: 'Era un compositor de fina sensibilidad. No es culpa suya que el lector actual carezca de oído para sus ritmos y sus rimas' [He was a composer with a refined sensibility. It is not his fault that the modern-day reader does not have an ear for his rhythms and rhymes] (1940, p. 327). Consequently, the theme of love has largely been ignored in productions that want to focus more heavily on the political and ideological aspects of the play. In this case, however, love is ubiquitous and not construed to be the exclusive preserve of romantic couples; harmonious relationships of all kinds are afforded a privileged role. In the wedding scenes, for example, all of the villagers happily sing and dance; Laurencia and Frondoso canoodle at the side before being dragged into a communal dance.

In sharp contrast, the revolt is violently staged and the Comendador's decapitated head is kicked around the stage as if it were a football. Laurencia, seated on a chair, tends it in an almost cannibalistic manner before throwing it on the floor as she kisses Frondoso in a savage romantic exchange in which the lips of both are coated with blood. Mengo then jumps off a chair to land on the Comendador's head, which is subsequently placed on a spike. At the end of this dark celebratory scene, all of the villagers leave the stage and Laurencia and her father are left alone. She is crying and he hugs her with the words 'mi hija' [my daughter]. By showing the villagers as loving and loved human beings, without shying away from the carnivalesque savagery of their actions, the production inspires that mixture of pity, fear and compassion that is axiomatic to the play's dramatic potential.

Ferdinand and Isabella are presented as a young and loving couple dressed in elegant ball gowns; they are seen to be cynical but neither cruel nor perverse. This is rather unnecessarily vocalized at the end when he says: 'A estos cansados villanos bien podemos perdonar, pues vinieron a dejar Calatrava en nuestras manos' [We can easily forgive these exhausted villagers, as they have come to leave Calatrava in our hands]. Then, in line with the prominence given to female characters throughout, the queen delivers the lines uttered by her husband in Lope's play text (2001, vv. 2442–9). This is the least successful part of the production and is symptomatic of the way in which Spanish theatre has an apparent inability to satisfactorily incorporate the secondary action into the body of the play.

This production formed part of an exchange – entitled 'Lope por Lope' [Lope for Lope] – with the CNTC who, in turn, offered a version of *El castigo sin venganza*. This initiative, which will be discussed in more detail in chapter five, was clearly construed as an olive branch and 'muestra de "normalidad" cultural' [demonstration of cultural 'normality'] following the 2004 general elections (Punzano, 2005). In addition to paving the way for a tentative rapprochement between Madrid and Barcelona, the Socialist victory also facilitated an exponential growth in the number of student and amateur productions.[42]

In one respect or another, all of these troupes or collectives are direct or indirect heirs of La Barraca and this legacy has undoubtedly contributed to the frequency with which *Fuente Ovejuna* has been staged. Furthermore, the PSOE have also always been keen to promote a culture of parenthesis through which they present themselves as the rightful heirs to the Second Republic. Given this backdrop, it is hardly surprising that in 2006 the Sociedad Estatal de Conmemoraciones Culturales [State Society for Cultural Commemorations] sponsored groups from four universities (Valencia, Murcia, Santiago and Carlos III in Madrid) to recreate La Barraca's repertoire and destinations in the twenty-first century.[43]

A similar ideological agenda underpinned the 2006 Almagro Festival, marketed as a celebration of the seventy-fifth anniversary of the proclamation of the Second Republic, much to the chagrin of some vocal opponents. The Bishop of Ciudad Real's objections to Carmen Linares offering a recital of songs made famous by the Second Republic are not completely without substance: 'no sería de recibo ofrecer este espectáculo en un lugar donde están enterrados 43 monjes dominicos que fueron asesinados por fuerzas republicanas' [it is not right to offer this performance in a place where forty-three Dominican monks are buried having been executed by Republican forces] (cited in Torres, 2006a).[44] They are certainly more convincing than the disingenuous justification offered by Hernández who claimed that productions of this kind are:

> aptas para todos los públicos y todas las ideologías [porque] [l]a relación entre teatro y República fue muy estrecha, hubo un tremendo resurgir de este arte. Hemos querido abordar una sección que nos habla de la vinculación entre el trabajo de los actores y su puesta en escena y la guerra. (cited in Torres, 2006b)

> [suitable for all audiences and all ideologies [because] the close relationship between theatre and the Republic meant that there was a huge resurgence in the art form. We have wanted to incorporate a section that speaks to us of the relationship between the actors' work and stage performances, and the war.]

It is culture's supposed claims to neutrality that can sometimes make it a valuable political weapon as is proven by the modern-day performance history of *Fuente Ovejuna* in Spain. The choice to have RNE broadcast a version of the play based on an adaptation by José A. Ramírez, originally performed on the Republican front in 1936, was clearly an attempt to surreptitiously reignite a political charge that had, seventy years earlier, been electric. If the Festival was generally interested in the relationship between theatre and the war as a purely cultural phenomenon, why not also broadcast the production that Pemán had admired so much?

Following what appeared to be a ceasefire, *Fuente Ovejuna* has once again become a symbolic and strategic prize to be fought over. The battle is clearly more civilized than it had been in the 1930s and 1940s, and the weapons and objectives have changed. Culture is no longer evoked as a form of praxis but as a manifestation of civilization. This has resulted in some dramatically effective and balanced productions, yet the equation can easily become as deceitful and politically charged as earlier attempts to patent Lope. Nevertheless, the play's iconic status and associations with key moments in national history afford it a privilege hardly ever bestowed on Golden Age plays: an almost guaranteed presence on the Spanish stage.

Conclusion

Fuente Ovejuna is arguably the only *comedia* to have a genuine performance tradition in the modern era. *El alcalde de Zalamea* and *La vida es sueño* may be staged on a regular basis but, with the occasional exception, productions tend not to enter into an active dialogue with their predecessors. In contrast, virtually every performance of Lope's play is engaged in a process Marvin Carlson refers to as 'ghosting', whereby 'the external associations that the continually recycled material of theatre brings in from the external world as well as from previous performances' perform a constitutive role (2004, p. 58).

Even before it was revived for the Spanish stage, *Fuente Ovejuna* was a haunted play. That this 'ghosting' has exerted an incredible force field is undeniable; how and to what extent this has enabled or stifled creativity and/or engagement with Lope and the nation's cultural past is more open to debate. It is paradoxical that the play text's actuality has ensured its continual presence on the Spanish stage, yet in performance this actuality has so often been resisted in an attempt to deliver a single univocal meaning. It is easy, therefore, to see Lope as a sacrificial lamb delivered as an offering to the grand political ideals of the last hundred years. Does the play, therefore, need to be rescued from the ghosts of its performance history?

This certainly appeared to be the view of a recent Spanish production directed by Laurence Boswell, associate director of the RSC, which followed the play text very closely and boasted of its post-ideological credentials in the programme: '*Fuenteovejuna* no pertenece a nadie, y es y siempre será de todos y cada uno de nosotros y de vosotros' [*The Sheep Well* does not belong to anyone in particular; it is, and will always be, the property of all of us and all of you] (Compañía Rakatá, 2009). On attending this version in Madrid just prior to completing this chapter, I realized that I had never seen a version of the play text which was not heavily cut performed in a way that did not appear anachronistic. In this case, despite being imaginatively staged and reasonably well acted, the onstage action was unengaging and the audience was visibly bored for the duration.

What is it that has prevented philologically faithful versions from triumphing on the modern Spanish stage? I would like to suggest that it is because *Fuente Ovejuna* presents two specific challenges that have not been adequately addressed. Firstly, in order for the two actions to have the unity many textual critics see as central to the play's artistry, practitioners and audiences alike would require a conceptual and intuitive knowledge of verse forms and seventeenth-century philosophical and political ideals that have been rendered obsolete by the absence of a wider performance tradition. Secondly, the vicissitudes of Spanish history have converted the Catholic Monarchs into such volatile icons that a hermeneutical chasm separates seventeenth- and twenty-first-century spectators. As a result, it seems difficult to see how a literal interpretation of the denouement could make dramatic or ethical sense to a contemporary Spanish audience. This is not to imply that a talented director will not discover a way of successfully performing the play in its entirety, but I suspect they will only be able to do so if and when they discover ingenious solutions to the challenges outlined above.

The most successful performances of the play, from La Barraca to CAT, have been those where the production has a strong personal vision and message to communicate. If we return to Bate's postulate that *Fuente Ovejuna* is open to multiple interpretations that can nevertheless not be perceived simultaneously, does this therefore imply that it is the role of the theatre practitioner to decide on a reading that they will then perform to an audience? This would accord with Howard Mancing's belief that 'the experience of reading a book is comparable not to the watching of a play but to participation in its performance' (2006, p. 196). The problem with this division of labour is that it makes the audience passive, when in reality the play's performance history suggests that the most affecting productions have been those that have actively encouraged the audience's response(s) to perform an unusually decisive role in the theatrical experience.

As we have seen, the play contains individual scenes that retain their effect even when removed from the wider dramatic edifice. *Fuente Ovejuna* may have been staged so frequently because of its amenability to different ideological agendas, but it would have had little or no propagandistic worth if it were not for its theatrical virtues which clearly have the capacity to stir audiences in a unique way. Paradoxically, as we speculated in the case of Luca de Tena's production and saw in the case of Hernández's, those characteristics that make the play a potentially valuable political tool also ensure that it communicates multiple and even contradictory messages. In other words, the play's performability, performativity and actuality are inextricably linked. It is surely in these relationships that, as Bate suggests, Lope's genius is to be found.

Chapter Three

Resurrecting lost traditions? Calderón's wife-murder plays and the CNTC

On 27 January 1986, the *BOE* announced the creation of a national company dedicated exclusively to the staging of the classics:

> que tiene como finalidad, por una parte cubrir el vacío que se venía produciendo en la difusión de obras del teatro clásico español y de otra, crea un ambiente de recuperación de los dramaturgos clásicos universales, desde los griegos hasta los del siglo XIX, cuyas obras tienen hoy en día algunas dificultades para su puesta en escena debido a la ausencia de una tradición ininterrumpida de creación e interpretación de los textos procedentes de este patrimonio teatral.

> [whose remit is, on the one hand, to cover the gap that has emerged in relation to the diffusion of Spanish classical theatre and, on the other, to create an environment for the recuperation of the universal classical dramatists – from the Greeks right up to the nineteenth century – whose plays currently have difficulty being staged due to the lack of an uninterrupted tradition of creation and performance of texts from this theatrical heritage.]

Under the direction of Adolfo Marsillach, the Compañía Nacional de Teatro Clásico debuted in April 1986 in Buenos Aires with a production of Calderón's *El médico de su honra*. The remit may have extended beyond the *comedia* but, with the exception of *La Celestina* (1988), it would focus exclusively on Spanish Golden Age drama until a production of Molière's *Le misanthrope* in 1996. In its first ten years, it staged a total of twenty-three works including six by Calderón, six by Lope and three by Tirso.

In this chapter, I will discuss to what extent there was a 'gap' that needed covering and, presuming there was, to what extent the CNTC has provided the remedy and been able to establish a 'tradition of creation and performance'. Tradition can also take on a radically different meaning in relation to Calderón's wife-murder plays. This subgenre has been instrumental in the forging of a black legend around Golden Age drama; the widespread assumption in Spain has been that they both document and endorse an inquisitorial society predicated on unwavering codes of honour.

Susan Fischer has already supplied a detailed study of Marsillach's production of *El médico de su honra* (2009, pp. 3–20). It is not therefore my intention to replicate this task here; instead I focus more specifically on its relationship to the two notions of tradition outlined above. It is the only CNTC production to have been staged twice; the revival with a different cast in 1994 thereby facilitates an assessment of their progress. In the second half of the chapter, I turn my attention to the company's subsequent foray into the world of wife-murder plays: Eduardo Vasco's 2008 staging of *El pintor de su deshonra*. This production opened in a society with different attitudes towards both the playwright and wife murder than it had twenty-two years previously; it is my aim to register some of these changes through detailed aesthetic analysis in order to offer some more general remarks about the standing of both Calderón and the company in twenty-first-century Spain.

The legacy of Calderón's wife-murder plays

Of all the Golden Age dramatists, Don Pedro is undoubtedly considered to be the most sombre and reactionary.[1] As Marsillach notes, 'se le acostumbra a mirar con recelo como si nos fuese a herir con el afilado acero de alguna honra mancillada o a machacarnos con el inquisitorial martillo de algún Auto Sacramental terrible y sermoneante' [one tends to view him with trepidation as if he is going to wound us with the vengeful blade of some tarnished honour, or to browbeat us with the inquisitorial hammer of some awful and doctrinal Corpus Christi play] (2003, pp. 192–3). His tragedies are studied in Spanish universities far more than his comedies (Arellano, 2002), and the lighter side of his dramatic output tends to be forgotten. Central to his macabre image are the infamous wife-murder trilogy – *A secreto agravio, secreta venganza*, *El médico* and *El pintor* – which share a common paradigm succinctly described by Bruce W. Wardropper:

> Circumstances lead a husband to suspect that his wife may be in some way unfaithful to him. The evidence in which he bases his suspicion is circumstantial. Eventually, however, he convinces himself that his suspicions are true. Appealing to a code of honour whose barbarous nature he himself recognizes, he stifles his love for his wife and kills her. (1981, p. 385)

To what extent the executioners love their victims is an issue to which I will later return. Beyond doubt, however, is that the return of a former suitor places each of the respective wives in a quandary between honour and love. The married women – with the arguable exception of Leonor in *A secreto agravio* – privilege the former but this is not sufficient to save their lives, or for their deaths to prompt the condemnation of a wider community who ostensibly endorse the violent actions of an over-zealous and paranoid husband.

In the case of *El médico*, Prince Enrique is reacquainted with Mencía when he falls off his horse near her rural home on his way to Seville in the company of his brother, King Pedro. He regains consciousness in her arms, but is unsettled when he hears of her marriage to Gutierre. The injured royal suitor pursues her relentlessly; she loved him in the past but resists his advances. She inadvertently incriminates herself in her attempts to conceal what is happening from her husband, who is tormented by honour that he personifies and addresses in soliloquy. Gutierre forces Ludovico to bleed Mencía to death; the latter then reports this crime to Pedro, who passes no judgement on Gutierre apart from to force him to marry Leonor, a former fiancée who he had left because he also suspected her of infidelity.

The notoriety of these dramatic uxoricides has not, however, generally been translated into performance in Spain, where they have been (in)conspicuously absent. They have never been filmed for television (Suárez Miramón, 2002), and are the only Golden Age plays to have been staged more regularly in the UK than Spain (Mountjoy and Wheeler, 2007). When *El médico* was performed at the Teatro Español in 1946, it was the first Spanish production since 1905 (Carrión, 2008, p. 430).[2] It would not be staged again until Marsillach's production in 1986, and was the only *comedia* to be performed more in France than in Spain during the Franco regime (Torres Monreal, 1974, pp. 331–46). *A secreto agravio* has only been performed once in modern-day Spain and this was at the hands of Cuban-American director René Buch, in 1983; the last attempt to stage *El pintor* prior to the CNTC's 2008 production took place in Barcelona in 1946.

This almost non-existent stage and screen history is clearly not unrelated to the largely negative reception of the plays on the page. In this respect, Menéndez y Pelayo again provides an important precedent. He was very dismissive of what he categorizes as the 'dramas de celos' [dramas of jealousy] that he compares unfavourably with *Othello*. He argues that the noble Moor is vindicated by Iago's trickery and his passionate love; Calderón's male protagonists commit premeditated murders and the plays' principal virtue is as curiosities that bear testament to this 'aberración histórica singularísima' [completely unique historical aberration] (1881, pp. 7, 15, 37). In a similar vein, Miguel de Unamuno would later note that 'los celosos matan sin besar como Otelo, sin amor, por conclusión de silogismos y en frío.' [the jealous men kill without Othello's kiss, without love, in cold blood spurred on by syllogisms] (1964, p. 85), while Azorín went as far as claiming that Calderón must have been inspired by an event in his own life (1995, p. 138). This negative comparison with Shakespeare together with the direct association between life and drama has been a widespread and very influential school of thought in Spain.³

Even when Golden Age playwrights were praised in an uncritical and general fashion, the wife-murder trilogy proved unsettling. Hence, *El médico* received generally positive reviews when it was staged at the Español in the early Franco period (*SIPE*, 1946), but the choice of text did raise some concerns. In an article originally written to coincide with the play's run, Pedro Laín Entralgo speaks of the 'inevitable repulsión estética y moral que en el hombre de hoy produce la figura del sangrador de su esposa' [inevitable moral and aesthetic repulsion that the figure who bleeds his wife to death will evoke in people today] despite admitting that he has not seen the production (1956, p. 182). He proceeds to compare the play – of which he says modern Spaniards cannot be proud 'porque somos hombres y cristianos' [because we are gentlemen and Christians] – with an Agatha Christie novel before dismissing the term 'dramas of jealousy': 'Más que un celoso apasionado, Don Gutierre es un redomado intelectual' [Don Gutierre is less of a passionately jealous man than he is a calculating intellectual] (pp. 185, 187). In the same year, the censor, Emilio Morales de Acevedo, raised similar concerns about *El pintor* and spoke of the 'imperativo categórico del honor conyugal de los tiempos pretéritos, sordo y ciego a reflexiones' [categorical imperative of conjugal honour from times past, deaf and blind to reflection].⁴

The tenets of these beliefs have, with a few notable exceptions, retained their credibility in Calderón's homeland to this day. As early as 1963, A. Irvine Watson noted how Spanish critics were refusing to follow a new trend in international criticism that suggested *El pintor* neither advocates revenge nor accepts the values of an honour-based society without question (p. 17).⁵ Patriarchal oppression has, however, largely been seen less in terms of the female victims than it has in relation to the black legend of Spain's imperial and inquisitorial past. As Manuel Durán and Roberto González Echevarría note: 'El catolicismo calderoniano, su indudable adhesión a la España del XVII, es decir a la España de la convalecencia contrareformista, no puede ser nunca soslayada en la península. En España la crítica no alcanza ni siquiera la pretensión de ser pura.' [Calderonian Catholicism with its undeniable adhesion to seventeenth-century Spain, that is to say to the resurgent Spain of the Counter-Reformation, can never be sidestepped in the peninsula. In Spain, criticism does not even aspire to be free from prejudice] (1976, p. 110).

Much critical ink has been spilled in the discussion of codes of honour and their relationship to what David D. Gilmore has termed '"libidinized" social reputation' in Spain and neighbouring Mediterranean states (1987, p. 11).[6] I suspect wife-murder plays have been subject to the opprobrium of successive generations because they are seen to provide evidence of the country's difference to much of the rest of Europe in largely negative terms. A compounding factor in modern-day Spain is that honour culture(s) are not seen purely in terms of a distant past but also in relation to the patriarchal culture of the dictatorship and its legacy. This is reflected, for example, in the following exchange in *Céfiro agreste de olímpicos embates* (see chapter one):

> Antonio – La mujer en Calderón tiene como ley suprema la fidelidad y la castidad.
> Maite – Sigue: lo estás mejorando.
> Pilar – ¿Y hacemos a Calderón? ¡Cavamos nuestra tumba!
> Antonio – Sois vosotros los que queréis cambiar el Auto por una comedia donde el honor es tan bárbaro que si yo lo aplicase, debería matar a media compañía por mirar a Maite.
> Juanjo – Según se la hubiera mirado.
> Antonio – Golosamente.
> Maite – ¿Y si yo le he dado pie?
> Antonio – Pues muerte para tí también y no sería castigado por ello. Calderón justifica en muchas de sus obras el crimen por celos, aunque sean infundados.
> Pilar – ¡Nos dan una subvención para representar a un maníaco homicida!
> Maite – Toda esa mentalidad es muy anticuada. El adulterio ya no se castiga.
> Antonio – Lástima.
> Maite – Facha. (Miralles, 1981, p. 23)

> [Antonio – The supreme law for women in Calderón is fidelity and chastity.
> Maite – Carry on. You're getting better at it.
> Pilar – So we do a Calderón? We'll be digging our own grave.
> Antonio – It's you lot who want to change the Corpus Christi play for a secular one in which honour is so barbarous that, were I to apply it, I'd kill half the company for looking at Maite.
> Juanjo – Depending on how they have looked at her.
> Antonio – With desire.
> Maite – And if I encouraged them?
> Antonio – Well you'd die too, and I wouldn't be punished for it. Calderón justifies crimes of passion in many of his plays, even when there are no grounds for jealousy.
> Pilar – They are giving us a subsidy to represent a homicidal maniac!
> Maite – This whole mentality is very out of date. Adultery is no longer punishable.
> Antonio – That's a shame.
> Maite – Fascist.]

Given this backdrop, it was a remarkably brave or foolhardy decision on Marsillach's part to mark the debut of the CNTC with *El médico*. He claims to have chosen the work because 'me parece que el concepto de honor puede dar lugar a un interesante debate' [I think that the concept of honour could give rise to an interesting debate] (cited in Cañas, 1986). The production – in opposition to what Melveena McKendrick terms the dominant Hispanic mode of reading 'the endings in the context of the plots as a whole as prescriptive exercises in male triumphalism' (2000b, p. 217) – implies that Calderón was critiquing a cruel and inhumane honour code. Hence, for example, dark sinister figures, who perform a pre-show ritual and often stalk the stage, appear to represent the social pressures that psychically imprison the protagonists; in sharp visual contrast, Mencía is clothed in white throughout.

Figure 6 Photograph by Ros Ribas of *El médico de su honra* (dir. Adolfo Marsillach, 1986), CNTC

As Fischer notes, Pedro is depicted not so much as a *deus ex machina* but as a desperately flawed human being. The king repeatedly appears distracted, despotic and malicious thereby precluding the equation of his final judgement with any kind of genuine ethical or dramatic closure (2009, pp. 15–18). Calderón self-consciously wove the two facets of the historical figure's renown for justice and cruelty into the narrative, and which of these qualities is seen to predominate will obviously affect whether or not we believe the playwright to be endorsing his final judgement.[7] In this case,

Marsillach clearly suggests that the baroque playwright considers Pedro to be, above all else, cruel and that we ought not therefore to see his resolution as positive or the ending as happy. This effect is compounded by an ominous and dissonant score that accompanies Gutierre as he reluctantly accepts Leonor's hand in marriage.

Conserving, creating and escaping tradition: the CNTC and *comedia* performance

In the same way that Marsillach's onstage interpretation of *El médico* differed from the doctrinal view, he was keen to distance himself from how classical drama had previously been staged in Spain. He contended that *comedia* performance had created a negative or even bogus tradition that needed to be dispelled. Hence, for example, he talks of how it made the task of establishing stable casts far more difficult and how:

> un actor justificó su negativa a contratarse con nosotros porque 'no quería pasarse un año con una espada al cinto'. En el fondo esta frase era algo más que una tontería. Estaba indicando el prejuicio que muchos de nuestros intérpretes tenían respecto a los clásicos: decorados ilustrativos, recitaciones enfáticas, gesticulación ampulosa, público rancio y, efectivamente, espadas al cinto. (2002, pp. 449–50)

> [one actor justified his decision to not sign a contract with us by saying 'I don't want to spend a year with a sword strapped to my waist'. This phrase represented something more profound than a mere off the cuff remark. He was indicating the prejudice many of our actors hold towards our classics: illustrative sets, emphatic recitations, overwrought gestures, a putrid audience and, precisely, swords strapped to the waist.]

Although there is undoubtedly a poetic truth in this anecdote, Marsillach refused to acknowledge alternative traditions. It is, I think, worth us taking the time to redress this historical injustice by describing the precedents that pre-dated the CNTC. In chapter one, we saw how Manuel Canseco's cooperative could be construed as a non-institutional dress rehearsal for a national company. Admittedly, a fairly traditional approach to staging and performance style meant that this was unlikely to dispel negative images of the type outlined above. Nevertheless, the work of a number of other practitioners who had worked abroad and/or had international links interrogated how the *comedia* could and should be performed.

José Estruch first staged Spanish classics in the UK with child refugees from the Basque country; it was used as a means to keep the memories of their native language and culture alive.[8] He subsequently ran the National Theatre of Uruguay alongside Margarita Xirgu; their productions included

Porfiar hasta la muerte and *El caballero de Olmedo*. The former was performed in Spain as part of Lope's centenary celebrations in 1962 (see chapter one), and the latter would be staged as a reposition in 1987 at the Almagro Theatre Festival. He stopped working as a practitioner on his return to Spain, to dedicate his energy and experience into pedagogy, primarily within (R)ESAD which – alongside classes given by Miguel Narros and William Layton as part of the TEI – was one of the few places where young actors could learn about the Golden Age and, more specifically, methods for reciting verse.

Lessons in verse nevertheless constituted something of a marginal activity. Former director of RESAD Juan José Granda Marín recalls from his student days in Estruch's classes that, even within the school, 'no podíamos evitar esa sensación de apestados' [we couldn't avoid that sensation of being lepers] and that 'todo eso del teatro clásico se observaba como una afición con poco futuro' [anything relating to classical theatre was looked upon as a hobby with very little future] (2000, p. 99). Estruch would himself note that a lack of genuine discipline and general laxity in RESAD meant that there was a huge artistic and intellectual deficit in comparison with his experiences in Montevideo (cited in Eines, 1984). It is clearly no coincidence that the *comedia*'s chief advocates in the early democratic period were those who had experience working abroad, and in systems that favoured stable and continual training and preparation.

It is from this conception that the value of the classics within a wider theatrical education and the importance of verse emerges. This provides one explanation for why Spanish classical drama has proved so successful in many (ex)communist states with, for example, Jerzy Grotowski's production of Calderón's *El príncipe constante* – arguably the most famous *comedia* staging of the twentieth century – taking place in Poland.[9] During both the dictatorship and the democratic period, there has been resistance to forging links with the Eastern bloc providing one explanation for why this is a much under-researched area of Spanish theatre history. Its legacy has nevertheless been promoted and safeguarded by the theatrical efforts made by a number of individuals.

Alicia Hermida, now a household name in Spain as a result of her appearance as the grandmother in the top-rated television series *Cuéntame cómo pasó*, is a veteran of *comedia* performance. She appeared in the 1960 Dido production of *La viuda valenciana* and was a stable member of the María Guerrero theatre throughout that decade. In spite of these mainstream credentials, she is also a militant communist with strong artistic and political links with opposition groups in countries such as Nicaragua and Cuba. In the early 1980s, she established a theatre school and collective, La Barraca, in collaboration with her husband, Jaime Losada. As the name suggests, this endeavour was inspired by the artistic and pedagogical vision of Lorca's troupe, and they have deliberately positioned themselves at the margins of the official Madrid theatre scene. In 1982, they staged a version of *La vida es sueño*, and *Fuente Ovejuna* was performed in 1986 under the auspices of the Jornadas in Almería (García Lorenzo, 1997, p. 120). La Barraca has gone into schools to work with both teachers and pupils on performing the classics, and Hermida has worked extensively as a verse coach.

Another figure key to a comprehensive understanding of Golden Age drama on the contemporary stage is Ángel Gutiérrez. Having left Havana for Asturias aged two, he was subsequently sent as a child refugee to Russia.[10] In his new adopted homeland, he staged a number of Golden Age plays such as Lope's *El maestro de danzar*. On his return to Spain in 1974, he also began to give classes at RESAD and in 1980 established the Teatro de Cámara, recruiting primarily among his students past and present. Over the coming years, they would stage *El maestro de danzar* in addition to Tirso's *Marta la piadosa* and *Los balcones de Madrid*. His vision of the pedagogical, social and artistic values of theatre training is very similar to that of Estruch and Hermida:

> El Gobierno debería pensar muy en serie [*sic*] que el futuro está en los jóvenes y la mayor preocupación debería estar en su formación, porque son los que mañana van a estar haciendo teatro y van a enseñar a otros. Para eso hay que enseñar a los jóvenes, para transmitirles un fuego que puedan ellos transmitir después. Hay que enseñarles que hay Lope de Vega y Calderón y Tirso y Valle. Estos son los planteamientos que yo tengo. (cited in Arce, 1986, p. 21)

> [The government should think very seriously about the fact that the future is in young people and its main concern should be in their training, because it will be they who will work in theatre in the future and who will go on to teach future generations. For this to happen, it is necessary to teach young people, to pass on a passion to them which they can then later transmit. We have to teach them about the existence of Lope de Vega, and Calderón, and Tirso, and Valle. These are the priorities that I have.]

In this respect, the CNTC might have been seen as a vital first step in providing the kind of artistic and institutional structure that maverick advocates of *comedia* performance had long been calling for; they nevertheless tended to maintain an at best ambivalent, and at worst hostile, response to the company. This is not altogether surprising considering that Marsillach claimed he had had to create a tradition out of thin air;[11] resentment was compounded by the fact that he was not primarily famed for his work with Golden Age drama,[12] and was therefore seen as something of an imposter. Alberto González Vergel, for example, has spoken of how:

> declaró en varias ocasiones que no le interesaban ni gustaban nuestros autores clásicos, sin embargo aceptó el nombramiento de director de la

Compañía Nacional de Teatro Clásico porque 'si no acepto yo, lo hará cualquier otro', según confesó a su amigo el músico Antón García Abril. Esta anécdota define su catadura moral y profesional. (cited in Salvat and Coll, 2001, p. 282)

[he declared on various occasions that he was neither interested in nor liked our classical authors. He nevertheless accepted the appointment as director of the National Classical Theatre Company because 'if I don't say yes, they'll just get someone else to do it', as he confessed to his friend, the musician Antón García Abril. This anecdote says all that needs to be said about his moral and professional nerve.]

Bearing testament to this view, Carlos Ballesteros claims to have been in negotiations in the mid 1980s with Madrid's city council over the erection of a seventeenth-century style *corral* next to the Español, but that the CNTC's new director sabotaged the plan because he viewed the project as unwanted competition (2007, p. 28). As we saw in chapter one, there was still a radical schism between advocates and detractors of the *comedia* in the mid 1980s. Marsillach's inability or unwillingness to ingratiate himself with some of the most prominent members of these advocates, alongside a controversial choice of play, ensured that the CNTC's debut took place in a context predisposed to hostility. *El médico* was staged first in Argentina before moving to Seville and then Madrid, where it was subject to such negative criticism in the press that Marsillach claimed he offered his resignation (2002, p. 460).[13]

It is however important to distinguish between reviews that objected to the specific performance and those that felt the general approach of the company was misguided. The most influential reviewer was *El País*'s theatre critic Eduardo Haro Tecglen, an anarcho-communist who has repeatedly stated his aversion to the *comedia*, and noted, for example, how:

No son fáciles, los tipos de Siglo de Oro. Quizá por su futilidad, por su sonsonete: porque muchas de sus obras no son gran cosa. Qué molesto es tener que respetar y admirar profundamente lo intranscendente, lo pequeño, la obra de paso. En el teatro se da mucho. (1999, p. 176)

[Those guys from the Golden Age aren't easy. Perhaps it is a result of their pointlessness, their lack of gravitas: because many of their plays are nothing to write home about. What a pain it is to have to respect and admire profoundly that which lacks transcendence, the insignificant, the workmanlike play. It happens a lot in the theatre.]

There is an ethical correlative to this view, and in line with the majority of Spanish academic critics, Haro Tecglen took for granted that the *comedia* reflected and endorsed the mores of the time.[14] Given this backdrop, and his close personal friendship with Marsillach, the line he takes in relation to the CNTC's debut is counter-intuitive: he praises the choice of play but lambasts the production. The reviewer criticizes Anglo-Saxon academics for offering revisionist readings that suggest the play contains an implicit irony and criticism. The 'negación histórica de la España negra' [historical denial of Spain's dark past] is, in his view, the result of an unwillingness to accept that the beauty of the play emerges from such moral degradation; according to him, a genuine appreciation must embrace the coexistence of the two facets. He praises the CNTC's audacity in staging a quintessential *comedia* in its entirety, whose absence from the stage in recent years is symptomatic of 'un cierto pudor, como un deseo de tapar esta cara fea de Calderón' [a certain reticence as if there were the desire to conceal Calderón's ugly side]. Nevertheless, he concludes that the production is not worthy of a national company: '[o]tra cosa es el resultado y la posible digresión ante él de si ésta es *la* o es *una* compañía clásica, si tiene en sus manos la medida y el reloj de la restauración o una capacidad de interpretación con la misma libertad que pueda tenerla otra' [the result is a different matter, which makes us think about whether this is *the* or *a* classical company; whether it is charged with painstakingly recuperating the past or whether it should be able to perform with the same freedom that any old company can] (1986).

In contrast, other critics had more specific objections that related to the production rather than the company. As Gutierre, José Luis Pellicena recited verse in a traditional grandiose style, and he proved very popular with critics and audiences alike (Vilches de Frutos, 2008, p. 341). This veteran actor had established his name in José Tamayo's Compañía Lope de Vega but, as Marsillach notes, his experience and skill was in many respects detrimental: 'José Luis era un estupendo actor tradicional incrustado en un proyecto que quería romper con la tradición' [José Luis was a magnificent actor from the old school embedded in a project that wanted to break with the old school] (2002, p. 454). A further source of complaint was Vicente Cuesta's performance as Pedro. Although, as noted previously, the choice to demystify kingship was a deliberate ethical and aesthetic choice, his exaggerated gestures combined with an accent and intonation that resembled that of a modern-day Madrid hoodlum detracted rather than reinforced this intention. These inconsistencies were symptomatic of the lack of a coherent aesthetic described by Julia Arroyo in the following terms:

> El breve diagnóstico sería: cierta confusa exposición del drama, un trabajo actoral de desigual convicción; un espectáculo, en fin, que parece surgir del extrañamiento con temor a ser aceptado, y un intento esforzado por presentar con renovada faz a nuestros clásicos, para que el público se sume con interés a un proyecto más que deseable. (1986)
>
> [The brief diagnosis would be: certain confusion in conveying the drama, an uneven set of performances from the actors. All in all, a distant and confused production that seemed fearful of not being accepted, and a too

laboured attempt to present our classics with an up-to-date face in the hope that the general public will greet a more than desirable project with interest.]

This review was unusual in its measured caution for, as Alberto Fernández Torres notes, '*El médico de su honra* ha sido recibido, por lo general, como si del examen de fin de curso de la CNTC se tratara' [*The Physician of his Honour* has generally been received as if we were dealing with the CNTC's end of year exam] (1987). The original staging of *El médico* may have struggled to pass this first test, but the company and its director were able to continue. Over the coming decade, Marsillach directed ten works himself and other, often high-profile practitioners (José Luis Alonso, Josefina Molina, Pilar Miró, Miguel Narros *et al.*), were invited to direct the other thirteen works.[15] During this period, the overriding ethos was that a new tradition ought to be grounded in *mise en scène* and performance style.

A far more conventional approach was taken in relation to performance texts, which tended to be prepared by writers with a literary rather than a theatrical background (e.g. Luís Antonio de Villena, Carmen Martín Gaite, Francisco Rico). Though individual words were changed, cuts were made, and occasionally scenes were transposed, the primary aim of these versions was to facilitate understanding. This was symptomatic of the fact that literary assessor Pérez Sierra construed radical overhauls not in terms of innovation but as indicative of a lack of competence and experience, noting how:

> se podan las obras a veces en exceso, aunque el motivo puede ser otro completamente distinto. Las compañías más modestas suelen practicar este abuso no sólo para descargar al público, sino también para facilitarse el trabajo, para hacer más alcanzable la obra a su capacidad de trabajo, para ponerla a la medida de sus fuerzas. (1999a, p. 8)

> [plays are often trimmed excessively, although the motive can be something else completely. The most modest companies tend to practise this abuse not only to relieve the audience, but also to make their job easier, to make the the play more amenable to their work ethic, to tailor it to their abilities.]

In many respects, this formula of textual fidelity combined with ostensibly audacious performance aesthetics proved successful; subsequent productions such as *Antes que todo es mi dama* charmed audiences in ways that the more austere *El médico* had failed to achieve. The company undoubtedly established a house style, but to what extent this constitutes the inauguration of a new performance tradition is more contentious. Although some actors appeared in multiple productions, there were no stable ensembles and the only attempt to establish a training scheme beyond the rehearsal room took place when Marsillach temporarily left to become director of INAEM in 1990.

In his capacity as acting director, Pérez Sierra established the ETC, a short-lived venture that yielded three modest productions: Lope's *El perro del hortelano* and *La noche toledana*, and Calderón's *El jardín de Falerina*.[16] This initiative was almost immediately dissolved when Marsillach returned to the helm with the following justification: 'hubo un momento en que un actor que estaba contratada en esta Compañía se marchó ... y la escuela no produjo un actor capaz de sustituirlo. Y yo me pregunté para qué sirve entonces esa escuela, si ya existe una Real Escuela de Arte Dramático' [there was a moment when an actor who had a contract with the company left ... and the school could not produce an actor capable of replacing him. And I asked myself what, then, was the point of the school if RESAD already existed] (cited in Rodríguez, 2002, p. 155). Roberto Alonso, assistant director of the CNTC at the time, has a rather different explanation:

> A mi juicio, esa escuela debería continuar, pero de hecho no es así, porque la creamos Rafael Pérez Sierra y yo, y en el 92 nos fuimos de la Compañía y la escuela desapareció con palabras textuales del anterior director, que dijo 'yo cuando vuelva me cago en la escuela'. (cited in Castilla, 2001, p. 268)
>
> [In my opinion, that school should have continued but this was not to be because Rafael Pérez Sierra and I created it, and we left the company in 1992, and the school disappeared with the previous director saying, and I quote verbatim, 'when I return, I'll screw the school over'.]

Whichever version of events we choose to accept, Marsillach's comments raise questions over the CNTC's ostensible *raison d'être*. How exactly was it resurrecting a lost tradition if it was reliant on an acting school that pre-dates its existence and, as we have seen, construed training in classical verse as a marginal activity not always taken seriously? The ECT's fate is not only indicative of the director's authoritarian and rebarbative approach, but is also symptomatic of the surreptitious appropriation of experience for the 'creation' of a new tradition. One of the company's most regular actors, Francisco Portes had, for example, formed part of Canseco's cooperative in the late 1970s, and many of the invited directors had forged and/or consolidated their reputations in the National Theatres during the 1960s. In many respects, this reliance on individuals trained in other institutions helped to dispense with the immediate need for an in-house training scheme. Hence, for example, Narros cast Carmelo Gómez in his first major role as Don Alonso in *El caballero de Olmedo* (1990) after having taught him at RESAD.

It was this combination of institutional support, collective experience and Marsillach's personal and professional charisma that secured a degree of popular and critical success. When *El médico* was restaged in 1994, there were a few cuts made to the 1986 version but the production was almost identical apart from the actors who were far more consistent. In general, there was an (in)conspicuous lack of grandiloquence and it was a sign of the company's new-found stature that it was able to attract Carlos Hipólito – a relatively young actor (b. 1956) who had by this date already established himself as one of Spain's most respected stage and screen actors – to play Gutierre; having trained with Narros and the North American William Layton at the TEI, he has claimed that 'el teatro clásico es la mejor escuela para un actor' [classical theatre is the best school for an actor] (1999, p. 78).[17]

For the CNTC regular, Pedro's villainy was intimated through performance intertextuality: Héctor Colomé's previous role had been as the Comendador in *Fuente Ovejuna*. Though his behaviour was ostensibly regal, outward appearances are belied by his appearing permanently distracted, thus neglecting his duties while indulging his whims in settings such as an Arabic bath. This was a far more sensual production in which a more coherent aesthetic allowed the actors to act through their bodies as much as their words. Leonor was very much presented as a Southern belle, while Adriana Ozores – the only actress to have genuinely forged a reputation through her multiple appearances with the company – expressed her desire with corporeal gestures that were far more inviting to the muscular Enrique than they were to the less conventionally attractive Gutierre.

The revival was something of a vindication and a swansong for Marsillach. In contrast to the play's first appearance, reviews were almost unanimously positive and there were none of the earlier complaints about the declamatory style(s).[18] This was not, however, so much the result of some miracle cure as it was of the imposition of a standardized house style that was increasingly accepted by press critics. When practitioners and critics flag up verse as a problem, they are rarely making a precise metrical or rhythmical observation; a general comment is usually invoked as shorthand for the fact they believe that something more fundamental is amiss.

The reposition of *El médico* largely bypassed verse as a semiotic system with the potential to communicate content and mood from the stage to auditorium; music was used in both 1986 and 1994 to guide the audience's emotions and sympathies in the way that different metrical forms would have done in the Early Modern *corral*. This is both the cause and consequence of a widespread antipathy to Castilian verse forms exemplified in the fact that, as Evangelina Rodríguez Cuadros notes, Spanish actors tend to compare their native octosyllables and endecasyllables negatively to Shakespearean blank verse without providing any justification. The CNTC compounded rather than dispelled this tendency, with Marsillach advancing, in both his productions and public statements, a false dichotomy between 'verse' and 'life' as if there were something inherently deathly about traditional Castilian metrical forms (1998, p. 494). Where the company did undeniably make headway is that actors increasingly gave the impression of having internalized rather than merely learnt their lines, and this seemingly facilitated communication with the audience.

On a smaller scale, neither did the staging of *El médico* prompt a widespread reappraisal of the play's content or meaning in the past or present. In the remainder of the twentieth century, there would be no subsequent productions of what Isaac Benabu has termed Calderón's 'morally "embarrassing" plays' (1994, p. 13), and *El médico* was included in a compendium of misogynist national literature (Ortiz, 1990, pp. 141–2). During the centenary of Calderón's birth, Antonio García Berrio added the following disclaimer in an otherwise sympathetic piece advocating the playwright's continued relevance:

> Pero en relación a la capacidad (o no) de los dramas de honor calderonianos para continuar movilizando las preferencias inteligentes y el gusto sensato de la modernizada sociedad española e internacional de nuestro tiempo, creo no equivocarme cuando considero que – tomados en bruto los dramas de honor y sin la punta de ironía secreta con que Calderón plasmaba y resolvía su problemática – la hoy ya tediosa guardarropía de los temas clásicos sobre la honra no moviliza intereses respetables, ni siquiera a título de pintoresquismo curioso. (2000, p. 20)

> [But as for the capacity of Calderón's honour plays to continue stimulating (or not) intelligent preferences and sensible tastes among contemporary Spanish and global societies, I think I am not wrong in saying that – the honour dramas taken at face value and without the secret point of irony with which Calderón infused and resolved his problematic set-up – what we now consider to be tedious apparel of the classical theme of honour will be incapable of generating respectable responses even in its capacity as an exotic curiosity.]

I would like to suggest that, in spite of some individual triumphs that include *El médico*, the CNTC was only partially successful in conserving, escaping and creating tradition(s). Furthermore, Marsillach's conflation and confusion of these functions was not only dishonest but arguably counter-productive in the long term. His personal, political and theatrical talents created a house style that challenged certain preconceived notions among audiences and critics of Golden Age drama on the contemporary stage; what they failed to do was establish a new performance tradition.

Calderón and the CNTC come of age?

José Antonio Campos, the new director of INAEM, has stated that when he offered Vasco directorship of the company in its eighteenth year, 'le pedí algo tan sencillo y apasionante como retomar el proyecto de Marsillach, pues es imprescindible recuperar su memoria y su propósito' [I asked him something as simple and exciting as reviving Marsillach's project since it is vital that we recuperate his memory and goal] (cited in *El correo*, 2004). Vasco shares this position and, whenever I have spoken to him, he has made it clear that he feels the CNTC had lost its way since his departure.[19] Nevertheless, with the exception of *Don Gil*, an entertaining romp through Tirso's play that consciously echoed Marsillach's earlier production,[20] there have been some radical departures.

As noted in chapter one, the company is no longer dedicated exclusively to *comedia* performance. Although this tendency respects the company's original statutes and the current legislative definition of a classic – 'Debe entenderse el teatro clásico en su más extenso significado y por tanto la política del INAEM estará dirigida a preservar todo el teatro clásico desde sus inicios más remotos hasta el romanticismo del siglo XIX' [Classical theatre should be understood in its broadest sense and INAEM's policy is therefore designed to preserve all classical theatre from its most remote beginnings right up to nineteenth-century romanticism] (*BOE*, 2006) – it does seem a shame that Golden Age drama has to cohabit in its new home when it is yet to establish itself firmly in Spain. In the editorial to the CNTC's *Boletín*, it is argued that they have been able to widen their repertoire because their earlier efforts have ensured that the performance of baroque drama is no longer 'una asignatura pendiente' [a pending matter] (2006a); as we have seen, this is not really the case.

Vasco differs from his predecessors in a number of important respects. At thirty-five, he may have lacked the status of José Luis Alonso de Santos or Marsillach but, unlike them, his reputation has been forged primarily through *comedia* performance. His relative youth also means that he belongs to the first generation of theatre practitioners to have no direct memory of Francoism, and to have had access to the various institutions that helped shape the theatrical landscape of democratic Spain. He graduated from RESAD and his own company, Noviembre, benefited from the funding available for the performance of classical drama and the increase in the number of theatrical spaces and festivals in which they could perform. Vasco is also far more willing to openly acknowledge and engage with earlier traditions of performance. He claims to have became interested in staging Golden Age drama as a result of seeing Marsillach's productions, and he has spoken of Estruch's importance: 'fue un personaje determinante para entender la evolución de la puesta en escena del teatro clásico en España' [he is a key figure vital to understanding the evolution of staging classical theatre in Spain] (CNTC, 2006a). He shares with the now deceased pioneer a commitment to stable troupes and education, with the CNTC for the first time in its history now being ensemble-based. Vasco has noted how a remarkable number of practitioners currently involved in *comedia* performance were trained in the short-lived ECT, and he has therefore been committed to providing a more stable heir to this earlier experiment in the guise of the Joven Compañía.

The young director has returned to Marsillach's energetic and financially rewarding practice of directing a considerable number of works himself. Although it may be a conscious decision, it is also indicative of the fact that he lacks his predecessor's cachet and/or contacts that there have been far fewer high-profile adaptors and directors than in the past. Vasco is not famed for any concrete ideological leanings, but he clearly shows a preference for people of his own generation and/or former colleagues from the independent sector (e.g. Yolando Pallín, Helena Pimenta, Lorenzo Caprile), and yet he has also shown a willingness to work with veterans of *comedia* performance. Pérez Sierra returned to the company for the first time since his resignation to work on the adaptation of *El pintor de su deshonra*, which also featured costumes designed by Pedro Moreno.

Of all the wife-murder plays, *El pintor* has perhaps the most sympathetic husband in the figure of Juan Roca, a middle-aged artist who marries Serafina, a much younger woman, in order to produce an heir. He and his servant, Juanete – who always attempts to tell stories and parables that he is never allowed to complete – arrive at the home of an old friend, Don Luis, who insists that they lodge with him. Their host lives with his daughter, Porcia, and is mourning the death of his son, Álvaro, who turns out to have survived and subsequently pursues Serafina whom he courted in the past. A fire breaks out at Don Diego's palace, and Juan leaves his wife in the hands of a dancer – Álvaro in disguise – who kidnaps her.

On realizing his loss and shame, Juan enters self-imposed exile, wandering aimlessly in search of casual work. Prince Ursino, who was once in love with Porcia but has now turned his attention to a mystery beauty who is in fact Serafina, commissions Juan to paint her. As the itinerant professional arrives with canvas in hand, she awakens from a nightmare and in a semi-conscious state grabs hold of her captor; Juan interprets this as proof of her infidelity and shoots them both. He makes no attempt to conceal this double homicide, but the other characters do not condemn his actions with even the victims' fathers accepting his actions as just. The Prince marries Porcia, and Juan resumes his aimless wanderings.

In 1986, domestic violence was rarely discussed in Spain but, in recent years, the number of women killed by their partners every year has become an increasingly visible and polemical social epidemic. As I have discussed elsewhere (Wheeler, 2008b), there is no evidence that rates of domestic violence are any higher in Spain than in other European states but it does have the unfortunate distinction of being a country in which this social ill has been systematically silenced, tolerated and even condoned. Most reviews of *El médico* were more concerned with discussing the merits (or lack thereof) of the nascent company to make detailed reference to the domestic murder on display. The one exception was academic and future director of the CNTC Andrés Amorós, who reproduced a number of familiar tropes in his objection:

> Quizá se pensó que la persistencia, en la España actual, de algunos crímenes pasionales mostraría su actualidad. Creo que no es así: poco tiene que ver la pasión de amor y celos que hoy puede sentir un joven con la frialdad implacable del código calderoniano, expresión de una sociedad basada en la apariencia. (1987)

> [Perhaps it was thought that the persistence in present-day Spain of some crimes of passion demonstrated its relevance. I do not think this is the case: the passion of love and jealousy that a young man may feel bears little resemblance to the cold intransigence of the Calderonian code, the manifestation of a society based on appearances.]

Discourse on the wife-murder plays in more recent years has increasingly highlighted the links between past and present by suggesting that these works provide a historical antecedent, even inspiration, for the Francoist dictatorship.[21] Ernesto Caballero's 2005 play *Sentido del deber*, loosely based on *El médico*, parodied traditional values by placing an all-female cast in a symbolic realm of the Francoist state: the barracks of the Guardia Civil. Here, Gutierre, affectionately known by his colleagues as Guti, is a hard-drinking member of this tight-knit right-wing fraternity who constantly reinforce his traditional notions of masculinity.

The oppressive and patriarchal nature of the dictatorship is indisputable: gender roles were heavily codified and the prevailing ideology bestowed upon men the right and responsibility to discipline women under their control.[22] The direct equation of honour and violence with a hermetically sealed sociocultural period is, nevertheless, reductive and the result of historical revisionism (see Wheeler, 2012c). Francoist discourse is not always as monolithic or rigid as it is often construed to be and, as we have seen, the events described in the wife-murder plays caused more outrage among critics in 1946 than they did in 1986. This is, perhaps, symptomatic of the fact that Spanish democracy has traditionally adopted a very passive attitude towards hierarchical gender relations. The left made little or no attempt to settle this deficit in the transition period (Threlfall, 1996, p. 116), and, since the ascension of the PSOE to government in 1982, far more emphasis has been placed on female visibility and emancipation in public rather than private spheres (Wheeler, 2008b, p. 180).

Vasco informs me that, in spite or perhaps because of his serious reputation, Calderón has the most loyal audience of all the Golden Age dramatists and that less publicity is required to sell tickets for productions based on his plays. He does, however, continue to occasion problems of a different kind for the CNTC, an icon of democratic Spain and cultural democratization. The director's decision to stage a wife-murder play often seen as emblematic of a bygone era when, to borrow a phrase from Manuel Fraga's infamous marketing campaign of the 1960s, Spain was different, is beguiling to say the least. This helps contextualize Pérez Sierra's claim that the director-general of theatre requested, unsuccessfully, that they change the ending of *El pintor* so as to make it more politically correct.[23] Although this clearly constituted a threat to the company's artistic independence, it was nevertheless in concordance with its cultural and political *raison d'être* for, as Purna Sen has noted:

> Modernisation theory posits gender relations as key indicators on the road from tradition to modernity; modernity that is exemplified by individualism and choice. Collective controls over individual actions through codes of shame and honour have been deemed remnants of backward cultures which have no place in contemporary societies and for those seeking to join the club of enlightened, secular and rational societies. (2005, p. 45)

This does raise the question of why Vasco made life potentially difficult for both himself and the CNTC. The programming does, however, appear less idiosyncratic and foolhardy when two factors are taken into account. Firstly, the young director has shown a strong preference for staging plays in which women are killed by men (*La fuerza lastimosa, El castigo sin venganza, Amar después de la muerte*), something he informs me is merely a by-product of his interest in Byzantine narratives. Secondly, the death of women at the hands of their male partners has received a hitherto unprecedented level of attention in Spanish society in recent years culminating with the controversial *ley integral de la violencia de género* [organic law on gender-based violence] in 2005.[24] This may help to explain the subtext of Calixto Bieito's 2004 production of Shakespeare's *King Lear*, which intimated domestic violence (see Delgado, 2006, pp. 136–50), and why there has been a small but significant resurgence in the performance of wife-murder plays in recent years.[25] Vasco has publicly claimed that this discourse was the determining factor in deciding to stage the play:

> Vivimos en un momento en que el maltrato a la mujer está tan al orden del día que encontrarse con una función en que todos están metidos en un engranaje del que no pueden salir y que al final castiga a los amantes, a una mujer que no tiene culpa, era especialmente atractivo, y el hecho de que los padres se vean obligados a perdonar me acabó convenciendo; que una norma social nuestra, que no hace tanto tiempo que ha desaparecido, esté reflejada tan al desnudo, tan cruentamente y que nos hable de nuestra historia sin tapujos; la ley del honor puesta en discusión y aplicada de la manera más drástica ... eso fue lo que acabó de convencerme. Por ahí podíamos encontrar una vía de contemporaneidad justamente sin tocar el texto para nada. (CNTC, 2008, p. 43)

[We are living in a time in which the abuse of women is so habitual that coming upon a dramatic work in which everyone is immersed in a vast web from which there is no escape – that ends by punishing the lovers and an innocent woman – was particularly appealing. The fact that the parents feel obliged to offer pardons was what ended up convincing me. That one of our social regulations which disappeared not all that long ago is reflected so bluntly, so cruelly, and that it speaks to us of our past without holding back in the least; the law of honour as an object of discussion and applied in the most drastic manner ... that was what ended up convincing me. This is the way in which we could find genuine relevance to today without touching the text in the slightest.]

What is interesting about recent sociopolitical developments in Spain, as far as wife-murder plays are concerned, is that they suddenly appear remarkably prescient by virtue of the very qualities for which they have traditionally been most heavily criticized. The new legislation rests on the basic tenet that individual misdemeanours are inextricably linked with wider social practices: 'La Ley asume la tesis de que la agresión a una mujer es una violencia estructural fundada en normas y valores sociales que encuentra su fundamento en las relaciones desiguales y jerarquizadas entre los sexos' [The Law assumes the premise that aggression against women is a form of structural violence whose root can be found in the unequal and hierarchical relationships that exist between the sexes] (Añón Roig and Mestre i Mestre, 2005, p. 35). Multiple studies have demonstrated that a character such as Juan Roca is a social rather than an autonomous being (e.g. McKendrick, 1993; Pym, 1998; Saffar, 1989); his modern-day counterparts are now construed to be similarly grounded in a collective that both enables and stymies their relationship to the self and others. According to both seventeenth- and twenty-first-century definitions, intimate partner violence is therefore now legally defined as an honour crime in Spain.

On this model, the ostensibly passionate nature of some male violence is little more than a false romanticization of a form of patriarchal aggression that is both the symptom and cause of unequal gender relations.[26] Amorós's distinction between the man who kills his partner in a jealous fit and the cold honour killing therefore disappears. Furthermore, the grounds and means by which Calderón's jealous husbands kill their wives in a clinical fashion without explicit censure from their compatriots potentially has more contemporary relevance than Othello's visceral act of homicide that is condemned by other characters and prompts his suicide.

On paper, therefore, the CNTC's production of *El pintor* boded well. The play's subject matter and theme clearly had the potential to touch an essential preoccupation or need in the audience. In addition, the cast had experience as an ensemble, as the majority of the actors had already collaborated on *El castigo sin venganza* and the *Tragicomedia de Don Duardos*, while Vasco had a series of experienced practitioners on hand to aid the transition from page to stage. Unfortunately, this transition was not to prove as smooth or successful as one might have hoped. The first thing to note is, as the table below demonstrates, how much was cut in comparison to Marsillach's earlier production:[27]

	El médico de su honra	*El pintor de su deshonra*
Primera Jornada (no. of lines/lines cut)	116/1020 (11.37%)	262/1080 (24.26%)
Primera Jornada (no. of lines/lines altered)	55/1020 (5.39%)	22/1080 (2.04%)
Segunda Jornada (no. of lines/lines cut)	98/1028 (9.53%)	185/1018 (18.17%)
Segunda Jornada (no. of lines/lines altered)	61/1028 (5.93%)	17/1018 (1.67%)
Tercera Jornada (no. of lines/lines cut)	69/905 (7.62%)	285/1041 (27.38%)
Tercera Jornada (no of lines/lines altered)	29/905 (3.2%)	16/1041 (1.54%)
Total (no. of lines/lines cut)	283/2953 (9.58%)	732/3139 (23.32%)
Total (no. of lines/lines altered)	145/2953 (4.91%)	55/3139 (1.75%)

Not only does this appear to contradict Vasco's claims that the play was relevant 'without touching the text in the slightest', but it also clashes with Pérez Sierra's ethics of adaptation. When I asked him about this apparent anomaly between theory and recent practice, his response was candid and pragmatic: the actors were not sufficiently skilled to perform the play in its entirety and, if he did not make the edits himself, they would later be made out of necessity by Vasco in the rehearsal period.[28] If this was indeed the case, then clearly something has gone seriously amiss with the CNTC's mission plan; twenty-two years after its debut, an experienced ensemble is seemingly less well equipped than their predecessors who were, in theory, laying the groundwork for future generations. A more specific problem in relation to *El pintor* is that, unlike for example *Fuente Ovejuna*, there are no secondary actions that can be readily excised and Calderón's dramatic works are so intricately and tightly constructed that any changes have to be made with extreme delicacy and care.

Unfortunately these issues came to the fore in a production that lacked cohesion, brought nothing new to the play for the *comedia* specialist, and probably would have been very confusing for anyone not familiar with

Calderón. The performance begins in a promising fashion. Most of the cast enters onto a relatively bare stage adorned with a simple wooden construction and a naval painting at the rear. Juan Roca, played by Arturo Querejeta, is dressed in black but his physical appearance and mannerisms suggest sobriety rather than anything more sinister. Although he is clearly middle-aged, he is far younger than his host Luis (Pepe Merino) who, accompanied by a soundtrack of waves, tells the story of losing his son in a touching and poetic manner.

Throughout the production, however, individual units are well performed but insufficient attention is paid to the specific rhythm and tone of many scenes and there is no sense of overall cohesion. Take, for example, when Serafina (Nuria Mencía) first tells Porcia (Eva Trancón) about her lost love. The two actresses have radically different declamatory styles. Mencía is completely non-naturalistic as she speaks at a very slow pace presumably in an attempt to suggest the solemnity of her words and their meanings. In contrast, her interlocutor – the only performer in this production capable of consistently respecting the metrics and rhythm of Calderón's verse while also effectively communicating content and emotion in a non-affected manner – speaks at a relatively normal pace. In a problem that is replicated elsewhere, the actors are also blocked in an unimaginative and static fashion. Porcia is initially positioned at the back of the stage while Serafina alternates between addressing her extensive lament at her friend and the audience. She then moves to the front of the stage where they sit together on a raised step. While Luis's stillness during his early speech was well suited to his tone, here the stasis of the two actresses fails to reflect the young bride's pent-up passion. As a result, it seems rather incongruous when she faints. This action is signposted by overwrought music that, rather than accompanying the action, calls attention to itself especially in the Pavón which does not have an orchestra pit; the musicians are consequently seated within the auditorium.

These attempts at tragic grandeur then clash with a frivolous tone prevalent elsewhere. Alan K. G. Paterson long ago noted how we can see, in Luis's house, the 'swelling rhythm of domestic comedy' (1969, p. 247), while Ellen C. Frye has more recently observed some striking parallels with Tirso's *El vergonzoso en palacio* (2003, p. 4). These comic tendencies and aspects are however exaggerated to the point of caricature. In this heavily edited version, the more complex lines relating to psychology and emotions are often the first to disappear. This is a pragmatic approach for their absence does not occasion any continuity problems while also often making long speeches shorter and therefore less challenging for both the actors and the audience. The consequence in the first act, for example, is that much of Álvaro's early speeches have been removed (1991, vv. 569–82; 914–50); he therefore seems a remarkably superficial character and his motivations and desire for Serafina are never altogether clear. In contrast, Juanete's pithy remarks cannot be readily edited and therefore, in relative terms, his presence is far more dominant on the stage than in Calderón's play text.

This propensity towards the comic is also exaggerated by turning the prince into a one-dimensional fool. Although the playwright clearly mocks this character whose overblown amorous verses turn him into a parody of the court suitor in love with love, 'Calderón is too excellent a dramatist to reduce his character to a farcical figure' (Paterson, 1969, p. 248). The portly Fernando Sendino is, however, dressed in a ridiculous buccaneer outfit, adopts an affected Italian accent and employs exaggerated physical gestures and verbal mannerisms to turn him into a clown. When he first appears on stage, followed by the equally rotund Celio in an identical costume and carrying an odd bouquet of flowers, this sartorially challenged royal suitor guides the offstage musicians as their instruments provide an accompaniment to his ruminations on love. He is then literally stopped in his tracks on seeing Serafina, and his statuesque pose is only broken when, in a routine repeated twice, Celio hits him with his hat.

These problems in tone and genre, and a tendency to eschew complexity in favour of superficiality, all coalesce in the climax to the second act, performed just before the interval. In the build-up to the party, the visibly intoxicated Celio and his master address Porcia at her balcony. In the middle of this exchange, her father arrives on stage in a space age costume while the prince continues to drink out of his hip flask and he and his servant soon break into song. A canvas then drops to reveal Álvaro, who has previously worn bright colours, dressed all in black. Costuming which plays against type is clearly designed to reflect the *mundo al revés* [world upside down] atmosphere of carnival but it is, to my mind, played out in a far too iconoclastic and unsubtle fashion. The whole cast arrives on stage in various atemporal costumes that are the epitome of what Roland Barthes terms 'the hypertrophy of a formal beauty without relation to the play' (1972, p. 44). Even more incongruously, the troupe then move forward in a horizontal

Figure 7   Photograph by Chicho of *El pintor de su deshonra* (dir. Eduardo Vasco, 2008), CNTC

formation as if they were on a catwalk rather than a theatre stage, begin to sing their lines, and one character even unleashes a set of balloons held on a wire suspended over the audience.

As this hothouse carnival atmosphere literally and metaphorically becomes more combustible, the production once again struggles to communicate this transition in a moving way. The 'mystery' dancer's prosthetic phallic nose is rather unsubtle and, while Álvaro's abduction of Serafina is dynamically staged, the production is more adept at communicating physical rather than emotional movement. Juan's dishonour is then suggested in a very literal fashion as he paces the stage but is surrounded by the masqued characters who all chuckle in a manner befitting pantomime. Querejeta then just shouts as he delivers his key speech. This actor made his debut in the company as Flores in Marsillach's production of *Fuente Ovejuna* and he played minor secondary roles until Vasco's arrival when he was promoted to the status of lead actor.[29] As the Duke of Ferrera in *El castigo sin venganza*, he was completely unconvincing as either a dissolute libertine or as a cuckolded husband bent on vengeance to the detriment of his own psychic wellbeing. He has up to this point performed Juan as a rather bland and harmless aesthete entering middle-age with no outward signs of intellectual or emotional disquiet; this makes the sudden lapse into histrionics appear exaggerated, forced and unrealistic.

Figure 8 Photograph by Chicho of *El pintor de su deshonra* (dir. Eduardo Vasco, 2008), CNTC

In the second half of the performance, more directly occupied with issues of honour and violence, this lack of aesthetic consistency or cohesion becomes both a symptom and cause of the absence of an ethical engagement that effectively negates the play's potential relevance to a contemporary audience. The educational handbook poses the following question: '¿Crees que el tema de esta obra puede trasladarse a nuestra época? El problema de la violencia de género, tan preocupante en nuestra sociedad, ¿guarda algún tipo de relación con la visión calderoniana de *El pintor de su deshonra?*' [Do you think that the subject of this play could be applied to our age? Does the problem of gender-based violence, so worrying in our society, bear any kind of resemblance with Calderón's vision in *The Painter of his Dishonour*?] (CNTC, 2008, p. 67). Based on the production alone, I would find this question virtually impossible to answer.

Any director who takes on the challenge of staging a wife-murder play in modern-day Spain ought, at least, to take into account the question of whether these *comedias* are part of the problem or solution. In this sense, they are potentially entering into a wider debate as to whether Calderón condones or censures the inexorable honour code to which he ostensibly subscribes. In other words, are these wife-murder plays capable of moving twenty-first-century audiences because they are products of the patriarchal structures that provide the breeding ground for gender-based violence and/or because they offer a critique/deconstruction of said structures? It was completely unclear to me whether, in performance, Vasco and his team had anything to communicate in this regard.

The end of the second act is a logical climax with which to end the first half; it was also used as an interval point in Laurence Boswell's production of the play with the RSC in the mid 1990s.[30] Here, however, the problem is that its relatively advanced position in the play text, together with the fact that the third act is the most heavily edited (over 27 per cent of the lines cut), makes the second half disconcertingly short with shifts in mood occurring at too rapid a pace.

El pintor differs from *El médico* and *A secreto agravio* in that there are far fewer soliloquies but there are a greater number of asides (Johnston, 2003, p. 243). These are employed at the beginning of act three as a means of mounting tension and to stress psychological isolation and what Charles Oriel has termed 'the tenuous nature of human relations in the communicative universe of Calderón's honor plays' (2000, p. 89). Hence, for example, Luis is inwardly tortured about the whereabouts and well-being of his friend Juan. In the editing process, however, most of these asides have disappeared and the effect is that the beginning of the third act eschews psychological complexity while rapid-fire exchanges take on the air of a *capa y espada* [cloak and dagger] comedy. This is bolstered by the physical appearance of Porcia brandishing a rifle in a comic pose as she ostensibly goes in search of her brother but secretly hopes to find the prince.

The challenge the production then faces is how, given this comic backdrop, to make the tragic denouement both performable and dramatically coherent. At the purely visual level, it is relatively elegantly staged. Serafina lies in a sober yet stylish nightdress that frames her beauty between two wooden constructions. On seeing this, her dishevelled husband who now wears an artisan's weather-beaten rags rather than the well-tailored suit of yore, goes down on one knee to deliver his lament. However, at the verbal and thematic level, the production is notably less successful. Querejeta clearly lacks the emotional calibration to deliver this kind of speech where 'the burdened conscience resorts to a desperate ultra-rational dialectic, a kind of private Inquisition or legalistic tourney' (Honig, 1972, p. 11). Then, as Serafina awakes, there is a ponderous delay as Álvaro enters from the rear of the stage and it is not clear how conscious a state she is in.

Juan, on being presented with this heart-wrenching spectacle, is, as a result of the 'incompatibility of honour and reasoning about dishonour' (Bryans, 1981, p. 278), seemingly unable to take any course of action other than to use his pistols to paint his last bloody canvas. The actor fails, however, to endow his character with any depth of personality and there is no sense of how his actions and words are motivated by passion and/or honour, or the complex interrelationships between the two emotions. Instead, he resorts to his default mode of shouting and employing exaggerated grimaces and physical expressions as if inner turmoil can be performed purely through outer agitation. This is precisely the style that Marsillach was looking to dispel. Furthermore, Vasco's leading man emulates a traditional performance style but without the technical or emotional skill of an actor such as Pellicena.

In marked contrast to the performance style, the execution of the lovers is then staged in a remarkably understated manner. As Serafina embraces Álvaro, a screen with an abstract red painting shields the action from public view. The pistols are shown in silhouette yet the sound of them being fired is so quiet that the audience cannot be completely sure of what has happened in a rather (anti)-climactic finale. This bathos could, however, be justified on dramatic and ethical grounds. If we follow the logic upon which the traditional reception of *Othello* and the wife-murder plays has been predicated, then Juan has more compelling and visceral evidence of his wife's supposed infidelity and is therefore more justified in his actions than his counterparts in other Calderón plays.[31] Therefore, if we apply what Antonio Carreño terms 'a sociology of closure' (1997, p. 44), it is clear that a more cathartic and less understated murder scene may well have eschewed the particular contemporary relevance that I have argued is inherent in the play.

Both Vasco's production and Calderón's play resist the grand gestures that led Brecht to reject tragedies for depicting catastrophe beyond criticism and thereby implying that things could not be other than described. As Melveena McKendrick notes, the endings of the wife-murder plays 'resist grand climatic gestures in favour of squalid personal and social adjustments which withhold completion, and instil a feeling of bemused revulsion instead of satisfaction' (2000b, p. 219). This lack of acquiescence in traditional aesthetic forms can either be seen as formal shortcoming or as an invitation to reflect on both the play and the social circumstances in which it was written and is now staged. In a statement that is equally applicable to the *comedia*, Jonathan Dollimore argues:

> This is not a transcendental awareness; the drama may incorporate the contradictions it explores. It is, then, a tragedy which violates those cherished *aesthetic* principles which legislate that the ultimate aim of art is to order discordant elements; to explore conflict in order ultimately to resolve it; to explore suffering in order ultimately to transcend it. All three principles tend to eliminate from literature its socio-political context (and content), finding instead supposedly timeless values which become the *universal* counterpart of man's *essential* nature – the underlying human essence. Measured against such criteria much Elizabethan and Jacobean drama does indeed lack aesthetic completeness and ethical/metaphysical resolution. But perhaps it has to be seen to lack these things in order to then be seen to possess real (i.e. historical) significance. (2004, p. 8)

In other words, the breaking of 'cherished aesthetic principles' has two possible consequences: the interrogation of content and/or the rupture of form. While the latter is arguably a necessary prerequisite of the former, that does not imply that it is a sufficient condition. The problem of the distancing effects in the CNTC's production is that they appear to be both the symptom and cause of confusion rather than reflection. There is no genuine consideration of how Juan relates psychically to himself or his community; thus there is no sense of what his very (un)dramatic actions are meant to convey or how they relate to either the seventeenth or twenty-first centuries.

A similar problem also befalls the production's resolution. In Calderón's play text, the final scene can be read as a very literal and shocking exercise of the law of the father but it is,[32] at best or worst, a pyrrhic victory for this small patriarchal community. Calderón depicts two grieving fathers alongside the prince who offers to marry a woman he has previously rejected in favour of another. Juan, as multiple commentators have noted (e.g. DiPuccio, 1989, p. 125; Soufas, 1984, p. 201), is a shadow of his former self, a man in tatters destined to continue his solitary and tormented aimless wanderings which Paterson argues will lead to suicide (1989, p. 130). All of this is completely absent from the stage where the actors line up in a horizontal formation and have light shone upon them as they read their individual verses, delivered as if they were costumed recitations of the text. While this expressionless style could, in theory, be a deliberate choice to show the ways in which honour acts as a stranglehold on individual desires and actions, here it comes across as both confused and confusing.

The refusal to engage with the psychological dimension of the play means that the audience has little emotional investment in the fates of the individuals on stage. Furthermore, the opaque performance style does not so much suggest the corseting effect of a bloody social code as the sudden realization that the play is meant to be tragedy. This is particularly problematic in reference to the prince, still in his buccaneer outfit, whose comic representation throughout means that he lacks the gravitas to act effectively as a *deus ex machina* and marry Porcia. This ominous and dark tone is reiterated in the curtain call where Juan's pistols and the red canvas are left on display.

In spite of my concerns about *El pintor*, the production received positive press coverage (e.g. García Garzón, 2008; Torres, 2008; Villena, 2008a), with a fairly representative review describing both the play and the performance as 'un visionario alegato contra la violencia de género' [a visionary diatribe against gender-based violence] (López, 2008). Although this is indicative of the fact that the sociopolitical conditions of the present may be poised to undertake a radical overhaul of the critical tradition of interpreting Calderón's wife-murder plays – and it would be an act of despotism on my part to declare that any opinion other than my own lacks validity – I am nevertheless sceptical about these assessments in that they merely repeat platitudes and information distributed by the company. In recent years, Spanish newspapers and magazines have drastically reduced the amount of space dedicated to theatre (Pérez Rasilla, 2008, p. 21); and I was unable to uncover even one detailed review. In what is arguably just one manifestation of the poor quality of much theatre criticism in Spain, the line between an article publicising a production and a critique appears to have been blurred.[33]

Critics such as Alfredo Marqueríe and Eduardo Haro Tecglen, who died in 2005, had an expansive knowledge of theatre. They may often have been rigid, obstinate and dogmatic but they also earned the respect, albeit grudging, of other critics and practitioners. Sadly, they are literally a dying breed. It is almost unthinkable to imagine that Vasco would have to resign because of a bad review as Marsillach thought he might have to do after *El médico* was given a critical mauling in *El País*. I am not calling for a return to this adversarial tradition but it is clearly preferable to the current state of affairs whereby the vast majority of reviews compare unfavourably with even the most sycophantic and superficial commentaries from the 1940s. Marcos Ordóñez – arguably Spain's most knowledgeable and articulate theatre critic – has paid relatively little attention to Golden Age drama.[34] This is indicative of the fact that *comedia* performance still exists at the margins rather than the centre of theatrical activity in Spain, and that the CNTC has yet to fulfil the remit with which it was first created: it was seemingly less well prepared at the age of twenty-two to approach a *comedia* than it had been when it made its debut.

Conclusion

In his autobiography, Marsillach claimed that *El médico* was the best production staged during his time as director of the CNTC (2002, p. 527). That this was their debut is, I think, indicative of him being more interested in, and successful at, individual triumphs than in establishing a new tradition. The fact that the company so quickly lost direction in the wake of his departure can be interpreted as a testament to his innovation and talent, and/or an indictment of his inability to equip classical theatre's new home with a sufficiently strong infrastructure to withstand the absence of its chief architect. Vasco, in contrast, has been far less successful on the stage but he will nevertheless bequeath a logistical legacy with potential waiting to be realized.

In mitigation, it ought to be noted that *El pintor* is a very complex and difficult play with which the RSC also struggled and for which they were often critically reproached, unlike the CNTC (Theatre Record, 1995). Furthermore, the Spanish production is, in my opinion, the worst to be staged by the company in recent years and is not, therefore, representative. This is indicative of the fact that, of the two permanent troupes, this cast appears to be the weaker. The other, which has focussed more heavily on comedies, has generally been far more accomplished; hence, for example, I have elsewhere concluded my discussion of Vasco's production of *Las manos blancas no ofenden* by suggesting that it achieves the 'dual feat of making an unfamiliar and convoluted plot involving multiple layers of transvestism intelligible' and that 'this process of *deleitar enseñando* [delighting through instruction] is a vital first step if *comedia* performance is to genuinely take root in Spain' (Wheeler, 2012b).

These disclaimers do not, however, dispel concerns over the inability to bring out the contemporary relevance of *El pintor*, a play that, due to a unique set of sociopolitical circumstances, clearly has much to say to modern audiences. Vasco, alongside directors of other Spanish National Theatres, was asked to leave in 2011. In general, his most creative work to date with Golden Age drama has been undertaken with Noviembre and Vasco's departure from the CNTC might therefore prove to be mutually beneficial. It is to be hoped that his talents will be deployed at least partially in the promotion of the *comedia* within other settings and that the incoming artistic director, Helena Pimenta, will be able to learn from the lessons of the past. If (and it is a big if) this is the case, the CNTC may finally be able to act its age and move beyond its arrested development so as to stage versions of Calderón, Lope and Tirso which do justice both to the playwrights and their twenty-first-century audiences.

Chapter Four

Cinema and Golden Age drama: the *comedia* goes to the movies

In Raul Ruíz's film *Mémoire des apparences* (1986),[1] a literary professor attempts to recall lines from *La vida es sueño*; the identities of the other members of his revolutionary group are encrypted in different lines. Struggling with the task, he visits the cinema repeatedly; the screen functions as a mnemonic device due to the underlying similarities in the different media. In fact, ever since Ramón Menéndez Pidal referred to a Lope play as a 'verdadero cinedrama' [genuinely cinematic drama] (1924, p. 541), commentators have persistently noted the cinematic quality of the *comedia*. Golden Age drama's cultural ubiquity in the seventeenth century finds its closest modern-day equivalent in film and, in terms of style, both artistic forms are characterized by rapid scene changes and an ostensible prioritizing of action over psychology.

In Paul Julian Smith's memorable phrase, '[i]f the past is another country, then Spaniards are frequent visitors' (2006, p. 11). To continue with the same metaphor, the written word is a popular mode of transport; Antonio Lara has claimed that two-thirds of the films shown on Spanish television and cinema screens are based on literary texts (2002, p. 2). Given these fertile preconditions, it would be logical to presume that there would be a thriving tradition of filming Golden Age drama for the silver screen. This is not, alas, the case. There have been relatively few adaptations; Lope heads the list with seven extant cinematic appearances but this relative popularity is placed into sharp relief when one considers that there have been ten adaptations each of *Don Quijote* and *Don Juan Tenorio*.[2] A recent monograph study of films based on Spanish theatre makes no mention of Tirso and dispenses with Calderón and Lope in six perfunctory lines (Gómez, 2000).

In this chapter, I trace the history of filming the *comedia*, examining specific screen adaptations, projects that were never completed and broader cinematic references to Golden Age plays. In the final part, I provide a detailed study of the production and reception of, at the time of writing, the most recent film based on a *comedia*: *La dama boba* (Manuel Iborra, 2006). I will attempt throughout to address the question of why a genuine tradition for filming Spanish national drama has never emerged, and suggest some of the ways in which cinema may have influenced the way in which at least some Spaniards view Calderón, Lope and Tirso.

Filming Lope and the Golden Age for the masses

La dama duende was filmed in 1919 as was *La moza de cántaro* in 1927, but there are no extant copies (Hormigón, 2002c, p. 68). Fragments of a silent film version of *El alcalde de Zalamea* can, however, be viewed at the Filmoteca. In 1935, the German director Constantin David directed *La musa y el Fénix*, a fictional recreation of the playwright's life and times. In spite of these one-off projects, there was no tradition that would provide the regime with a positive example to emulate or a negative precedent to dispel.

As with theatre, cinematic activity was concentrated in Republican zones during the Civil War (Triana-Toribio, 2003, p. 32). This is not to say that the Nationalists were unconcerned with an art form whose mass appeal and propagandistic potential far outweighed other media. Its influence made it a valuable weapon which, it was believed, could be manipulated for both edifying and nefarious means.[3] Thus, an order made by the Nationalist command on 2 November 1938 justified censorship in the following terms:

> Dado que el cinematógrafo ejerce una innegable y enorme influencia sobre la difusión del pensamiento y sobre la educación de las masas, es indispensable que el Estado vigile siempre que haya algún riesgo que pueda apartarle de su misión. (cited in Puigdomènech, 2007, p. 12)

> [It is essential – given that the cinema has an undeniably and enormous influence on the diffusion of ideas and the education of the masses – that the State is vigilant whenever there is any risk that might divert it from its mission.]

This logic persisted following Franco's victory and censorship was far stricter for cinema than it was for theatre or literature (Neuschafer, 1994, p. 11). While it is undeniable that the regime was reactive in terms of dispelling what were seen to be dissident or perverse elements, what is more debatable is the extent to which it actively sought to use cinema as a means through which to inculcate its ideology. According to Juan Miguel Company Ramón:

> A diferencia de las dictaduras nazi-fascistas, nunca existió aquí un proyecto definido y perfilado para elaborar un cine de exaltación franquista debido, es claro [*sic*], a la pluralidad de opciones existentes en el bloque dominante

de los ganadores de la contienda civil cuyos intereses irán surgiendo a la palestra al hilo de la evolución y reubicación de sus fuerzas y vectores dirigentes en el tablero político. (1999, p. 184)

[Unlike the Nazi-fascist dictatorships, there was never here a set or elaborately designed project to develop a cinema that would exalt Francoism. This is due, of course, to the plurality of options that existed within the victors of the civil conflict whose interests would variously come to the fore as different nexus of power and policy makers evolved and repositioned themselves within the political arena.]

Although it is undoubtedly true that there was no single concerted effort to turn cinema into a propaganda machine, it was nevertheless prioritized by the regime. The national economy would not return to the relative prosperity of 1936 until 1954, yet the film industry recovered at a much earlier stage (Diez Puertas, 2002, p. 325). Important subsidies were established and protectionist orders were set in place to limit the number of foreign films that were shown.

There was a widespread belief that the combination of Spanish history and celluloid were a match made in heaven that could provide an important medium for proselytizing at both national and international levels.[4] From the pages of the state-run Falangist film magazine *Primer Plano*, Fernández Ardavín spoke of how: 'Nuestra historia, nuestro arte, nuestra literatura, nuestras leyendas poéticas, nuestros romances medievales, nuestro paisaje rico y variado y nuestros hechos gloriosos son un filón inagotable para crear un espléndido cine capaz de imponerse en el mundo' [Our history, our art, our literature, our poetic legends, our medieval ballads, our rich and varied landscape and our glorious real-life events are an inexhaustible goldmine for the creation of a splendid cinema with the capacity to conquer the world] (cited in Alcaroz, 1943).

Nevertheless, the mere call for Spain to produce works capable of aesthetic colonialism is symptomatic of the fact that there were not as many nationalistic or historical films being made as the Falange would have hoped. Depending on the exact definition, somewhere between twenty and sixty-four of the 437 films produced in the 1940s can be classified as being examples of *cine histórico* [historical cinema] (Monterde, 2007, pp. 90–1). This belies the popular misconception that Spanish cinema of the time was the exclusive preserve of religious and historical epics that have retrospectively become particularly powerful symbols of the culture and age in which they were made. As Stephen Marsh notes, in reality '[t]he vast majority of Spain's filmic production of the period [1939–51] consists of popular comedies, melodramas, costume dramas that are often set in the 19th century, and musicals' (2006, p. 2).

In fact, Lope made his post-war film debut in the light musical comedy *Aventura* (Jerónimo Mihura, 1944) scripted by theatre critic Alfredo

Marquerie. The narrative tells of an urban theatre company that travels to a remote Aragonese town to stage *Peribáñez*. Lope's play is performed and the film's central plot consciously echoes the *comedia*. Ana, a beautiful young cosmopolitan actress, is besotted with her new home and finds her own Peribáñez in the guise of a local farmer, Andrés. Where the film is remarkable is that it mocks her idealization of the countryside by deconstructing the myth of the rural idyll. In moral terms, it is also very daring in that the peasant is married and has a child; this does not prevent him from wanting to run away with the actress, although she ultimately rejects him out of compassion for his wife.

During the Civil War, the Generalitat de Valencia – effectively a Communist institution at the time – had plans to make a superproduction of *Fuente Ovejuna*. It was originally hoped that Jean Renoir would direct the film, but he was unable to travel to Spain. The project was subsequently offered to Francisco Elías but the Nationalist victory ensured that filming never commenced (Caparrós Lera, 1992, p. 54). Then, in 1942, Carlos Arévalo began his attempts to film Lope's play. I have been unable to unearth any archival evidence for why this never materialized. However, Pepe Coira's contention that it was most likely a result of the regime's documented aversion to authoritarian narratives at the end of the World War, combined with their lack of faith in the director to deal with such sensitive material, is highly plausible (2004, p. 118). It has been argued that Arévalo's earlier *Rojo y negro* (1942) is 'el único filme de auténtica concepción falangista que se ha realizado' [the only genuinely Falangist film to have been made] (Fernández-Cuenca, 1972, p. 168),[5] and cinema's ability to be widely distributed clearly entails potentially negative as well as positive consequences.

Three years after the collapse of Arévalo's project, Antonio Román voiced an interest in filming a high-budget screen version of *Fuente Ovejuna*. Although he had for a short time been director of La Barraca when they had performed Lope's play, he was, in the eyes of the establishment, an exemplary figure (see Huerta Calvo, 2011). His most recent film had been the hugely patriotic and successful *Los últimos de Filipinas* (1945), and he had earlier worked as a hired screenwriter on the infamous *Raza* (José Luis Sáenz de Heredia, 1942), written by the *Caudillo* himself as an idealistic retelling of his own family history. José María Pemán wrote the screenplay for *Fuente Ovejuna*, and Román made every effort to ensure that the film was 'politically correct'. This is reflected in his choice of three advisors: Major General Luis Bermúdez de Castro gave counsel on military matters; Father Antonio Figora on religious matters; and Cayetano Luca de Tena on locations and sets.

The film was given a shooting permit in August 1946 and awarded the category of 'national interest' by the state administration.[6] This level of official support, the fact that the film had the largest set ever erected for a national production, Román's reputation and a famous cast ensured strong media coverage. In one of his earliest film roles, Fernando Rey plays Frondoso but the star of the picture was undoubtedly Amparo Rivelles, popularly known as Amparito or 'la cara más bonita del cine español' [the prettiest face in Spanish cinema] (Comas, 2004, p. 122).[7]

Despite its official support, Ramón did have some problems with the censors. They objected to Laurencia's use of 'maricones' (replaced by 'maritones') and to the original ending where the Catholic Monarchs march into Portugal in a bellicose manner (Fernández Colorado, 1997, p. 216). The first change was a result of not wanting to corrupt or offend the domestic market,[8] while the second was designed so as not to suggest any Spanish imperial ambitions to the outside world now largely under the control of the Allied powers.

The shooting of the film was plagued by bad weather and there were persistent rumours of financial difficulties. *Fuente Ovejuna* was eventually premiered in a gala presentation in Burgos on 10 October 1947, and then opened in Madrid on 20 November at the Cine Coliseum. Although a few reviewers were disappointed by the heavily hyped set design, quite justifiably so, the film was predictably very well received by critics. From the pages of *Primer Plano*, López Rubio spoke of 'uno de los mayores éxitos del cine español' [one of the greatest successes of Spanish cinema] and 'este gran esfuerzo de nuestro cine' [this great effort of our cinema] (1947), while Gómez Tello praised it for projecting, with sincerity and panache, Lope's original vision: 'Un pueblo entrañable, vigoroso, con una convincente frontera de su orgullo y su justicia y con un sentimiento de fidelidad que – ¡ay! – era lo que se torcía en unas versiones teatrales mugrientas y tumultuosas de las que más vale no acordarse' [A warm resolute community that presents a convincing front of pride and justice with a sense of fidelity that, alas, was precisely that which was perverted in some repulsive and unruly theatrical versions that we would do better to forget] (1947).

The film itself, though enjoyable, is hardly subtle and is a prime example of 'papier mâché' films that 'tend to be characterized by an exaggerated interpretative style and an artificial and grandiose aesthetic, with entire sets made out of papier mâché – hence the genre's name' (Pavlović, 2009, p. 75). The Spanish studio CIFESA, run by Vicente Casanova and designed as a Spanish version of the Hollywood majors with its own star system, specialized in this genre dominated by historical epics such as *Inés de Castro* (1944), *Locura de amor* (1950), *Agustina de Aragón* (1950), *La leona castellana* (1951), etc.[9] *Fuente Ovejuna* was not produced by CIFESA but both Román and Rivelles were on Casanova's roster, and the presence of the Catholic Monarchs ensures that it is at least as much a historical picture as it is a literary adaptation.

Román's biographer claims that *Fuente Ovejuna* is the director's most overtly political film (Coira, 2004, p. xiv), and it clearly accords with Rob Stone's description of how 'Spanish cinema was being used to rewrite the past and dictate the present in order to posit Francoist Spain as the culmination of a struggle through the ages and a beacon of sinlessness in an otherwise pagan world' (2002, p. 39). For a modern-day viewer, it is also unintentionally comic in its deployment of what Alejandro Yarza has termed 'totalitarian kitsch aesthetics' (2004, p. 50).

Early in the film there are scenes, not present in Lope's play text, of a local priest criticizing Fernán Gómez's behaviour; the Comendador does not appreciate this polite admonishment and rather melodramatically smashes the communion chalice. The Catholic Monarchs are idealized to a degree not even intimated by Lope; when Ferdinand doubts whether they can go to *Fuente Ovejuna* because of the weather, Isabella stands firm claiming: 'No hay justicia de tiempo seco y justicia de tiempo de agua. Más pronto corre el mal ejemplo que las nubes' [There is not justice for dry weather and justice for wet weather. Bad habits travel faster than clouds]. On hearing the inhabitants' stories, there is not the pragmatic acquiescence of the play text but a maternal sigh of 'pobre gente' [poor people] followed by shots of mass celebration as the monarchs pass through the town.

Fuente Ovejuna thereby lends itself to being interpreted as a paradigmatic example of a didactic genre unequivocally manipulated for propagandistic purposes. It is in these terms that Román is remembered if at all in Spain (Galán Blanco, 1990, p. 249). Although it is clear that, at the very least, the film had an ideological subtext, how effectively this goal was realized is harder to gauge.

As Raymond Carr notes, '[w]ith more cinema seats per capita than any other European country, the Spain of the '40s and '50s was a nation of cinema addicts' (1980, p. 139). As a correlative to this view, a deterministic model is often adopted and it is assumed that Spanish cinema patrons of the time were passive victims in constant need of a prescribed fix. A doctoral study on historical cinema of the time submitted in 2005 cites José Antonio Maravall's theory as an incontestable given and suggests that films were the *comedias* of their day: 'la cultura durante el franquismo funcionó de la misma manera que la cultura del barroco' [culture during Francoism operated in the same way as baroque culture] (González, p. 56). A cursory glance at the reports of premieres and gala performances in official publications like *Primer Plano* may appear to support this argument although their compulsive discourse of enthralment does suggest a basic insecurity. Equally, their reports are predominantly based on special grand occasions in Madrid and Barcelona; to what extent would these reactions be replicated across the nation in radically different environments?[10]

In the context of a repressive dictatorial regime, cinema-going was one of the few genuinely democratic activities. Unlike the theatre, the price of tickets was not prohibitive and it was the only socially acceptable entertainment venue for women to attend on their own (Bosch and Rincón, 1998, p. 115). Furthermore, matinee performances were mainly frequented by women and former Republican combatants who had been denied work permits and therefore had nothing else to do (Labanyi, 2000, p. 165). These factors are not purely anecdotal because, as Elizabeth Cowie notes:

> images are not transparent and do not reflect a reality prior to and other than them; on the contrary images are polysemic and without fixed meaning until organised as a statement. Meaning only arises in the construction and circulation of the representation. (1997, pp. 18–19)

It is for this reason that issues of agency continue to be central to theories of spectatorship (Aaron, 2007, p. 1). How free, for example, might at least some former Republican combatants have been to negotiate subversive readings through the presence of Soviet cinematic techniques deployed in the wedding scenes where montage is used in a series of rapid edits that alternate between crowd scenes, the bride and groom, and tableaux of different forms of collective revelry? The film's sexual politics also lend themselves to multiple and potentially contradictory readings. According to Isolina Ballesteros, 'nunca ha sido la mujer tan omnipresente y visible en las pantallas de cine ni tan ausente e invisible en la reconstrucción política y social del país' [never have women been so omnipresent and visible on cinema screens nor so absent and invisible in the country's social and political reconstruction] (1999, p. 54). This paradox is manifest throughout Román's film where, for example, Isabella takes on a more far prominent role than Ferdinand. Bernard P. E. Bentley has suggested that this is largely a consequence of the Castile-centric view of the time (2004, p. 335). An additional explanation is provided by Jo Labanyi's observation that the focus on women in Spanish cinema of the 1940s is symptomatic of a desire for national reconciliation (2000, p. 164). In this case, Isabella's depiction as a compassionate maternal figure rather than a monarchical power base served the political exigencies of the time by delivering a less bellicose image of Spain both at home and abroad.

The queen's role is heavily determined by her gender yet she nevertheless represents a woman with authority. It is by no means clear how female spectators would have responded to a character endowed with an exponentially greater degree of agency and power than they would have been able to exercise in their everyday lives. This radical indeterminacy is even more explicit in the case of Laurencia; she is the film's main character and the casting of Rivelles is not incidental. Many theorists have convincingly argued that the presence of stars enables spectators to negotiate meanings in collaboration with the filmic text (Cook, 1993; Dyer, 2004; Stacey, 1994). This process acts as an obstacle to the deterministic model because, as Christine Gledhill argues, 'star images reconcile, mask, or expose ideological contradictions' that open 'up the possibility for divergent or oppositional readings by different audiences' (1991, p. xiv).

As with Isabella, Laurencia's agency and femininity are both stressed. While much of her famous diatribe is removed, the film visualizes what occurs when she is kidnapped by the Comendador. In a series of medium shots, we see her resisting his advances as she attempts to defend herself by biting him. However, as a woman, she is unable to physically overpower him. Her face is bathed in light and takes on the air of a sacrificial martyr, reminiscent, for example, of how Jaime the priest is filmed in *Raza* prior to his execution at the hands of Republican forces. Clear parallels can therefore be established with older Spanish artistic traditions. According to Peter N. Skrine:

> The real martyrs of the baroque age were priests and soldiers; the martyrs so often depicted in its literature and painting, however, were beautiful young women, and understandably so. This springs less from any deep psychological and erotic motivations than from its instinct for the allegorical dimension; its readiness, that is, to accept figures that are half-human, half-personification. (1978, p. 65)

A similar process is, I would suggest, in operation in *Fuente Ovejuna*, where Laurencia/Rivelles represents the *patria* in peril. Not surprisingly, the potential martyr is able to escape the Comendador's rapacious grasp as she jumps through the castle window and falls a great distance into the river below. This quintessentially Spanish actress functions here as a kind of metonym for the heroic value inherent in the work as a whole; self-abnegation through death is construed as more honourable than violation. Not surprisingly, Laurencia survives the perilous escape thus providing an ideal pretext to show Amparito in revealingly wet attire while remaining within the realms of moral propriety.

In one respect, Laurencia adheres to a traditional patriarchal model in that her strength and fortitude are demonstrated through her ability to protect her purity and family's honour against the advances of a predatory male. Yet, at the same time, the film does not prioritize how this will affect her male relatives but instead treats her as an entity in her own right. It bestows female suffering with a forceful visual image within a social context that generally sought to silence women's voices. Equally, the actress who incarnates the *patria* epitomized a lifestyle antithetical to the values of self-abnegation and thriftiness with which the general female population was being inculcated. As Labanyi notes, '[t]he glamour associated with such active, expressive female stars may have been escapist, but it also kept alive the belief that things could be otherwise' (2000, p. 168). Within a few years of the film's release, 'the prettiest face in Spanish cinema' would leave the motherland and head for Mexico, partly as a result of the intrusive media coverage of her various romantic liaisons.

Until more research has been done on spectatorship in 1940s Spain, these questions over how audiences identified with on-screen images and the extent to which they were free to negotiate their own perhaps subversive meanings are largely speculative.[11] However, audiences definitely exercised their freedom in one regard: they generally rejected Spanish national cinema and showed a marked preference for films made in the US (Bosch and Rincón, 1998, p. 114). There were a small number of home-grown successes but *Fuente Ovejuna* was not among them. It was a commercial disappointment which financially ruined Román's production company, Alhambra; furthermore it was the first of the director's films not to be awarded a prize by the Sindicato Nacional Español [National Spanish Union] (Coira, 2004, pp. 125–6).

This lukewarm response did not prevent a document produced in 1949 by the Diplomatic Information Office from containing multiple stills from the film alongside the proud boast that '[f]or this type of picture – which may be produced with whatever pomp may be desired – Spain is a fountain of dazzling inspiration' (1949, p. 14). The report is tragicomic in its parochial vision. Prior to addressing the major issue of how the national cinema needs to enter into major distribution networks before it will be able to modernize its studios and improve its cinematic techniques (p. 24), it proudly boasts of how:

> Spanish cinematographic art has a style of its own which is unmistakable. It is made up of the Spanish truths which inspired Cervantes and Lope de Vega, Velázquez and Goya, St. Teresa of Jesus, and Father Francisco de Vitoria. For this very simple reason, the national content of the pictures being made in Spain and by Spaniards is bound to interest and astonish the world at large. (p. 21)

In the years of autarky, the national cinema industry seemed to constantly believe that worldwide success was just on the horizon and that this would facilitate a mutually beneficial exchange of Spanish spiritual values for material wares from abroad.[12] Thus, ploughing public and private money into high-profile and costly historical films such as *Fuente Ovejuna* was seen as an investment for the future. This was also the motivation behind the next adaptation to which I will now turn.

Repackaging a Spanish myth for national and international audiences

Don Juan (José Luis Sáenz de Heredia, 1950) is ostensibly the epitome of the most reactionary form of Spanish cinema from the dictatorship period. It was produced by CIFESA and directed by José Luis Sáenz de Heredia, the man behind *Raza* and *Franco, ese hombre* (1964), who stopped directing films in 1976 because he did not approve of the cinema or the politics of the time (Abajo de Pablos, 1996, p. 9). Furthermore, as Labanyi convincingly argues (2003), the film was an attempt to reclaim a Spanish myth that had been desecrated by the *Adventures of Don Juan* (Vincent Sherman, 1948) starring Errol Flynn, which presented the Spanish queen as one of the eponymous hero's amorous conquests.

Ironically, as was the case with the triumphant Real Madrid football team of the time, this patriotic grandstanding was facilitated by the presence of foreign players: in this case the Portuguese Antonio Vilar as Don Juan and the French starlet Annabella as the English Lady Ontiveros. This is symptomatic of a film that 'attempts to have it both ways: that is, to draw on the pleasures of Hollywood spectacle while paying lip-service to Nationalist values' (Labanyi, 2003, p. 147). Spanish sensibilities may have been offended by foreign usurpation of a national myth but it was the character's stature abroad that made him so amenable to a cinematic makeover for:

> it is precisely Don Juan's internationalism that makes him such an important figure for an industry which was still hopeful of establishing a *niche* with films that would appeal in international markets as well as to compete with Hollywood in domestic spheres. Like a wayward prodigal son returning after a long journey through foreign lands, Don Juan is gathered back into the Spanish fold. (Wright, 2005, p. 416)

The importance of this international dimension is demonstrated by the fact that the distributor, Chapalo films, successfully used Don Juan's premieres in France and Italy as grounds to receive a dubbing license for foreign films. An internal report by the Ministry of National Education dated 8 November 1950 notes: 'Es indudable que nuestro "cine" está alcanzando éxitos sobresalientes, incluso fuera de España, gracias a la protección y ayuda oficial, y realizando temas tan importantes de nuestra historia y literatura' [It is undeniable that our 'cinema' is, even outside Spain, achieving outstanding successes with important subjects from our history and literature as a result of protectionist measures and official subsidies].[13] Pride was taken in the fact that it became the first Spanish film to compete at the Venice Film Festival since the end of World War Two, and this was taken as evidence that the tide of international opinion was at last turning in favour of Spain. This optimism then turned sour when the film failed to win any awards in what was assumed to be an anti-Spanish conspiracy (Gómez Tello, 1950).

Don Juan may have his origins in a dramatic work attributed to Tirso but he has taken on a mythical role without parallel in the *comedia*,[14] and has spawned a seemingly endless number of stage and screen adaptations that usually bear little if any resemblance to *El burlador de Sevilla*.[15] One advantage for a film-maker of a non-static myth is that it allows more scope for adaptation. In the opening credits Sáenz de Heredia claimed:

> Esta película no está ceñida a ninguna obra determinada de las muchas que han tratado la figura de Don Juan. Pretende ser una versión nueva del legendario burlador español, aunque en esta se hayan conservado de las otras, aquellos rasgos del personaje que más eficazmente lo definen. A Tirso de Molina que creó el personaje y a Don José Zorrilla que le dio la máxima popularidad dedicamos admirativa y reconocidamente nuestra intento.[16]
>
> [This film is not tied to any specific work among the many that have incorporated the figure of Don Juan. It aspires to be a new version of the legendary trickster of Seville although it has retained from its predecessors those character traits that best define him. The fruits of our efforts are dedicated, with a mixture of recognition and admiration, to Tirso de Molina who created the character and to Don José Zorrilla with whom he reached the height of his popularity.]

Beyond the character himself, the film does reveal some similarities with the play attributed to Tirso, especially when Don Juan seduces unsuspecting women who believe him to be their paramours. Equally, although his servant is called Ciutti as in Zorrilla's version, in terms of character he is closer to Catalinón from *El burlador*. However, the narrative is largely invented. The English Lady is a match for Don Juan in terms of both promiscuity and ingenuity. She is contrasted with Inés, a religious Spanish girl who, much to the dismay of the distraught and isolated foreign aristocrat, causes Don Juan to genuinely fall in love and repent prior to his death. The denouement, replete with a 'gallery of absorptive poses, a reification of Catholic imagery crystallised or petrified into position' (Wright, 2005, p. 430), is closer to the redemptive narratives of Tirso's *El condenado por desconfiado* or Calderón's *La devoción de la cruz* than *El burlador*.

The narrative's ostensible conservatism has led, once again, to the film being largely dismissed by modern Spanish critics as an aesthetically redundant and anachronistic piece of propaganda (e.g. Fernández, 2000, pp. 524–5).[17] It is, however, so excessive in every respect that it enabled me to thoroughly enjoy it as a camp melodrama. Furthermore, as Sarah Wright notes, 'at the end of the film we are left with the feeling that Don Juan's Christian rebirth has been tacked on, a hasty Catholic redemption after almost two hours of sexual shenanigans' (2005, p. 431). In a familiar pattern, the ending cannot simply annul the body of the film. The glamorous furs that drape both Vilar and Annabella are ostentatious and the unprecedented specularization of both stars is remarkably explicit; this is a likely explanation for the film's commercial success both at home and abroad (Labanyi, 2003, p. 151).

Don Juan would, however, prove to be a swansong and represents the end of an era. Films of this ilk would be classified alongside historical films, and the vogue for these came to an abrupt end with the spectacular commercial failure of *Alba de América* (Juan de Orduña, 1951) starring Rivelles as Isabel in a film about Columbus's adventures in the New World (Mira Nouselles, 1999).[18] Cinema may have remained a popular pastime in early 1950s Spain with over three hundred million cinema admissions per year being the norm (Vincendeau, 1995, p. 466), but the national film industry was in crisis and this led to calls for a radical change in direction.

The end of an era: recreating the *comedia* in the age of realism

As early as 1952, Eduardo Ducay had been complaining that historical films were becoming passé and made Spain look insular when the international tide was turning towards realism. This point was reiterated by José María García Escudero at the famous Salamanca talks (1954, p. 11), where Juan Antonio Bardem also spoke disparagingly about how Spanish cinema 'sigue siendo un cine de muñecas pintadas' [continues to be a cinema of painted dolls].[19]

It is at this crossroads that the next two *comedia* adaptations, *La moza de cántaro* (Florián Rey, 1952) and *El alcalde de Zalamea* (José G. Maesso, 1954), would be released. That they were still considered as potential hits is indicated by the fact they both opened at very high-status cinemas in Madrid: the former at the Gran Vía and the latter at the Roxy A.[20] Unfortunately, however, neither were artistic or commercial successes, and their failure in all likelihood served to discourage future adaptations.

La moza de cántaro's second screen outing was directed by arguably the most important Spanish film-maker of the silent era who had made the landmark *La aldea maldita* (1930). He had subsequently worked in Nazi Germany but then returned to Spain in an attempt to try and help rebuild the national cinema industry. However, by this stage he was already past his prime, and he specialized in *españoladas* that delighted in the kind of kitsch and sentimental images of Spain that Luis García Berlanga was to parody in *Bienvenido Mister Marshall* (1953).[21] In many respects, these films are the closest cinematic equivalents of José Tamayo's theatrical extravaganzas, and the emphasis on music and melodrama is such that *La moza de cántaro* has more in common with Ladislao Vajda's 1952 cinematic adaptation of the *zarzuela Doña Frasquita* – itself loosely based on Lope's *La discreta enamorada* – than it does with a standard literary adaptation.

The film had a relatively high budget for the time and, according to the producers, it had enjoyed critical and commercial success in Italy and Argentina prior to its domestic release. This fact was successfully used to argue that the censor's original category of interest level B ought to be elevated to level A.[22] In retrospect both the film's apparent success and high budget are surprising because, as a critic recalling the film in 1962 noted, 'pecaba de pobreza de medios y falta de ritmo eficaz, por lo que no obtuvo los resultados apetecibles' [it suffered from a lack of resources and a suitable rhythm; as a result it did not achieve the desired results] (Jiménez Smerdou, 1962, p. 12).

The star of the film was Paquita Rico, a singer by profession who was known together with Carmen Sevilla and Lola Flores as one of *Las Tres Marías*; in Terenci Moix's words she was 'el perejil de todas las salsas' [the icing on every cake] (1993, p. 21). Her celebrity status and appeal among lower-class audiences was seen to be crucial to the film's appeal. According to the trade magazine *Cine Asesor*:

> Atractivo el título de esta película, cuyo reparto encabeza una artista taquillera, como lo es Paquita Rico, el anuncio de este film despertará expectación y su estreno se esperará con interés, máxime si se exhibe antes algún traylers que, al recoger las canciones de la protagonista, aumentarán el deseo de verlo [*sic*]. (1954b)

> [With its appealing title and a cast headed by a box-office star such as Paquita Rico, the announcement of this film will generate expectation and its release will be anticipated with interest, especially if trailers featuring songs by the protagonist – which will increase the public's desire to see it – are screened in advance.]

The commentator qualifies these remarks by observing that 'la película en sí no es una obra de arte' [the film, in itself, is not a work of art], and it is difficult to disagree with this assessment. Lacking in any dramatic coherence or depth, the film is structured so as to allow Rico to burst into song with the flimsiest pretext. Her strong vocal chords are not, unfortunately, matched by acting skills. Rey eschews the more complex and dark aspects of Lope's play text that tells the story of Doña María who kills a man to defend her father's honour, and is then forced to disguise herself as a peasant girl, Isabel, to escape recriminations. For example, the sexual aggression María suffers when disguised as a servant is shrouded in risible farce.

Furthermore, the melodramatic aspects of the plot are exaggerated beyond any reasonable grounds of credulity. María/Isabel's beauty is such that the king, Philip IV, falls in love with her. He visits Isabel at night and says that when a king is in love, he wants to be thought of not as a monarch but as a suitor. Isabel then reveals her true noble identity and Philip says that her father was correct to have described her, earlier in the film, as 'la más bella flor de Andalucía' [Andalusia's most beautiful flower]. At this point, María/Isabel's suitor, Don Juan, crashes through the window intent on challenging the king. Once informed of his rival's true identity, however, Juan goes down on one knee and says how he loves María. Philip asks María if this love is reciprocated, and on hearing that it is, he graciously relinquishes his role as a suitor and judiciously acts as a king, saying that they will marry and that he will be the best man. This then provides the perfect opportunity for a celebratory and mawkish final wedding scene.

Not only was the film an artistic failure but it failed to live up to its commercial promise. According to the Filmoteca's admittedly not always reliable statistics, only one hundred and fifty-nine tickets were sold for this film with a total gross of twenty-five euros and seventy-four cents.[23] Even if this figure is not completely accurate, it is certain that the film's theatrical release in Madrid only lasted ten days (*Espectáculo*, 1954). Given this disastrous showing, it is perhaps not surprising that Rey would soon leave film-making to open a bar in Benidorm decorated in 'typical Spanish' style and aimed at tourists (Sánchez Vidal, 1991, p. 342), and that it would be nearly twenty years until Lope returned to the big screen.

CIFESA produced the next marginally more successful *comedia* adaptation, this time of Calderón's *El alcalde de Zalamea*. Jesús Saiz went to the Instituto de Investigaciones y Experiencias Cinematográficas [School of Cinematographic Theory and Practice] in 1950 and asked its director, Serrano de Osma, for his best student. As Maesso recalls:

> Y Serrano le dice que lo razonable en tal caso es que sea el número Uno salido de la Escuela el que pueda ser más adecuado, lo lógico es que sea el número Uno, y no lo dijo por mí, se atuvo a las calificaciones, en suma, se comportó formalmente. Y, de otra parte, yo creo que él pensó que ni Bardem ni Berlanga hubieran aceptado una obra clásica, que no tenía nada que ver con el neorrealismo que querían hacer a machamartillo. Y, bueno, a mí eso no me importaba nada, porque pensaba que si te ofrecían hacer una obra clásica, era cuestión de ponerse manos a la obra, tratar de sacar adelante el texto clásico y, por tanto, yo consideraba que se podía hacer. (cited in García de Dueñas, 2003, p. 196)

> [And Serrano said that the reasonable thing to do in a case such as this would be to choose the student with the highest mark, that this would be logical. He did not say it to favour me personally but rather went by the marks; all in all, he behaved in a formal manner. And, on the other hand, I don't think that he thought either Bardem or Berlanga would have accepted a classical play that had nothing to do with the neo-realism that they were so insistent on doing. And, well, this did not bother me at all because I thought that if one was offered a classical play, it was simply a question of getting

started, of trying to do something with the classical text and, as such, I thought that I could do it.]

Although willing to accept the commission, the director hardly seems enthused by the prospect of filming Calderón's play. The narrative, concerned with the complex interplay between duty, honour and interpersonal ties, focusses on the disruptive presence of soldiers billeted in a town. Captain Álvaro lodges with Pedro Crespo and his two children: Isabel and Juan. Although her father tries to hide her presence, the captain discovers Isabel and rapes her. Crespo subsequently begs him to marry her and restore the family honour; Álvaro refuses on the basis that they are peasants, and therefore his social inferiors. The dishonoured father is elected mayor of Zalamea, and he uses his authority to execute the captain. Don Lope is infuriated to hear that a local politician has garrotted one of the men under his military jurisdiction; he swears revenge, but softens on learning the full story and, more decisively, that the offending mayor is his friend.

Maesso's artistic freedom was, in reality, circumscribed within certain predefined limits. He could not alter the script that had been prepared by Manuel Tamayo and the studio had already cast the film with two of its biggest stars: Alfredo Mayo and Manuel Luna (2003, pp. 199, 203). The former, 'un mito estelar concebido desde y para el Régimen' [a mythical star conceived by and for the Regime] (Company Ramón, 1999, p. 178), was the lead in *Raza* and specialized in playing sexually attractive military heroes while the latter had begun his career in the theatre and subsequently specialized in playing villains for CIFESA. In *El alcalde*, they are interestingly cast against type as Mayo plays the captain and Luna is Pedro Crespo.

The film itself is unremarkable and a competent, albeit unadventurous, vision of Calderón's work. The visual style now appears terribly dated largely as a result of being almost exclusively shot in the studio. One exception was the scene where the king arrives on horseback, filmed in Franco's residence El Pardo. According to Maesso, the censors insisted that he extend this sequence by including a shot-reverse-shot when he had originally just filmed it through a single image (cited in García de Dueñas, 2003, pp. 200, 210–11). The dramatic tension is almost exclusively drawn from a Manichean dualism between the Edenic paradise of Zalamea and the disruptive force of Álvaro. The former is communicated with a series of hackneyed images: a gaggle of excitable but wholesome girls saying their prayers; and a folkloric singalong during a performance by the theatrical troupe. The latter is contrasted with the soldiers' drunken song that ends in a fight.

Although the script was written in prose, the actors delivered their lines, as they had done in *Fuente Ovejuna*, in a grandiose manner designed to foreground their stylized literary value. Ducay, who professed to be an admirer of Lope and Calderón, claimed from the pages of *Objectivo* (a new

Figure 9   Still from film of *El alcalde de Zalamea* (José G. Maesso, 1954)

radical film journal) that this approach ensured that cinematic adaptations were superficial and their modest results would discourage future productions:

> Lo que nunca es válido es la medianía, dar cal y arena. Reducir verso a prosa, intentando además que aquél suene en ocasiones, para que el espectador quede complacido ocasionalmente con tal o cual frase, tal o cual palabra o situación. En España esta solución ha sido a [*sic*] generalmente usada, con resultado monótonamente malo ... En estas cuestiones de cine de época, nuestro cine ha llegado a un amaneramiento altamente pernicioso. Todo se hace con arreglo a la misma fórmula, hay un vicio de producción, un tipo 'standard'. (1954)

> [What never works is the halfway house that is neither fish nor fowl. To reduce verse to prose but to retain it in parts so that the viewer is pleased from time to time with this or that phrase or situation. In Spain, this is the approach that has generally been taken with singularly bad results ... As far as period films are concerned, our cinema has reached a level of affectation that is highly detrimental. Everything is done according to the same formula; there is a vice in production, a kind of house style.]

Ducay rather overstates his case but his criticism is certainly valid in part. Nevertheless, as César Oliva notes in a fascinating article that examines different cinematic adaptations of the play to try and identify some characteristics of different acting styles, 'Luna es una sorpresa, pues consigue una verdad expresiva honda y profunda' [Luna is a surprise as he is able to achieve an intense and profound mode of expression] (2002b, p. 44).

The film received some good reviews from more traditional publications (e.g. P, 1954; J. B., 1954), but these voices were nowhere near as vociferous or voluminous as they had been for earlier productions of this kind.[24] Official endorsement was also singularly lacking and CIFESA's appeal to have the film's status raised to the category of National Interest was refused; the reason given was that, from the formal perspective, it lacked the requisite accomplishment.[25] The censor also objected to the scene where Isabel is raped in a barn; Maesso protested but agreed to only show the incident in an elliptic and fleeting manner so as to underplay the sexual dimension. The film was equally unpopular with audiences and its theatrical run only lasted for two weeks (*Cine Asesor*, 1954a). Maesso's film was to prove to be the last of a dying breed in a decade in which '[r]ealism would in fact gradually displace the historical cinema as the favoured vehicle for a national cinema' (Triana-Toribio, 2003, p. 57).

Given that we are at the end of the era, it is worth briefly recapitulating the chief characteristics of films based on the *comedia* in the early years of Francoism. Firstly, with the possible exception of Maesso, they were made by directors approved of by the regime and who made films that promoted a patriotic and essentialist image of national identity. Secondly, they starred popular lead actors whose success was, at least in part, derived from them representing specific qualities associated with being Spanish. Thirdly, verse was adapted into prose and the play texts were simplified in terms of both plot and diction. Fourthly, they refused to grapple with the darker edges of the play texts as is exemplified by the softening of both physical and sexual violence.[26] Fifthly, there is an attempt to remove any potential ambiguity from the denouement. This ruse is often achieved by affording an increased prominence to a monarch who is idealized to a far greater degree than in the source text.

The ones that got away

Ever since Arévalo failed in his attempt to bring *Fuente Ovejuna* to the big screen, there have been a sizeable number of *comedias* that have failed to be completed and/or shown in Spain. In 1945, when Spanish cinema in general was in crisis and CIFESA was experiencing financial difficulties, their chief rival, Suevia films, hoped to take advantage of the situation and thereby become the leading Spanish studio. Their head of operations,

Césareo González, announced four ambitious projects including an adaptation of *El burlador de Sevilla*. These films would never be made as the studio increasingly turned its attention towards other genres that it was hoped would secure a foothold in the international market (Castro de Paz, 2005, p. 54).

The same studio also received a shooting permit in 1948 to film a version of *El alcalde de Zalamea* directed by Eusebio F. Ardovia with the famous theatre actors Enrique Borrás and Rafael Calvo slated to take the lead roles.[27] This project never bore fruit, and neither was the play filmed by Pesca Films, based in Barcelona, who were also granted a license for Ricardo Gascón to make a version that was to star Rafael Calvo but not Borrás.[28] At the time of *Don Juan*'s release, magazines such as *Primer Plano* were filled with advertisements for CIFESA's upcoming version of *La vida es sueño* which never materialized.[29] This is likely the result of the fact that the studio was in buoyant health in 1950 but was in trouble in 1951 and, by 1952, was in crisis (Fanés, 1983, p. 211).

While these projects were probably thwarted by prosaic realities, the regime was also assaulted from all sides by deviant adaptations. The Spanish diaspora exiled in Central and South America staged a large number of Golden Age classics in the early post-war period. In addition, they were involved in three screen adaptations: *La dama duende* (Luis Saslavsky, 1945); *La viuda celosa* (Fernando Cortés, 1946) which was an adaptation of Lope's *La viuda valenciana* by Max Aub; and *El condenado por desconfiado* (Manuel Altolaguirre, 1955).[30]

The first of these films, based on a very free adaptation of Calderón's comedy and set in the eighteenth century, was by far the most successful from both a critical and commercial perspective. It was released in France, and was picked up for distribution in Spain by CIFESA (Emiliozzi, 2003, p. 81). In 1948, it was screened in Madrid as the Argentinean entry to a Hispanic Film Festival. It has, nevertheless, been described as 'una película leal, un arma de guerra contra Franco' [a loyal film, a weapon of war to be wielded against Franco] (Núbila, 1960, p. 54); it is not therefore surprising that it did not win any prizes, and that it was subsequently banned in Spain.[31]

In 1956 the East German production company Defa-Film released a German-language version of *El alcalde de Zalamea* entitled *Der Richter von Zalamea* (Martin Hellberg, 1956), that cut 90 per cent of the original text and focusses on the sexual relations between Álvaro and Isabel.[32] It seems unlikely that this film would have been approved by the censor or that it would have found an audience in Spain at the time; it is therefore not at all surprising that there is no record of any attempt being made to release the film in Calderón's native land.

It was not just the traditional 'enemies' of Spain that were not allowed to offer their vision of the classics to cinema-goers. Prior to making his neo-realist masterpiece *Surcos* (1952), awarded the National Interest prize in preference to *Alba de América* in a decision that García Escudero claims lost him his job (1995, p. 14), the Falangist José Antonio Nieves de Conde set out to direct a cinematic adaptation of *La Estrella de Sevilla*. An initial copy of the script adapted by Gonzalo Torrente Ballester submitted by Premator producers received a very negative appraisal; the majority of the censorship board advised prohibition citing, among other reasons, its democratic sentiments, anti-monarchical narrative and distasteful combination of humour and vile actions.[33] Considering that '[a]fter mid-1945 the Caudillo's only concerns with the Falange was to keep it quiet' (Payne, 1961, p. 242), the project's problems are most likely to be a result of antipathy felt towards the director than any genuine reservations over the *comedia*.

This is borne out in an incredible letter sent by Torrente to Don Gabriel García Espina (General Director of Theatre and Cinema). In his attempt to salvage the project, the writer clearly feels that Lope is his trump card. He complains that a certain Señor Grau who headed the board responsible for the decision was not even aware that he was dealing with a masterpiece of the Golden Age. On realizing his mistake, he apparently suggested the script be resubmitted and that he would make sure he was absent on the day that a decision was made. Torrente, not satisfied with this solution, says that he feels that it would be best to personally intervene:

> Hay muchas razones para que tome en este asunto el interés que me tomo. Tú, lo mismo que yo, habrás comprendido que una bagatela puede alcanzar importancia extremada. La Oficina Oficial de Censura <u>no puede</u> desautorizar el rodaje de una película basada en *La estrella de Sevilla*, que con razón o sin ella, está reputada como uno de nuestros mejores dramas históricos (véase Menéndez y Pelayo), que, con razón o sin ella, pasa por ser de Lope de Vega. Acaso los sacerdotes que han juzgado el guión ignorasen absolutamente estas circunstancias, y, por lo tanto, no previesen en que la prohibición de rodaje o el veto una vez hecha la película podía dar materia a una desagradable campaña contra nosotros en el extranjero. ¿Imaginas los titulares? 'La Censura de Franco prohíbe un drama de Lope de Vega'.[34]

> [There are many reasons why I take the interest that I have in this matter. You will have understood as well as I do that a silly trifle can blow up out of all proportion. The Official Censorship Office <u>cannot</u> prevent the shooting of a film based on *The Star of Seville* which, rightly or wrongly, is considered to be one of our best historical dramas (see Menéndez y Pelayo) and, rightly or wrongly, is attributed to Lope de Vega. Perhaps the priests who judged the script were completely unaware of these circumstances and thus did not take into account that the prohibition of the shooting of the film or a ban once it has been made could lead to an unpleasant campaign against us abroad. Can you imagine the headlines? 'Franco's censors ban one of Lope de Vega's dramas'.]

With a combination of nepotism and corruption that was hardly unknown in the censorship department, Torrente suggests that if a shooting permit were to be provided, then 'la casa "Mercurio films" (como sabes, la Paramount camuflada)' [the firm 'Mercurio films' (as you know, Paramount in disguise)] would take charge of the production. He then apologizes to 'querido Gabriel' [my dear Gabriel] that, for the first time, 'me haya convertido en un pelmazo' [I have become a pain in the neck]. Either his own and/or Lope's clout was not as strong as Torrente had hoped, for the project never went ahead; not surprisingly its prohibition failed to make the front pages of foreign newspapers.

El príncipe encadenado [*The Prince in Chains*] (Luis Lucia, 1960)

The next *comedia* film adaptation was a very free adaptation in prose of *La vida es sueño* shot in Technicolor by a director, Luis Lucia, who was famous for having discovered child stars such as Rocío Dúrcal and Marisol and specialized in melodrama and musicals.[35] Lucía has cited it as his best film although it perhaps ought to be borne in mind that this claim was made when he thought that it had been lost forever (Generalitat Valenciana and Filmoteca Valenciana, 1986); copies have subsequently been recovered.

Calderón's play's is a philosophically dense meditation on human nature and the limits of free will. A royal father, Basilio, locks away his son from birth as a result of a tragic prophecy in which his tyrannical offspring makes him kneel before him. Basilio subsequently repents and decides to release his son to provide him with an opportunity to prove himself; Segismundo acts as a tyrant and is returned to his prison tower where he is told that his experiences in the outside world were but a dream. The play is largely about Segismundo learning to become a man through both reason and the love of beauty, which he begins to appreciate when Rosaura stumbles upon the secluded tower in which he is imprisoned. A rebel soldier subsequently raises an army to release the royal prisoner and wage a war against his father. Basilio is defeated but his son subsequently bows down before him and relinquishes his power, which his father subsequently returns to him.

As the title of the film suggests, it bears little relation to the play on which it is ostensibly based but it does retain certain narrative strands. Set in Poland, but filmed in Cuenca, it works best as an entertaining historical romp. Burmann once again designed the sets but the production values, shortness of Rosaura's skirt and Javier Escrivá's dyed blonde hair which earned the film the moniker *El príncipe oxigenado* [*The Peroxide Prince*] (García de Dueñas, 2003, p. 191), immediately plunges the viewer into an alternative visual universe from earlier adaptations. The film clearly has an eye on the international market and, perhaps understandably for an aspiring blockbuster, Lucia alters the original so as to turn it into both an action film and melodrama whose narrative is clearly built around a series of grand battle scenes.

Figure 10   Still from film of *El príncipe encadenado* [The Prince in Chains] (Luis Lucia, 1960)

The film opens around Segismundo's tower where soldiers arrive in a village in search of a wild horse. They are warned by the local villagers, who are dressed in primitive garb, that evil spirits haunt what they call *el valle de la muerte* [the valley of death] from which they claim nobody returns alive. The first soldier who enters is struck down dead and the camera cuts to a sniper with a crossbow and spears assaulting the trespassers. There is then a flashback to the king and queen of Poland celebrating their victory; the euphoric atmosphere is deflated however by her having a negative premonition about her unborn son. Astrologers interpret the dream and, in the next scene, we see the king holding his infant son while he is informed of his wife's death. The young Segismundo is then shown being taken off by Clotaldo on a white horse.

On his initial release, Segismundo's first action is to free all of his fellow prisoners, which prompts an argument with the king in which Rosaura verbally attacks Basilio for his parental mistreatment. The young couple are forced to flee the palace and, in their wanderings, they chance upon a family and he says how his dream is to have one with her; she rebuts his offer claiming that he has a destiny to follow. They subsequently join forces with the savages seen at the beginning of the film who live in the forests that surround his former prison. Basilio comes forward and asks Segismundo to return to the palace. His son refuses and even throws a sphere defiantly at his father but Basilio is eventually able to convince him by saying that if he remains a fugitive then he will have to renounce everything including Rosaura. Segismundo's desire to become a family man proves to be his downfall as he is drugged and returned to the tower.

He is taken prisoner, but Rosaura is able to round up an army constituted of the prisoners that he earlier released. The film's climax is provided by an extended battle sequence filmed with a mixture of medium close-ups and panoramic views designed to showcase both the mass spectacle and the dustbowl setting that is more reminiscent of a spaghetti western than Poland. Segismundo wins this battle and his father comes in front of him and kneels down before him. They are reconciled and the final shot is of Segismundo and Rosaura, replete with her ubiquitous miniskirt and helmet, standing together at the peak of a mountain.

El príncipe encadenado opened on 20 December 1960 with the tagline 'una joya de la literatura española convertida en auténtica joya del séptimo arte' [a jewel of Spanish literature now turned into a genuine jewel of the silver screen]. *Primer Plano* were predictably over-optimistic in their bullish boasts that 'esta producción que honra el cine español ... ha de encontrar mercados fáciles fuera de nuestras fronteras' [this production that honours Spanish cinema ... should easily find a place in markets beyond our frontiers] (J. S. R., 1960). The film nevertheless proved to be a sizeable box-office hit over the festive season in the domestic market; unlike in the US and elsewhere in Europe, cinema attendance in Spain was not in decline at the beginning of the new decade (Camporesi, 1994, p. 70).[36]

It was also critically well received, and went on to win a series of awards. These included the highest accolades from the *Revista internacional del cine* and the Círculo de Escritores Cinematográficos [Circle of Film Critics] in the category of best Spanish film; it also won the National Prize for cinema.[37] Nevertheless, some critics questioned the decision to film a Golden Age play at the dawn of a new decade and Calderón's name was no longer seen as advantageous. In a generally positive review, José A. Pruneda noted:

> Que el film tiene defectos es casi obvio, dada su naturaleza. El mayor, seguramente, radica en la misma obra teatral; esto es, en pensar si el *El príncipe encadenado* es el tipo de cine que la España de 1960 merece; pero salvando esto, que a mi parecer es perfectamente salvable, la película peca

de cierta grandiosidad barroca y de cierta pobreza narrativa en alguna de las escenas de masas. (1961)

[That the film has its defects is almost inevitable given its very nature. The greatest stems from the play itself; that is to say, in thinking *The Prince in Chains* is the type of cinema that Spain deserves in 1960. But even if this is salvageable, as I think it is, the film suffers from a certain baroque grandeur and narrative paucity in some of the crowd scenes.]

The fact that the film is anomalous in terms of both *comedia* adaptations and Spanish national cinemas helps explains why *El príncipe encadenado*, despite its success, has been almost completely forgotten both in Spain and abroad. It is only ever shown on Spanish television in graveyard slots – it was most recently broadcast at 0.45 on Canal Nostalgia on 30 May 1999 – and it does not, for example, warrant even one single mention in Sally Faulkner's monograph on Spanish cinema of the 1960s (2006). Given the climate of the time and the general move away from Golden Age drama, it is perhaps not surprising that there would be no more cinematic *comedia* adaptations made in Spain during the remainder of the decade.

The *comedia* in Spanish homes: television and Golden Age drama

Although Lope, Tirso and Calderón may have been absent from the big screen, they found a new home in the small screen that would, over the course of the decade, cease to be a luxury item; 'only one per cent of Spaniards had TV sets in 1960, by 1970 the TV audience embraced 90 per cent of the nation' (Carr, 1980, p. 162). It is beyond the remit of this study to discuss these adaptations in detail but a brief overview is required in order to place in context two productions released for the cinema in the early 1970s.[38]

Throughout the 1960s, two theatre slots (Gran Teatro and Estudio 1) provided a forum for filmed *comedias*. Both were very popular and the latter, created by Juan Guerrero Zamora, ran for fifteen years and, at its peak, had a remarkable audience of 7,364,000 viewers (Suárez Miramón, 2002, pp. 575–6). The productions have not, admittedly, aged well. TVE have recently released both *Don Gil de las calzas verdes* and *Peribáñez* on DVD. They feature very basic sets that are, in many cases, clearly made out of cardboard and they have been heavily edited so that they run for just over an hour and the soliloquies in the latter are rather ridiculously done as voice-overs.

The inauguration of Teatro de siempre in 1967 came about after Manuel Fraga visited the corral in Almagro; he immediately contacted Salvador Pons (director of TVE2) and asked him to devise a programme that could showcase this unique venue thereby providing the *comedia* with a more hospitable abode. As noted in the first chapter, in its second season in 1968 it featured a series of productions filmed in the Almagro corral: *El rufián castrucho*, *La dama duende*, *La villana de Getafe* and *El gran teatro del mundo*. According to Andrés Peláez Martín, '[e]l éxito de estas grabaciones fue tan extraordinario que desde algunas tribunas públicas se pidió que debía ser la primera cadena de TVE la encargada de dar a conocer este teatro a toda España' [the success of these recordings was so extraordinary that some public forums called for the state broadcaster's first channel to take charge of disseminating this theatre to the whole of Spain] (1997, pp. 22–3).

Although this unique form of televised evangelism would never take place, the *comedia* did continue to be broadcast. Josefina Molina, a renowned film-maker, directed a version of Lope's virtually unknown *La prudente venganza* that was transmitted in 1970. As Manuel Palacio notes, projects of this kind were 'verdaderas experiencias innovadoras e insólitas como nunca se han visto en toda la historia de la televisión en España' [genuinely innovative and unusual experiences that have never been seen at any other stage in the history of Spanish television] (2005, p. 127). It is within this context that we must understand the next two cinematic adaptations of the *comedia* that were produced by TVE primarily for television but also granted theatrical releases: *Fuente Ovejuna* (Juan Guerrero Zamora, 1972) and *La leyenda del alcalde de Zalamea* [*The Legend of the Mayor of Zalamea*] (Mario Camus, 1973).

Guerrero Zamora's credentials were, in theory, impeccable: he founded Estudio 1, had directed an hour-long version of *Fuente Ovejuna* for Lope's centenary and many other Spanish and foreign classics for the small screen.[39] Television audiences had also had the opportunity to watch *Fuente Ovejuna* more recently as Teatro de siempre transmitted a version in 1967 directed by Vicente Llosa (Suárez Miramón, 2002, p. 586). However, Guerrero Zamora distanced himself from earlier small-screen versions by claiming a political motive for making the film: 'propuse "*Fuenteovejuna*". ¿Por qué? Implicaba una gran trascendencia social su contenido, que además no suelen tener las obras clásicas' [I suggested *Fuenteovejuna*. Why? Because its content is of great social significance and, furthermore, this is not typical of classic works] (cited in Caravajal, 1972).

Fuente Ovejuna performed respectably at the box office but was markedly less successful in other respects. It is too long, and, in sharp contrast to Román's film, not only refuses to eschew violence but clumsily foregrounds even the most latent hint of aggression in Lope's play text. For example, there are extended torture scenes and we see the Comendador rape three women: María, Marcela and Manuela.[40] The censors objected to the film claiming that it betrayed both Lope and Spanish history: 'no solamente no era fiel al espíritu de la tragedia de Lope de Vega, sino que deformaba ésta, ambientando la acción de una forma inadecuada al interés histórico-político, acentuando tintes rayanos con la leyenda negra española' [in addition to being unfaithful to the spirit of Lope de Vega's tragedy, it also deforms it, locating the action in a setting that ill-serves our political and historical interests, exaggerating as it does certain aspects to the extent that they verge on the black legend surrounding Spain's past].[41] The censor ordered some substantial cuts which, following lengthy negotiations, the producers accepted much to the chagrin of Guerrero Zamora who was sufficiently offended that he did not attend the film's premiere.

In line with the director's avowed aim, the film focusses on the social and psychic effects of a community ruled by fear. Unfortunately, however, it is for once difficult to disagree with the censor's assessment; any political motivation is undermined by aesthetic shortcomings characterized by one representative critic as 'mera falta de oficio cinematográfico' [a basic lack of cinematic competence] (Sánchez, 1972). The use of verse in film was a constant source of consternation with, for example, the reviewer from *Cineinforme* noting how the film compares unfavourably with Román's earlier version because:

> aquella producción, con todos los defectos de la época, hay que reconocer que era más 'cine' que ésta de ahora. Guerrero Zamora se ha limitado a hacer teatro, y para que nada le falte se le ha dejado incluso el verso, con todo lo anticinematográfico que el verso resulta. (A. F., 1972)

> [we have to recognize that that film, with all the defects of the age, was more 'cinematic' than this present one. Guerrero Zamora has simply made canned theatre and, to make sure that nothing is left out, he has even retained verse whose effect is quintessentially anti-cinematic.]

Subsequent adaptations would prove that verse is not a priori anti-cinematic and the problem is not in its inclusion but rather in its application. In this case, it ruthlessly exposes the limitations of most of the cast while technical ineptitude prevents the director from applying restraint to the risible theatrics on display. This is evident, for example, at the end when we cut from seeing the Comendador's corpse being paraded as if it were a roasted pig by the villagers to a bloody Flores informing the Catholic Monarchs with a grandiose delivery straight out of Román's film about what has taken place. The camera registers his bloody appearance in a series of close-ups that, for no apparent reason, focus on different fragmented parts of his face. At the end of his speech, he passes out and an obviously dubbed Ferdinand responds in a wooden and unemotional manner.

Fortunately, *La leyenda del alcalde de Zalamea* was a far more successful outing. In fact, if we accept, as I think we must, that film 'with its own codes, both cinematic and non-cinematic, may be regarded not as a violation but as a "selective interpretation" of the original' (Evans, 1997, p. 2), then it is arguably the most accomplished *comedia* adaptation ever made. In contrast to earlier productions, it emerged from the progressive end of the Spanish political system and for example has been described by Smith as 'a family drama turning on the rape of a daughter' that 'shows how even conservative classics were open to discreet redirection in the allegorical mode by an oppositional director' (1996, p. 26).

Camus would in the early 1980s become a household name in Spain with a series of high-profile literary adaptations including *La colmena* (1982) and *Los santos inocentes* (1984). The Cantabrian film-maker began his career as a screenwriter for Saura on *Los golfos* (1959) and *Llanto por un bandido* (1963). His directorial debut, *Los farsantes* (1963), is a social realist depiction of a troupe of impoverished actors whose largely commercially unsuccessful repertoire includes Golden Age plays and, by the early 1970s, Camus had a reputation as a serious and left-wing film-maker. As Pedro Crespo he cast Francisco Rabal, who had made his name in José Tamayo's company in the 1950s but had gone on to work with Luis Buñuel and was a vocal opponent of the regime. Fernando Fernán-Gómez who had directed and/or starred in a number of films associated with the Nuevo Cine Español [New Spanish Cinema] played Don Lope.

The project was inadvertently an offshoot of *Fuente Ovejuna*; Mario Arosio, a producer from the Italian state television channel RAI, had already bought the rights to screen Guerrero Zamora's film and was interested in producing another Spanish classic. He then contacted Pons at TVE who in turn commissioned Antonio Drove as screenwriter and Camus as director with a sizeable budget of seventeen million pesetas (Frugone, 1984, p. 107). The latter claims that Spanish cinema was in crisis and that the market was generally controlled by the distributors much to cinema's detriment: 'Por eso acepté trabajar para TVE ... Como tal organismo solvente y con una producción prolongada, es la única firma que puede enfrentarse con una cierta garantía con el mundo de cine' [This was why I agreed to work for TVE ... As a solvent entity with continual production, it is the only signature that guarantees anything in the world of cinema] (cited in Castro, 1974, p. 113).

Drove had previously reworked *comedias* by Calderón such as *La devoción de la cruz* into police stories. He claims that his respect for the playwright and for the film-maker Douglas Sirk, who had written of his admiration for *El alcalde de Zalamea*, resulted in an anxiety of influence (1995, p. 41). This was only relieved when the screenwriter pinned two notes onto his wall: 'Calderón de la Barca es mucho mejor escritor que yo, pero yo sé un poco más de cine que Calderón'; 'Sirk sabe mucho más que yo de cine pero el que tiene que escribir este guión soy yo' [Calderón de la Barca is a much better writer than me, but I know a little more about cinema than Calderón; Sirk knows much more about cinema than I do, but I am the one who has to write this script] (pp. 74, 75). He then proceeded to write the first page of the first draft.

His is a very free adaptation that owes at least as much to the play attributed to Lope as it does to the more canonical version by Calderón.[42] Hence, Crespo makes frequent references to his recently deceased wife and he has three daughters: Isabel, Leonor and Inés. The latter two, as in Lope's version, willingly have sexual relations with the captains in the belief that they will marry them while the former, as in Calderón's version, is a paragon of virtue who is abducted and raped.

A doctoral thesis on literary adaptations directed by the Spanish filmmaker – sometimes referred to as the 'Richard Brooks español' [the Spanish Richard Brooks] (Portalo, 2002) – concludes: 'lo que nos parece más destacable de esta pasión del cineasta Mario Camus por la novela y por la novela realista en particular es su afán de centrar siempre a un personaje en su ambiente natural' [what emerges most clearly from the film-maker Mario Camus's passion for the novel and the realist novel in particular is his desire to always situate a character in their natural surroundings] (Martínez Aguinagalde, 1996, p. 669). This same emphasis is evident in this formally intricate *comedia* adaptation by Drove that undertakes an interrogation of masculinity through its focus on Pedro Crespo and his relationship with his family, community and home town.

In terms of both theme and aesthetic, *La leyenda* could almost be classified as a western with its focus on male pride, homosocial relationships and the use of a small community under threat as a metaphor for national concerns.[43] The film was shot in a village outside Cáceres and the barren landscape – often registered through a series of impressive long shots that, ironically for a film designed for television, can only be fully appreciated on the big screen – resembles the cinematic Almería on display in many of the spaghetti westerns of the 1960s. Equally, the soundtrack by Antón García Abril, which Camus regretted with hindsight (Frugone, 1984, p. 109), was designed to outdo Ennio Morricone who had written the iconic theme tune to *The Good, the Bad and the Ugly* (Sergio Leone, 1966).

This tone and register and the independence from the *comedia* is established in the captivating opening sequence. Don Lope rides into town on horseback and, in a scene that anticipates the famous opening of *El crimen de Cuenca* (Pilar Miró, 1980), a blind troubadour who will reappear throughout the film both as a narrator and character recites the conflict between Pedro Crespo and Lope in the form of a *romance de ciego* [ballad of the blind].[44] In a synaesthetic display of force, soldiers beating drums are then shown in a series of long shots which reveal the vast landscape surrounding the town; their advance is only halted with the arrival of the king. At this point the blind man quickly summarizes the story before the camera cuts to the beginning of the narrative that will subsequently be unravelled in a predominantly linear form.

As noted, the film is largely a character study and Drove notes how 'intenté hacer de Pedro Crespo un personaje más contradictorio y conflictivo que el de Calderón, aunque traté de conservar, al mismo tiempo, la enorme fuerza y la dimensión gigantesca que tiene' [I endeavoured to make Pedro Crespo a more contradictory and argumentative character than in Calderón although, at the same time, I tried to retain his tremendous force and gravitas] (cited in Marías, 1975, p. 24). The film resembles a western in that it is about a man's individualistic rights to defend his land, property and family. In terms of his attitude to an inexorable code of honour, Francisco Rabal's performance is reminiscent of John Wayne's performance as Ethan Edwards in *The Searchers* (John Ford, 1956).

This code may ostensibly be designed to protect families and communities but it also comes at a terrible cost. In the course of the film, Crespo is on the verge of slaying three of his children: Leonor, Inés and Juan. On discovering his two daughters exchanging letters with two captains, he vows to kill them; they are only saved by Lope's timely intervention. He orders Juan to be sent to prison for acts of vigilantism (drawing a sword against the captain and attempting to kill his sister). Although he might, he claims, have pardoned another individual for a similar offence, he argues that he cannot in this case because he would be seen to act as a father not as a mayor. Lope once again takes on the role of the mediator and says that Juan, as a soldier, falls under military jurisdiction; he will therefore take responsibility for his punishment.

As suggested by his actions, Fernán-Gómez plays Don Lope as an equally proud but more benign patriarch. When he first appears and approaches the prison to rescue the captains, the script specifies that, 'flameado por las antorchas y el humo parece un viejo ángel justiciero' [illuminated by flame torches and smoke, he takes on the appearance of an Old Testament angel bent on a quest for justice] (Drove, 1972, p. 3). Although he cuts an impressive physical figure on horseback, he subsequently limps and complains incessantly about his leg, which was wounded in Flanders. He adopts an avuncular role to both Juan and Isabel, regaling the latter with jewels. There is clearly a warm relationship between him and Pedro, and the film is rather over-sentimental in their initial farewell where they embrace while very melodramatic music is played on the soundtrack.

A clear distinction is drawn between the two soldiers who seduce the wayward daughters and Isabel's assailant. This was a deliberate ploy by Drove who sought to avoid a Manichean narrative by 'dejando su aspecto menos caballeroso y más tramposo al sargento que le acompaña, y su aspecto más golfante a los otros dos capitanes' [transferring his less gentlemanly and more deceitful side to the sergeant who accompanies him, and his more loutish side to the other two captains]. In other words, he claims, 'intenté darle la máxima dignidad posible' [I tried to imbue him with the maximum possible dignity] (cited in Marías, 1975, p. 24). This prominence is manifested for example in the visualization of him being garrotted, which is shown in silhouette.

Quite apart from the ethical issues raised by presenting a rapist in a positive light, no such subtlety of characterization is afforded the female characters. Inés and Leonor are, from the outset, depicted as two frisky and impetuous cauldrons of pent-up eroticism while Isabel, the best looking of the three,[45] is chaste and obedient. When she discovers that her sisters have eloped with the soldiers, she runs into her father's arms and talks tearfully of how they have been 'deshonradas y por su gusto' [dishonoured and by choice]. These differences are further foregrounded in the film's central action sequence. The camera shows Inés and Leonor in a state of post-coital bliss trying to embrace their respective beaus but they are violently pushed away. Pedro, who is searching for the recently abducted Isabel, sees the two captains and charges at them. The camera then cuts to dawn, where we see Isabel running over a mountain. She sees Pedro tied to a tree and she cuts him loose; he says 'Vamos a casa. ¡Qué nadie nos vea!' [Let's go home. Where nobody will be able to see us!]. As they reach Zalamea, he is leading the horse with her sitting upon it. She has her head down and cannot meet any of the villagers' eyes. He instructs her to go to her room and informs her that as the offence was public, so too will the vengeance be.

Isabel, played by Rabal's real-life daughter Teresa, is pliant and obedient; she construes her honour and will only in terms of her father. At the denouement, Pedro sends his two other daughters off to be nuns; when they are left alone, she asks him '¿Qué ha de ser de mi?' [What will become of me?]. Her father answers that he is old and does not want to be left alone so she will look after him; this is clearly construed as a 'happy ending' yet no genuine consideration of what she might have wanted is explored. This western may be about individual human rights and dignity but these are clearly coded as male.

Both Camus and Drove anticipated criticism and controversy from Spanish reviewers due to the fact that their version deviated so heavily from the original play texts (Castro, 1974, p. 118; Marías, 1975, p. 24). Nevertheless, the film was generally well received and Drove was amused by the reaction to his attempts to ward off criticisms of betraying Calderón by referencing Lope: 'casi nadie se dió cuenta de mi maniobra, llegando algún crítico muy serio a hablar de "la donosura del estilo de Lope de Vega" en escenas que había inventado yo por complete' [hardly anybody realized what I had done, with one critic even speaking very earnestly of 'Lope de Vega's elegant style' in scenes that were completely of my own invention] (cited in Marías, 1975, p. 24). He goes on to note that foreign critics advanced a more intelligent debate. *La leyenda* was the first TVE production ever to be broadcast on French television and Italy's RAI, and it was very well received (Sánchez Noriega, 1998, p. 165). It also had a relatively successful theatrical release in Spain which came as a surprise to Camus: 'Lo hice para televisión y no pensé que pudiera tener el éxito que está teniendo' [I did it for television, and it never occurred to me that it would be so successful] (cited in Santos, 1973).

With radically different results, the two film and television adaptations of *comedias* made by TVE in the early 1970s both mark a significant change in direction from earlier screen adaptations. Directors with an oppositional political agenda self-consciously divert from the play texts on which they are based often to focus on the darker and more violent aspects that resist neat dramatic closure. Related to this is the renewed emphasis on sexual and political violence that is not rejected or resolved unproblematically by the presence of an actor and/or character seen to embody the essential virtues of the Spanish character. Especially in the case of *La leyenda*, the film showed that, in the right hands, *comedia* adaptations could, at least on the small screen, find an international audience. This should have provided an important precedent but unfortunately the relations between TVE and cinema were still rather sporadic and lacked a clear infrastructure or direction and so it was not to be (Torreiro, 1995, p. 374).

El mejor alcalde, el rey (Rafael Gil, 1973)

This Spanish-Italian co-production starring Italian actress Simonetta Stefanelli based on a script in prose by José López Rubio, a previous recipient of the National Prize for Theatre, is a product of its time that also casts its glance back to more traditional adaptations. Despite a decent output, national cinema was in crisis and reliant on subsidies in the early 1970s. This led to a vogue for co-production that had clear advantages considering the precarious state of the national film industry: primarily, shared costs and common markets (Utrera Macías, 2002, p. 81).

Gil is often dismissed on political grounds in Spain where he is seen to be a quintessential Francoist film-maker.[46] In the early 1970s, he had already made films based on texts by a broad spectrum of writers including Unamuno, Galdós and Azorín. Nevertheless, to a certain extent his version of *El mejor alcalde* also anticipates a general trend towards adapting medieval and Golden Age texts during the 1970s for non-literary reasons: '[t]odos estos trabajos trataron de aprovecharse de la carga erótica de las narraciones, para resaltarla y convertirla en el principal atractivo de las películas' [all of these works tried to appropriate and maximize the erotic charge of the narratives in order to turn them into the films' major selling point] (Navarrete-Galiano, 1999, p. 83).[47]

Gil also offered a political and artistic motive for making the film: 'Es el tema social que refleja la obra de Lope. Es un alegato sobre la justicia, el poder de unas clases, el sometimiento de otras en un mundo más próximo a nosotros' [It is the social aspect that is reflected in Lope's play. It is a paean to justice, about the power of some classes and the subjugation of others in a world that is very close to our own] (cited in Rubio Gil and Gil, 1998, p. 237). In Lope's play text, Élvira is abducted by her overlord Tello on her wedding day. Her jilted fiancé Sancho appeals to the king, who brings justice by executing the lascivious noble – who has subsequently raped the young bride – thereby allowing the young couple to marry.

In line with the trend of other Spanish literary adaptations of the time, and in contrast to adaptations of the *comedia* from the 1940s and 1950s, *El mejor alcalde* foregrounds the sexual and violent aspects. The film was classified as being suitable only for patrons over the age of eighteen, or over the age of fourteen if accompanied by an adult. This restrictive rating was at odds with the principles that underpinned these projects as attempts to increase awareness and knowledge of Spain's cultural patrimony; as one of the censors wrote in his report on *El mejor alcalde,* 'aunque hubiese sido mi deseo darla para 14 y menores' [though I would have liked to classify the film as suitable for 14 and under], this proved impossible 'dado que está hecho de manera bastante tosca y la personalidad del Conde es tan bárbara y cruel' [given that it is shot in a rather crude tone and the count's character is so barbaric and cruel].[48]

Gil's film is visually reminiscent of Roman Polanski's controversial film adaptation of *Macbeth* (1971) which had recently enjoyed great success in Spain. Tello's castle is presented as a decadent den of iniquity, and his moral depravity is indicated through his grotesque and uncontrolled carnality. Early on, there is a cut from an idyllic village scene to a banquet of Bacchanalian excess where Tello unceremoniously gorges on food and drink; later on, the camera lingers on the greasy and fleshy contours of his body as he washes. An incestuous subtext is introduced between Tello and his sister, Feliciana, who also shows a sexual interest in Sancho. While Tello lusts after Élvira, he gives Felicana permission to have sex with Sancho who is, at the time, being tortured. Following some explicit torture scenes, a subplot, not present in the play text, is introduced where Feliciana comes to Sancho's rescue and rather fetishistically tends his wounds. She then goes to kiss him, but is sharply rebuked as Sancho strangles her. The scene where Élvira is violated is also depicted in graphic detail as, although the camera cuts away before the actual rape can take place, there is a long scene where we see Tello ripping off her clothes and then reporting to his sister: 'No me importa que llore. Estoy acostumbrado' [It doesn't bother me that she cries. I'm used to it].

The film was generally well received by critics who commended López Rubio's adaptation for 'la actualización de los diálogos, de los que se ha eliminado el empaque literario' [the modernization of the dialogue, from which all literary excess has been shed] (Sánchez, 1974) while also praising 'la corrección en la factura técnica de un veterano y equilibrado profesional que conoce muy bien su oficio' [the technical prowess of a veteran and well-grounded professional who knows his trade very well] (Soria, 1974). Lorenzo López Sancho was even more enthusiastic in his appraisal: 'Hay un cine histórico en el que es positivo unir, como lo hace Rafael Gil, la evocación de una época y de un arte con la belleza viva de una peripecia humana que resiste por su propia fuerza a la erosión de los siglos' [There is a type of historical cinema in which it is a good thing to combine, as does Rafael Gil, the evocation of a period and its art with the vibrant beauty that bears testament to changes in human circumstances but, by virtue of its own vitality, resists the erosion of the centuries] (1974). Despite her praise for the film, Ángeles Maso nevertheless lamented:

> Esta producción hispano-italiana, está sin duda destinada a interesar más en el extranjero que en España. Porque más allá de nuestras fronteras, saborean mejor las esencias de la España del Siglo de Oro. Ejemplo: los elogios que la prensa extranjera dedicó a la última adaptación de *El alcalde de Zalamea*, cinta que pasó aquí casi inadvertida. (1974)

> [This co-production between Spain and Italy is undoubtedly destined to be received with more interest abroad than in Spain. This is because they better appreciate the essence of Spain's Golden Age beyond our frontiers. An example: the praise bestowed on the latest adaptation of *The Mayor of Zalamea* abroad, a film that went almost unnoticed here.]

Her prognostications were to prove correct and the film, although not a disaster at the box office, failed to win any major prizes and was less commercially successful than the producers had hoped. It was no coincidence that the director's next two films would be modern-day literary adaptations (Rubio Gil and Gil, 1998, p. 101). The time was not necessarily ripe for *comedia* adaptations and in any case, as the regime entered its final throes, Lope was perhaps not in need of patronage from a figure so closely associated with Francoism.

A conspicuous presence and/or an inconspicuous absence: the *comedia* and Spanish cinema in the democratic period

After *El mejor alcalde, el rey*, it would be over twenty years before another director made a film based on one of Lope's plays. In fact, in the interim

Spain did not produce a single film based on the *comedia*. This was largely a consequence of the fact that, in the transition period, Golden Age drama was often construed as a reactionary art form that had enjoyed special treatment under Franco. Nevertheless, the absence of traditional adaptations did not imply that seventeenth-century dramatists were not present, at least in spirit, in the cinema of the time.

Carlos Saura appears to draw on *La vida es sueño* and *El gran teatro del mundo* as an inspiration in *El jardín de las delicias* (1970) and *Ana y los lobos* (1973) respectively. Subsequently, in *Elisa, vida mía* (1977), the director made the allusions clearer by including a scene of the father teaching *El gran teatro del mundo* in a convent school. Marvin D'Lugo construes this as the strategy of an oppositional film-maker rejecting old Spain (1991, pp. 146, 228). Saura himself has, however, refuted this interpretation and his explanation is far more straightforward: 'The truth is that if the film refers to this work, it's because I find it truly marvellous. I always tend to use things in my films which I find pleasing without worrying too much about whether they are necessary or appropriate' (cited in Willem, 2003, p. 48).

Saura was seemingly, however, in the minority in film circles. Spanish cinema was in crisis for much of the late 1970s and its most successful commercial output was largely *destape* movies. There nevertheless existed a strong desire for a new kind of national cinema that, as in the 1940s, would present an image of a spiritually regenerated Spain in domestic and foreign markets:

> Among the liberal middle classes it was popularly held that the cinema industry had to be helped because the new democratic Spain needed a new democratic national cinema which would announce and explain to the world at large the death of the old Spain and bring the nation together. This cinema was expected to emerge as soon as the crisis was overcome. (Triana-Toribio, 2003, p. 109)

Although this new cinema would largely be based on literary texts, the *comedia* would not be among them. Beyond any antipathy possibly felt towards Calderón, Tirso or Lope, this is also undoubtedly the result of a 'very culture-specific need to recuperate a past which for forty years had been hijacked and aggressively refashioned by Francoism' (Jordan and Morgan-Tamosunas, 1998, p. 16). Hence the dominant majority of texts adapted for the cinema revealed 'la voluntad de recuperación histórica' [the desire for historical recuperation]; over half the films produced in the transition period were set between 1931 and 1977 (Monterde, 1989, pp. 47, 56).

This tendency would be further accentuated with the ascension of the PSOE to power and the appointment of film-maker Pilar Miró to the role of Director-General of Film. She passed the controversial Miró Law, which focussed state investment on a small number of 'quality' films in the early 1980s; although it did arguably improve the standard of cinema in Spain, the system generally failed to deliver films that appealed to the public and was rife with nepotism.[49]

Not surprisingly in this climate, both the *comedia* and Spain's imperial past were of little interest on the big screen; following the Socialist victory, Golden Age drama also disappeared from state television (Suárez Miramón, 2002, pp. 582–3). In fact, Spain's once glorious past now only appeared as the object of ridicule in adolescent, albeit entertaining, comedies such as *Cristobal Colón, . . . de oficio descubridor* (1982), *Juana la loca . . . de vez en cuando* (1983) and *El Cid Cabreador* (1983).[50]

Although the trend for costly and prestigious literary adaptations from the twentieth century dissipated as the decade progressed, there was no return to earlier periods in history. The one major exception was *El rey pasmado* (Imanol Uribe, 1991) an ambitious production with a three hundred million peseta budget set in the period of Philip IV and shot in quintessentially Castilian towns (El Escorial, Toledo, Madrid, Salamanca, Ávila). Critics were surprised firstly by the fact that, after such a long absence, the Golden Age had returned to the big screen and, secondly, by the fact that a film set in this period could be entertaining.[51]

¡Un Lope que arrasa! [A Lope that cleans up]: El perro del hortelano (Pilar Miró, 1996)

There were three primary factors that helped resurrect the Spanish phoenix in *El perro del hortelano*.[52] Firstly, the birth of the CNTC had raised awareness and interest in Spanish classical drama. Secondly, the success of Kenneth Branagh's *Much Ado about Nothing* (1993) and Jean-Paul Rappeneau's *Cyrano de Bergerac* (1990), especially among young people, had proven that there might be an audience for this kind of film adaptation. The third and probably decisive factor was the formidable and tenacious nature of the film's director. As Juan Antonio Pérez Millán recalls:

> la inmensa mayoría de los amigos con quienes comentó la idea respondieron – respondimos – de forma muy singular: que era una locura, que el cine español no estaba en condiciones de permitirse ese lujo, que el público huiría despavorido de una película dialogada en verso, que Shakespeare era Shakespeare y Rostand había sido, en esa ocasión . . . Gérard Depardieu, mientras que, por desgracia, los autores del Siglo del Oro español sonaban sobre todo a libro de texto de bachillerato. (2007, p. 247)

> [the vast majority of her friends, me included, responded to the idea in a singular manner: that it was madness, that Spanish cinema was in no condition to permit a luxury of this kind, that the public would run away

petrified from a film featuring dialogue in verse, that Shakespeare was Shakespeare and that Rostand had, on this occasion, been ... Gérard Depardieu while, unfortunately, the writers from the Golden Age had, above all, connotations of A-Level textbooks.]

Though lacking a substantial tradition in Spain, Shakespeare adaptations provided Miró with inspiration and confidence. In an article in *El Mundo*, Miró reminisced on the formative impression left by Renato Castellani's *Romeo and Juliet* (1954), the first Shakespeare adaptation she had ever seen, and the importance of other adaptations by Orson Welles and Branagh (Miró, 1997). Her appreciation of these productions created in her an acute case of Shakespeare envy. She argued elsewhere that 'no valoramos lo que tenemos' [we don't value what we have] and that while 'nadie se extraña cuando se adapta a Shakespeare ... todo el mundo se sorprendió cuando pensamos llevar al cine a Lope de Vega' [nobody bats an eyelid when Shakespeare is adapted but everyone was surprised when we thought of bringing Lope de Vega to the big screen] arguing that 'si esta película no se ha rodado antes es porque somos demasiado críticos con lo nuestro' [the reason that this film has not been shot before is that we are too critical of our own heritage] (cited in Montero, 1996). In light of this observation, it is rather ironic that there seems to be no record of Miró making concrete reference to previous film adaptations of the *comedia*, and she incorrectly claimed that *El perro* was the first to be done in verse (cited in Muñoz, 1996). Screenwriter Pérez Sierra actively tried to distance the film from what he termed 'aquellas versiones vulgarizadas de los dramas de Lope y Calderón' [those dumbed-down versions of Lope and Calderón's dramas] (1996: 108). This cultural amnesia was also reflected in the film's press coverage.

Finding money for the project was an uphill struggle but the producer, Carlos Ramón, was eventually able to raise the film's budget of 271 million pesetas through ministerial support, contracts with television channels, distribution advances and bank subsidies; filming commenced in Portugal in June 1995.[53] Five weeks into the shoot, however, Ramón went bankrupt due primarily to his lack of experience as a producer and the financiers' scepticism over whether audiences would pay to go and see a *comedia* in verse. The Portuguese crew harboured fears that they would never be paid and decided to take the film's costumes as insurance.

Following some anxious negotiating, the thought that a film facing bankruptcy would have an adverse effect on future productions in Portugal led three of the largest producers in Spanish cinema (Enrique Cerezo PC, Lola Films and Cartel) to invest in the project and shooting resumed in August 1995. It seems, however, that they were interested in protecting Spanish cinema as an industry and had little interest in Lope or the project itself. This sentiment was voiced at an official dinner where lead actor

Carmelo Gómez recalls that the producer, Cerezo, told José María Aznar's wife, Ana Botella, that there was no money to be made from the Spanish classics.[54]

Even on completion, the film faced further obstacles. It was not chosen as part of the official selection in the 1996 San Sebastian Film Festival. Although it was shown out of competition, most critics did not even bother to attend. Nevertheless 'tuvo una gran acogida. El público siguió el verso con interés y coronó la proyección con una ovación cerrada' [it was very well received. The audience followed the verse with interest and, at the end, gave the film a standing ovation] (Galán, 2006, p. 383). This was the first major intimation that Lope's palace comedy about the on-off relationship between Diana, Countess of Belflor and her secretary, Teodoro, might be able to seduce a late-twentieth-century audience.

The curators of the Argentine Mar de Plata Festival were present at the screening and chose to include the film in its official programme, where it would ultimately win the highest prize, the Ombú de Oro. It was only on receiving this foreign accolade that the film was given a release date at home. Largely as a result of Miró's status among Spain's cultural elite, its domestic release in November 1996 was nevertheless a veritable media feast. Aznar held a lunch for the director and her cast while the king, a personal friend of Miró, attended the premiere (Pando, 1996).

Now that it had finally been released, *El perro del hortelano* achieved the rare feat of charming critics and audiences alike. It was the ninth most successful film at the Spanish box office in 1996 and the sixth in 1997 (Canning, 2005, p. 81), ultimately grossing over three million euros. It was markedly more successful, both artistically and commercially, than *Tu nombre envenena mis sueños* (1996), a film set in the Civil War period that Miró shot largely with the same cast and crew while the Lope adaptation was in hiatus.[55] Against all expectations, it was also far more light-hearted and popular than Gerardo Vera's adaptation of *La Celestina* (1996) starring Penélope Cruz. As a film-maker, Miró succeeded in delivering what had generally eluded her as director general: a prestigious and accomplished literary adaptation with mass appeal. Reviewers heaped praise not only on the work itself but also on its cultural significance as a film that presented a Golden Age play to a mainstream audience, thereby establishing a precedent for future adaptations.[56] While there is an element of hyperbole in such appraisals, its critical and commercial success undeniably renders it a triumph.

The film is unique in terms of *comedia* performance within Spain in that no other project has been capable of harnessing so much collective experience. Miró's ministerial tenure may not have exactly favoured the *comedia* but, by the time she made *El perro*, she had directed a series of classic works for the small screen,[57] and had worked for the CNTC. Her film *El pájaro de la felicidad* (1993) even included a segment of *La verdad sospechosa* being performed. Pedro Moreno, who provided the costumes, had also worked for the CNTC, as had cinematographer Javier Aguirresarobe.

As noted in the last chapter Gómez received his first major break with the CNTC's *El caballero de Olmedo* (1990). Ana Duato who plays Marcela had appeared in the company's *Fiesta Barroca* (1992). Although Emma Suárez (Diana) had no experience with classical drama, and had in fact failed an audition with Marsillach (Aguirre, 2008, p. 616), her pairing with Gómez is arguably the film's masterstroke. At the time, they were two of Spain's best and most famous actors and their appearances together in a series of films directed by Julio Medem had yielded an intertextual sexual synergy in which Suárez tended to provide a dominant sexual foil to Gómez's curious hybrid of masculinity, intelligence and reticence. This on-screen chemistry was particularly well suited to Lope's tantric narrative. Irrespective of their experience, the actors all received extensive training from Alicia Hermida.

Pérez Sierra, not for the first time, was instrumental in resurrecting the Golden Age. He claims that he removed more verses than he would have done in a theatrical version of the play (1999b, p. 95). Nevertheless, in terms of the number of lines cut, the screenplay is remarkably loyal to Lope's play text and, as Phyllis Zatlin has argued, 'the resulting film script is very verbal and is marked by very rapid speech'. In relation to other cinematic adaptations, it 'may be placed at the transposition end of our spectrum' (2005, p. 179). That a mainstream audience was still able to follow the film with relative ease is testament to the strength of the performances and the seductive vivacity of non-verbal signifiers such as the lavish palace settings and Diana's array of costumes.

Where Miró does make a concession to her audience is in terms of genre. When asked why she had chosen this play in particular, she answered: '[p]rimero es una comedia, que llegan mejor al público que un drama; y contaba una historia actual, además de ser un texto realmente hermosísimo' [firstly, it is a comedy which always appeals more to the public than a drama; furthermore, it is a story with contemporary relevance as well as being a genuinely beautiful text] (cited in Gil, 1996). The play text is, however, a 'dark comedy' (Moir and Wilson, 1971, p. 52). Teodoro's servant, Tristán, invents a false biography for his master by duping an ageing aristocrat, Ludovico, into believing that the secretary is in fact his long lost son. This pleases Diana because it provides a socially sanctioned fiction that enables her to marry for love. Fearful however that Tristán will reveal her husband's true identity, Teodoro has to convince her not to have him killed; far less fortunate is the secretary's previous fiancée, and the countess's lady-in-waiting, Marcela, who is coerced into marrying a man she does not love. The film, nevertheless, eschews the darker edges of Lope's play and, as I have noted elsewhere:

costume functions alongside other semiotic systems (mise-en-scène, star presence, choice of scenes, music) to transfer attention away from the axes of class to gender divides. This transferral ensures that a narrative of desire, repression and evasion is assimilated into the world of romance, a place where quotidian impediments are kept at bay. (Wheeler, 2007: 277)[58]

Peter W. Evans has argued that it was the cinematic adaptation's configuration of amorous relations that provided much of its appeal: 'The film's endorsement of the centrality of Lope's heroine, its desire to explore the tensions of gender and romance, are sustained by the new Democracy's redefinitions of subjectivity and the relations between the sexes' (1997, p. 11). *El perro* has the potential to offer a powerful romantic charge while simultaneously undertaking an exploration of female subjectivity and sexuality that resists the charge of anachronism. In this regard, the internalization rather than the imposition of social rules and norms is central to the play's modernity. This is facilitated by two factors that help distinguish this *comedia*. Firstly, there are no male blocking characters and it is a woman who is very much in charge, albeit within the framework of a patriarchal system whereby Diana is under pressure to accept marriage proposals from either Ricardo or Federico, two buffoonish but eligible noble suitors. Secondly, although issues of class are paramount, the ostensible mismatch between the countess and her secretary is not presented as the result of mistaken identities as is often the case in comedies from the Golden Age.

Diana's battle is therefore predominantly psychological; she does not care about Teodoro's status but she is nevertheless acutely sensitive to how it will be seen by others. In other words, the play is about an unusually powerful female whose position might theoretically be seen to imbue her with freedom yet that very same position makes her particularly vulnerable to judgement and criticism. Representations of women of this kind abound in Spain with the ubiquitous presence of the *prensa rosa* [celebrity magazines] whose staple diet include 'nobles damas salidas y bastardos sin denominación de origen' [randy female aristocrats and bastards with unaccredited backgrounds] (Sánchez Díaz, 2000, p. 28).[59]

This prominence continues to be a mixed blessing in the modern-day context; it ensures a certain visibility but it can easily make women subject to a harsh scrutiny in which their gender and physical appearance often eclipse their professional or social role.[60] Women who operate within the public sphere are almost automatically converted into celebrities. The terrain that members of what Maria Antonia García de León has termed 'élites discriminadas' [elites subject to discrimination] (2002, p. 38) have to negotiate therefore has antecedents in a play that 'is much less a reflection of reality than a multi-focussed interpretation of a world that cannot define itself in substantial terms' (Torres, 2004, p. 199).

The parallels that can be established between Diana and both Miró and characters from the director's earlier films have led some commentators to interpret this film adaptation in largely biographical terms. As both Mercedes Maroto Camino and Elaine Canning have noted, the director has a seemingly personal investment in the countess who is presented in a more positive light than Marcela whose suffering is underplayed so as to focus on Diana's anxiety and frustrations (2003, pp. 16–17; 2005, pp. 85–6). As a result, Esther Fernández and Cristina Martínez-Carazo have gone as far as claiming that 'se sintió identificada Miró con la protagonista y se reinscribió a sí misma en la comedia lopesca' [Miró identified with the protagonist and reinscribed herself in Lope's comedy] (2006, pp. 319–20).

Interpretations of this kind undoubtedly contain a kernel of truth but they can also lead to the romanticization of the solitary artist, and thereby bypass the collaborative nature of cinematic endeavour; as we have seen, this was vital to the film's success. Furthermore, Pérez Sierra claims the director had originally intended to shoot Calderón's *No hay burlas con el amor* and that it was only as a result of his insistence that she turned to *El perro* (1996, p. 109). This is ironic, considering that in Spain the resulting film 'tendrá más de testamento cinematográfico de Pilar Miró que de comedia palatina de Lope de Vega' [will be remembered more as a Pilar Miró film than as a palace comedy by Lope de Vega] (García Santo-Tomás, 2000a, p. 390). In recent years, the film has been broadcast many times on television, and multiple editions of the film released on VHS and DVD have sold out almost immediately (Ramón Fernández, 2003, p. 28).

El perro may have seduced audiences at home but its international standing was far less prominent. According to trade magazine *Variety*: 'Theatrical prospects appear minimal, but stately production values and attractive leads should secure quality TV bookings for this tiny frock piece' (Rooney, 1996). This assessment proved to be accurate. The film was shown at a number of festivals but did not receive extensive international distribution. In Italy, where Branagh's adaptations are very popular, it struggled to find an audience. After being screened in the open market in Cannes, it was booked into five screens in France but the distributor admitted that its commercial prospects were very limited (EFE, 2000). It is difficult to recoup the investment in a costly production of this kind from the domestic market alone; a general lack of interest at the international level was an obstacle insufficiently taken into account by those who optimistically predicted a major revival for the Golden Age on the silver screen.

El perro del hortelano 2? This time it is personal

Following the domestic success of *El perro del hortelano*, Miró was engaged in a number of different projects. She staged *El anzuelo de Fenisa* for the CNTC and, having previously filmed Princess Elena's wedding in 1995, made preparations to direct the wedding of the younger royal princess, Cristina, on 4 October 1997. In addition, she was planning to film a version of Strindberg's *Miss Julie* also to star Gómez and Suárez.[61]

In the long term, however, she planned to adapt both *El castigo sin venganza* and *El caballero de Olmedo* for the big screen and reunite much of the same cast and crew who had worked so successfully together on *El perro*. Pérez Sierra claims that the producers were contrite following Miró's unexpected triumph yet they were unwilling to give the green light to *El castigo sin venganza* because it was felt that a tragedy, especially of this kind, would not be commercial.[62] Health would tragically avert what a lack of support from the industry may not have done; Miró died of heart-related problems on 19 October 1997. She remained resolute to the end. According to Hermida, the director told her twenty days before her death that the filming of *El castigo sin venganza* would, one way or another, definitely go ahead.[63] Miguel García-Posada substantiates this view in an open letter published in *El País* about Miró and her proposed Lope adaptation:

> Pero no pudo ser, y ahora esa herencia está esperando a alguien con talento capaz de hacerse cargo de ella. Alguien con talento, pero también con la tenacidad que la caracterizaba. Por muy increíble que resulte, a comienzos de este año último de su vida, digo bien, a comienzos de este año no tenía productora para hacer *El castigo sin venganza*, según me decía en la citada carta, donde despachaba el asunto con elegancia y voluntad de hacer frente a todas las dificultades (comenzar la batalla, escribía ella). (1997)
>
> [But it could not be, and this inheritance now awaits someone with talent to become its custodian. Someone with talent; but also someone with the tenacity that characterized her. Incredible as it may seem, at the beginning of this last year of her life or, better said, at the beginning of this year, she did not have a producer with whom to work on *Punishment Without Revenge*. This is what she told me in the letter I have previously made reference to in which she approaches the matter with elegance, and a willingness to face all the difficulties that lay ahead (to commence battle, as she wrote).]

Nobody would, however, rise to the challenge and another decade would pass before the *comedia* received another cinematic makeover. The nearest approximation to a sequel was the teenage comedy *Menos es más* (Pascual Jongen, 2000), designed as a vehicle for the stars of the popular television series *Al salir de clase*. The narrative is a very loose modern-day adaptation of *El desdén con el desdén*, a play whose narrative shows some marked similarities to *El perro*. The film follows the adventures of a group of aspiring actors who work in a theme park in Seville where they perform scenes from Moreto's play. Somewhat predictably the plot of the *comedia* is then played out in 'real life' as the nerdish Carlos infatuates the beautiful but distant Diana by feigning lack of interest.

From a practical perspective, however, if Miró was going to have to enter into battle to make *El castigo*, the chances of any other warriors of lesser reputation and resolve taking her place was, in retrospect, unlikely. Although most of the Spanish film-makers I have spoken to express no particular animosity towards the *comedia*, neither do they seem particularly enthused as they invariably discuss the budgetary limitations of Spanish cinema.

Iciar Bollaín, for example, was offered a commission to direct a film version of *La dama duende* for Calderón's centenary. She did not refuse on principle but rather, she has told me, because the successful completion of the project required a level of financial commitment and security that she was not confident the producer could provide.[64] There were also attempts to film a high budget biopic of Lope. This project was passed around numerous Spanish directors and producers; it was, however, a Brazilian film-maker, Andrucha Waddington, who would direct the international co-production, *Lope*, a historical epic released in Spain in September 2010.[65]

The success of *El perro del hortelano* proved that it was possible for a *comedia* to reach a broad audience many of whom may never have stepped into a theatre or read a seventeenth-century play in their lives. What it did not provide was the kind of easily reproduced formula that is so attractive to the industry, especially in the context of Spain where film criticism, production and reception remains in the grips of what Susan Martín-Márquez has termed 'tenacious auterism' (1999, p. 47). The film may not have been the exclusive matrimony of its director, but the unique fusion of her and Lope, two 'monsters of nature', delivered an unusually strong gene pool.

Filming the *comedia* in the age of text messaging

Although it would take nearly ten years following the success of Miró's film for another *comedia* to be given a cinematic makeover, Tirso, Calderón and Lope were not absent from the big screen. While there have always been films that have included extracts or references to the *comedia* within their narratives, this trend has become more pervasive in recent years. This may well be the result of the increased prominence given to the *comedia* but it also probably because the inclusion of fictions within fictions has appealed to directors who often employ this device in an attempt to add a deliberate self-conscious or postmodern spin to their films.

In *Don Juan, mi querido fantasma* (Antonio Mercero, 1990), a tale of the legendary seducer reappearing as a ghost and replacing the lead actor in a production of *Tenorio* being performed in Seville for All Saints' Day, a performance of *La discreta enamorada* is woven into the narrative.[66] Generally, however, the play that is most frequently referenced is *La vida es sueño*. This is symptomatic of the fact that this is seemingly the one *comedia* about which all Spaniards, irrespective of age or class, have at least a passing knowledge. A number of recent films feature dialogue and/or characters from the play: *Sólo se muere dos veces* (Esteban Ibarret, 1997); *Niño nadie* (José Luis Borau, 1997); *Issi/Dissi (Amor a lo Bestia)* (Chema de la Peña, 2004).

In these screen appearances, the play is the source of friendly ridicule and/or is associated with pseudo-intellectuals/artists.[67] Hence in *Niño nadie* for example, a group of cultural dilettanti who congregate in Madrid's Círculo de las Bellas Artes decide to stage *La vida es sueño*. The actress whose recently deceased husband is financing the production is inspired by Núria Espert's recent performance as Hamlet to take on the role of Segismundo. This is considered to be a wise decision by the group as it is collectively agreed that Calderón's masterpiece contains no decent female roles! The ensuing satire is painfully realistic in parts. When the exploitative producer is asked what he is bringing to the table, he responds 'la subvención' [subsidy] while the actors are seen to buy their own bouquets of flowers for the opening night on which the audience clap too enthusiastically in an attempt to mask their boredom. This trend is not, however, specific to the *comedia*. Humorous references of a similar kind have also formed part of other films engaging with the literary canon; Lorca has, for example, been similarly mocked in *El otro lado de la cama* (Emilio Martínez Lázaro, 2002).

Éxtasis (Mariano Barroso, 1996) is more profoundly indebted to *La vida es sueño*. The narrative not only contains scenes from the play specially staged in the Teatro Romea in Murcia, but Calderón's narrative is also re-enacted in the non-theatrical sections of the narrative. The dedication to William Layton who taught Barroso and much of the cast – including lead actor Javier Bardem – also provides a clue as to where this interest in Golden Age drama may have originated. It would, in fact, be a director with a similar educational background who resurrected the *comedia* for the twenty-first century. Iborra, originally from Alicante, had specialized in Lope when he trained as an actor at the TEI in Madrid. It was Layton's former colleague, Miguel Narros, who subsequently suggested he ought to film a version of Lope's play as it addressed, in an inventive and beautiful manner, the perennial subject of Iborra's films: love.[68]

La dama boba tells the story of two sisters, one a bluestocking and the other an idiot, who exasperate their father, Octavio, with their respective excesses: pedantry and stupidity. Finea's scant mental capacities are counterbalanced by her economic wealth as her uncle, fearing her unable to attract a husband, has left her a substantial dowry. A match is found in Liseo, wealthy as result of his adventures in the New World, who is nevertheless more attracted to Nise whose haughty intelligence has led her to rebuff suitors including Laurencio who switches his allegiance to Finea when he realizes the financial implications. A series of typical *capa y espada* complications ensue, but are nevertheless resolved through the marriage of both sisters; in the process, love provides the means through which both young women shed their respective excesses.

The play is far better known in Spain, where it has been staged consistently throughout the twentieth and twenty-first centuries, than *El perro del hortelano* was when it was filmed.[69] Alberto González Vergel had previously directed a version for television, and there are multiple scholarly editions of a play that is also 'one of the few of Lope's comedies to have been seriously assessed by critics' (Thacker, 2007, p. 48).[70] As Miró's experiences demonstrated, its being a comedy immediately improves its commercial prospects; it is by far the most successful national genre at the domestic box office and appeals to both men and women (Fernández Blanco, 2005, pp. 9–11). In addition, there are certain similarities and continuities between *capa y espada* comedies and modern-day Spanish cinema. It is not simply a linguistic overlap that led to a new subgenre, invented in the early 1980s with films such as *Ópera prima* (Fernando Trueba, 1980), being labelled as the *Nueva Comedia Madrileña* [New Madrid Comedies]. As with so many Golden Age *comedias*, their narratives focus on the amorous adventures of a recently created urban elite who, unlike in the 1940s, are now the prime cinema audiences in Spain (Fernández Blanco *et al.*, 2002, p. 64).[71]

In comparison to Miró's ordeals, the passage from page to screen was relatively smooth. Edmundo Gil, the producer with whom Iborra usually works, admitted that he was not particularly enthused by the project. He found the play text dense and impenetrable, but he was willing to back the film if they could find additional investors and if Iborra could pen an intelligible adaptation. Both of these conditions were met as TVE agreed to provide 50 per cent of the budget as part of a proposed plan to buy the rights to a Spanish classic on an annual basis.

The film's ostensibly gynocentric narrative may here have worked in the project's favour because state television has broadcast an unprecedented number of programmes with lead female roles since the Socialist victory in 2004 (Palacio, 2007, p. 76). The strong female roles provided a good fit for the mainstream and arguably cosmetic feminism that is now firmly embedded in Spanish film production and consumption.[72] The importance of this characteristic as a marketing tool is reflected by the fact that, despite bearing little relation to the film, the synopsis in the press book states, '*La dama boba* está ambientada en el siglo XVII y centra la trama en dos hermanas que se evaden de la sociedad machista de la época de dos formas muy distintas. Una, a través de los libros, y la otra, haciéndose la tonta' [*Lady Nitwit* is set in the seventeenth century and the plot centres on two sisters who circumnavigate the macho society of the age in two very different ways. One through books and the other by pretending to be stupid] (DeA Planeta, 2006).

Iborra and Gil were able to raise a budget of three million euros (Balseyro, 2005). Although this is not insubstantial, it is relatively small for a historical drama. The project was nevertheless aided by the fact that an old friend of Iborra was in charge of the recently created Ciudad de la Luz in Alicante; he was keen for someone he knew and trusted to be the first to shoot there as a kind of trial run. Iborra therefore had access to a world-class studio, subsequently used by Antonio Banderas and Francis Ford Coppola among others, at a heavily discounted rate.

Although Miró's film had failed to establish a precedent, it still constitutes the benchmark against which all other adaptations will be judged; hence the publicity surrounding the film foregrounds the connection with *El perro del hortelano* and most reviewers have compared the two works. Like Miró, Iborra also had a feeling of cultural belatedness and comments he made at the film's premiere at the Malaga Film Festival in March 2006 were almost verbatim copies of the kind of observations that she had made ten years earlier:

> Sería maravilloso que esta película sirviera para que todos los años pudiéramos hacer uno o dos filmes sobre Lope, Calderón o Zorrilla ... a todos nos gusta ver las películas de Shakespeare que hacen los ingleses, pero es que nosotros tenemos clásicos y textos maravillosos que se deberían hacer, y no estaría mal que se convirtiera en un hábito. (cited in Camacho, 2006)
>
> [It would be marvellous if this film served as an impetus for us to make one or two films every year based on the works of Lope, Calderón or Zorrilla ... all of us enjoy seeing the Shakespeare adaptations that the English produce, but we also have classics and texts that ought to be filmed, and it would be no bad thing if this were to become a habit.]

The context however had changed. Despite the presence of the occasional literary adaptation – for example *Lázaro de Tormes* (Fernando Fernán-Gómez and José Luis García Sánchez, 2001), *El caballero Don Quijote* (Manuel Gutiérrez Aragón, 2002) and the hugely successful historical epic, *Juana la loca* (Vicente Aranda, 2001) – 2006 proved to be a watershed year in terms of Spanish cinema's approach to the past. With the release of *Teresa, el cuerpo de Cristo* (Ray Loriga), *Tirant lo Blanc* (Vicente Aranda), *Los Borgia* (Antonio Hernández) and, most importantly, *Alatriste* (Agustin Díaz Yanes), Spain's early modern history dominated national cinema to an unprecedented degree. I will offer a critical appraisal of *La dama boba* before returning to the question of if and how it can be meaningfully compared to these other films.

Iborra has cut roughly a third of the play text with the first act being the most heavily edited yet he remains remarkably loyal to Lope's verse with only the occasional word being changed, often for little discernible reason; for example 'Bien le puedes abrazar' [You could well embrace her] (2006: v. 915) is replaced by 'Bien le puedes saludar' [You could well greet her]. The meaning of the former would not be obscure to a twenty-first century audience, and it is not clear that any semantic or thematic twist is provided by the addition of the latter.

Considering that most Shakespeare adaptations have used no more than 25 to 30 per cent of the original text (Jackson, 2000, p. 17), the film remains relatively faithful to Lope's play text. Perhaps understandably and justifiably for a product aimed at a mainstream audience, the vast majority of lines that relate to poetic theory have been excised. For example the first scene of act two, in which Duardo, Fineo and Laurencio discuss love and the latter evokes both Plato and Aristotle in his echoing of Ovid's theory that love is the best teacher, has disappeared completely.

In terms of characterization, Otavio has been turned into a woman – as has a secondary character, Miseno – and Iborra concentrates on the central love story between Finea and Laurencio. This is emphasized by stripping Nise and Liseo of their servants thereby divesting them of opportunities to discuss their thoughts, actions and emotions. Indicative of this new hierarchy is also the deletion of the scenes in Illescas where Leandro informs Liseo of Finea's wealth and stupidity. Thus Liseo is ill-prepared when he first meets his fiancée and, because it is his first appearance, the viewer is encouraged to view him through Finea's eyes.

While all these changes can, I think, be justified within the logic of the film, at least some have been introduced as a result of practical necessity. By setting the play exclusively in and around Octavia's house, the need for filming in multiple locations is reduced, as is the cost. Secondly, the decision to present a maternal rather than a paternal figure enabled Iborra to cast his long-time partner Verónica Forqué in the role.[73] This is symptomatic of a broader problem that plagues this production and Spanish cinema and theatre in general. While Miró's film was a collaborative effort that benefited from a broad range of expertise, Iborra seems to have been reluctant to look beyond his own personal fiefdom.

Despite the fact that his grounding in Lope was as an actor rather than director or screenwriter, he wrote the script on his own. José Coronado (Laurencio), introduced at the producer's behest, had starred in Narros's production of Calderón's *El gran mercado del mundo* but he was unique among the cast for having experience with theatre of the period, and for not having worked with Iborra on previous occasions.[74]

Figure 11   Backstage still from *La dama boba* (Manuel Iborra, 2006)

While most British or American actors will have at least a rudimentary knowledge of Shakespeare, Spanish film-makers can make no such assumption when it comes to filming their national classical drama. Actors may have little or no knowledge. Silvia Abascal had previously appeared alongside Coronado in a successful television version of *Don Juan Tenorio*, and had performed *Romeo and Juliet* on stage. Nevertheless, this young actress (born in 1979) told me that she was aware that neither her previous performances nor her training in Spanish drama schools had prepared her for playing Finea: 'mi conocimiento sobre Shakespeare es mucho más amplio. En la escuela sus obras son de las más trabajadas y citadas por los actores' [my knowledge of Shakespeare is much broader. In schools, his plays are the ones that actors work with and quote from the most].[75] Hermida was once again contracted to train the actors but she was only given fifteen days to work with them. While both she and Abascal are very positive about their fruitful working relationship, the veteran actress claims that Coronado and Roberto San Martín (Liseo) barely attended her classes while she never even met Forqué.[76]

In terms of characterization, if we were to apply what Robert Stam has referred to as 'fidelity criticism's discourse of loss' (2005, p. 20), it would be easy to be very dismissive of the film. Liseo and Nise are turned into comic caricatures; the former is shown to be a camp, affected fop while the latter is depicted as a sexually repressed bluestocking who only needs the slightest hint of a Gongoresque conceit to be brought to the cusp of orgasm. She first appears when Laurencio woos her and so the audience never sees her as an *esquiva*; indicative of this change of emphasis is that Iborra changes one of Laurencio's lines in the play text from 'discreta Nise' [wise Nise] (v. 1967) to 'divina Nise' [beautiful Nise]. The more learned sister's diminished role alongside the removal of most of the literary references effectively reduces Duardo and Feniso to being little more than extras. A reference by Laurencio's servant Pedro to Clara as being 'más taimada/que boba' [more sly than stupid] (vv. 735–6) has been cut and the serving girl is presented throughout the film as an innocent playmate for the simple Finea.

Equally, Otavio is no longer the voice of common sense that he had been in Lope's play text (Larson, 1973, p. 50). By recasting him as a woman, any genuine sense of paternal threat and/or intimacy is lost, and the character is rendered in a rather inconsistent and unsatisfactory manner. Forqué plays her as a mass of nervous hysteria and Octavia is, in many respects, depicted as an unsympathetic character with an almost autistic unawareness of her daughter's emotional needs. Nevertheless, the actress also evokes the 'personal warmth and sympathy conveyed almost exclusively by facial expression' that Robin Fiddian has identified as being central to her star persona in the 1980s (1999, p. 248).

As Pierre Sorlin notes, 'when language is used in the cinema it forms part of a whole: the raw material of cinematic expression is an indissoluble combination of picture, movement and sound' (2001, p. 27). While Iborra's film undeniably simplifies the psychological and literary aspects of Lope's play text, what may be construed as the silencing of old voices can also be seen as paving the way for the creation of new vistas. In terms of directorial style however, it is surprisingly unadventurous. The narrative is almost exclusively unveiled through the use of medium and shot-reverse-shots. Typically the long shot is used to reveal the multiple locations facilitated by the cinematic medium and their absence is perhaps indicative of the fact that the film did not have at its disposal the kind of sumptuous landscapes on display in *El perro*. In contrast, the close-up tends to be employed to reveal a character's inner emotions but Iborra instead opts for a technique that is rarely used in modern-day adaptations: the filmed soliloquy. Although it is consistent with the theatrical and non-naturalistic aesthetic of the film, I am not convinced that this device is effective.

Where the film often excels, however, is in terms of performance style and *mise en scène*. For better or worse, Iborra does not seem to take either himself or the Golden Age all that seriously and delights in what James E. Holloway Jr has referred to as 'the apparently superficial comedy of *La dama boba*' (1972, p. 255). A love of old-fashioned glamour is reflected in the sensuous focus on a series of outlandish alternative period costumes provided by Lorenzo Caprile who has worked with the CNTC but is best known for designing wedding dresses for royal and/or celebrity marriages such as those of Princess Cristina and Marta Sánchez. In the press book, he writes:

> A partir de una rigurosa investigación histórica, asesorado en todo momento por los conservadores del Museo de Traje, dejé volar mi imaginación para remarcar en cada personaje no sólo su carácter y su temperamento sino esa idea de juego infantil, de divertimiento, de cuento con final feliz que la propia historia me sugería. De ese modo, y de acuerdo con el director Manuel Iborra, huí en todo momento de esa idea realista, un poco tópica, del siglo XVII español oscuro, negro y tenebroso... (DeA Planeta, 2006)
>
> [Having undertaken rigorous historical research assessed at every stage by specialists at the Costume Museum, I allowed my imagination to take flight; I wanted to bring out not only the personality and temperament of every character, but also the idea of infantile play, of fun, of a fairytale with a happy ending, which the plot itself suggested to me. In this way, and in agreement with the director Manuel Iborra, I always eschewed that realist and somewhat stereotypical idea of seventeenth-century Spain as always being dark, black and sinister.]

This approach is well suited both to Iborra's avowed aim to direct a film that was 'suavemente teatral' [lightly theatrical] because, as Christopher Breward notes, 'aside from its role in sustaining a coherent semblance of naturalism, screen dressing has also contributed to (and sometimes disrupted) those processes of acting and plot narrative which link cinema back to preceding theatrical and literary genres, whose modes of communication have been far from naturalistic' (2003, p. 131).

A sense of self-conscious play-acting works particularly well within the context of a *comedia* that is theatrical in content as well as form. Hence, for example, both the play and the film address femininity as the product of an educational process. The simulated nature of non-essential gender categories is literally visualized on screen as we see Finea being harangued into taking on her feminine role as various layers of costume and apparel are forced on her prior to her first meeting with Liseo. Later, it is her appearance in a striking red Roman outfit during her dance that sways her original suitor's affections away from Nise. By the end of the play and film, Finea is so clearly in control of her constructed feminine persona that she anticipates and reflects film theorist Mary Ann Doane's observations that '[t]he masquerade, in flaunting femininity, holds it at a distance. Womanliness is a mask which can be worn or removed' (1992, p. 235).

The stage and screen history of *La dama boba* has, in fact, been inextricably linked with female performance. Lope wrote the role of Nise specifically for Jerónima de Burgos (Zamora Vicente, 2006, p. 28), and Felipe Pedraza Jiménez has argued that it was the arrival of great actresses such as Margarita Xirgu at the beginning of the twentieth century that was instrumental in the play's resurrection on the Spanish stage (CNTC, 2003, p. 19). In her mastery of verse and Finea's emotional transition, Abascal proves herself to be a rightful heir to her illustrious predecessors. Given her talent, it is unfortunate that the film's rather one-dimensional focus on the comic aspects of the play does not allow her the opportunity to deliver some of Finea's most moving lines. Most of her lament about having to forfeit Laurencio (vv. 1669–1789) has, for example, been cut.

As noted, the film focusses primarily on the relationship between Laurencio and Finea. Instead of presenting the former's lack of pecuniary means as a weakness, as Helena Pimenta had done in her 2002 stage production for the CNTC, Iborra delights in Laurencio's rakish qualities that allow him to live by the skill of his wits. Coronado – who, as Chris Perriam has elsewhere noted, 'must be the epitome of the old-style leading man to a significant segment of the audience' (2003, p. 201) – takes on an appearance reminiscent of Depp's portrayal of Jack Sparrow in *Pirates of the Caribbean: The Curse of the Black Pearl* (Gore Verbinski, 2003). It is no coincidence that both actors have played Don Juan (see note 66) and, in these more recent roles, they both appeal to traditional notions of masculinity while simultaneously mocking them with a degree of self-conscious and carefully calibrated camp that is associated with a performance-based approach to life and actions.

As a result of Finea's childish innocence for much of the film, Abascal is, in spite of her good looks, far less of an erotic spectacle than Coronado. From his first appearance pushing past passers-by with sword in hand so as to reach Nise, he delivers a virtuoso performance. Without shying away from the character's mercenary motivations, Coronado provides a vitriolic rush of physical prowess, sexual potency and verbal wit that charms the audience into forgetting his motivations and bypassing the question of 'si Finea no será más boba que nunca entregándose a un pretendiente tan oportunista.' [if Finea might not be more stupid than ever for handing herself over to such an opportunist suitor] (Gaylord, 1992, p. 76). This performance makes perfect dramatic sense because, as César Oliva notes about Laurencio:

> Es un desalmado, pero con apariencia maravillosa. Un rico venido a menos, que quiere recuperar su posición social. No podemos ridiculizarlo en tono exagerado porque Finea *se debe enamorar de él*, como haría cualquier espectadora. En rasgos externos es el chico que a todas enamora. La justeza o equilibrio de su exposición no es nada fácil. Es un sinvergüenza, pero protagonista. (1997, p. 47)

> [He's a rogue, but with a marvellous appearance. He is a rich man fallen on hard times, who wants to regain his social position. We can't ridicule him in an exaggerated fashion because Finea *has to fall in love with him*, as would any female member of the audience. In terms of physical appearance, he is the young man that makes all the women fall in love with him. Getting the

balance of his depiction spot-on is no easy task. He is shameless, but he is also the leading man.]

Central to Laurencio's attraction is his quintessentially cinematic relationship with Pedro that ably translates the master–servant relationship for a modern-day audience. In his edition of the play text, Diego Marín argues that Pedro is a less developed servant than in most *comedias* because he cannot perform the function usually assigned to characters from his social class as:

> este papel corresponde al criado del galán más digno – el típico amante noble –, mientras que Laurencio, el galán apicarado, no necesita del completo materialista que suele proporcionar el criado-gracioso, por cuya razón el papel de Pedro se limita a destacar la ruindad de su amo. (2005, p. 51)
>
> [this role befits the servant of the most dignified leading man – the typical noble lover – while Laurencio, the picaresque leading man, does not require the materialist counterpart usually provided by the servant-clown; this is why Pedro's role is limited to highlighting his master's baseness.]

Iborra, however, showcases the capacity that performance has for bringing to life even the most seemingly marginal characters in the text by recasting the Finea–Clara and Laurencio–Pedro relationships into the cinematic idiom by creating bonds that do not so much foreground class distinctions as the desire that Clara and Pedro have to emulate their sparring partners. This works to excellent comic effect while also exaggerating the protagonists' already forceful personalities. After resolving to turn his attention from Nise to her sister, he is given the perfect opportunity when Finea has her money stolen by some errant thieves – whether they are in the employ of Laurencio is not clear – who he then pursues. Both he and Pedro then deliver their first verbal amorous advances in the middle of a sword fight. Later, when the respective lovers are hidden in the secret attic, Pedro tries rather less successfully than his master to adopt the role of a swashbuckling suitor, and Clara imitates her mistress's amorous responses by paying careful attention to the precise motions of her tongue before venturing to kiss her beau.

Throughout the film, Laurencio wears the same trademark outfit of black trousers and white shirt and he always carries a sword. He adopts an androgynous pirate glamour that is nevertheless rooted in an archetypal masculinity which finds its polar opposite in the emasculated Liseo. Although San Martín, a Cuban, has previously starred as the object of sexual desire, in *Habana Blues* (Benito Zambrano, 2005), here he wears rouge and showcases a vast array of ridiculous costumes that are clearly designed to feminize his character. In a very Lopean conceit, love teaches Liseo to take on his appropriate gender role as, when he and Nise are eventually reconciled, he dons a more sober outfit that clearly echoes Laurencio. As in Lope's play, the film simultaneously appears to subvert and uphold essential gender categories. Nevertheless, the coexistence of traditionally masculine and feminine traits renders a spectacle of male bodies that requires a new 'critical paradigm', evoked by Santiago Fouz-Hernández and Alfredo Martínez-Expósito, which 'will necessarily have to consider men as spectacle-driven, exhibitionist, masochistic, passive and narcissist; it will have to consider their masquerades and their bodies' (2007, p. 2).

As with many of the play's characters, the film has its faults and can often appear slightly confused and inconsistent, but despite or perhaps even because of this it is both unique and worthy of recognition. With the exception of Abascal, Lope's verse is delivered in a rather haphazard fashion yet one advantage of most of the actors knowing each other so well is that there is a genuine sense of bonhomie on display with some excellent screen chemistry. Through its use of swashbuckling action, eroticization of the male body, appropriation of Hollywood-style tropes and uncynical belief in the transformational power of love, the film is a distant relation of *Don Juan* and is the most straightforwardly fun and enjoyable *comedia* adaptation since Sáenz de Heredia's unintentionally camp classic.

The initial critical reaction appeared to be positive as it won a series of high-profile awards at the Malaga Film Festival,[77] but this honeymoon period was short-lived as subsequent reviews were lukewarm at best. *El País* referred to 'una ambientación muy cómoda, pero de andar por casa' [a very pedestrian and unchallenging *mise en scène*] (Torreiro, 2006) while Javi Vara complained of how 'podría haberse hecho hace 20 años en el mal sentido de la hipótesis' [it is no compliment to say that this film could have been made twenty years ago] (2006). More recently, Carlos Aguilar has dismissed it as a film that 'cae en los peores parámetros del teatro filmado, harto lejos de lo que debe suponer una reinterpretación cinematográfica del original' [falls into the worst excesses of filmed theatre, far removed from what a cinematic reinterpretation of the original should entail] (2007, p. 315).

If *La dama boba* has not been an unqualified success with the critics, then it has proven even less popular with audiences. While it received healthy media exposure and opened on 24 March on some of the most high-profile screens in both Madrid and Barcelona, the number of screens it was shown on was quickly reduced and it was seen by only 69,669 spectators. This is only marginally more people than the CNTC stage production that was performed 92 times to a total of 43,922 people with an average of 87 per cent of the tickets being sold on any given night (CNTC, 2003, p. 73). Whatever we choose as our point of comparison (Shakespeare adaptations, the director's previous work, literary adaptations of Spanish literary works, comedies in general), there is no doubting that the film was a commercial failure. In a country still dominated by Hollywood, it was only the forty-second most successful Spanish film at the domestic box office and it does not even figure in the list of best-selling DVDs.[78]

Prior to the film's release, Spain's best selling film magazine, *Fotogramas*, spoke of '[e]l loable riesgo de Manuel Iborra en *La dama boba*: reivindicar a Lope de Vega en tiempos del SMS' [the admirable risk of Manuel Iborra: to revive Lope de Vega in the age of text-messaging] (2006). In purely financial terms, this risk has not paid off. Despite the presence of actors who appeal to different generations and high-profile cameos from veteran actor Antonio Resines alongside young television star Paco León, Spanish mainstream audiences have once again rejected the *comedia*.

Elaine Canning has concluded that 'textual modifications may not have been welcomed by *lopistas*, but "theatrical acting"' in Iborra's *La dama boba* may have dissuaded members of the Spanish public from turning out to see it at local cinemas' (2006, p. 170). In a similar vein, Verena Berger has criticized the film for an apparent inability to establish a relationship with present-day concerns, alongside its historical incongruity which she highlights with reference to a sword fight between Octavia and Liseo (2009, pp. 66, 71). There is undeniably an element of truth in these appraisals but it is important to add that overtly theatrical acting is problematic for both *culto* and *vulgo* audiences because it is seen to represent an anachronistic style of film-making that has specific negative temporal and political implications.

As noted, 2006 marked the first sustained return to the seventeenth century since the Franco years. The most high profile example was *Alatriste*, based on an incredibly successful series of novels revolving around the eponymous anti-hero, a soldier fighting at home and in Flanders. This international co-production starring Hollywood's Viggo Mortensen had the highest budget in the history of Spanish cinema. Its release was a national event that constituted a paradigm shift in both national film production and representations of the Golden Age. This cinematic outing has probably been responsible for introducing a higher number of Spaniards to the *comedia*, albeit in a superficial fashion, than any other event in history. A very popular exhibition in the Plaza Mayor based around Alatriste's Madrid gave details of the *corrales*. Although, unlike Quevedo, no seventeenth-century playwrights appear in the film, a scene from *El perro del hortelano* is performed. This, in itself, is testament to Miró's success since the novel on which it is based features instead a scene from *El arenal de Sevilla* (Pérez-Reverte, 1996: 190).

What distinguished *La dama boba* from the period competition of 2006 is that all of the other films made an active effort to distance themselves from earlier productions. This reaction against earlier cinematic traditions was key to the acceptance of these twenty-first-century historical films. Hence, Juan Ferrer wrote in his review of *Alatriste*:

> Crónica de amores en tiempos de cólera; de soldados sin lustre; de batallas en el infierno y de un imperio edificado sobre la miseria, tanto económica como moral. Bajo estas consignas, transita el desencantado Diego Alatriste, vaso comunicante entre la España harapienta y la insidiosa, taimada y conspiradora corte del funesto rey Felipe IV, al que los libros de historia del Movimiento elevaron a la categoría de gran monarca y así se aprendió en las escuelas de los niños de posguerra. (2006)

> [A chronicle of love in the time of cholera; of downtrodden soldiers; of battles in hell; of an empire constructed on moral as well as economic degradation. These are the terms in which the disenchanted Diego Alatriste operates. He is our entry point into the poverty-stricken, insidious, treacherous and sly court of Philip IV, a king who brought ruin, but whom the history books of the Movement – used to teach children of the post-war period in schools – elevated to the status of a great monarch.]

I would like to suggest that by presenting a more light-hearted and colourful version of the Golden Age, *La dama boba* came to be irrelevant, outdated and therefore deemed unworthy of attention by audiences, film critics and *comedia* specialists alike; by presenting a comic vision of the nation's cultural and historical past, *La dama boba* inadvertently subjected itself to aesthetic as well as ethical censure. Hence, for example, we have already seen the negative references made by press critics to its temporal and theatrical limitations that were construed not only as anachronistic but also as bordering on the offensive. In other words, Iborra's film and arguably Lope has seemingly been interpreted as the kind of film which Spanish cinema ought to be fighting against.

This provides one likely explanation as to why no attempt was made to promote *La dama boba* even among non-mainstream international audiences. Although TVE was able to sell its television series of *Don Quijote* at a global level (Kercher, 1997), the specialist international market is seen, correctly or not, to be far less interested in Lope. *La dama boba* was neither screened at international festivals nor were English subtitles included on the DVD release.

Given the largely negative reception afforded to Iborra's film, it is not perhaps surprising that TVE have not continued with their plan to provide funding and buy the rights to a *comedia* adaptation once a year. The failure of a film of this calibre to capture the popular imagination does not inspire faith in the commercial viability of the *comedia* 'in the age of text-messaging' even if there may be an explanation for this failure.

Technological advances can nevertheless open as well as close doors. At the time of writing, a very liberal adaptation of *La vida es sueño* is about to be shot digitally on location in Spain, the US and Brazil by Paula Ortiz.[79] This relatively low-budget project, partly funded by Amnesty International and Abbey-Santander, follows on from an English-language theatrical production that has been staged by the same team both in New York and at Almagro.[80] The creative team claim that the cinematic version is inspired by a variety of international films. This project, whose natural home is more likely to be found in galleries or cultural centres than multiplexes, is destined to circumvent the particular pitfalls that beset the production and reception of Iborra's film; whether it will stumble upon others of its own remains to be seen.

Conclusion

The cinematic careers of Golden Age dramatists have been sporadic at best. They have been the servants of many masters who have sought to appropriate their works for a variety of agendas. Only very occasionally has this favour been returned with adaptations that genuinely attempt to render their plays as cinematically credible works suitable for modern-day audiences.

The first Shakespeare adaptation to make a considerable return on its investment was Baz Luhrmann's *William Shakespeare's Romeo and Juliet* in 1996 (Holland, 2000, p. xvii). Given this, the challenges facing his relatively anonymous Spanish counterparts are evident. The cost of expensive period makeovers is prohibitive when it is unlikely to be recouped at the domestic box office and the chances of major international distribution are slight. More positively, as Miró and Camus have proved, challenging does not necessarily mean impossible. *La leyenda del alcalde de Zalamea* may subsequently have been unfairly sidelined but, at the time of its release, it was able not only to set a new standard in *comedia* adaptations but also to secure that most elusive of prizes: a receptive international audience.

Nevertheless, prior to *El perro del hortelano*, Spanish audiences had tended to respond indifferently to films that have either disappeared from the popular imagination or survive only as icons of a bygone age. Adaptations produced in the early Franco years are clearly more conservative than the play texts on which they are based and are therefore liable to reinforce ingrained prejudices about the *comedia*. They also suffer a double and paradoxical ignominy in that they are paradigmatic examples of popular Spanish cinema under the dictatorship that were never actually that popular. As *La dama boba* showed, the spectre of these productions is such that any film which attempts to resurrect Golden Age drama for contemporary audiences has to make an active effort to distance itself from the black legend of its predecessors if it is not to be rejected by critics and audiences alike.

Chapter Five

Locating Spanish classical drama in (inter)national contexts: Almagro, the CNTC and the RSC

In theory, this book is primarily concerned with performance in the national as opposed to the international sphere. Nevertheless, in an increasingly transnational world, the local and the global can no longer be seen in opposition and their relationship is worth probing. The three detailed case studies which compose this chapter each focus on a major institution, and will attempt to locate the *comedia* within (inter)national contexts. These are designed to facilitate a discussion on if and why Spanish theatre's location in broader cultural currents underpins the nature and mechanics of performance; and how the standing of Golden Age drama at home and abroad impact on each other.

To begin, I discuss the RSC's Golden Age season in Madrid. In a manner akin to the way that Spanish music fans and bands invariably reference another popular and symbolic British import as Los Rolling,[1] the RSC tends to be affectionately called La Royal. This is symptomatic of the way in which the foreign company has been fetishized as a symbol of everything that Spain lacks by successive generations of theatre critics and practitioners. My interest is less in detailed aesthetic analyses than in examining how the season – and in particular an English-language version of *El perro del hortelano* [*The Dog in the Manger*] – was received in Madrid, and what, if any, lessons and precedents it might provide for Spaniards wanting to stage their own classical drama.

I then move onto an analysis of the reception of Lope, Calderón and Tirso in the autonomous regions. In relation to the CNTC's dual status as a National Company based in Madrid, I question whether its identity is grounded in the city or the state, and analyse why and how efforts have been made in recent years to focus on the latter. These attempts include, but are not limited to, high-profile co-productions with Catalan companies. I interrogate the motives underlying these and, to borrow a phrase from the title of David George's 2002 book, ask to what extent Barcelona and Madrid can be seen as rivals and/or collaborators in specific relation to *comedia* performance.

In the final section, I discuss the current standing of the Almagro International Theatre Festival that began as a modest venture in 1978. This was originally the pet project of the then Director-General of Theatre, Rafael Pérez Sierra. It would not, I suspect, have surprised anyone if these annual meetings had been discontinued following his departure, and their longevity and expansion are therefore in need of explanation. There are, I will argue, two primary explanations: the growth of domestic tourism and the emergence of a new form of officially-sanctioned state culture. An understanding of these two aspects is, I will suggest, essential for a genuine understanding of the realities underpinning the production and reception of *comedia* performance in twenty-first-century Spain.

Teaching an old dog new tricks?

In 2004, the RSC staged a season consisting of the following plays from the Golden Age: Tirso's *Tamar's Revenge*; Cervantes's *Pedro the Great Pretender*; Sor Juana's *House of Desires* and Lope's *The Dog in the Manger*. This major undertaking was largely the brainchild of Laurence Boswell, 'the period's most important pioneer on the British stage' (Boyle and Johnston, 2007, p. 11). By the time the season arrived in Madrid for the Festival de Otoño, the actors had performed together for nearly a year to a largely rapturous response in the UK. British reviewers revelled in the discovery of a lost dramatic canon and audiences and critics alike responded most positively to the works by Lope and Sor Juana.[2]

Boswell had first staged *The Dog* as a student in Manchester during the 1980s, and it is not surprising therefore that the work was included in the season, or that he directed it himself. Furthermore, the play fulfilled the criteria he applied for inclusion: quality, contemporary relevance, rich and complex themes, and good female roles (cited in Mountjoy, 2005a, pp. 173–4). Unlike recent Spanish productions, the success of Miró's film would not perform a determining influence on the production or its reception.[3] It was the company, rather than Lope or the play, which ensured tickets for performances at the Español sold out instantly, and this foreign production received a level of press coverage that is very rarely afforded a performance of a *comedia* in Spain.[4]

The merits of the production have been elaborated upon elsewhere;[5] my discussion will rather be oriented around what Boswell has termed 'a genuinely intercultural moment' (cited in Johnston, 2007b, p. 152). Without wanting to take away from this not inconsiderable achievement, offstage politics in Madrid – of which the British contingent was perhaps at least partially unaware – undeniably contributed to the dramatic frisson of the play's performance. Following Alberto Ruíz Gallardón's win in the municipal elections, there was a complete administrative overhaul in the arts administration in Madrid and, among the changes, Mario Gas replaced the antiquated Gustavo Pérez Puig as director of the Español.[6] The opening night of *El perro* was a veritable communion of Spain's theatrical elite and virtually all of them were sympathetic to Gas's appointment.

Within this context, the historic British company's arrival in the Spanish capital was clearly mutually beneficial. The RSC's international activities have tended to limit themselves to workshops (Lichtenfels and Hunter, 2002, p. 51), and a presence in the English-speaking world. Thus the status attached to an invitation to perform in Madrid was not insignificant, and was perhaps underestimated among Spanish practitioners and politicians predisposed to construe the RSC's visit as a source of pride, and confirmation of the status of both Gas and the national theatre. Furthermore, as noted in the first chapter, the state of *comedia* performance was at a particularly low ebb in 2004 and this helps to contextualize Catherine Boyle's account of the reaction:

> midst the rapture and the laughter, drama and tragedy that filled the theatre in that week, all of which heralded a re-discovery of great literary and theatrical gems through the eyes of a foreign other, there was a profound melancholy that came from a shared memory of rupture. (2007, p. 72)

This summary is certainly borne out in most reviews. Ignacio Amestoy, for example, noted: 'El periodista de un gran diario londinense le preguntó al cronista esta semana qué le parecía la Royal con su "programa español". El cronista no pudo contestar otra cosa que: "un gran ejemplo para España y los españoles"' [This week, a journalist from one of the great London daily newspapers asked this columnist what they thought of the RSC's 'Spanish season'. The only answer that the columnist could give was: 'a great example for Spain and for Spaniards'] (2004). What Boyle perhaps does not take into account, however, is that national self-flagellation is a discursive characteristic of Spanish press critics. In *El Mundo*, Javier Villán went as far as to speak of how the production was a success '[p]ese a los recelos que uno pueda tener sobre Lope' [in spite of the reservations that one might have about Lope]. He subsequently implies that the RSC had triumphed in spite of rather than because of the play:

El teatro popular de Lope destinado al vulgo apuntala siempre el orden moral y político de su tiempo. En *El perro* ... se mantiene la supremacía de clase. El final feliz se articula sobre un engaño que avala la capacidad manipuladora del criado, aunque no subvierte el orden de valores. Pero lo que importa es la visión de esta comedia palaciega de la Royal Shakespeare: magistral; se impone el virtuosismo interpretativo y el ingenioso juego con el espacio escénico. (2004)

[Lope's popular theatre aimed at the masses is, without exception, predicated on the moral and political order of his time. In *The Dog* ... the supremacy of the class system is upheld. The happy ending is based on a trick that vouches for the servant's manipulative talents, but does not subvert the overall value system. But the important thing is the RSC's vision of this palace comedy: magnificent; carried by the virtuoso display of acting and ingenious use of stage space.]

Beyond such platitudes and generalities, what Spanish critics were seemingly unable to articulate, with honourable exceptions (Armiño, 2004; León Sierra, 2004), was where Spanish practitioners were going wrong and what the RSC was doing right. In other words, of what did this 'great example' consist and what exactly could it teach Spaniards? It is this question to which I will now turn.

I do not believe that this production is necessarily the most accomplished *comedia* performance that I have seen but it does undeniably excel in one respect: the intensity and precision of the psychological charge that circulates between the characters, actors and spectators. There is an unfortunate tendency in Spain to establish a series of false dichotomies that have had a stifling effect: fidelity/theatricality; archaeology/adaptation; respect/liberty; entertainment/solemnity.

While making cuts and changes can be symptomatic of a lack of professionalism, as we saw in reference to *El pintor de su deshonra* in chapter three, it can – as has been the case with *Fuente Ovejuna* – be used a means for 'seizing dramatic writing as an *agency* of performance' (Worthen, 2010, p. 67). Faithful versions have, with notable exceptions, tended to be staged out of obligation; insufficient thought or imagination has been dedicated to 'the dialectical tension between its identity as poetry and as performance' (2010, p. xiv). It is, to my mind, an undeniable albeit perhaps unfortunate truth that the best *comedia* productions I have seen in Spain have often been those that have taken most liberties with the text.

There have been a number of radical overhauls of *El perro*. Hence, for example, the Machado brothers' 1931 adaptation – available for consultation at the Fundación Juan March in Madrid – is a heavily edited and simplified version,[7] which was staged by the ECT to lukewarm reviews as part of the Almagro Festival in 1989.[8] More successful in terms of both content and audience numbers was Magüi Mira's production – based on a revamped version of Lope's play text by Emilio Hernández – that opened in 2002 and, as I have argued in more detail elsewhere:

> succeeds in transporting Diana's dilemma into a contemporary framework by supplying the convincing thesis that fashion and sex appeal operate as modern-day psychic equivalents to what honour might have meant to a seventeenth-century lady of standing. (Wheeler, 2007, p. 283)

The adaptation retains Lope's original language, although heavily edited with many scenes and exchanges excised completely. Spanish critics often considered this tactic as being, at best, a 'necessary evil' to engage a modern-day audience. The artistic and commercial success of the production proved that it was not evil; what the RSC would prove was that it was not necessary either. This claim does, nevertheless, have to be nuanced in reference to both the liberties afforded by translation, and the company's history and the precise manner in which its reputation has been forged.

One, although by no means the only, attraction of staging Shakespeare in Spain is that many translations are written in prose and are therefore easier for actors to understand and perform. In a similar vein, the RSC was under less pressure in Madrid in terms of verse delivery than their Spanish counterparts would be; firstly, because most of the audience is not hearing their native language and, secondly, translation allows a level of flexibility not permitted by the original. This latter consideration nevertheless has to be understood within the context of the company's veneration of the text as the origin and guarantor of quality. In a manner akin to the CNTC under Marsillach's direction, ostensible stage radicalism has been couched in the security of the page as defined by Margaret Jane Kidnie: '"Text," as currently understood within a dominant ideology of print, is indifferent to, even antithetical to, performance: a performance is "of" the text; the text stands alone' (2005, p. 104).

In a rhetorical manoeuvre unlikely to succeed in the Spanish context in relation to Calderón, Lope or Tirso, Alan Sinfield notes how the RSC have cannily navigated between reverence and relevance:

> The central idea of Shakespeare, so far from affording some control over what it is that the plays might represent, is actually used to justify at least sufficient interpretive scope to secure relevance. Then, conversely, the relevance of any particular production is guaranteed by the fact that it is Shakespeare, who is always relevant. The circle seems unbreakable. The RSC has, from the start, fostered this potent combination of relevance and the real Shakespeare by announcing its respect for the scholarship which seems to authenticate the process. (1994, p. 199)

This provides one explanation as to why they sought the cooperation of academics to advise on the Golden Age season. These included David Johnston who was commissioned to write a translation of *The Dog* that he described as being 'probably as faithful as the related demands of speakability and performance will allow' (cited in RSC, 2004, p. 17). He may be rather slippery in his choice of terms yet it is at least partially true. What he presumably wants to suggest is that he has attempted to translate the text according to philological criteria of fidelity where possible, but has dispensed with this method when, in his opinion, it produces a translation that would render the play incongruous and/or awkward on the stage.

His approach is, in many respects, the polar opposite of that adopted by Hernández because he does not edit the text yet he does alter Lope's verses. The latter adaptation is clearly an artistic license facilitated by the use of a language that does not belong to the playwright.[9] Johnston's generally respectful approach is reflected in the fact that the version was sufficiently close to the original that the possibility of using Lope's original for surtitles in Madrid was considered; his literary input nevertheless grounds his objection to this approach as a negation of both his and the Company's creative role.[10] Beyond the individual case in hand, this tension brings to the fore the inherently relative nature of fidelity as regards both historical and linguistic translation.

The RSC were able to explore 'what today we would call the psychological dimension, that obscure layer that lies between what people say and what they hide' (Johnston, cited in RSC, 2004). The play's narrative is relatively static and belies Lope's reputation for being more concerned with action than characterization.[11] Beyond the intrinsic character of the play text and the fidelity of Johnston's translation, a number of additional factors allowed for a level of textual and character analysis that simply would not take place in Spain: extensive rehearsal periods; a stable ensemble; and the collaboration between academics and practitioners.

Kathleen Jeffs (Mountjoy) has documented these processes in detail (2005b and 2008). She discusses, for example, how Boswell sought to unlock the first act by suggesting that the key is identifying the difference between envy and jealousy while actors engaged in a process of psychological exploration and debate that finds its correlative in the work done by academics at their desks. Hence, they discussed the individual emotional and practical motivations that differentiate Diana's two noble suitors who, in other productions, have generally been performed as undifferentiated and interchangeable buffoons. As a result, even an ostensibly minor character such as Anarda was fleshed out – appearing as a sycophantic seething mass of animosity – to a degree that I have not seen elsewhere. More substantially, the actors' skill alongside their apparent physical and psychic inhabitation of their roles facilitated a control of emotional registers that allowed the play to deliver genuine tragicomedy.

The visual aesthetic of Boswell's production was generally very dark and sombre and, as Susan Fischer notes, 'black, tight-fitting period costumes with ruffs gripping the neck carried implicitly the idea that, although the play is set in Naples, its spirit is that of post-Tridentine, inquisitorial Spain' (2009, p. 225). This image is bolstered with burning candles and the fact that all of the characters wear at least one crucifix with some also having rosaries. As I have argued elsewhere, when a recognizably foreign work is staged in British theatre, 'the shedding of its linguistic origins often co-exists with the desire to highlight the work's social-cultural origins' (Wheeler, 2010, p. 829). Considering that the black legend of Spain's imperial past is still deeply imbedded in the UK (Wheeler, 2006 and 2009), this visual iconography is both an obvious yet effective way of familiarizing a British audience with a play and dramatist that are likely to be unknown to them. With the exception of Mauro Armiño, who spoke in passing of 'una visión tópica de lo español' [a stereotypical image of all things Spanish] (2004), this approach was seemingly accepted by the local critical community.

In all fairness, the dark *mise en scène* also functions as an effective counterpart to Rebecca Johnson's performance as Diana, that foregrounds the darker reaches of desire which are seen to underpin her sadomasochistic treatment of both herself and those around her. This mood and aesthetic is also lightened by the presence of comedy. In this respect, the chemistry and timing on display demonstrated that the time the ensemble spent together reaped dividends. Take, for example, Teodoro's uttering with exasperation 'I have no idea what's going on' after taking dictation from Diana (Johnston, 2004, p. 81). While on the page this line delivers a sly chuckle at best, Joseph Millson's delivery brought the house down on a nightly basis.

But the comic centre of the play was undeniably provided by Tristán. From the moment he appears on stage, looking as if he were a hyperactive turtle as he carries a small table on his back, he is a kinetic mass of physical and mental activity that enables the kind of complicity between stage and auditorium that is very specific to the theatre. When he first refers to Teodoro as Icarus, Simon Trinder places the emphasis in his speech in such a way that no prior knowledge of the myth would be required in order to follow his meaning. This complicity reaches its climax at the end when he implores the audience to keep Teodoro's false biography secret.

The RSC was thereby able to avoid the trap into which many, although by no means all, Spanish productions fall: either playing excessively for laughs or encasing the seventeenth century within a corset of solemnity. As early as 2005, Boswell had spoken of how he would like to direct a *comedia* in Spanish with a native cast: 'And as soon as I do that, I would use the complete original text. I think that it is a very dangerous thing to underestimate your audience' (cited in Mountjoy, 2005a, p. 174). This approach clearly worked in relation to his English production and represents an attempt to superimpose the RSC's ideology and working methods into the Spanish context;

nevertheless, his equation of quality and textual fidelity belies the processes of transmission through which we have access to the *comedia*.

As J. E. Varey notes, although there are more modern editions of English than Spanish Early Modern plays, the reverse is true in terms of original manuscripts (1990, p. 100). This is attributable, at least in part, to the fact that:

> No sólo los actores, sino también los mismos dramaturgos, consideran sus textos como artefactos maleables, escritos para ser puestos al día, suprimiendo o añadiendo detalles o episodios enteros, actualizando el texto con referencia tanto a las circunstancias históricas y políticas como a las condiciones escénicas del día. Es posible, pues, que en vez de un original haya varios. (pp. 107–8)

> [It was not only the actors but also the dramatists themselves who considered their texts to be malleable artefacts, written to be updated, removing or adding details or entire episodes, bringing the text into the present. There were as many references to the historical and political circumstances as to the stage conditions of the day. It is possible, therefore, that rather than there being one original, there are various.]

In other words, a textual hierarchy by which Johnston's translation – to cite just one example – is assumed to be inherently more pure than Hernández's reworking is undermined by historical as well as theatrical determinants.

At one stage, Boswell was in negotiation with the CNTC to work with them but Eduardo Vasco did not want to restage a work that was now the most regularly performed *comedia* across Spain,[12] while his British counterpart felt that for his first foray into the Spanish language, he needed to work with a text of which he had encyclopaedic knowledge.[13] In the end he opted to work with Rakatá, a modest company based in San Sebastián de los Reyes, and contracted Vicente Fuentes – who has trained actors in the CNTC over recent years – to work with the actors on the verse that he saw as central to the production's success:

> There seems to be a lack of consensus in Spanish theatre about verse-speaking. There are so many different opinions and theories, but the actors tell me that they get no real guidance from directors and that in fact the performance issues that verse poses aren't really considered at all in the rehearsal process. In other words, verse-speaking is something actors end up struggling with individually. So the first two weeks here we spent working on a company approach as to how the actors were going to speak the verse. (cited in Johnston, 2007b, p. 148)[14]

In spite of the linguistic barrier it therefore seemed that Boswell was applying the communication model that had worked so successfully in the RSC to a Spanish production. Lead actress Blanca Oteyza spoke enthusiastically to the press about this working process and praised the way in which the British director 'cuenta la historia sin pelos en la lengua' [tells the story as it is, with no sugar-coating] and how '[l]os ensayos han sido enormemente enriquecedores. No habla español, pero conoce tan bien la obra . . . incluso la métrica' [the rehearsals have been hugely enriching. He doesn't speak Spanish, but he knows the play so well . . . even the verse metrics] (cited in J. B., 2007). Unfortunately, however, the communication seemingly broke down and, as I have discussed in more detail elsewhere, 'the acting was generally far inferior to that of the RSC production and there was a virtual absence of either dark sexual passion or the pace of comedy' (Wheeler, 2011b, p. 189).

In commercial terms, the play was a success with its two-week run at the Albéniz theatre in Madrid being a complete sell-out. This traditional large nineteenth-century theatre did not benefit the performance as its vast auditorium and poor acoustics arguably forced the actors to overact and inhibited the complicity between actors and spectators so essential to the earlier success. Boswell's preference for unedited versions ensured a similarly long performance time in both cases (RSC: three hours with an interval; Rakatá: one hundred and fifty minutes with no interval). This had not previously been a problem but here the duration of the play proved interminable as the British director delivered what Spanish theatre practitioners are so often accused of: a faithful but boring and unimaginative rendition of a classical text.

Furthermore, the RSC has not capitalized on the success of its Golden Age season at home. There was talk of a follow-up season but this has yet to materialize, while it has achieved less than might be hoped in terms of raising the *comedia*'s profile. When Jonathan Mumby staged *Life is a Dream* at the Donmar Warehouse – a subsidized theatre with a loyal audience and a relatively small performance space – he was given the go ahead, but only on the condition that he was able to recruit a star to take the lead role.[15] While a moment of intense and profound intercultural fusion undoubtedly occurred in 2004, whether this will prove to be more than a holiday romance remains to be seen.

Beyond Madrid: a transnational approach to the centre and periphery

Even before the CNTC made its debut in Seville, Marsillach noted how there were suspicions that it was a surreptitious ploy to impose a centralist discourse on autonomous regions that, in the paternalistic language of Francoism, might be termed the provinces:

> Parece como si el término 'nacional' estuviera mal visto. Lo cierto es que muchas veces no sólo parece sino que lo es: las autonomías se miran

corriendo los estatutos y los contribuyentes el bolsillo. Nos quedan secuelas del antiguo régimen: ni Madrid es siempre la odiada bota centralista ni todo lo estatal está forzosamente deteriorado. Por extraño que suene, una Compañía Nacional de Teatro Clásico puede nacer desde la buena fe y hasta incluso el sentido común. (1986, p. 35)

[It seems as if the term 'national' is looked upon negatively. What is certain is that the effects of this perception are often very real: the autonomous regions see their statutes disappearing before their very eyes as does the individual taxpayer their fiscal contribution. We retain the negative legacy of the previous regime: neither is Madrid always that much-hated centralist parasite nor is everything which is state-run automatically compromised. Strange though it may sound, a National Classical Theatre Company can be born out of good faith and even common sense.]

This problem is exacerbated in reference to *comedia* performance which, as we saw in the first chapter, is disproportionately Madrid-based. This is a marked contrast to the case of Shakespeare where 'translations into Spain's other languages (Catalan, Basque and Galician) have even made his plays the standard-bearers of nationalist causes in the country's most fiercely independent regions' (Gregor, 1998, p. 422). Hence, for example, '[e]ven during the early years of the Franco dictatorship, clandestine editions of new Shakespeare translations were published in Barcelona, and he has continued to be translated, performed and celebrated right up to the present day' (Buffery, 2007, pp. 19–20). The emblematic Teatre Lliure, which opened in 1976, staged eleven plays by Shakespeare in its first thirty years, but none by Calderón, Lope or Tirso (Graells, 2007). Early Modern Castilian, in other words, is often perceived as something of a foreign language, but not one that always invites translation.

It is ironic, therefore, that it would be Calderón – the Golden Age playwright most indelibly linked in the popular imagination with nationalistic and centralist discourses – who would prompt the CNTC's first serious attempt to engage with institutions and practitioners outside the capital. At an event held at the company's house theatre in Madrid on 17 January 2000, Andrés Amorós highlighted that *El alcalde de Zalamea*, directed by Sergi Belbel, constituted an important milestone: this co-production with the TNC was the first time that the Catalan company had performed a Spanish classic in Castilian.[16] In fact, two out of the CNTC's three centenary productions emerged primarily from Catalonia; it is, therefore, worth examining why and how this came to be.

There may well be an element of mistrust or even resentment towards Golden Age drama in Catalonia,[17] but it is an exaggeration to assume that its presence has been non-existent and/or imposed. Marsillach himself was born and raised in Barcelona and it was during a performance run of *El alcalde de Zalamea* that the city's mayor officially renamed the theatre in the

Plaza Urquinaona the Teatro Enrique Borrás (Vila San-Juan, 1956, p. 286). More substantially, Ricard Salvat is an instrumental figure in the history of both Catalan theatre and *comedia* performance. He supported both through his columns in Tele/eXpres,[18] bridged the worlds of the page and stage in the history of art department at the University of Barcelona where he held a chair in theatre,[19] and ensured that actors received extensive training in the classics in the Escola d'Art Dramàtic Adrià Güal, which he formed alongside Maria Aurèlia Campany in 1960.[20] His ethos, which remained constant throughout his professional career, is succinctly described in the following statement given near the end of his life: 'No soy centralista, pero no concibo que un catalán se forme en teatro sin conocer a Calderón' [I am no centralist but I cannot see how Catalans can be trained in theatre without being familiar with Calderón] (cited in Simón, 2003, p. 157).

When Salvat was director of the Teatro Nacional de Barcelona [National Theatre in Barcelona] during the early 1970s, he made sure to programme Lope's *El caballero de Olmedo*. This institution provided a precedent for the TNC which would not open until 1996. Nevertheless, the switch from Castilian to Catalan, alongside an ostensibly small semantic shift, marks an important ideological and geographical difference. The earlier institution was reportedly established by Manuel Fraga in the 1960s in response to complaints that, if Madrid had two national theatres, then Barcelona should have at least one (Buffery, 2006, p. 196). In other words, it was a Spanish national theatre located in Catalonia; the TNC, in contrast, is the theatre of a nation without a state. Its first director would be Josep Maria Flotats who received his training in France and Germany after fleeing Francoist Spain to return to Catalonia amid considerable fanfare in 1983.

As Lourdes Orozco notes, 'the return of Flotats to the Catalan theatrical scene proved to be highly controversial because of the special treatment that the Generalitat devoted to him at the expense of other practitioners' (2006, p. 214). Between 1980 and 2003, Jordi Pujol of the centre-right and nationalistic CiU was president of the Generalitat and – as Kathryn Crameri has demonstrated throughout her book on the subject (2008) – cultural policy has taken an important role in the forging of late-twentieth-century Catalan identity. This has been true of elite as well as mass forms of cultural expression: 'it was not only the media in Catalonia that was highly politicized by the Catalan government, culture and theater in particular also fell into the hands of the Convergència's nationalist ideology' (Orozco, 2006, p. 213).

Flotats was Pujol's choice for the TNC, and the theatre was seen by many to be a puppet for the latter's nationalist and political ambitions (Antón, 2004). Between 1998 and 2002, the proportion of co-productions between the TNC and other companies was around 35 per cent (Castells, 2002, p. 156). However, in line with the Generalitat's general policy of prioritizing international over national links, there was a 'penchant for inviting European directors to bring prestige to Catalan-language projects' and, in spite of some isolated high-profile initiatives, 'there continue to be complaints that the Catalan national theatre space offers insufficient opportunities to companies from the rest of the Spanish state' (Buffery, 2006, p. 204). This is in sharp contrast to a mission statement made by Flotats just after the opening of the theatre:

> La profesión de toda España tiene las puertas del TNC abiertas. Quiero que haya la mayor comunicación posible con todos los teatros y que surjan proyectos comunes, mucho más allá de la simple invitación mutua. Aquí se harán producciones en todos los idiomas. Es el TNC y se da prioridad a la lengua catalana. Pero, como ya he dicho con Pujol delante, el día que montemos un Calderón se hará en castellano. Lo contrario resultaría una estúpida dilapidación de esfuerzos. (cited in J. A., 1997, p. 45)
>
> [The TNC's doors are open to professionals from every part of Spain. I want there to be the best possible communication with every other theatre and for joint projects to emerge which go far beyond mutual invitations. Here, we will do productions in every language. It is the TNC and the Catalan language will therefore be prioritized. But, as I have already said in Pujol's presence, when we come to stage Calderón, it will be in Castilian. To do anything else would be a stupid waste of time and effort.]

In at least one respect, this promise would be fulfilled in Belbel's production of *El alcalde de Zalamea*. There are a number of reasons why this production came about. One explanation offered by Salvat – who has some grounds for feeling marginalized by the institutions of democratic Catalonia even if his constant attempts to inscribe himself as central to almost any recent development in theatre, alongside his predilection for conspiracy theories and hyperbole render his claims problematic – is that Pujol was forced into staging the play as a result of a campaign undertaken by the author Antonio Gala, which raised concerns about whether young people in Catalonia were learning Castilian properly (cited in Simón, 2003, p. 157). More substantially, Belbel was associate director of the CNTC that, considering its lack of stability and continuity at the time, was in need of outside help to commemorate such an emblematic event as the centenary. From the Catalan perspective, there is no equivalent to the Spanish Golden Age in drama (George, 2002, p. 11), and a refusal to engage with Calderón in 2000 might have been interpreted as a sign of open hostility.

The second Catalan engagement of the centenary year was *La vida es sueño*, a joint venture between the Teatre Romea and the CNTC in which the former was by far the more dominant partner. Calixto Bieito, appointed artistic director of the Barcelona theatre in 1999, had already staged the play in English at the Edinburgh Festival and the Barbican prior to his production in Castilian. As a result of his Shakespeare productions in

English, Spanish and Catalan – and, more recently, his operatic career – he may, in Maria Delgado's words, be the director from Spain 'who finally breaks into the visible European axis of *auteurs* forging dissident, eclectic readings that highlight rather than erase the contradictory or contentious elements of the work staged' (2006, p. 107).

It is somewhat embarrassing for the CNTC that Bieito received very positive reviews abroad for his work with the Spanish classics,[21] when the company had in the past received a lukewarm response in the UK.[22] The Catalan director has also implicitly undermined the company in public interviews where he has declared an interest in directing works in Castilian: 'Hay gente que escribe muy bien en España, y además nos queda todo un trabajo de recuperación del Siglo de Oro' [There are people who write very well in Spain and, furthermore, we still have a mighty task ahead of us in recuperating the Golden Age] (cited in Francisco, 2002). As discussed in chapter three, the CNTC has been unable to satisfactorily address the latter challenge.

It would have been fascinating to see how this recuperation process might have taken place if Bieito had been allowed to assume artistic control of the CNTC in the mid 1990s (see chapter one). Delgado has identified the following performance constants in his multilingual Shakespeare productions:

> Bieito's approach is never simply an issue of unquestioningly 'updating' the work in question. Rather his productions are always dependent on a series of cultural juxtapositions which recast the work through a complex modern-day reference system, providing uncomfortable readings that rediscover the theatricality of the medium, and stimulate enquiry into the ways these cultural works shape how we see and, crucially, how we act. (2006, p. 108)

This accurate and insightful description is equally applicable to his staging(s) of Calderón's best-known play. *La vida es sueño* is the *comedia* with the highest number of different extant *original* editions (Vega García Luengos, Cruickshank and Ruano de la Haza, 2000, p. 13), and Bieito immediately confounds expectation by basing his performance script not on the canonical play text designed at the time for publication but a much earlier performance script.[23] This move is symptomatic of a production that focusses somewhat incessantly on the construction of *La vida es sueño*'s theatricality.

Modern-day productions of the play have tended to make a concerted effort to distance themselves from the pomp associated with productions from the Francoist period; hence, for example, the CNTC's 1996 production directed by Ariel García Valdés deliberately eschewed any sense of grandiloquence in stage design and declamatory styles. Bieito breaks with the general consensus in modern-day *comedia* performance that verse ceases to be problematic when the audience understands the content and is unaware of its presence. From the opening scene where Rosaura explains her plight, the actors frequently recite their lines so quickly that it is challenging to understand all or even any of what they are saying. The director has claimed that this is a deliberate choice and yet:

> people kept asking why the characters were talking so fast as this stopped them from understanding the text. My answer was that it's impossible to understand the text because even if you're reading it you can't really understand it as you need a dictionary close by to really comprehend the meaning of the sentences. It's the same with Shakespeare. The sound of the words is like a song; it's like music. You can't ignore this and just concentrate on what each word means. (cited in Delgado, 2004, p. 74)

Bieito showcases a rhythmic sensibility throughout, complemented by his choice of Alicia Hermida as assistant director; as Eduardo Pérez-Rasilla has analysed in reference to Carlos Álvarez Novoa's performance as Basilio (2006), the actors were sufficiently versatile and skilled in the musicality of verse that they were able to convey different moods and ambience through more than semantic content. That the declamatory style closely resembled traditions nurtured in the dictatorship period was indicative of the deliberate cultivation of a Francoist aesthetic. The director, a long-time resident of Catalonia who was nevertheless born in Burgos, claims that his images of authority and repression are forged through childhood memories, and that he wanted 'aprovecharlo para componer este cuento tenebroso con una magia oscura y castellana' [to take advantage of it to compose a sinister tale with that dark Castilian magic]. He set out to recast Poland in collaboration with stage designer Carlos Pujol: 'tiene mucho que ver con Castilla, así que picamos piedra escocesa y hicimos un círculo de grava que podría ser la piedra de El Escorial después de caer una bomba' [it is very similar to Castile, and so we made a gravel circle by breaking up Scottish stones so that they had the appearance of what the rocks from El Escorial might look like after a bomb had fallen] (cited in CNTC, 2001, p. 99).

In line with this aesthetic, Clotaldo – Segismundo's guardian in the tower – is dressed in a military outfit and is depicted less as a benevolent instructor than a man obsessed with regulations and order. When he informs Basilio that intruders have entered Segismundo's prison, he becomes increasingly irate as this transgression impedes him from expressing himself in an intelligible manner; his diatribe only comes to an end when the king slaps him repeatedly in the face. The production in its entirety can be read as an interrogation into the audience's complicity with the performativity and performability of both fascism and Calderón's play text; a mirror that hangs above them in an increasingly precarious manner implicates them both visually and metaphorically in the onstage action. The performance is self-consciously Brechtian in style throughout; hence, for example, Roger Coma's deliberately exaggerated gestures and declamatory style often giving the impression that he is depicting an actor performing Astolfo – the play's chief villain, a Machiavellian prince who attempts to usurp Segismundo's claim to the throne – rather than the actual character.

This is a virtuoso production with much to admire. Personally, however, I found it unengaging and somewhat adolescent in its desire to call attention to its transgressions in scenes such as the one where the king recites his principal soliloquy naked, much to the chagrin of Astolfo who repeatedly attempts to cover him. What I did, however, find fascinating was Bieito's willingness to actively engage with precisely the kind of tradition that the CNTC has actively sought to disavow. Perhaps the director's outsider status not only makes him more predisposed to reinscribe the past in a radically new context, but also more immune from censure even if his aim is clearly to interrogate rather than reproduce historical and historicizing tropes; hence, for example, the willingness to celebrate Calderón's play text while showing its amenability to be appropriated by a totalitarian regime such as Francoism.

That this overt politicization is the exception rather than the norm in *comedia* performance is reiterated in the TNC's second foray into the Castilian classical canon with a production of *Fuente Ovejuna*, staged as part

Figure 12   Photograph by Ros Ribas of *La vida es sueño* (dir. Calixto Bieito, 2000) CNTC and Teatre Romea

of an exchange with the CNTC. Both theatres were passing through symbolic transitional phases at the time. Vasco had recently been made artistic director of the latter, while 2005 marked Domènech Reixach's final year at the helm of the TNC prior to the ascension of Belbel. Since Pujol departed the presidency of the Generalitat in 2003, there had been attempts at cultural normalization and *Fuente Ovejuna* was largely the result of an agreement signed between INAEM and the TNC on 21 March 2005 to increase collaboration.

Illustrious *madrileño* Juan Mayorga prepared the adaptation for Catalan Ramón Simó who directed a cast that he claimed was comprised of 'algunos actores que son los mejores de España, pero desconocidos a este lado del Ebro' [some of the best actors in Spain who are, nonetheless, unknown on this side of the River Ebro] (cited in Albesa, 2005). While the onstage politics were minimized with a renewed emphasis on human relationships (see chapter two), the production – like the town of Fuente Ovejuna – was both the product and cause of political reconciliation. The need for linguistic and cultural reconciliation was vocalized by Simó who argued that:

> Cataluña no tiene por qué cerrarse a los clásicos castellanos, ya que una de las riquezas de Cataluña es que todo el mundo entiende el castellano. Por tanto, es como si hiciéramos una obra de Shakespeare, pero sin tener que traducir el texto al catalán . . . Éste ha sido un primer paso, aunque también nos gustaría que los intercambios no fueran sólo a través de la cultura castellana, sino también de la catalana. Las obras catalanas deberían representarse también en el resto de España. (cited in Corroto, 2005)
>
> [Catalonia has no reason to close itself off from the Castilian classics since one of Catalonia's assets is that everyone understands Castilian. It is therefore as if we were to stage a Shakespeare play, but without having to translate it into Catalan . . . This has been a first step, although we would like exchanges to be done through Catalan as well as Castilian culture. Catalan plays should also be staged in the rest of Spain.]

Borrás may have performed a Catalan season in Madrid in 1904 (George, 2002, pp. 60–1), but the likelihood of this occurring in the twenty-first century especially within the context of a high-profile National Theatre is limited at best. Furthermore, this mutual invitation hardly constitutes the kind of joint venture that Flotats had previously advocated. It was, however, symptomatic of Vasco's political savvy and a genuine commitment to moving beyond Madrid. Since 2004, many of the CNTC's productions have premiered outside the capital and the director has claimed that:

> se trata de una política deliberada que pretende indicar que el adjetivo nacional no representa un simple adorno del nombre de la compañía. Hemos estrenado en Zamora, en Alicante o en Sevilla y, por supuesto en

festivales como Almagro y Alcalá de Henares. Todos los españoles pagan los mismos impuestos y todos tienen idéntico derecho a asistir a estrenos absolutos de la compañía. (cited in *El País*, 2008)

[this is a deliberate policy designed to show that the adjective 'national' represents more than a decorative adjunct to the company's name. We have premiered in Zamora, in Alicante and in Seville; and, of course, in festivals such as Almagro and Alcalá de Henares. All Spaniards pay the same taxes and therefore have an equal right to attend the company's absolute premieres.]

While this level of activity beyond Madrid is to be applauded and means that, for the first time in its history, the CNTC can lay claim to being a National Company in more than name, it also provides a practical solution to a very literal structural problem Vasco inherited: the continued unavailability of the Teatro de la Comedia. As Amestoy has recently lamented:

Es sorprendente que la compañía emblemática del teatro español tenga que sobrevivir en el Pavón, un lugar que podría ser complementario, una tercera sede, nunca el mascarón de proa. Tres teatros tiene la Comédie! [*sic*] Urge tomar decisiones ... Una asignatura pendiente de la CNTC es la del establecimiento de correspondencias e intercambios con las grandes compañías de todo el mundo. ¡Ni a la Royal Shakespeare Company ni a la Comédie Francaise [*sic*] se las puede traer al Pavón! (2008)

[It is surprising that Spanish theatre's emblematic company has to make do in the Pavón, a site which could be an adjunct, a third space but never the flagship theatre. The Comédie has three theatres! Decisive action is called for! ... A pending matter for the CNTC is the establishing of mutual invitations and exchanges with the world's major companies. You cannot bring the RSC or the Comédie Française to the Pavón!]

These objections may be rather excessive in their obsession with status and prestige but it is undeniably true that the company's temporary home, although a perfectly acceptable medium-size theatre, does not have the characteristics that one would expect from a company of the CNTC's stature and repute. A pretty standard Italianate theatre, it has no obvious historical value while its location in Lavapiés, a multiethnic area of Madrid, is the kind of area in which one would normally expect to find fringe and experimental drama.

Although the Pavón might not be a suitable venue for the RSC, Vasco has opened its doors to a broad range of Spanish practitioners. Rafael Rodríguez has, for example, been instrumental in resurrecting *comedia* performance in the Canary Islands – not traditionally a hub of theatrical activity – with 2Rc Producciones, whose output includes *La verdad sospechosa* and *El perro del hortelano*.[24] Vasco took notice of these regional achievements and invited the director to stage Lope's *¿De cúando acá nos vino?* with the

Figure 13   Photograph by Nicolas Trémouilhe of Pavón Theatre

National Company in 2009. He also utilized the fact that the PP now controlled both Madrid and Valencia city councils to coordinate a landmark exchange with the Teatres de la Generalitat, which involved the latter having a well-received residency in the Pavón over Christmas 2009 with a production of *La viuda valenciana* directed by Vicente Genovés.

The replacement of an antiquated and chauvinistic discourse with an increasingly democratic and communicative non-centric approach can, nevertheless, have disabling as well as enabling consequences. Vasco has announced that the Teatro de la Comedia will, when it reopens, retain the architectural divide between stage and auditorium. This is perhaps surprising, considering that this design style is anachronistic in terms of both original performance traditions and contemporary thinking. As Maurice Hindle notes, '[m]ost new theatres these days are replacing the "two room" division of spaces produced by the old-style proscenium arch with more prominent stages bringing actor and audience closer together in "one room"' (2007, p. 5). Hence, for example, the current director of the RSC Michael Boyd has cited the introduction of thrust staging as one of his major priorities.[25] The Spanish director has nevertheless defended the decision by claiming that 90 per cent of theatres in the country are based on the Italianate model so any major innovations in the capital would force them to adapt productions when they toured. There is some logic in this claim. The *comedia* tends not to be performed in innovative theatrical spaces such as the Matadero in Madrid or the Mercat de les Flors in Barcelona and, in spite of their individual charms, the vast majority of theatres in Spain are, in fact, remarkably homogenous in terms of basic design. Even the *corral* in Almagro, which in many respects resembles the Globe in London, has a proscenium arch and provides no standing room for modern-day groundlings.

Nevertheless, to my mind at least, an important part of the CNTC's *raison d'être* is to instigate change and innovation even if this does occasion inconvenience. Its inability or unwillingness to do so in this case is, in my opinion, symptomatic of a broader problem: existing at the margins of international theatre, it is now carrying out the somewhat belated task of moving away from an antiquated model of the centre defining the periphery. As Bieito's production of *La vida es sueño* has shown, it is a distinct possibility that figures emerging from what was once seen as the margins may enter global networks with greater ease and skill. The CNTC's attempts to balance the admittedly challenging demands placed upon it in its attempts to move beyond Madrid and become a genuinely (inter)national company have, as we have seen, been partially successful at best.

The *comedia* as a cultural commodity: Almagro and heritage tourism

Until Almagro was given international exposure as a result of Pedro Almodóvar's film *Volver* (2006), this small provincial town in La Mancha, with just under nine thousand inhabitants, was best known for theatre; more specifically for its beautifully conserved sixteenth-century *corral*. On 29 May 1954, its theatrical doors reopened for the first time in the modern era with a performance of Calderón's *auto sacramental, La hidalga del valle*, directed by Gustavo Pérez Puig. A plaque at the entrance says that it was declared a historical monument by the Ministry of National Education in 1955 and, coinciding with a boom in tourism, the venue was used throughout the decade for a variety of activities including beauty pageants and medieval dinners (Peláez Martín, 1997, p. 21).

It would not be until the 1980s, however, that the Almagro Festival established itself as a major player in Spain's cultural calendar. While it had begun as a series of *Jornadas* accompanied by performances, it was now a Theatre Festival that incorporated academic discussion under its aegis. The ascension of the PSOE to government in 1982 facilitated its consolidation, and it adopted something approaching its current guise. As a result of regional devolution, it ceased to be the exclusive patrimony of the state and

1983 proved to be a landmark year with productions by companies from Spain, Italy, France, Portugal and America. It was a mark of the esteem in which it was now held that the new minister of culture, Javier Solana, attended, as did the vice-president of Italy and cultural attaches from France and the US. Largely as a result of this foreign intervention, Almagro would from 1984 onwards be defined as an International Festival envisaged as a symbol of cultural and political normalization.

There are clear antecedents to this project in the more established European festivals described by Dennis Kennedy in the following terms:

> In a Europe absorbed with social and material reconstruction, the post-war festivals often identified spiritual recovery as essential to their foundation and demanded pilgrimage as a necessary part of the experience. The first examples, the Edinburgh International Festival and the Avignon Festival, set out in the summer of 1947 to revive a fading European memory and used Shakespeare to return to the cultural high ground. (2000, p. 4)

Avignon and Edinburgh also provided attractive summer holiday destinations for wealthy tourists. Stark economic realities would not have made large-scale projects of this kind tenable in the post-war period in Spain; the closest equivalent to the European festivals – and the most obvious antecedents for Almagro – were the (in)famous Festivales de España where productions, rather than spectators, had to travel.

In 1989, the festival was moved from September to June/July in order to coincide with the holiday season, and its development must be understood in relation to changes in Spain's tourist industry for which Franco's death had created a number of challenges and opportunities. On the one hand, it allowed for a hitherto prohibited degree of efficiency and productivity in regional tourism planning (Ivars Baidal, 2004). On the other, the industry was a vital part of its economy and yet Spain's incorporation into the international community brought into sharp relief the problems of coastal over-development and the challenges of offering sustainable tourism. As M. Robinson notes, this was particularly problematic because, '[a]way from the historic cities, towns, villages and coastal centres, interior Spain has a shortage of "formal" attractions to absorb tourists' interests' (1996, p. 413).

One possible solution was cultural tourism, which was also advantageous for a number of additional reasons. Firstly, it provided a good fit for international trends, as Marlene K. Smith has analysed in some depth, the sector identified and consolidated as one of the major future growth areas in Europe at the time (2003, p. 31). Secondly, it provided a good fit for lifestyle changes. Improvements in the domestic economy meant that by the early 1990s Spaniards were, for the first time, becoming mass consumers of their own tourism (Stewart, 1992). As Paul Julian Smith notes, unlike most leisure activities, cultural visits were consistently on the increase throughout the decade (2006, p. 101); it would, therefore, be crucial to the festival's growth and survival that it cater not only to *comedia* specialists and aficionados, but also to 'the increasing number of Spaniards who seem to find visiting historical monuments a leisure activity appropriate to moneyed, modern life' (2006, p. 108).

The effects of this new emerging demographic can also be seen in other initiatives and the state's increased willingness in the late 1980s and early 1990s to invest money in the classics and their commemoration, supporting, for example, the reopening of Lope's house in Madrid as a museum. The villages of Zalamea and Fuente Ovejuna also resurrected an old custom of staging huge outdoor performances of the plays that helped immortalize their towns in the national psyche.[26] There is, however, a potential downside to this boom in subsidized *comedia* performance for, as Susan Bennett notes, '[w]hile state support might make cultural products available to more people, the range available for consumption will be limited by the state's conception of what constitutes (suitable) art' (1997, p. 88).

One explanation for why heritage tourism caught on so rapidly is that '[i]n the Spanish view of things, culture, like education, is axiomatically good' (Hooper, 1995 p. 322). As a result, Spanish policymakers and practitioners do not generally have to concern themselves with the charges of elitism or objections to promoting a purely middle-class view of culture which are sometimes raised in the UK around Shakespeare performances. In Pierre Bourdieu's terms, the rules of the cultural game are very different:

> Culture is a stake which, like all social stakes, simultaneously presupposes and demands that one take part in the game and be taken in by it; and interest in culture, without which there is no race, no competition, is produced by the very race and competition which it produces. The value of culture, the supreme fetish, is generated in the initial investment implied by the mere fact of entering the game, joining in the collective belief in the value of the game which makes the game and endlessly remakes the competition for the stakes. (1984, p. 250)

When the notion of culture is accepted without question, as in the case of Spain, the overriding question concerns what constitutes culture and, yet again, subsidies and inclusion in official events perform a crucial role for they are often construed as an assurance of quality. This provides one explanation as to why productions that form part of annual state or municipal schemes regularly sell out in advance yet seemingly fail to ignite a wider interest in Golden Age drama. In other words, critics and audiences only appear to be willing to embrace the *comedia* in predefined contexts that are largely dependent on official manifestations of democratic culture. Stage and screen adaptations are often judged not so much for their artistic merits as to what they represent as cultural fetishes. This localization of success is clearly both a symptom and cause of Luciano García-Lorenzo's claim that no private company could stage a classic without a subsidy (2007a, pp. 94–5).

Subsidized theatre in democratic Spain constitutes a paradigmatic illustration of Frederick Schauer's observation that the 'traditional ontology of coercive governmental interference has in recent years become sufficiently inclusive to recognize that governments may often operate (and thus restrict) indirectly as effectively as it operates directly' (1998, p. 150). The irony, as Joan Ramón Resina argues, is that the contemporary Spanish state tends to defend and define itself against the dictatorship's culture of overt 'coercive governmental interference':

> The dominant narrative strategy has been to simulate a temporal division in what is patently a political one. Adjoining the boundary on the wrong side are the particular cultures, on which diminishing and demeaning descriptions of folklorism, provincialism and self-absorption are heaped to justify their expulsion from the bounds of the universal (i.e. state sponsored) culture. Irrespectively of their function, contents or significance, particular cultures are consigned to an inert temporality whose effect upon them is to liquidate any claims to viability and relevance. (2000, p. 11)

Golden Age drama occupies an ambivalent position in this temporal–cultural division for it exists on both sides of the boundary. This helps to explain the reluctance to engage with past precedents, and clearly has a decisive effect not only on production but also on reception. In chapter four, we saw the danger in being consigned to the category of 'inert temporality' in relation to the critical and commercial failure of the film adaption of *La dama boba*. An implicit chastisement of a similar kind can also be detected in a review of *Fuente Ovejuna* staged in the eponymous town in 1992 for the first time in thirty years: 'Los fuegos artificiales inundan la plaza mayor del pueblo. Las campanas de la iglesia repican sin cesar, ante el júbilo de todos. Una ovación cerrada: "lo hemos conseguido". Podría ser una escena de *Calabush*, la película de Berlanga, pero es Fuente Ovejuna.' [The fireworks inundated the town's main square. The church bells rang ceaselessly to accompany the mass celebration. A standing ovation: 'we've done it'. It could have been a scene from Berlanga's film *Calabush* but it is Fuente Ovejuna] (Pascual, 1992, p. 2). Subsequent productions have tended to focus less on the play's folkloric and regional elements, and more on its relation to contemporary social and political matters.

It has been essential to Almagro's growth and reputation that it has actively aligned itself with international rather than national traditions. This rise and consolidation was inextricably linked with the Socialist conception of democratic culture and it is, therefore, no surprise that the festival was less prominent between 1996 and 2004 when the PP were in government. On the left's return to power, José Luis Rodríguez Zapatero became the first leader in the democracy to specifically discuss culture in his inaugural address: 'El destino de un pueblo depende del valor que sus gobiernos dan a la cultura. Por ello me propongo que la cultura se sitúe en las cuestiones de Estado' [The fate of a nation depends on the value that their governments place on culture. Because of this I propose that culture becomes a matter of state] (2004, p. 7). In the second half of this section, I would like to discuss the approach taken by Emilio Hernández who was made director of the festival in the wake of the Socialist victory in 2004. He has stated his desire for Almagro to become 'la capital europea del teatro clásico' [the European capital of classical theatre] (cited in López Antuñano, 2007, p. 101), and has defined the criteria for inclusion as follows:

> Que no se repitan las compañías, que se produzca una rotación para que no existan compañías estables del Festival. Sin embargo, el problema con el que nos encontramos es que no existe mucha variedad en propuestas de teatro clásico. También queremos seguir programando compañías extranjeras y que se realice un proceso de intercambio. (p. 100)

> [That the same companies are not always repeated, that there is a rotation so that there are not permanent festival companies. The problem, however, is that there is not a great deal of variety on offer as far as classical theatre is concerned. We also want to continue programming foreign companies and to participate in cultural exchanges.]

The *comedia* may have been instrumental in staking Almagro's claim as a cultural tourist destination but its role is no longer clear: its problematic status at home means that it is not widely performed and its relative obscurity at the global level does not necessarily encourage the profile and collaboration now being actively sought.[27] Nevertheless, Golden Age drama was afforded an unusual prominence in the thirty-first edition of the festival. In a detailed article on the productions staged that year, I conclude:

> In terms of *comedia* performance in modern-day Spain, the 2008 Almagro Theater Festival was unprecedented in both intensity and range ... This ought to be a cause for celebration but, as we have seen, quantity was not matched by quality. With a few notable exceptions, productions did little to sharpen the specialist's appreciation of canonical or lesser-known works, and it is difficult to imagine that they would make the general public more inclined to further explore Golden Age drama. (2012b)

I was not alone in my misgivings, and reputed director Adrián Daumas – whose production of *El castigo sin venganza* provided one of Almagro's highlights in 2003 – entered into a very public dispute with Hernández. He has criticized the festival's director in a very personal manner through his blog; and in a published newspaper article, he claimed that '[h]abría que prescindir de Emilio Hernández como director y hacer que el Festival vuelva a tener pocos espectáculos pero de una gran calidad' [we must get rid of Emilio Hernández as director and ensure that the festival returns to its previous custom of having a few high-quality productions] (cited in Otto, 2008). The debate hinged as much on differing notions of success as it did on the particularities and individuals concerned.

In spite of my reservations, Hernández clearly achieved his goal of generating cultural tourism and raising the festival's profile in 2008. There were sales of nearly eighty thousand tickets; this equates to a 3 per cent increase from 2007, and an average occupancy of 85 per cent (EFE, 2008b). The desire to establish international links was obvious with a substantial amount of the festival's budget dedicated to securing prestigious companies from abroad. The director also held a party for the EU ambassadors in the German diplomatic offices in advance of the Festival where guests were greeted by actors from Denis Rafter's company dressed as ladies and knights. As a result of British company Cheek By Jowl's receiving a prize, the festival was discussed on BBC Radio Four in the UK.

Hernández's predecessor, Luciano García Lorenzo, had boasted that over twice the number of people who buy tickets visit the town during the festival (2005, pp. 50–1), and Almagro's mayor, Luis Maldonado, has referred to the event as 'uno de nuestros principales motores tanto a nivel social como económico' [one of our principal generators as much at the social as at the economic level]. For a town of Almagro's size, the effect on the local economy is considerable. Day trippers may travel by train but the intense heat of La Mancha ensures that performances tend not to begin much before eleven in the evening. As a result, visitors without a car tend to have to stay in the town itself as there are no late trains and the sole taxi driver does not work late in the evenings. Hotels are thereby able to charge premium rates that are often double or triple the standard tariff during the festival period. Furthermore, as Hernández notes, culture is 'una de las industrias que pueden tener más futuro en España' [among the industries that could have the best prospects in Spain] and '[e]s tan alto el número de espectadores que si no repercute ahora, repercutirá después, ya que la gente viene a hacer simplemente turismo porque se le ha despertado el interés tras venir a ver teatro' [the number of spectators is so high that if the effects are not felt immediately, they will be in the future; people will simply come here as tourists having had their interest piqued by coming to the theatre] (cited in EFE, 2009b).[28]

These arguments clearly provide a justification for the amount of public money invested in the festival. However, one of the many complaints I hear from Spanish practitioners about Hernández is that he has placed too much emphasis on what Alison J. McIntosh has termed 'the experiential dimensions of consumption' (2007, p. 237), and has turned Almagro into a classical theme park. This impression is bolstered by the increased prominence of street displays and performances that, while effectively broadening the potential audience, also run the risk of diverting attention away from investment, both financial and artistic, in stage productions.

In other words, we might object that the *comedia* is understood as cultural capital in the commercial rather than the artistic sense. This phenomenon is hardly specific to Almagro or Spain, and there has been widespread criticism of theatre festivals around Europe – Edinburgh in particular (see Harvie, 2005) – for subscribing to what Priscilla Boniface and Peter J. Fowler diagnose as 'cultural commodification as a cure for all' (1993, p. 2). Susan Bennett has, nevertheless, provided an important caveat for those of us who might be predisposed to rally against the commercialization of culture:

> Where the context is tourism, it would seem that the play is but one thing among many that produce, confirm, and encourage a register of experiences that cumulatively allow for the pleasure that underwrites the spectator's presence. This conclusion is not to serve the cause of wringing our collective scholarly hands over the fate of Shakespeare performance but to understand an economic and cultural reality – one that, rather surprisingly, assumes the viability of theatre in the twenty-first-century marketplace. (2005, p. 507)

In relation to Almagro, the priority ought not to be to lament the fact that it is no longer necessarily programmed or designed with the *comedia* specialist in mind, but to realistically assess to what extent recent transitions may enable or stifle Golden Age drama in performance. In spite of my concerns, it does nevertheless provide an umbrella for a number of key events that would probably not take place if it were not for the festival. It supplies, for example, one of the rare opportunities to recognize past achievements with annual awards given for lifetime achievements. Since 2005, these have been selected in what appears to be a fairly judicious manner with Pérez Sierra and José Tamayo receiving just recognition for their vast contribution to *comedia* performance. This can also be a forum in which to promote publications that have important scholarly and historical value; the homage given to Ángel F. Montesinos also served as a book launch for his memoirs on which I based much of my discussion of his landmark yet largely forgotten production of *La viuda valenciana* in chapter one.[29]

In terms of actual performances, patience and money is required to separate the wheat from the chaff but audiences are still able to attend accomplished and enjoyable productions; in a year as lean as 2008, there were opportunities to see *Las manos blancas no ofenden* and *Chrónica de Fuente Ovejuna*. Whether many of those present would have had the opportunity or inclination to see them if they did not form part of a wider experience is not clear; it is similarly debatable as to how viable these productions would be if it were not for such high-profile residencies. To cite a concrete example,

Dan Jemmett's engaging, albeit stylistically uneven, production of *El burlador de Sevilla* from the same year sold out in Almagro; three months earlier, I had watched it in the company of fewer than thirty other spectators, all over the age of sixty, as part of its initial run at the Abadía. This was in spite or perhaps because of the fact that the tickets were far cheaper in Madrid. The interesting question to arise from this observation – and to which there is no definitive answer – is if it were not for the existence of Almagro and its kind, would productions elsewhere fare better, or would they simply disappear?

Rather than bemoan the seemingly inevitable direction that large theatre festivals are taking – and over which we have little if any control or influence – I think that the efforts of scholars and practitioners alike would be better directed at attempts to curb excesses and optimize Golden Age drama's chances within this existing framework. In many respects, Almagro is following broader pan-European trends but an important distinction can nevertheless be detected in relation to what has been termed 'the arm's length principle'. According to Robert Hewison, this has acted as a buffer against despotic behaviour in the UK: 'A convention has been established over the years in arts patronage that neither the politician nor the bureaucrat knows best' (1995, p. 32). There has been an unwillingness to apply this principle in Spain where cultural decisions are often made for sectarian reasons, and are subject to political interference at both the local and state level.

Hence, for example, performances in Fuente Ovejuna are reliant on municipal funding, and have become the plaything of warring factions. Isabel Pérez from the PP cancelled a production that had been organized by the previous administration when she became mayor in 1999; Agustín Martín from the PSOE would repeat this strategy four years later. Isidro Rodríguez Gallardo had already begun rehearsals of a production that ought, theoretically, to have appealed to a left-wing administration: it was designed to promote European citizenry through the inclusion of non-professional actors from different countries (García-Martín, 2004, pp. 115–16). The new mayor publicly claimed that there were no funds available but, according to Rodríguez Gallardo, openly told him that he had no intention of inheriting projects from a predecessor especially when the individual in question was female![30]

In terms of large public institutions, artistic directors are often political appointments, yet in other respects they have an unusual level of power because they are not generally answerable to a board which, when it does exist, often has little more than symbolic worth. This, combined with the economic advantages of working within public rather than private theatres, automatically makes them liable to charges of nepotism of which they are often guilty. Vasco has not been immune from disgruntled moans among the theatrical community about who he has chosen to contract;[31] complaints have, however, been far more vociferous and widespread in relation to Hernández's controversial administration in Almagro. He was, for example, criticized in 2008 for effectively contracting himself – alongside his wife, Magüi Mira, as assistant director – by staging his production of *El burlador de Sevilla* in a prime location at the height of the festival. It is also widely believed that he did not invite the very popular production of *La viuda valenciana* to participate in the 2009 edition because Mira, a native of Valencia, had wanted to direct a version of the play herself, and Hernández was angered by the competition. Whether or not this anecdote is true is largely incidental: the fact that he was believed capable of making such a decision is indicative of a severe lack of confidence in the current administration, and a lack of transparency in its decision-making processes.

In an exception to the general trend outlined above, Hernández was dismissed by the festival board in February 2010 due to mounting debts, charges of nepotism, a lack of financial transparency and personal differences. It is unlikely that this decision would have been taken if it were not necessitated by the current economic crisis that is ill-suited to the director's ambitious market-driven response. It does, however, at least provide the possibility to reflect on the criteria for inclusion in the festival and serves as a hopefully productive indictment on the power currently invested in individuals, which might encourage the compartmentalizing of specific responsibilities. I hope that this might provide a fertile climate in which to focus on a series of more modest productions that nevertheless seek to engage with the Golden Age in a less cosmetic manner than has been the norm. I am, however, very much aware that the rules of cultural play and heritage tourism entail that *comedia* performance will be but one, and by no means the most important, consideration among many.

Conclusion

As José M. Magone notes, [s]upport for European integration has become probably one of the most salient features of Spanish political culture' (2009, p. 58), and this has clearly been reflected in theatrical policy. Certainly in relation to the staging of Golden Age drama, subsidized culture and European integration are not the panacea that they are often assumed to be. This is firstly because the practices and productions of international institutions are often accepted too uncritically with insufficient account being taken of their potential weaknesses; and secondly because the attempt to integrate a foreign model into the Spanish context can be invigorating but, as has too often been the case, is not always implemented successfully as a result of local peculiarities.

Principal among these is the disproportionate level of power and influence held by agents of official culture. One common lesson that can, I think, clearly be learned from these three discussions is that policymakers, audiences and practitioners alike have placed too high a premium on their often unquestioning acceptance of state-endorsed theatre. This control, exacerbated by the suspect practices fostered by the infrastructure of cultural institutions, often functions as an indirect form of censorship with clear antecedents in the dictatorship. A major difference lies, however, in the fact that regional devolution entails that cultural power is no longer so highly concentrated in the capital.

This is a double-edged sword as regards Golden Age performance. In one regard, a conscious or subconscious association of Calderón, Lope and Tirso with centralist discourses can lead to their marginalization, but it also provides the occasional new forum or approach to the way in which they are staged. This is most evident in relation to Catalonia, arguably the most international of Spain's autonomous regions. When he ran the Théâtre de l'Europe in France, Lluis Pasqual directed more works from the Spanish dramatic canon that he had at home (Bradby and Delgado, 2002, p. 22); in addition to works by Lorca and Valle-Inclán, he also staged Lope's *El caballero de Olmedo*. As we have seen, it would be his former assistant director and protégé, Calixto Bieito, who would then promote Calderón abroad while opening an unusually challenging debate over his theatrical and ideological meaning in contemporary Spain.

These figures are, however, the exceptions rather than the norm. David Bradby and Annie Sparks have noted how in contemporary French theatre, the 'reinterpretation of classic plays, ranging from Shakespeare and Molière to French Farce, has become the accepted way for young directors to make their mark' (1997, p. 48). This is a less established practice in Spain and, even when it does occur, it is rarely in relation to a *comedia*. Even Bieito's efforts with Golden Age drama pale in comparison to the energy he has invested in reinterpreting Shakespeare for the contemporary stage. This leaves the national classical canon in a somewhat precarious situation: lacking an institution with the RSC's prestige, it is reliant on individual efforts along with support from the various institutions that have ensured its presence on the contemporary stage but nevertheless reproduce strategies that have arguably been instrumental in its marginalization.

Conclusion

This critical survey of Golden Age drama in contemporary Spain is but one of the many that could have been written; the constraints of space and time have meant that I have, by necessity, focussed on certain areas at the expense of others. Television adaptations, for example, might have been analysed in greater depth and I have only mentioned radio plays in passing. Another area in need of further attention is the use of Golden Age drama in schools. How, for example, have controversial new education laws – introduced in 2006 by the PSOE to hand over power to the different autonomous communities – affected how and where Calderón, Lope and Tirso are taught? There is also major research to be done into the work of Republican exiles with the *comedia*, along with the relationship between practitioners in Latin America and Spain during the Franco period; the wealth of material on this topic suggests that it might be best dealt with as a collaborative rather than individual project.

The five studies that comprise this book have, however, at least placed us in a better position to address some of the questions I raised in the introduction. I asked, for example, to what extent Maravall and his followers were influenced by the social and historical climate in which they wrote. As we have seen, the propagandistic interpretation is in fact a more accurate reading of stage and screen versions produced in the 1930s, 1940s and 1950s than it is of the play texts themselves. Imperial monarchs, for example, perform a much more prominent and less ambiguous role in cinematic adaptations than they do in the *comedias* on which they are ostensibly based.

Although Maravall and Díez Borque are undoubtedly the most refined and influential exponents of their school, the central tenets of their argument were already in place by the time they wrote. As I have argued in more detail elsewhere (Wheeler, 2012a), it is, I think, self-evident that the political experiences of living under a dictatorship – whose official culture included the performance of the national classics – helped to forge a view of the theatre as a weapon deployed in a surreptitious offensive waged against a passive audience. What this equation between past and present fails to take into account is that baroque and Francoist mass culture differ in one very important respect: the former was, unlike the latter, extremely popular with its audience over a sustained period of time. One of the principal reasons that *comedia* performance never caught the modern-day popular imagination in Spain as it had in the seventeenth century was that it was staged not so much as art but as propaganda.

Marvin Carlson's concept of 'ghosting', to which allusion was made at the end of the second chapter, can, therefore, be applied in general to the reception of Golden Age drama in modern-day Spain for it provides a salient example of how theatre (in this case on the page, stage and screen) can function as a kind of 'memory machine':

> All reception is deeply involved with memory, because it is memory that supplies the codes and strategies that shape reception, and, as cultural and social memories change, so do the parameters within which reception operates, those parameters that reception theorist Hans Robert Jauss has called the 'horizon of expectations'. (2001, p. 5)

The ghosts of Francoism in association with the tradition of *comedia* performance supplied a specific repertoire of codes and strategies for reading Golden Age drama that had delivered a rather idiosyncratic set of conclusions about its role in the seventeenth century. That this occurred thirty years ago is not, perhaps, surprising; what is more perplexing is that the same 'memory machine' remains in operation and there has not been a radical overhaul of the 'horizon of expectations'. For example Eduardo Haro Tecglen, just prior to his death, spoke of how '[l]os autores, con los corrales llenos de públicos, eran un poco como los de la televisión en tiempo de Franco: unos propagandistas del régimen' [the writers, with the theatres bustling with crowds, were a bit like the stars of television in Franco's time: propagandists of the regime] (2005).

This absence of horizon shaking is, I believe, indicative of a failure to transform a tradition of performance into a performance tradition. In the UK, we are so accustomed to seeing Shakespeare staged that any interpretation of a play automatically has to compete with images from multiple performances that readers/spectators will have seen; in Spain, the lack of a genuine performance tradition ensures that the competition is heavily loaded in the textual critic's favour.

The CNTC and Almagro Festival have both given Golden Age drama a certain symbolic value, but a spectral residue nevertheless haunts both the past and present. This corrosive force negates the possibility of identifying precedents in a tradition of performance that has been politically and artistically nullified in its entirety, while simultaneously leading modern-day performances to actively define themselves in contrast to their predecessors.

This breakdown in communication between successive generations actively discourages the construction of broader hermeneutical bridges between the seventeenth and twenty-first centuries, while the *comedia*'s ambivalent status helps to explain why Calderón, Lope and Tirso are more problematic national treasures than Cervantes, García Lorca or Valle-Inclán.

It is no coincidence that *Fuente Ovejuna* and *El perro del hortelano*, two of the best known and most regularly performed *comedias*, are also viewed with less suspicion by practitioners and audiences alike. This is indicated by the fact that they are the Golden Age plays with productions emerging from the widest cross-section of theatrical companies and geographical origins. The fact that they have not always had such canonical status reveals the contingency of reception. Hence, for example, if *El perro* – or indeed, *La villana de Getafe* – had been more widely known during the dictatorship, it is unlikely that José María Díez Borque would have spoken so broadly of how:

> en el extremo del aristocratismo y la intransigencia social, defenderá que el humilde nacimiento se descubrirá siempre, por más que se ascienda socialmente lo que implica un determinismo social que acepta de forma inquebrantable. (1976, p. 258)[1]

> [from the perspective of extreme aristocratism and social intransigence, he ensured that a humble birth was always discovered; however much anyone climbed the social ladder, he applied a form of social determinism rigorously and without exception.]

This critic's faux pas is a cautionary warning to us all that the corpus of Golden Age plays is so expansive that we need to be cautious about establishing monolithic conclusions of any kind. In a parallel universe where alternative *comedias* had achieved canonical status, our opinions and prejudices about Lope, Calderón and Tirso might be very different indeed. What, for example, would have happened if instead of Calderón's wife murder plays, some of Lope's spousal abuse *comedias* were more famous. *La desdichada Estefanía*, with its clear parallels with *Othello*, replete with its contrite and passionate husband and Iago-esque figure, could potentially have enjoyed a healthy stage life. At the opposite end of the spectrum, Golden Age drama might have been seen in an even darker light if *Los embustes de Celauro*, *El honroso atrevimiento* or *Ello dirá* were better known.[2] In these outrageous comedies, tragedy is only averted at the last minute through the marriage and/or reconcilement of women with physically abusive men, who in many cases are also rapists.

In this life, however, Spanish classical drama remains, to a large extent, foreign and unknown in its country of birth. It would be a betrayal of the basic principles of reception theory on which the book is predicated to make a romantic call to return to the plays as *they are in themselves*, and dispense with their symbolic connotations. Nevertheless, there is a pressing need for the demystification of multiple symbolic layers that, paradoxically, requires memory and amnesia in equal measure. How this is to be achieved is far from clear, but until this process is seriously set in motion, the national dramatists who were arguably the most prolific of any country are destined to retain a minor position in national as well as global canons.[3]

Notes

Introduction

1. The first drama degree programme in the United States was established in 1914 and a department made its debut in the English university system in 1947 (Shepherd and Wallis, 2004, p. 7).
2. Nearly thirty years ago, Andrés Amorós noted the discrepancy in the fact that there was an Instituto de Estudios Shakesperianos [Institute for Shakespearean Studies], funded by the British Council, associated with the University of Valencia, and yet that there was no equivalent department dedicated to Lope or Calderón (cited in Oliva, 1980, p. 32). This observation was accompanied by a whole series of complaints such as 'La institución española descuida gravemente el teatro como fenómeno cultural y social' [Spanish institutions are seriously negligent in their attention to theatre as a social and cultural phenomenon], and that 'el estudio del teatro se limita a la consideración literaria de los textos teatrales, como mero apéndice de los estudios de historia de la literatura española' [the study of theatre is limited to the literary study of theatrical texts; as a mere appendix to studying the history of Spanish literature]. These are reprinted in Oliva, 1980, pp. 50–2. A few years later, Ricard Salvat would complain that '[l]a falta de facultades de ciencias teatrales en nuestro país se está notando cada vez más' [the lack of theatre departments in our country is becoming increasingly obvious] (1984, p. 133).
3. Links between the two worlds have traditionally been closer in Barcelona, largely as a result of the efforts of El Institut del Teatre [Theatrical Institute]. However, at least since the appointment of Hermann Bonnin as director in 1970, Golden Age drama has played a very small role. This is but one manifestation of the marginalization of the *comedia* in modern-day Catalonia which will be discussed in more detail in chapter five. Within the Madrid context, it is to be hoped that this cultural belatedness might, at least in part, be overcome through the recently inaugurated Instituto del Teatro de Madrid that has been established as a partnership between Complutense and Abadía theatre under the directorship of Javier Huerta Calvo, but this remains to be seen.
4. One notable exception from the former camp was Victor Dixon who has, over the course of his academic career, translated and staged many *comedias* in English. Similarly, Alicia Sánchez who has worked as a director, actress and verse coach proved to be a much needed representative of the theatrical community in 2008; not only was she present throughout the *Jornadas* but she also delivered

a very insightful paper on the challenges facing actors who want to appear in productions of Golden Age drama.
5   See essays contained in the collection by Bass; Burningham; García de la Rasilla; Pratt and Hegstrom; and Sieber (2006).
6   See Mariscal, 1990 for a good overview and critique of Parker's school of critical thought.

Chapter 1

1   A good general guide to theatre performed during the Civil War is provided by McCarthy, 1999. For details of *Fuente Ovejuna*, see chapter two. An unpublished dissertation by García-Martín is a good source of information on productions of *Numancia* during the Civil War (2004, p. 203–7), as is Gagen, 2008. For more information on the work of La Barraca and Misiones Pedagógicas with the classics, see Suelto de Sáenz, 1964. For recent scholarship that does examine theatre in the Nationalist zone, see London, 2007; and Dennis and Peral Vega, 2009.
2   A collection of articles and essays compiled by Julio Rodríguez Puértolas offers a wide selection of pieces that express this sentiment (1987).
3   It was precisely this kind of staging, designed to combine religious and national exaltation that, ironically, caused the *autos sacramentales* to be banned by a decree of Carlos III in 1765; it was felt that their increasingly elaborate staging was overriding their religious content. They would not be performed again until a 1927 production in Granada at the hands of Gallego Burín and Manuel de Falla. For more detailed studies of the performance of *autos sacramentales* from 1939 onwards, see García Lorenzo, 2002a; and García Ruiz, 1997b.
4   For more details of this production, see Escobar, 2000, pp. 114–24.
5   For a good overview of how censorship operated, see Bernal and Oliva, 1996, pp. 22–5; Neuschafer, 1994, pp. 46–54; and O'Connor, 1966 and 1973. The censor's guidelines have been reproduced in García Lorenzo, 1981, pp. 229–98.
6   It is worth remembering, however, that similar legislation was in operation in England at the same time. Until the abolition of the Lord Chamberlain's Men in 1968, all new plays had to be submitted for approval (Jongh, 2000, p. ix).
7   Lluch was a firm Catholic who had worked with Rivas Cherif and Alberti previously. He had connections with Republicans early in the Civil War though his strong Catholicism and the fact that he had ended the war as a prisoner of the Republicans served to make him a suitable first director of the Español. From before the conflict, he had been advocating the need for a National Theatre that would rely heavily on the classics. For more details, see Aguilera Sastre, 1993; and García Ruiz, 2010.
8   An indispensable guide to these two theatres detailing the periods 1939–62 and 1960–85 respectively, is provided by a two-volume collection edited by Andrés Peláez Martín (1993, 1995). Nathalie Cañizares Bundorf has written the definitive guide to the María Guerrero theatre (2000). Juan Aguilera Sastre examines the debates that surrounded the creation of the National Theatres from 1900 to 1939. The last chapter details how the Español came to be a National Theatre (2002, pp. 333–56).
9   In theory, from 1942 onwards, the classics were meant to be the exclusive preserve of the Español but Escobar, director of the María Guerrero, felt that they constituted essential training for actors and they therefore remained a

constant, albeit reduced, presence in the theatre's programming (Cañizares Bundorf, 2000, pp. 215–17).

10 For more details on how the concept of a director emerged and changed in Spain, see Cornago Bernal, 2001; Delgado, 2012; González Ruiz, 1949, pp. 31–8; Higuera, 1992; and Hormigón, 2002a.

11 This is symptomatic of the fact that 'although Franco despised the ideologies espoused by leftist Republicans, he and his followers studied the left's methods carefully and co-opted them for their own well-orchestrated campaign of cultural unification, a unity they hoped would one day lead to a Spain that was "una, grande y libre"' [one, great and free] (Holguín, 2002, p. 195). For further information on Burgos and Burmann who were the most important stage designers for the classics in this period, see Martínez Roger, 2003, and Burmann, 2009 respectively. The latter is, as the author feely admits, largely based on Beckers, 1992.

12 Two collections of the writings of the critic Alfredo Marquerie offer a good overview of how the National Theatres operated and how their practices differed from those of other companies operating at the time (1942, 1944a).

13 By 1952, the Madrid Diplomatic Office claimed in an official document that each National Theatre had a million peseta annual subsidy (1952, p. 173).

14 For a full list of this company's performances, see Gallén, 1985, p. 400.

15 For a general guide to the TEUs, see García Lorenzo, 1999. Ruiz Carnicer, 1996 contains useful background information on the TEUs and their changing relationship with the SEU.

16 The timing of this event and the choice of plays are not surprising. 1941 was the year that 'marked the apogee of the Spanish alignment with the Axis' (Payne, 2008, p. 145). Equally, Calderón has traditionally found particular favour among German critics and theatregoers. As Henry W. Sullivan argues, this was particularly true of this period: 'In the Third Reich, Calderón's theatrical popularity did not diminish. Indeed, the worst of reasons – Calderón's supposedly anti-Semitic concern for *limpieza de sangre*, his submission to absolutist rule, his portrayal of the legal revolutionary *Führer* Segismundo drawing his authority directly from the people – all contributed to his general acceptability in Nazi eyes' (1983, p. 341). This helps explain why, as John London notes, 'Spanish Golden Age drama amounted to almost one per cent of all productions performed in the Third Reich (approximately double the percentage proportion of the years 1929–1933)' (2000, p. 229).

17 Considering Lope's views on stagecraft, it seems unlikely that he would have agreed with Luca de Tena on this matter. In a prologue to the sixteenth *parte* of his works, he stages a dialogue between *teatro* [theatre] and a *forastero* [stranger]. At one point *teatro* says the following: 'Yo he llegado a gran desdicha, y presume que tiene origen de una de tres causas: o por no haber buenos representantes, o por ser malos los poetas, o por faltar entendimiento a los oyentes; pues los autores se valen de las máquinas, las poetas de los carpinteros, y los oyentes de los ojos' (1860, p. xxv) [A great misfortune has befallen me, and its origins can be presumed to originate in one of three causes: either the actors are bad, or the playwrights are, or the audience lacks understanding when they listen; the impresarios rely on machines, the dramatists on carpenters, and the listeners on their eyes.]

18 Though his approach was clearly a product of the time, Luca de Tena never changed his attitude to the classics. In an interview in 1991 while he was

directing Lope's *El caballero de milagro,* he used exactly the same example of *Las Meninas* to justify his theatrical approach (Santa-Cruz, 1991, p. 35).

19 As London has argued, '[w]ith a total circulation of between one million and two million copies during 1939–63, the dailies had a widespread potential. Their theatrical critics represented the most immediate response to the works in question' (1997, pp. 23–4). He offers a good overview of how and why reviews were generally conservative and not very well written (pp. 158–62).

20 This was actually a very different theatre audience to the one proposed by Felipe Lluch when the Español and María Guerrero initially became National Theatres: 'Creemos en un teatro para el público, no en un "teatro de público". En un teatro para las masas populares, no en un "teatro de masas" ni en un "teatro de arte", sino en el arte del teatro. Creemos en un teatro que sea como el del siglo de oro, "una escena para todos", según lo define Plaudl.' (1940) [We believe in a theatre for the general public not a 'popular theatre'. In a theatre for the masses, not a 'mass theatre' nor an 'art theatre', but rather in the art of theatre. We believe in a theatre that will be like those of the Golden Age, 'a stage for all', in Plaudl's definition.]

21 The Archivo General de la Administración in Alcalá de Henares currently holds all the censorship files for theatrical performances. These records, available for consultation, usually contain the performance script and descriptions of the production. The censor's comments are also included.

22 The versions of most plays used by the National Theatres are available for consultation on request at the CDT in Madrid. The archive has also published a very useful guide to the play scripts from the National Theatres, with their corresponding file numbers, held in the archive (1995).

23 González Ruiz claims, for example, that he took out the line where Casilda calls her husband a 'noble toro' [noble bull] because he thought that the audience would not interpret it as a compliment, as Lope intended, but rather as smutty innuendo that would invite inappropriate laughter in a serious scene (1943).

24 I am indebted to Mercedes del Carmen Carrillo Guzmán's recent doctoral thesis (2008) on the musician. See pp. 332–43 for an in-depth analysis of his contribution to *Peribáñez*.

25 For more details on Borrás and his career, see George, 2004; Román, 1995, pp. 37–45; and Vila San-Juan, 1956.

26 For more details on Rambal, see Delgado, 2003, pp. 66–89; Martínez Ortiz and Sirera, 1989; and Román, 1995, pp. 85–91.

27 For more details of Tamayo's career, see Checa, 2003; Compañía Lope de Vega, 1966; Peláez Martín, 1991; and Ruiz García, 1971. These publications also feature pictures and photographs of many of Tamayo's productions.

28 There had been previous initiatives to encourage poorer people to the theatre. The prices for Escobar's extravaganzas in 1939 had been accessible with complimentary tickets for *La vida es sueño* offered to Nationalist soldiers (Escobar, 2000, p. 121). Later, a Popular Theatre Campaign was established in July 1948. The scheme eventually reached the María Guerrero in 1956 where ticket prices were reduced to eight, five and four pesetas. *El alcalde de Zalamea* was among the works on offer. The scheme was very popular but, unfortunately, it only lasted ten days and was never repeated (Cañizares Bundorf, 2000, p. 205). The festivals provided the most sustained example of state-subsidized ticketing by the regime.

29 For more details on this production, see a special report prepared by *Teatro* (1953). Included are photographs that give an inkling of how extravagant a production it must have been, alongside a photograph of the people present at

the official presentations. The concordat was a pivotal event in Spain's attempts to gain international respectability by stressing the regime's Catholic as opposed to fascist or totalitarian nature (Powell, 1995, p. 21).

[30] For more details of this visit, see Martín Rodríguez, 2004.

[31] For an excellent discussion on the role of *Teatro* in the 1950s, see Torres Nebrera, 2004.

[32] Luca de Tena went so far as to suggest that directors ought to be rewarded not with prizes but instead with the opportunity to stage an *auto sacramental*. This was because any director lucky enough to have the opportunity to stage one had a huge amount of money and resources at their disposal; as noted, they were also virtually immune to criticism (1953b).

[33] The letter also claims that, prior to the 1955 version, the play had not been performed since 1827. A request is also made for them to rent the María Guerrero at the reduced rate that was offered to the Sección Femenina; she claims that the standard rate is prohibitive. There is no reference to this request being granted although the production was approved for over 16s and also for airing on the nascent RTVE. In 1961 the production was also approved to move to the Teatro Reina Victoria.

[34] Fernández Montesinos also claims José Luis Alonso used to attend performances by the group in search of potential actors and that Carmen Bernardos's performance in this Lope play later led to her being cast in a lead role in *El anzuelo de Fenisa* (2008, p. 49).

[35] See Martín Gaite, 1994, for a description of mating rituals and social taboos in this period.

[36] For a more detailed discussion of women's status as both capitalist and spiritual agents, see Morcillo, 2000, pp. 55–76.

[37] For a discussion of this in relation to Lope's early comedies, see Thacker, 2008.

[38] For more details see Higuera, 1995; Morales, 1967; and Fernández Montesinos, 2008, pp. 60–80.

[39] For more details of this earlier centenary, see Aguilera Sastre and Lizarraga Vizcarra, 2001, pp. 59–82.

[40] For a discussion of this production, see Álvaro. 1963, pp. 132–9.

[41] For a multimedia performance history of this play see García Lorenzo, 2007b.

[42] For more details of this production, see Azcona Navarro, 1999.

[43] Piñar, one of the most fascist members of Franco's inner circle, retained the Civil War rhetoric of the victorious and the vanquished throughout, and would in a few years form the ultra right-wing *Fuerza Nueva* as a reaction to the increased liberalization of the Spanish state (Romero Salvadó, 1999, pp. 155–6).

[44] Many of Quinto's reviews of productions of the classics have been reproduced in a collection of his journalism (1997).

[45] For example, José María Rodríguez Méndez, when writing about Lope, spoke of 'el ignominioso vapuleo de un autor clásico merecedor de todos los respetos' [the shameful public vilification of a classic author who warrants our utmost respect] (1972, p. 187), and concluded: 'Mejor es que duerman los clásicos antes que maltratarlos tan despiadadamente de palabra y obra' [It is better that our classical authors remain asleep than to abuse their words and plays in such a merciless fashion] (p. 188).

[46] For extensive material on this production, see Hormigón, 2002b, pp. 457–506.

[47] For more details of this production see Oliva, 1975, pp. 64–74.

[48] Antonio Zapatero Vicente has also claimed that the TEU Zaragoza had thought of performing a version, with a similar approach to the one later adopted by

49 Castilla, during the 1959–60 season. He does not explain why this idea never materialized (1999, p. 203).
49 For an exhaustive selection of these foreign press reviews, see *Yorick*, 1965.
50 I will discuss Marsillach and his relationship to the classics in more detail in chapter three. For details of Alonso's work with the classics, see Hormigón, 1991; and Rubio Jiménez, 1995. In reference to Narros, see Amestoy, 2002; and for Gónzalez Vergel, see Facio, 2008; and Gónzalez Vergel, 2003.
51 Francisco Álvaro demanded to know: '¿qué necesidad tenía el director del teatro Español, Miguel Narros, de "meterse" de manera iracunda e irrazonable, con *Don Juan Tenorio*, de Zorrilla, al exhumar la obra de Tirso?' [Why did the director of the Teatro Español, Miguel Narros, feel the need to 'meddle' in an unreasonable and irate manner with Zorrilla's *Don Juan Tenorio* by exhuming Tirso's play?] (1967 p. 151).
52 For more details of the critical reaction to this play, see Álvaro, 1971, pp. 27–36.
53 For more details of his different productions of *La vida es sueño*, see Peláez Martín, 1991, pp. 147–50.
54 For an illuminating discussion between various critics on this production, see Álvaro, 1977, pp. 25–32.
55 For a good overview of theatre of the transition period, see Díaz Díaz, 2000.
56 By November 1978 the controversy had reached parliament and the Socialists demanded explanations of where public money invested in theatre was being spent (Pérez Coterillo, 1979, p. 4).
57 See García Lorenzo and Peláez Martín, 1997, for a comprehensive history of the Almagro Festival. For a brief overview, see García Lorenzo, 2002b.
58 For a more detailed discussion of the role of returned exiles in revitalizing the classics, see Wheeler, 2011a.
59 Ricard Salvat has been one of the few to speak out against this pact (1999, p. 109).
60 In his first season, Marsillach programmed Francisco de Rojas Zorrilla's *Abre el ojo* at the CDN. In the late 1970s, students at RESAD worked for three years with their teachers and then staged a play for the public. Having previously performed Lope de Rueda's *Medora*, they chose to stage Calderón's *La fiera, el rayo y la piedra* in 1979. The production was popular with critics and audiences alike. For more details of this production and subsequent works with the classics by RESAD, see García May and Rodríguez, 1990.
61 For more details on the critical response to the production, see Álvaro, 1980, pp. 111–15. In his autobiography, Fernán-Gómez talks about his generally negative experience with the production although this had more to do with his personal and professional situation than the play itself (1999, pp. 495–502).
62 For more details on the production of *Casa*, see Madroñal, 2002.
63 For more details of this version, see Fischer, 1986.
64 The highest grossing was Ibsen's *El pato silvestre* at the María Guerrero.
65 I have found records of two additional productions (Juan Antonio Quintana's *El mágico prodigioso* and Carlos Ballesteros's *Mejor está que estaba*) from outside the capital but the centenary celebrations were, nevertheless, primarily a Madrid phenomenon.
66 Various non-theatrical events took place for the centenary. For more details of these along with critical reactions to the productions themselves, see Álvaro, 1982, pp. 73–98.
67 For more details of this production see Ladra, 1985.
68 From this period on, we can be more confident in our judgement of productions as many performances were recorded and can be viewed at the CDT. A list

of available recordings can be viewed on their webpage: http://documentacion.teatral.mcu.es/.

69 José María Pemán, described by Gerald Brenan in the 1940s as 'the leading publicist and author laureate of the regime', was an (in)famous Francoist writer and intellectual (1987, p. 135). A regular on Spanish television, he was popularly known as *el segundo Séneca* [the second Seneca] or *el Séneca español* [The Spanish Senaca]. As Nigel Griffin correctly pointed out to me, the latter term is rather pleonastic considering that Seneca was in fact born in Spain.

70 For more details of the critical reaction to the play, see Álvaro, 1984, pp. 117–21.

71 For a detailed analysis of Hormigón's text, see Bergmann, 1994.

72 This was not the first time that Ángel Facio had embarked on such a project. In 1965, he had, with his avant-garde group Los Goliardos, staged a work entitled *Farsa del triunfo del Sacramental*, described as 'una visión crítica y revitalizadora al cadáver putrefacto de un auto sacramental' [a critical and revitalizing vision of the putrefying corpse of a Corpus Christi play] (Pipirijaina, 1974, p. 26).

73 For a discussion of this play and its relation to other variations on the Don Juan myth undertaken by Spaniards exiled as a result of the Civil War, see Aznar Soler, 1998; and Lonsdale, 2011.

74 State investment in the theatre increased exponentially through the early and mid 1980s. In 1978, the UCD spent 353.3 million pesetas on theatres, this had increased to 547.5 million in 1982; by 1985, the PSOE's official budget was 2,887 million (Oliva, 2002a, p. 229).

75 From 1960 to 1985, in official theatres, four hundred and ninety-two titles were premiered, and of these, only thirty-nine were works from the Spanish Golden Age. Material on these productions is available for public consultation at the CDT in Madrid.

76 This information is given on the DVD that accompanies CNTC, 2006b.

77 Brook explains one distinction between a living and a deadly theatre in the following terms: 'In a living theatre, we would each day approach the rehearsal putting yesterday's discoveries to the test, ready to believe that the true play has once again escaped us. But the Deadly Theatre approaches the classics from the viewpoint that somewhere, someone has found out and defined how the play should be done' (1990, p. 17).

78 For an attack on Socialist cultural policy that singles out Marsillach and the CNTC, see Rodríguez Méndez, 1993. This book-length rant dismisses almost everybody involved in the Spanish theatre establishment as being at best a dimwit and at worst a fraudulent megalomaniac. Although it is hardly scholarly and is unintentionally hilarious, it does, nevertheless, contain some kernels of truth.

79 For more details of this production see Fischer, 2009, pp. 21–41; and Morales Astola, 2003, pp. 149–83.

80 For more details of this production, see Fischer, 2009, pp. 93–116.

81 See Fischer, 2009, pp. 59–79 for more details of this production. For an interesting discussion of the changes made to the text in the adaptation by Francisco Brines, see Romera Castillo, 1993.

82 For more details of this production, see Fischer, 2009, pp. 77–92.

83 Interview with the author conducted in Madrid on 20 August 2007.

84 In 1995, fifteen private companies asked for government subsidies to stage Golden Age drama; thirteen of these companies were successful. Nonetheless, the 379,400,300 pesetas they were awarded still represented less than the CNTC budget for the year (Castilla, 2001, p. 255).

85   These statistics have been gathered from the *Anuarios* produced by *El público* in association with the CDT. These are available for consultation at the CDT. The number of productions in any year reflects the number of works that premiered. According to the CDT, they collect information on all professional and university companies, alongside productions by established amateur groups. While it is almost inevitable that the occasional small-scale project will be missed, these statistics nevertheless provide us with the opportunity to have a more accurate quantitative overview than has hitherto been the case. I have awarded one point for productions solely based on a playwright's work and half a point if the playwright's work has been used, alongside other authors, in a performance. Unfortunately, the *Anuarios* changed the way they collated information in 1997 so that they followed calendar rather than theatrical years. As such, there is a brief period – the last few months of 1996 – not accounted for. For the most recent years, I am very grateful to Gerardo del Barco for allowing me access to the internal database.

86   In his analysis, based on the number of performances of Lope and Calderón in Madrid between 1985 and 1999, Díez Borque calculates that there were 1,048 performances of Lope, 1,045 of Calderón and 380 of Tirso de Molina (2004, p. 213).

87   In his characteristic polemic style, Rodríguez Méndez has denounced this canonization of these authors under the Socialists, and compared the smugness with which their productions are staged with the exaltation of nationalist plays in the early Franco period (1990). For a more balanced view of how Lorca has been performed under the Socialist government, see Delgado, 2008; and Smith, 1998, pp. 105–38.

88   For general information on Shakespeare in Spain, see González Fernández de Sevilla, 1993.

89   Antonio Serrano is the only academic who, to my knowledge, has consistently raised the troubling question of whether the different regions have an interest in the *comedia* (e.g. in Castilla, 2001, p. 265). Picking up from his concerns, Salvat acknowledges and laments this fact: 'no hay voluntad de plantearse todo esto. Y es terrible, porque los gallegos, los catalanes o los andaluces no hacen nada más que empobrecerse' [there is no desire to address all of this. And it is terrible because the Galicians, Catalans and Andalusians are only impoverishing themselves] (1999, p. 119). Javier Huerta Calvo mentions companies based in the different autonomous regions but shies away from discussing the scarcity of non-Madrid based productions (2006, pp. 85–7).

90   For details of companies and practitioners working in *comedia* performance in the period immediately before the CNTC, see García Lorenzo, 1987.

91   Fernando Urdiales, the founder of Corsario notes how 'para mí supuso una crucifixión real. Los compañeros de viaje de la izquierda, algunos colegas de profesión, y otros, fueron intransigentes con nuestra decisión que, curiosamente, estaba basada en criterios que iban más allá de lo estético. Se trataba de rescatar un acervo casi olvidado de nuestra cultura, que el nacional-catolicismo se había arrogado como propio, pero cuya potencia era y es de primer orden' [it constituted a genuine crucifixion for me. My comrades from the left, some professional colleagues, and others, were intransigent as regards our decision, which curiously enough was based on criteria which transcended the purely aesthetic. It was an attempt to rescue a rich and almost forgotten pool of our culture that National-Catholicism had appropriated as its own but whose power was and continues to be first rate] (cited in Dirección General de Promoción e

Instituciones Culturales, 2007, pp. 60–1). This book, and accompanying DVD, also offers a definitive history of the company.

92 For more details on Zampanó, see Cifo, 1990.

93 This was the culmination of a long struggle for the director to stage this work. He had programmed it as director of the Español, but was then forced to abort it due to a breakdown in diplomatic relations between Spain and Morocco. He had later planned to film a version for TVE but, after finding locations, it was decided that the project would be too costly. See Ferrol, 1988, for more details.

94 Details of this company and their various productions are available, with video clips, on their excellent and informative website: www.aldabaproducciones.com

95 Interview with the author conducted in Madrid on 7 April 2008.

96 This iconic play written and directed by Alonso de Santos about life in a libertarian post-dictatorship Spain is arguably the most famous and emblematic dramatic work to have been written in Spain in the 1980s. For more details of the director's career, see Santolaria Solana, 1998.

97 See Oliva, 2000, for more details of the different centenary productions and activities.

98 For more details of these three productions, see CNTC, 2001.

99 For more details of this production, see George, 2006.

100 For more details of this production, see Alonso de Santos, 2007.

101 For more details of this production, see Fischer, 2009, pp. 117–33.

102 One notable exception was González Vergel's 1997 production for the Riojales Town Council that took place after the director's project had been rejected by the CNTC (Morales y Marín, 2008, p. 129).

103 For the director's view of this production, see Alonso de Santos, 2002.

104 See CNTC, 2002, for more detailed statistics.

105 Considering the lack of attention and disregard shown by the PP to the theatre, and the arts in general, this is not surprising; they merged, for example the Ministries of Education and Culture.

106 For a detailed review see Monleón, 2005.

107 In real terms, the budget is actually higher because National Theatres do not have to pay income tax on their ticket sales.

108 For more details of this production, see Fischer, 2009, pp. 134–59.

109 For a more details analysis of this production, see Wheeler, 2012b.

110 More details can be found on RESAD's very informative website: www.resad.es

111 For more details of this production and its reception, see Paun de García, 2008.

112 The following works by Tirso, Lope and Calderón were staged by a mixture of public, private and student companies: *Desde Toledo a Madrid, Don Gil de las calzas verdes, Amar después de la muerte, El mágico prodigioso* (two productions), *El caballero de Olmedo, Fuente Ovejuna, El burlador de Sevilla*.

113 Less positively, with the exception of *El burlador de Sevilla*, works attributed to Lope, Tirso or Calderón were absent from the Festival de Teatro Clásico de Olite held in the Basque Country between 18 July and 3 August.

114 In 1969, Pasolini said that he hoped to make the play into a film (cited in Stack, 1969, p. 143). This was not to be, but it was the only one of the director's plays to be staged in his lifetime (in 1973). *Calderón* has recently been published in Spanish in *PA* (Pasolini, 2009). For more discussion, see Huerta Calvo, 2002 and 2009; Mateo, 2009; and Van Watson, 1989, pp. 45–57.

115 For a detailed review of this production, see López Sancho, 1988.

116 For more details of this edition, see Martin, 2009.

117 For more details of this production, see Víllora, 2009.

Chapter 2

1. It is accepted practice to write both *Fuente Ovejuna* and *Fuenteovejuna*. I have opted for the former but, when quoting, I respect the original author's choice.
2. For a general discussion of the play's national and international reception and performance, see Gagen, 1993; García Santo-Tomás, 2000a, pp. 331–72; Kirschner, 1977a and 1979, pp. 13–27; Monleón, 1987; and Pedraza Jiménez, 2002. For details of the play's performance in Russia, see Weiner, 1982; and for Germany, Banús and Barcenilla, 2005, p. 272; and Seliger, 1984. Interesting discussions of specific productions in the UK, the US and Chile are provided by Edwards, 2007; Farrán Gravés, 1989; Hodge, 1963; and Weimer, 2000a and 2000b respectively.
3. Jack Weiner has speculated that Lorca may well have heard about these adaptations from Rafael Alberti, who visited the Soviet Union in 1932 to study theatre and staging techniques (1982, p. 220).
4. This information comes from Sáenz de la Calzada, 1976, pp. 65–6, who played the Comendador in this production and whose book tells the story of La Barraca. This production has received more scholarly attention than any other *comedia* performance. For more details of Lorca's version and his work with the classics, see Byrd, 1984; Delgado, 2008, pp. 28–31; Edwards, 2007; Gagen, 1993; Holguín, 2002, pp. 105–67; Huerta, 1987; Oliva, 2008; Stainton, 1998, pp. 403–20; and Suelto de Sáenz, 1964.
5. See, for example, Armas, 2006; Darst, 1995; Fiore, 1966; Hall, 1974; Herrera Montero, 1989; Kirschener, 1979; McCrary 1961; Parker, 1953; Rozas, 1981; Ruiz Ramón, 1997, pp. 50–93; Spitzer, 1955; Varey, 1976; and Wardropper, 1956.
6. This, for example, is the case with Suzanne W. Byrd, who claims, in the most detailed study of the production: 'De ningún modo la supresión del argumento secundario perturba el objectivo primordial de la pieza lopesca ... En todos los sentidos, La Barraca hizo de *Fuente Ovejuna* una obra maestra del teatro, artística y conmovedora. Tanto que llegó a ser el drama de España en cualquier época, porque expresa verídicamente el brío español ante el vicio y la injusticia' [In no way does the excision of the secondary action distort the primary objective of Lope's piece ... In every respect, La Barraca's production revealed *The Sheep Well* to be an artful and moving theatrical masterpiece. This is manifest in the fact that the play can embody the drama of Spain in any age; because it genuinely expresses Spanish brio in the face of vice and injustice] (1984, pp. 16–17).
7. Lorca and productions of this kind helped to secure the play's fame in the UK, where Joan Littlewood, for example, staged the play with her Theatre Workshop. Years later, Ruth Fainlight and Alan Sillitoe, who lived for an extended period in Mallorca, would also write a metatheatrical adaptation/translation of the play set in the Teatro Lara in Madrid, in which some Republican soldiers seek refuge to sleep but are recruited to help a depleted troupe of actors perform Lope's play, which tells the story of the people defying the forefathers of fascism who are 'not only the sworn enemies of the Spanish people, but of all the world' (1969, p. 4).
8. From the outset of the Civil War, the Church had been awarded responsibility for education and teaching while the Falange largely secured its influence through its appropriation of the mass media (Alted, 2000, p. 217).
9. This is particularly clear in this case, considering how little we know about the original staging of the work (Kirschner, 1979, p. 14). For a hypothesis on how the play might have been staged in the seventeenth century, see Takahashi Nagasaka, 2000.

10 In reality, as Peter W. Evans notes, '*Fuenteovejuna* is very much simultaneously a stylised version of history and a complicated aestheticised formulation, both conscious and unconscious, of contemporary political and sociological realities' (1990b, p. 111). For further discussions of the relationship between history and the play, see Cabrera and Morós, 1991; Carter, 1977; Cascardi, 1997; Hall, 1985, pp. 11–18; MacKay and McKendrick, 1986; Marín, 2001; Villegas Ruiz, 1990; and Welles, 2000, pp. 70–115.
11 File no. 1306 in the CDT.
12 For more details on the cast and credits of the major productions of *Fuente Ovejuna* staged between 1939 and 1999, see García Lorenzo, 2000, pp. 103–5.
13 File nos 1307–8 in the CDT.
14 As Günter Berghaus has noted, our knowledge about theatre orchestrated by the Falange in Spain is heavily under-researched: 'The very existence of a fascist cultural policy and theatrical practice has been repeatedly negated; documents have been destroyed, and access to archival material is often restricted' (1996, p. 6).
15 In further proof of the play's adaptability to different performance contexts, a left-wing version was published by the Dutch during the occupation (London, 2000, pp. 232–3).
16 Multiple stills are available for consultation at the theatre library in the Fundación Juan March.
17 In a recent interview, Luca de Tena recalls how: 'Fue la primera vez que goberné los grupos, grupo por grupo. El movimiento de cada actor, de cada comparsa, estaba planificado. Si eran ocho grupos, numeraba del uno al seis y al ocho cada grupo; cada uno tenía una misión precisa. Dibujé un gran plano de colores con los movimientos, y los encuentros, y las paradas, y las salidas y las entradas' [It was the first time that I controlled groups, group by group. The movement of every actor, every troupe of extras, was planned. If there were eight groups, I numbered each group from one to six, or one to eight; each one had a set mission. I drew up a big plan where different colours indicated the movements, the encounters, the breaks, the exits and the entrances] (cited in Baltés, 2008, p. 178).
18 For a concise overview of the role of women under Franco, see Folguera Crespo, 1997.
19 In its two runs at the Español beginning in October 1944 and June 1947 respectively, the production registered 12,145 spectators. This was, according to records held internally at the CDT, the most for any Spanish *comedia* in the National Theatres during the dictatorship – it did of course have the advantage of being staged twice – with Lope's *La discreta enamorada* coming in at a close second with 12,059 spectators over its two runs in 1945 and 1946. I would like to thank Gerardo del Barco for allowing me access to these internal databases.
20 See Marañón, 1952, for an interesting argument about how rural audiences unfamiliar with the *comedia* were more receptive than their better-educated urban counterparts.
21 2,453 verses in Marín's edition (Vega Carpio, 2001).
22 The anti-communism that served Spain so well in the Cold War context was one of the few constants in the generally Heraclitean political ideology. So too was an attitude of veneration towards Isabella. The inauguration of the Institute for Hispanic Culture took place symbolically on 12 October 1951 during the quincentennial of her birth (Resina, 2005, p. 168), and in 1958 attempts were made for her beatification (Caba, 2008, p. 176). As late as 1972, an official

document was sent to Rome with the hope yet again that she might be declared a saint. This document is reprinted in Álvar Ezquerra, 2002, pp. 274–85.

23 A recording of the play with much of the same cast and based on the same version was later issued by RCA records, and is available for consultation at the Sala Barbieri in the Biblioteca Nacional; the actors are impressive both in their mastery of verse and emotional range.

24 The director occupies an ambivalent place in Spanish theatrical history for he has been construed as a plaything of the regime yet he was also instrumental in having controversial foreign playwrights staged. Francisco Umbral has argued convincingly that, as an impresario, he was an expert strategist who knew how to negotiate under difficult circumstances: 'fue dúctil y sabio con la censura, jugó al posibilismo, les daba un *Fuenteovejuna* a cambio de un rojo y un Buero Vallejo a cambio de una legión romana de Pemán' [he was flexible and clever with the censor, he played with the possibilities contained within the system. He would offer them a production of *The Sheep Well* so as to stage a work by a left-wing playwright; a Buero Vallejo play for one of Pemán's Roman legions] (cited in Valverde, 2006).

25 No. 1040A, 1962.

26 For an overview of the critical reaction, see Álvaro, 1963, pp. 78–83.

27 For more details, see Álvaro, 1982, pp. 224–85.

28 Even before 1975 this had been a popular trend. Then, in the post-1975 period, irreverent works were frequently staged (Hernanz Ángulo, 1999, p. 102).

29 There has been some critical debate over whether Laurencia is actually raped. Her dishevelled appearance on her return seems to suggest that she has been, although Dixon has offered a convincing argument that, for a contemporary audience, Lope's precise physical descriptions would not have warranted this conclusion (1988). The narrative of *El mejor alcalde, el rey* (see chapter four) proves that, at least in Lope's dramatic universe, it was possible for a man to marry a woman who has been sexually violated. Frondoso later suggests that this was not the case here (2001, vv. 2410–13). This is, however, said in front of the other villagers and, if the assault did in fact take place, it is still plausible that she has not told her husband and/or that he does not want his neighbours to know. A more cynical reading is offered by Robert Archer who suggests that she deceives the villagers by crying rape so as to propel them into action (1990, pp. 117–18).

30 Antonio Valencia claimed that 'se quiso original y puesta al día y ha resultado un indigesto experimento, penoso de contemplar de principio a fin' [it has tried to be original and contemporary, but it has resulted in an indigestible experiment, painful to watch from start to finish] (cited in Álvaro, 1979, pp. 244), while Ángel Fernández Santos was even more scathing in his attack: 'Montar *Fuenteovejuna* en estas condiciones linda con la irresponsabilidad' [Staging *The Sheep Well* in these conditions borders on the irresponsible] (cited in Álvaro, 1979, p. 246).

31 A copy of the script is available in German (Fassbinder, 1976). For more details of the original production, see Iden, 1976.

32 On the first point see, for example, Allatson, 1996; Camino, 2004; Cañadas, 2005, pp. 137–83; Larson, 1991; López Estrada, 1989; Smith, 1993; Swietlicki, 1992; Weimer, 1996; and Worley Jr., 2003. On the second, Carter, 1977; Herrera Montero, 1989; Lauer, 1997; and Stroud, 2008.

33 Unless otherwise noted, all of the information about this production comes from an interview between the author and Emilio Hernández conducted in Madrid on 16 September 2008.

34 As Margaret L. King notes in her magisterial pan-European study of women in the Renaissance, '[t]he honor of a city, like that of a family, could be ruined by rape. The violation of chastity in wartime, prohibited by the custom of the day, added to the humiliation of the defeated' (1991, p. 30).

35 This issue is exacerbated when an all-female cast is being directed by a man who is also in charge of the company.

36 This has resulted in women suffering on multiple levels: 'Palestinian women living in the West Bank . . . face the oppression of two systems: the patriarchal (sociocultural) and Israeli occupation (political). Palestinian women have been expected to combat the occupying forces to accept patriarchal hegemony' (Shalhoub-Kevorkian, 2003, p. 584).

37 For a representative selection of reviews of the productions, see Urzáiz Tortajada, 2006.

38 Subsequent to Arafat being elected President in 1996 and the formation of the Palestinian National Authority, all sports, cultural and social events required a police permit (Aburish, 1998, p. 312). Hernández claims that Arafat's Minister of Culture came to watch the production in Seville and said that it would be impossible to perform in Palestine not as a result of the violence but due to the onstage nudity. An unfortunate side effect of this decision is that it in all likelihood consolidated the director's association of nudity with artistic freedom.

39 Hence, for example, one of Spain's most outspoken communists, the dancer Antonio Gades, has performed a ballet based on the play with the Spanish National Ballet, both at home and abroad, since the early 1990s. The company he founded has continued to include it in their repertoire since his death in 2004.

40 For a more detailed analysis of the production, see Wheeler, 2011b, pp. 191–6.

41 These are not restricted to the village scenes and are, as Marsillach's production intelligently picked up on, frequently used in exchanges between Ferdinand and Isabella. Critics who argue that the play is essentially about love include Feito, 1981; Pring-Mill, 1962; Spitzer, 1955; and Wardropper, 1956 and 1978.

42 In 2006, the Grupo de teatro Candilejas, based in Cadiz, who have previously staged Calderón's *La vida es sueño* and *Casa con dos puertas mala es de guardar*, performed the play outdoors in Argüelles (Madrid). This company was the brainchild of a literature teacher; they rehearse in a Carmelite school of which many of the members are alumni. For more details see www.candilejas.cadiz.com. *Fuente Ovejuna* was also performed by the Aula de Teatro de la Universidad de Murcia in the same year. Then, in 2007, the Asociación Las nueve menos cuarto, which emerged from the Escuela Municipal de Teatro de Los Corrales de Baena, staged a version directed by Anabel Díez. In April 2008, an amateur production of Lope's play by a local group was also staged as part of the Jornadas Cervantinas in Toledo (EFE, 2008a).

43 For more details, see www.lasrutasdelabarraca.es

44 For a balanced discussion of the Church's role as both victims and aggressors in the Civil War, see Lannon, 1987, pp. 198–223.

Chapter 3

1 For an overview of modern-day perceptions and readings of Calderón, see Pérez-Magallón, 2002; Regalado, 1995; and Wardropper, 1982.

2   For excellent studies of the reception of *El médico*, see Armendáriz Aramendía, 2007; and Vitse, 2007.
3   A. Gónzalez Palencia offers a more balanced version of Menéndez y Pelayo's reading but still nevertheless concludes that 'Calderón no analiza detalladamente la pasión de los celos, y por eso sus celosos son inferiores a Otelo' [Calderón does not analyse the passion of jealousy in any detail, and this is why his jealous men are inferior to Othello] (1943, p. 26). Ángel Valbuena Prat, who prepared the version of *El médico* for the Español, would later write that '[l]as venganzas de honor, pues, correspondían a hechos sangrientos de la España de la época. Los narradores de sucesos coetáneos nos informan de terribles realidades' [the honour vengeances relate to the bloody happenings of the Spain of the time. Contemporary accounts inform us of terrible real-life cases] (1956, p. 319). Ramón Menéndez Pedal, nevertheless, came to an opposite conclusion predicated on similar underlying assumptions: '[e]ste siglo de verdadero anti-honor ha hecho difícilmente comprensible el drama de honor' [this century which is resolutely anti-honour means that the honour drama is difficult to comprehend] (1958, pp. 150–1).
4   Box no. 36/11187.
5   Artiles, 1967, for example thought that the plays reflected the mores and practices of the time. An early and important exception to the general rule that Spanish critics were more predisposed to assume that Calderón is uncritically reflecting the prevailing ideology is provided by Francisco Ruiz Ramón in his introduction to the text (1968). Somewhat surprisingly, a similar position was subsequently adopted by José María Díez-Borque (1978). For a good overview of the issues surrounding the debate over the relationship between stage and real-life wife murders alongside extensive bibliographical material, see Cruickshank, 2003, pp. 23–4; and Stroud, 1990, pp. 14–15. Scott K. Taylor has very recently taken the debate in a new and, to my mind, strange direction by blaming dramatists for giving seventeenth-century Spain a bad name: 'The only evidence to suggest that Castile was an especially violent, misogynist, honor-bound society were the plays of Lope de Vega and Calderón' (2008, p. 225).
6   See, for example, Peristiany, 1966; Pitt Rivers, 1977; and Schneider, 1971.
7   As Nigel Griffin notes: 'An audience's view of the character of Pedro – not, as we have said, a king brought on at the end of Act III as a device but rather a fully-fledged and fully-flawed character in the play – will condition the view they take of his apparent tolerance of Gutierre's actions . . . and will, by extension shape their response to the play as a whole' (1994, p. 111). For more detailed discussion of Pedro's role in the play, see Kirby, 1981; Soufas, 1981; and Thiher, 1970.
8   For more information on Estruch, his conception of the need for acting schools and his work with the classics, see Eines, 1984; Festival International de Teatro, 1989; Guerenabarrena, 1986; Herrero, 2011; Moral, 1987; Rojo, 1987; Torres, 1991; Trancón, 1990; and Vicente Hernando, 1999.
9   For more details of this landmark production see Aszyk 2009; Baczyńska, 2009; Matyjaszcyk Grenda, 2008; and Quaknine, 1968.
10 Insufficient work has been done on Gutiérrez's work. The best source of information that I am aware of is an in-depth interview: see Bodelón, 1994.
11 Marsillach seemingly applied the same amnesia to his own productions. He directed *Los locos de Valencia* in the late 1950s and later as part of the Second National Theatre Campaign. Although the 1986 version was not a revival, the director once again used a version prepared by Juan Germán Schroeder. In the

programme, Marsillach contests the hypothetical claim that he was inspired by his earlier version rather too heartily. He argues that it was staged more than twenty years ago (no mention is made of the revival in 1969); that he is not even sure of when exactly it was performed; and that there are no extant records of the production. As he goes on to state: '[q]uiero explicar con todo esto que no me acuerdo de lo que hice con *Los locos de Valencia* en 1959 y que no existe, por lo tanto, el menor riesgo de que hoy vuelva a hacer lo mismo' [what I want to explain with all of this is that I don't remember what I did with *Madness in Valencia* in 1959 and there is not, therefore, the slightest risk of me repeating myself in the present day] (CNTC, 1986).

12 He had appeared as an actor in *El hospital de los locos*, and in Tamayo's versions of *Peribáñez* and *La cena del rey Baltasar*; he had also directed Lope's *Los locos de Valencia*. There was nothing beyond these intermittent projects to suggest that he had a specific interest in the *comedia*, and García Escudero claimed in 1966 that Marsillach resigned from his post as director of the Teatro Español because he was denied the opportunity to stage non-classic works (Pérez de Olaguer, 1966). In all fairness, this does not necessarily imply any antipathy to the classics as it may just reflect a belief that he ought to have the right to choose his own repertoire. For more details on his career and involvement with the CNTC, see *ADE*, 2002; Hormigón, 2003; Marsillach, 2002; Oliva, 2005; and Pedraza Jiménez, 2006.

13 For a good overview of the critical reaction, see Fernández Torres, 1987; and Vilches de Frutos, 2008, pp. 340–1.

14 Hence, for example, in a subsequent review of *El alcalde de Zalamea* from 2001, he would write, '[n]unca dejo de espantarme de nuestros antepasados cuando veo un drama clásico, y sobre todo de la herencia que guardamos de ellos, atenuada o simplemente disfrazada' [I never cease to be scared by our ancestors when I see a classical drama and, above all else, of all that we preserve of them in a diminished or merely disguised form] (2001). For access to a broad selection of his reviews and articles, see http://www.eduardoharotecglen.net/blog/.

15 See Fischer, 2000 and 2002, for good historical overviews of the CNTC's first fifteen years. The various publications produced by the CNTC (primarily the Cuadernos and Boletines) offer a comprehensive, albeit partisan, history of the company. There are too many of these publications to list here but more details can be found at their webpage: http://teatroclasico.mcu.es/.

16 For more details about the school and how it functioned on a practical level, see Cuevas, 1990.

17 Narros and the North American Layton have trained many of Spain's best actors. For more details of their methods and alumni, see Villena, 2002, pp. 34–6.

18 A detailed and fairly representative review is provided by Pérez-Rasilla, 1994.

19 Unless otherwise noted, all of the information about the company and this production of *El pintor* derive from an interview conducted by the author with Eduardo Vasco in Madrid on 17 December 2007.

20 This homage was evident, for example, in the use of the same iconic street map of Madrid as a backdrop.

21 Hence, for example, a recent Spanish obituary of the actor Glenn Ford speaks of how the actor striking Rita Hayworth's character in *Gilda* was sufficient for him to become a legend in a culture that continued to have 'Calderón al fondo' [Calderón in the background] (Villán, 2006).

22 This is reflected, for example, in a popular proverb: 'La mujer casada y honrada, la pierna quebrada y en casa' [The honourable married woman, at home with a broken leg]. Women under Franco were subject to 'patria potestad' and, until 1958, a man was legally entitled to kill his wife or daughter if he caught her in the act of adultery while his own maximum penalty was exile (Brooksbank Jones, 1997, p. 76).

23 Interview with the author conducted in Madrid on 14 April 2008.

24 For more details of the law and changing attitudes to domestic violence in Spain, see Wheeler, 2008b.

25 In 2005, *Las ferias de Madrid* – a Lope play that ostensibly subverts the honour code when a patriarchal figure kills his son-in-law when the latter asks the former to kill his daughter as the result of a suspected infidelity – was performed for the first time in many years. In 2007, Isidro Rodríguez Gallardo staged a version of *El médico* that, he told me on 10 September 2008, was inspired by the controversy over gender-based violence. César Barló directed a version of Lope's little-seen wife-murder play, *Los comendadores de Córdoba*, the following year in Almagro.

26 As Miguel Lorente Acosta contends: 'Los celos, en el fondo, son un mecanismo que persigue el control de la otra persona y, en parte, muestran el miedo, la inseguridad y la dependencia del que los ejerce. Es por eso que son una buena excusa para el hombre, una explicación suficiente para la mujer, una adecuada justificación para la sociedad y una atenuante o eximente lícita para la Justicia' [Jealousy, deep down, is a mechanism that pursues the control of another person and, in part, reveals the fear, insecurity and dependence of the individual who applies it. This is why it is a good excuse for men, an adequate explanation for women, a suitable justification in society's eyes, and a mitigating circumstance or legitimate excuse for the justice system] (2001: 73).

27 I have classified a line as having been cut when it has simply been excised from the text. I have not considered a line to be altered if a modern word with a similar definition has been used and the original versification has been conserved. Any other changes have, however, been classified as alterations. I also consulted different editions of the text and have considered lines to have been cut or changed only if this applies to all modern editions.

28 Interview with the author conducted in Madrid on 14 April 2008.

29 He played Osorio in *Don Gil* (1994); Don Arias in *El médico de su honra* (1994); Beltrán in *El acero de Madrid* (1995); Clarín in *La vida es sueño* (1996); Don Arias in *La Estrella de Sevilla* (1998); and Leonardo in *Peribáñez* (2002).

30 For more details of this production, see Fischer, 2009, pp. 179–202.

31 The grand patriarch of Anglo-American Hispanism, A. A. Parker has, for example, observed: 'What, one may ask, would any man do if, like Juan Roca, he were to find his abducted wife in the arms of another? It would need no acquaintance with or training in Spanish seventeenth-century *pundonor* to feel, under the stress of emotion, the instinctive urge to violence' (1962, p. 237).

32 As Laura Bass notes, '[a]lthough ties of blood have been severed by death, homosocial bonds, so frequently invoked in the play's first act, are reaffirmed' (2004, p. 202).

33 This is symptomatic of wider global trends. Michael Billington observed how, in the UK press, theatre reviewing 'no longer enjoys the primacy it once did' (2002, p. 55); in the North American context, Richard Brustein refers to some intellectuals who wrote about theatre a generation ago before issuing the following lament: 'We don't have people of that calibre who even go the theatre, let alone write about it' (cited in Bentley, Brustein and Kauffmann, 2009, p. 318).

34 This is made evident if you look at the space dedicated to Calderón, Lope and Tirso in comparison with, say, Lorca, Valle-Inclán, Shakespeare or Molière in his collection of writings on the theatre (2003).

Chapter 4

1 For more details about the film, see *Cinéma*, 1986; and Phillipon, 1987.
2 There have been various films of Calderón's works made abroad and there have been more screen adaptations of his plays than of Lope's in total. However, within Spain, Lope has a slight lead. For more details on all screen adaptations of the *comedia* see Calvo Sastre, Millás and Papell, 2005. This book, which provides an exhaustive catalogue of films based on Spanish literary works, has a chapter dedicated to film adaptations of Golden Age dramatic works (pp. 48–52).
3 This is, of course, reminiscent of debates surrounding the theatre in the seventeenth century (see Cotarelo y Mori, 1997).
4 For a detailed overview of how the censorship system functioned, see Estivill, 2009; Gil, 2009; González Ballesteros, 1981; and Gubern, 1981 and 2005. For a more general discussion of how the state protected national cinema in this period, see Castro de Paz, 2002, pp. 23–31; Monterde, 1995; and Pozo, 1984, pp. 44–9.
5 For a discussion on the controversy that surrounded the release of this film, see Elena, 2009.
6 The box numbers of the censorship files for Román's film are 36/03317 and 36/03299.
7 In the early post-war period she was 'la indiscutible estrella número uno del cine español' [the indisputable number one star of Spanish cinema] (Comas, 2004, p. 124), with her salary often exceeding that of the directors she worked for (Rodríguez Fuentes, 2002, p. 315).
8 Ramón also filmed a version with the offending word included for international distribution beyond the peninsula (Coira, 2004, p. 123).
9 For more information on CIFESA, see Fanés, 1982.
10 Bosch and Rincón's description of the cinema is far removed from the glitz of the *Gran Vía*: 'The cinema was cheap, warm in winter and cool in summer. There were movie theatres in every neighbourhood of the large towns, and at least one in most of the rural villages. In these pre-television times, entire families could escape the tribulations of daily life, as well as the asphyxiating cultural climate, by going to the cinema. Parents with young children and babes in arms went together, their meagre suppers carried in bags; admitted free, the children were expected to fall asleep after eating their sandwiches, while their parents spent the next three hours absorbed by the screen' (Bosch and Rincón, 1998, pp. 113–14).
11 This deficit should be settled at least in part by the upcoming books on the subject, based on oral accounts of cinema-going in Spain during the 1940s and 1950s, headed by Jo Labanyi and funded by the AHRC.
12 Vicente Casanova claimed at the time, for example, that *Don Quijote* would get a wide release in the US; of course it never did (Fanés, 1982, p. 191).
13 All this information is contained in the censorship file for *Don Juan*: box no. 36/04716.

14 For a discussion on the contested authorship of Don Juan, see Rodríguez López-Vázquez, 2002; and Parr, 1999.
15 The most exhaustive list of variations of the Don Juan myth is provided by Singer, 2003. For an analysis of Don Juan in the cinema see Fernández, 2000.
16 As Sarah Wright notes, 'Zorrilla's version is the one that holds sway in Spain' (2007, p. 9); throughout Franco's regime it would be performed annually on All Saints' Day. For a brief overview of the performance history of *Don Juan Tenorio* on the Spanish stage, see Oliva, 1998.
17 One exception is a spirited and somewhat reactionary defence of the film by Luís Pérez Bastías and Fernando Alonso Barahona in a book entitled *Las mentiras sobre el cine español* (1995, pp. 89–90).
18 For more details on this film and its failure, see González, 2005, pp. 137–57.
19 The transcript of the Salamanca discussions can be found in Pozo, 1984, pp. 134–9.
20 The Gran Vía cinema opened in 1944, had 1,018 seats and was thought of as one of the best in Europe, while the Roxy A opened in 1952, had 1,000 seats and was a popular site for premieres (Cebollada and Santa Eulalia, 2000, pp. 264, 363).
21 Kathleen M. Vernon defines the *españolada* as 'a hybrid genre of romantic comedy and/or melodrama incorporating regional, primarily Andalusian song and dance'; as she goes on to note it has generally been derided/dismissed by critics from both ends of the political spectrum (1999, p. 249).
22 Box no. 36/03460. In the documentation, they claim that the budget was 3,662,960.10 pesetas.
23 The Filmoteca's box office statistics are available on-line at http://www.mcu.es and are quoted in euros.
24 A sample of reviews from different national newspapers reproduced in *Espectáculo* reveal that the critical reaction was, in general, lukewarm at best (1954).
25 Box no 36/03469.
26 This trend of sugar coating was not restricted to Spanish classical drama; in 1955, it was prohibited that Juliet commit suicide in the film version of *Romeo and Juliet* (Taibo I, 2000, p. 84), thereby inadvertently making the narrative closer to Lope's version of the tale, *Castelvines y Monteses*.
27 Box no 36/04698.
28 Box no 36/04716.
29 The desire to bring *La vida es sueño* to the big screen is seemingly perpetual in Spanish cinema and is reflected, for example, in Edgar Neville's *Producciones Mínguez S.A*. In this play, a financier says he will only provide money to a struggling studio during the Second Republic if they film Calderón's masterpiece, much to their chagrin: 'No se recuerda de persona viva que haya pagado su butaca para ver *La vida es sueño*' [I cannot think of anyone alive who has paid for a seat to see *Life is a Dream*]. For more details on this play and its relation to *La vida es sueño*, see Green, 2007.
30 For more information on Altolaguirre, a poet and ex-director of La Barraca, see Gutiérrez Mandado, 2003; and Sánchez Vidal, 2003.
31 See Wheeler, 2011a, for a detailed analysis of the film and its reception in both Argentina and Spain.
32 For a discussion of this film (in German), see Wischnewski, 1956.
33 Box no 36/04572.
34 For a discussion of the arguments for and against attributing the play to Lope, see Parrack, 2008; and Rodríguez López-Vázquez, 1996.

35 For more details of the director's career, see Gantes, 2006; and Generalitat Valenciana and Filmoteca Valenciana, 1986.
36 In a report produced by and for the industry in which films' box office takings are awarded six ratings ranging from *pésimo* [dreadful] to *excelente* [excellent]. *El príncipe encadenado*'s showing was rated as *bueno* [good] (the second highest category) (*Documentos cinematográficos*, 1961, p. 203).
37 For a full list of the film's prizes see *Revista intenacional del cine*, 1961.
38 For more information on Golden Age drama on Spanish television, see Suárez Miramón, 2002.
39 For more details of this earlier production, see Guerrero Zamora, 1962.
40 Thomas Austin O'Connor has written an excellent article on the changes that Guerrero Zamora has made to Lope's play text (1997).
41 Box no 36/04224.
42 For a discussion of whether Lope did write the play attributed to him, and also a comparison of that play and Calderón's version, see Escudero Baztán, 1998.
43 My understanding of the western and how it relates to this film has been greatly aided by Buscombe, 1993; and Cameron and Pye, 1996.
44 Drove claims that he was given license to adapt most of the play into prose but that he was told that he ought to retain the most famous verses (1994, p. 73). There are many reversions to verse throughout the course of the film but by placing some of the play's most iconic phrases in the troubadour's mouth (e.g. 'el alma es solo patrimonio de Dios' [the soul belongs to God alone]) the screenwriter helps ensure that they will not unnecessarily obstruct the narrative flow while also employing a formally sophisticated framing device that foregrounds the role of popular tradition in artistic creation and justifies the inclusion of *legend* in the film's title.
45 The script specifies that Leonor is 'muy guapa, pero con esa belleza inexpresiva y muerta que denota la estupidez' [extremely pretty but with that kind of inexpressive and unresponsive beauty that suggests stupidity] while Inés 'en cambio, no puede decirse que sea muy guapa. Ni siquiera que sea guapa' [in contrast, could not be described as very pretty; not even as pretty] (Drove, 1972, p. 18).
46 He received more national prizes from the regime than any other director, and at the time of his death in 1986, he was planning to make a film of the dictator's life.
47 These films include *Libro de buen amor* (1975), *La lozana andaluza* (1976) and *El Buscón* (1979). The critic even goes as far as to say that these films would not have been made if it was not 'por su trasfondo pseudopornográfico' [for their pseudo-pornographic subtext].
48 Box no. 36/04445.
49 For a good analysis of the Miró law, see Puigdomènech, 2007, pp. 42–53. See Ballesteros, 2001, for a good overview and analysis of literary adaptations under the Socialists.
50 The first of these, which registered over a million and a half admissions at the cinema, suggested that Columbus was bisexual and, at one time, earned money by performing as a drag artist. It also focussed on the Catholic Monarchs' ineptitude and immorality and showed the Inquisition, among whose number was a friar played by Alfredo Mayo, offered Nazi salutes as they went about their task to expel the Jews.
51 Diego Muñoz y Miguel Bayón spoke of how, '[c]asi desde los tiempos de Cifesa no se contaban historias de reyes en el cine español' [monarchical stories have

hardly been told in Spanish cinema since the days of CIFESA] (1991) while Rafa Fernández was pleasantly surprised: 'El cine sobre ese momento histórico (Felipe IV en 1620) está asociado a lo farragoso, pero aquí es chispeante y divertido' [Cinema about this historical moment (Philip IV in 1620) generally has a bad name, but here it is lively and fun] (1991).

52 This was not the first time that *El perro del hortelano* had been filmed. It had been shown on Spanish television in a version directed by Fernando García de la Vega but the only review I have been able to find of it describes it as being 'mal, mal, muy mal' [bad, bad, very bad] (Zeta, 1966). In 1977, the Soviet director Yan Frid directed a Russian-language version of the play, *Sobaka na sene*, for television.

53 My account of the filming process is based on by far the most detailed and insightful overviews available: Galán, 2006, pp. 273–83; and Pérez Millán, 2007, pp. 247–70.

54 Interview with the author conducted in Madrid on 22 April 2008.

55 For an insightful comparison of the two films, see Allinson, 1999.

56 The film received unusually wide press coverage. For an exhaustive list of reviews, see *Nosferatu*, 1998, p. 110.

57 For details of these, see Nieva de la Paz, 2001, p. 256.

58 I have refrained from discussing the film's artistic merits in detail in this chapter because there are already various studies that offer detailed readings of the film. In addition to my own article, see Allison, 1999; Alonso Veloso, 2001; Barros, 2008; Canning, 2005; Díez Ménguez, 2002; Escalonilla López, 2002; Fernández and Martínez-Carazo, 2006; García Santo-Tomás, 2000b; Jaime, 2000, pp. 210–31; Mañas Martínez, 2003; Nieva de la Paz, 2001; Pérez Millán, 2007, pp. 247–70; Thiem, 2009; and Zatlin, 2005, pp. 177–80.

59 The collective sales of *Lecturas, Semanas, ¡Hola!* and *Diez Minutos* are more than all other Spanish magazines put together; since 1997, this boom has been reflected on television with Diana's funeral and royal marriages being broadcast (Falcón Osorio, 1998, pp. 34, 52).

60 Female politicians are, for example, frequently asked questions such as whether they would go topless (Cruz, 2004, p. 73). Miró, who worked as an image consultant for Felipe González and the PSOE prior to their first election win, would later defend herself when prosecuted for using public money for her wardrobe by claiming that the demands made on public men and women's dress were radically different. She demonstrated this point in a visible fashion by always wearing the same tuxedo at public events while she was under investigation. For a good general discussion of Miró's career as a pioneering female director not lacking in enemies, see Martín-Márquez, 1999, pp. 141–82. For a sympathetic discussion of how her gender and status were used against her, see Triana-Toribio, 1998.

61 Interview with the author conducted in Madrid on 22 April 2008.

62 Interview with the author conducted in Madrid on 14 April 2008.

63 Interview with the author conducted in Madrid on 29 August 2007.

64 Interview with the author conducted in Madrid on 17 December 2007.

65 For more details of this film and an opportunity to view the trailer, see www.lopelapelicula.com. It is beyond the timeframe of this book to discuss this film, but I plan to write about it in a future article.

66 Golden Age dramatists are, however, more invisible in *Don Juan DeMarco* (Jeremy Leven, 1994), an American film in which Johnny Depp is sectioned because he believes himself to be Don Juan and his psychiatrist to be Don Octavio. While a copy of *El burlador de Sevilla* is shown in his room, the absence of Tirso's name on

the front cover is more likely a result of Tirso's relative anonymity in the global marketplace rather than a coded reference to the text's contested authorship.
67 This association can be traced back at least as far as *La reina zanahoria* (Gonzalo Suárez, 1977) where an eccentric millionairess renames her Eastern European psychotherapist who she also turns into her butler and possibly lover Segismundo.
68 Unless otherwise noted, all information on the film is taken from a series of interviews conducted by the author with Iborra that took place in Madrid between April and August 2007.
69 *La dama boba* was, we know, a resounding success when it was first staged and it has had a continuous performance tradition throughout the twentieth century and is, for example, Lope's most popular comedy in America (Hernández Araico, 2000, p. 81).
70 For a brief but good overview of the play's reception and afterlife, see Gómez Sierra, 2003, pp. 369–72. A more detailed analysis is provided by CNTC, 2003.
71 The plot lines of highly successful films such as *Bienvenido a casa, El otro lado de la cama, A mi madre le gustan las mujeres, Café sólo o con ellas* treat love as a centrifugal force that motivates both human and narrative actions. These films depict an ensemble of young men and women living in the metropolis, whose amorous attachments change throughout the course of the narrative, and who successfully navigate a series of potentially dangerous scenarios in order to arrive at resolution in the end through marriage or a stable relationship.
72 For a discussion of the representation of women in the play, see Gómez Torres, 1996; Heigl, 1998; and Soufas, 1997.
73 The absence of mothers in the *comedia* is likely a result of the resistance to cast older actresses. As Melveena McKendrick notes, '[m]any not surprisingly retired as they got older and parts dried up, because then, as now to some extent, the careers of women players were far shorter than those of men' (2006, p. 82). The continuation of this gender imbalance is demonstrated by the fact that, in real life, Forqué (born in 1955) is of the same generation as Coronado (born 1957) and they last appeared on screen together in *Salsa Rosa* (Manuel Gómez Perreira, 1992) as potential love interests.
74 Silvia Abascal (Finea) had, for example, played Forqué's daughter in *El tiempo de la felicidad* (Manuel Iborra, 1997) and has more recently appeared as her niece in *Enloquecidas* (Juan Luis Iborra, 2008).
75 Interview with the author conducted in Madrid on 20 April 2008.
76 Interview with the author conducted in Madrid on 29 August 2007.
77 Abascal was voted best actress for her depiction of Finea; Lorenzo Caprile won the award for best wardrobe; and Macarena Gómez and Roberto San Martín were recognized in the category of best supporting roles.
78 All figures courtesy of the Ministry of Culture website.
79 For more details of this project see www.lavidaessueno.com
80 For more details of this theatrical production, see Wheeler, 2011b, pp. 189–91.

Chapter 5

1 They are of course referring to the Rolling Stones.
2 For an overview of the reception to the season in the UK, see Fischer, 2005.
3 When I asked Boswell whether he had seen Miró's film and whether it had been

an influence, he answered that he had seen it but that it was so 'utterly crap' that it had not left any impression on him. Email to the author, 18 August 2008.

4   This was not the first time that Spaniards had been presented with the play in a foreign language; in 2002 a French company, *La Traverse*, had performed it in Almagro with a translation by Fréderic Serralta and under the directorship of Hervé Petit.

5   The most detailed and best study of this production is Fischer, 2009, pp. 220–42. Fernández, 2006, also gives some valuable insights.

6   For more details of these changes, see *PA*, 2005.

7   There are, for example, no references made to Icarus. Ricardo and Federico hardly appear. Equally, Ludovico only makes his first appearance at the denouement, and we do not see Tristán providing a spin on Teodoro's fantastical genealogy.

8   For a detailed and intelligent review of this production, see Pérez-Rasilla, 1989.

9   This is, of course, necessitated by the translation process but his flexibility when it comes to replicating precise images or syntax is demonstrated when compared to Dixon's earlier translation that was used, albeit without permission, for the English subtitles on the video release of Miró's film. For a comparison of the two translations, see Fischer, 2009, p. 222–4.

10   For a discussion of the debates surrounding this decision, see Johnston, 2007a; and Mountjoy, 2007.

11   Robert Pring-Mill observed long ago that 'the action does stem from a psychological postulate' (1961, p. xxvii); *El perro* is one of Lope's most static plays. It has an unusual number of soliloquies and, according to Victor Dixon, there are more sonnets than in any other play by Lope (1995, pp. 132–3).

12   Unless otherwise noted, all of the information about Vasco and the company is from an interview conducted by the author with the director in Madrid on 17 December 2007.

13   Email to the author sent on 18 August 2008.

14   Spanish actors do now have at their disposal a very detailed and somewhat dense guide to reciting verse: Cantero, 2006.

15   Mumby told me this at the *Out of the Wings* conference held in Oxford on 18–19 March 2010. He also reported that ticket sales were low until it was announced that Dominic West, famous for his appearances in the television series *The Wire*, would play Segismundo.

16   For more details of this production, see Fischer, 2003.

17   This can often be read implicitly in newspaper columns and reviews. Hence, for example, the only newspaper I am aware of to give Miró's film adaptation of *El perro del hortelano* a negative review was *Avui* in which Jordi Costa claimed it was no more accomplished than the old Estudio 1 productions and that '*El perro del hortelano* no és, probablement, el millor argument per defensar la igualtat del teatre clàssic espanyol davant, posem per cas, Shakespeare' [*The Dog in the Manger* is probably not the best argument for defending Spanish classical theatre's equal standing with, for example, Shakespeare] (1996).

18   For a collection of these columns here, see Salvat, 1974.

19   For more information on his pedagogical activities, see Ciurans, 2009; Olivar, 2009; and Serrano, 2009.

20   For more information on the school, see Ferrer and Rom, 1998, pp. 34–49.

21   It was well received by critics and audiences alike in the UK, which led it to being performed in the Brooklyn Academy of Music in New York, where it had positive reviews from publications such as the *New York Times* (Pedraza Jiménez cited in

CNTC, 2001, pp. 28–9). For a selection of reviews from home and abroad, see CNTC, 2001, pp. 103–17. For a comparison of the Spanish and English-language productions, see Fischer, 2009, pp. 173–7.

22 After seeing Marsillach's production of *La Celestina*, Michael Billington was particularly scathing: 'Having hit spectacular highs with imports from Japan and the Soviet Union, Edinburgh's official programme comes back to earth with a lacklustre Spanish offering' (1989).

23 This version based on what is referred to as the Zaragoza edition has been published in an excellent modern edition, painstakingly prepared by J. M. Ruano de la Haza (Calderón de la Barca, 1992).

24 For more details of the company, see Mateo, 2006; and Reina Ruiz, 2010.

25 The director stressed this and the use of ensembles as his major priorities when he addressed the Oxford Union on 30 May 2008. The RSC's production of *El perro* at the Swan in Stratford was so inclusive and intimate largely as a result of recent evolution in theatrical and architectural approach. This was manifest by the fact that at least some of its charm and immediacy was lost when it was performed in spaces with a more traditional demarcation between stage and auditorium.

26 See García-Martín, 2004, for more details of amateur productions in Fuente Ovejuna (pp. 109–18) and Zalamea (pp. 149–75).

27 Two attempts were, however, made to raise the international standing of the festival and Golden Age authors with high-profile productions. Hernández attempted to lure Almodóvar back to Almagro to make his professional theatrical debut with a version of Lope's *La dama boba*. The former told me that scheduling difficulties prevented this from taking place and that it would happen at some point; representatives of the latter's production company, *El Deseo*, informed me that this definitely was not the case. In 2008, I translated an adaptation of *Cardenio* – a play attributed to Shakespeare that appears to be based on an incident in the Quixote – by a playwright from Seville, Antonio Álamo, for a potential dual language co-production between the Almagro Festival and the RSC. The project went through various further mutations before opening in English, and without the participation of the Spanish festival, in Stratford in April 2011.

28 This is generally accepted by most economic experts. As William Chislett notes: 'Tourism plays such a vital role in the Spanish economy (it generates around 10% of GDP and employs roughly one in every 10 people) that it would be unwise to do anything that seriously harmed the country's image as a Mecca for tourism, and yet Spain is also striking to promote a more 'serious' (cold) image in order to help exports and make the country known for other achievements and not just as a fun playground' (2010, p. 20).

29 For an account of the ceremony, see Alonso, 2008.

30 Interview with the author conducted in Madrid on 19 September 2008. The 2004 production did not ultimately go ahead but the play was once again performed in 2006.

31 See, for example, Daumas, 2005; and Martín Bermúdez, 2006.

Conclusion

1 Maravall does mention *El perro* but argues that it was conservative because it showed that people could rise in exceptional cases if they did not threaten the

basic tenets on which the hierarchical system was predicated (1972, p. 59). For a reading of the play inspired by Maravall, see Herrero, 1974.
2   I entertain this hypothetical scenario in Wheeler, 2011c.
3   There are individual territories such as Poland where Golden Age playwrights are canonical, but this is very much the exception rather than the rule. For a good overview of the *comedia* outside Spain, see Huerta Calvo, 2008.

Works Cited

Aaron, Michele (2007). *Spectatorship: The Power of Looking On*. London: Wallflower.
Abajo de Pablos, Juan Julio de (1996). *Mis charlas con José Luis Sáenz de Heredia*. Valladolid: Quirón Ediciones.
ABC (1951). 'Teatro de la comedia'. *ABC*, 18 January: 4.
Aburish, Said K. (1998). *Arafat: From Defender to Dictator*. London: Bloomsbury.
ADE (1983). 'Bases para una política teatral para el trabajo con los clásicos'. *Pipirijaina*, 24: 55–65.
— (2002). 'Adolfo Marsillach o el pudor de la maestría'. *ADE*, 90: whole issue dedicated to Adolfo Marsillach.
Adell, Alberi (1967). 'Lope, Osborne y los críticos'. *Ínsula*, 247: 7.
A. F. (1972). '*Fuenteovejuna*'. *Cineinforme*. December: 14.
Aguilar, Carlos (2007). *Guía del cine español*. Madrid: Cátedra.
Aguilera Sastre, Juan (1993). 'Felipe Lluch Garín, artífice y iniciador del Teatro Nacional español'. In Andrés Peláez (ed.), *Historia de los Teatros Nacionales (1939–1962)*. Madrid: CDT, pp. 40–67.
— (2002). *El debate sobre el Teatro Nacional en España (1900–1939): ideología y estética*. Madrid: CDT.
— and Isabel Lizarraga Vizcarra (2001). *Federico García Lorca y el teatro clásico: la versión escénica de La dama boba*. Logroño: Universidad de la Rioja.
Aguirre, Arantxa (2008). 'Emma Suárez'. In Arantxa Aguirre (ed.), *34 actores hablan de su oficio*. Madrid: Cátedra, pp. 601–22.
Agustín Puerta, Mercedes (1998). 'Moda, modernidad y modelos de mujer. Algunas revistas femeninas: *Letras, Telva, El Hogar y La Moda*'. In Emilio J. García Wiedemann and María Isabel Montoya Ramírez (eds), *Moda y sociedad: estudios sobre educación, lenguaje e historia del vestido*. Granada: Centro de Formación Continua de la Universidad de Granada, pp. 19–30.
Albesa, Isaac (2005). 'Simó: *Fuente Ovejuna* no tiene nada que ver con las revueltas actuales'. *Diari de Tarragona*, 22 June: 1.
Alcalá, Juan de (1952). 'Pulso teatral de Madrid'. *El noticiero universal*, 7 October: 8.
Alcaroz, Juan de (1943). 'La obra de los escritores españoles en la pantalla', interview with Fernández Ardavín. *Primer Plano*, 4 July: unpaginated.
Allatson, Paul (1996). 'Confounding convention: "women" in three Golden Age plays'. *B.Com*, 48.2: 261–73.
Allinson, Mark (1999). 'Pilar Miró's last two films: history, adaptation and genre'. In Rob Rix and Roberto Rodríguez-Saona (eds), *Spanish Cinema: Calling the Shots*. Leeds: Trinity and All Saints, pp. 33–45.
Alonso, Alejandro (2008). 'Presentación de las memorias de Ángel F. Montesinos y homenaje en el Festival de Teatro Clásico de Almagro'. *ADE*, 122: 299–301.
Alonso de Santos, José Luis (2002). '*Peribáñez y el Comendador de Ocaña*'. In Felipe B. Pedraza Jiménez, Rafael González Cañal y Elena Marcello (eds), *La comedia villanesca y su escenificación: Actas de las XXIV Jornadas de Teatro Clásico Almagro 10*,

11 y 12 de julio de 2001. Almagro: Festival de Almagro and Universidad Castilla-La Mancha, pp. 53–67.
— (2007). 'Sobre mis puestas en escena en la Compañía Nacional de Teatro Clásico'. In José Romero Castillo (ed.), *Análisis de espectáculos teatrales (2000–2006)*. Madrid: Visor Libros, pp. 27–34.
Alonso Veloso, María José (2001). '*El perro del hortelano*, de Pilar Miró: una adaptación no tan fiel de la comedia de Lope de Vega'. *Signa: Revista de la Asociación Española de Semiótica*, 10: 375–93.
Alted, Alicia (2000). 'Notas para la configuración y el análisis de la política cultural del franquismo en sus comienzos: la labor del Ministerio de Educación Nacional durante la guerra'. In Josep Fontana (ed.), *España bajo el franquismo*. Barcelona: Editorial Crítica, pp. 215–29.
Álvar Ezquerra, Alfredo (2002). *Isabel la Católica: una reina vencedora, una mujer derrotada*. Madrid: Temas de hoy.
Álvaro, Francisco (ed.) (1961). *El espectador y la crítica: el teatro en España en 1960*. Valladolid: Francisco Álvaro.
— (ed.) (1963). *El espectador y la crítica: el teatro en España en 1962*. Valladolid: Francisco Álvaro.
— (ed.) (1967). *El espectador y la crítica: el teatro en España en 1966*. Valladolid: Francisco Álvaro.
— (ed.) (1971). *El espectador y la crítica: el teatro en España en 1970*. Madrid: Prensa Española.
— (ed.) (1977). *El espectador y la crítica: el teatro en España en 1976*. Madrid: Prensa Española.
— (ed.) (1979). *El espectador y la crítica: el teatro en España en 1978*. Valladolid: Francisco Álvaro.
—, (ed.) (1980). *El espectador y la crítica: el teatro en España en 1979*. Valladolid: Francisco Álvaro.
— (ed.) (1982). *El espectador y la crítica: el teatro en España en 1981*. Valladolid: Francisco Álvaro.
— (ed.) (1984). *El espectador y la crítica: el teatro en España en 1983*. Valladolid: Francisco Álvaro.
Amestoy, Ignacio (2002). 'Miguel Narros, en el filo del teatro'. In Luciano García Lorenzo and Andrés Peláez Martín (eds), *Miguel Narros, una vida para el teatro*. Almagro: Festival de Teatro Clásico de Almagro, pp. 13–53.
— (2004). 'La royal en Madrid y Encinar en Venecia'. *El Mundo*, 30 October: 32.
— (2008). 'El Parnasillo: Gallardón y los clásicos'. *El Mundo*, 26 April: 12.
Amorós, Andrés (1987). 'La Compañía Nacional de Teatro Clásico'. *Ínsula*, 485–6: 33.
Anderson, Benedict (1991). *Imagined Communities: Reflections on the Origin and Spread of Nationalism*, 2nd ed., London: Verso.
Antón, Jacinto (2004). 'Cultura inicia por el TNC la reordenación del teatro público'. *El País* (Barcelona ed.), 28 February: 1.
Añón Roig, María José and Ruth Mestre i Mestre (2005). 'Violencia sobre las mujeres: discriminación, subordinación y Derecho'. In Javier Boix Reig and Elena Martínez García (eds), *La nueva ley contra la violencia de género*. Madrid: Iustel, pp. 31–63.
Aragonés, Juan Emilio (1973). 'El tartufismo que la juventud corea', review of *Marta la piadosa*. *La estafeta literaria*, 15 December: 41.
Arce, Carlos (1986). 'Ángel Gutiérrez, un maestro que vino del frio'. *El público*, 29: 20–1.

Archer, Robert (1990). 'El pueblo, los reyes y el público: el pragmatismo dramático en *Fuente Ovejuna*'. In Roy Boland and Alun Kenwood (eds), *War and Revolution in Hispanic Literatura*. Melbourne: Voz Hispánica, pp. 109–19.
Arellano, Ignacio (2002). 'Canon dramático e interpretación de la comedia cómica del Siglo de Oro'. In Enrique García Santo-Tomás (ed.), *El teatro del Siglo de Oro ante los espacios de la crítica: encuentros y revisiones*. Frankfurt and Madrid: Vervuert and Iberoamericana, pp. 357–77.
— (2004). 'Algunos problemas y prejuicios en la recepción del teatro clásico español'. In José María Díez Borque and José Alcalá Zamora (eds), *Proyección y significados del teatro clásico español: homenaje a Alfredo Hermenegildo y Francisco Ruiz Ramón*. Madrid: Sociedad estatal para la acción cultural exterior, pp. 53–77.
Armas, Frederick A. de (2006). 'A woman hunted, a city besieged: Spanish emblems and Italian art in *Fuenteovejuna*'. In Margaret R. Greer and Laura R. Bass (eds), *Approaches to Teaching Early Modern Spanish Drama*. New York: MLA, pp. 45–52.
Armendáriz Armendía, Ana (2007). 'El sentido y los sentidos'. In Pedro Calderón de la Barca, *El médico de su honra*, ed. Ana Armendáriz Armendía. Frankfurt and Madrid: Universidad de Navarra, Vervuert and Iberoamericana, pp. 11–227.
Armiño, Mauro (2004). 'Entre el honor y los celos', review of *The Dog in the Manger*. *La razón*, 25 October: 68.
Arroyo, Julia (1986). '¡Cuidado con los clásicos!', review of *El médico de su honra*. *Ya*, 26 October: 43.
Artiles, Jenaro (1967). 'La idea de la venganza en el drama español del siglo XVII'. *Segismundo*, 5–6: 9–38.
Aszyk, Urszula (2009). '*El príncipe constante* de Calderón-Slowacki-Grotowski: notas sobre el proceso de constitución de un mito teatral del siglo XX'. In Karolina Kumor (ed.), *De Cervantes a Calderón: estudios sobre la literatura y el teatro español del Siglo de Oro*. Warsaw: Instituto de Estudios Ibéricos y Iberoamericanos de la Universidad de Varsovia, pp. 113–26.
Auslander, Philip (2004). 'Postmodernism and performance'. In Steven Connor (ed.), *The Cambridge Companion to Postmodernism*. Cambridge: Cambridge University Press, pp. 97–115.
Ayanz, Miguel (2004). 'A los pies de la mejor escena de Europa'. *La razón*, 9 October: 42.
Ayllón, José (1952). 'La interpretación de los clásicos'. *Ínsula*, 75: 12.
Azcona Navarro, Alfonso (1999). 'TEU: 1960–1963'. In Jesús Rubio Jiménez (ed.), *Teatro universitario en Zaragoza (1939–1999)*. Zaragoza: Prensa Universitaria de Zaragoza, pp. 215–47.
Aznar Soler, Manuel (1998). 'El mito de Don Juan Tenorio y el teatro del exilio español de 1939'. In Ana Sofía Pérez-Bustamente (ed.), *Don Juan Tenorio en la España del siglo XX: literatura y cine*. Madrid: Cátedra, pp. 271–88.
— (1999). 'El teatro universitario en Barcelona durante el franquismo (1939–1975)'. In Luciano García Lorenzo (ed.), *Aproximación al teatro español universitario (TEU)*. Madrid: Consejo Superior de Investigaciones Científicas, Instituto de la Lengua Española, pp. 111–37.
Azorín (1995). *El cinematógrafo: artículos sobre cine y guiones de películas 1921–1964*, eds José Payá Bernabé and Magdalena Rigual Bonastre. Valencia: Pre-Textos.
Baczyńska, Beata. (2009). 'El teatro barroco español y Jerzy Grotowski'. In Karolina Kumor (ed.), *De Cervantes a Calderón: estudios sobre la literatura y el teatro español del Siglo de Oro*. Warsaw: Instituto de Estudios Ibéricos y Iberoamericanos de la Universidad de Varsovia, pp. 127–34.

Bajo Martínez, María Jesús (1999). 'Tres décadas del teatro universitario en Sevilla'. In Luciano García Lorenzo (ed.), *Aproximación al teatro español universitario (TEU)*. Madrid: Consejo Superior de Investigaciones Científicas, Instituto de la Lengua Española, pp. 223–33.

Ballesteros, Carlos (2007). 'La interpretación en verso'. In Antonio Serrano (ed.), *En torno al teatro del Siglo de Oro: Jornadas XXI-XXIII (Almería)*. Almería: Instituto de Estudios Almerienses, pp. 27–36.

Ballesteros, Isolina (1999). 'Mujer y nación en el cine español de posguerra: los años 40'. *Arizona Journal of Hispanic Cultural Studies*, 3: 51–70.

— (2001). 'Convergencias y alianzas culturales: las adaptaciones fílmicas de obras literarias en el período socialista'. In Isolina Ballesteros, *Cine (ins)urgente: textos fílmicos y contextos culturales en la España posfranquista*. Madrid: Ediciones Fundamentos, pp. 153–74.

Balseyro, Sergio (2005). 'Manuel Iborra será el primer director en La Ciudad de la Luz con *La dama boba*, en verano'. *La verdad*, 2 June: 40.

Baltés, Blanca (2008). 'Cayetano Luca de Tena: dirigir en los años cuarenta'. *ADE*, 120: 171–82.

Banús, Enrique and María C. Barcenilla (2005). '¿Vive el teatro del Siglo de Oro? Los "clásicos" en la programación de los teatros europeos'. In Carlos Mata and Miguel Zugasti (eds), *Actas del Congreso 'El Siglo de Oro en el nuevo milenio'*, vol. 1. Barañáin: Ediciones Universidad de Navarra, pp. 263–74.

Barros, Sandra R. (2008). 'La mujer en sus espacios: Lope de Vega, Pilar Miró y la reconfiguración cinematográfica'. *Espéculo: Revista de estudios literario* 38, electronic Journal (http://www.ucm.es/info/especulo/numero38/lopegen.html).

Barthes, Roland (1972). 'The diseases of costume'. In Roland Barthes, *Critical Essays*, trans. Richard Howard. Evanston: Northwestern University Press, pp. 41–50.

Basic, Robert (2005). 'Agustín Díaz Yanes: *Alatriste* es una película de sentimientos con acción'. *El correo*, 3 November: 74–5.

Bass, Laura (2004). 'To possess her in paint: (pro)creative failure and crisis in *El pintor de su deshonra*'. In Frederick A. de Armas (ed.), *Writing for the Eyes in the Spanish Golden-Age*. Lewisburg: Bucknell University Press, pp. 185–211.

— (2006). 'Costume and the *comedia*: dressing up *El vergonzoso en palacio* in the classroom'. In Margaret R. Greer and Laura R. Bass (eds), *Approaches to Teaching Early-Modern Spanish Drama*. New York: MLA, pp. 61–8.

Bate, Jonathan (1997). *The Genius of Shakespeare*. London: Picador.

Bayón, Miguel (1983). 'Lo moderno del amor', review of *La Dorotea*. *Pipirijaina*, 25: 93–4.

Beckers, Ursula (1992). 'La escenografía teatral de Sigfrido Burmann'. Unpublished dissertation, Universidad Complutense.

Benabu, Isaac (1994). '"Who is the protagonist"? Gutierre on the stand'. *Indiana Journal of Hispanic Literature*, 2.2: 13–25.

Benach, Joan-Antón (2005). '*Fuente Ovejuna*', review. *La vanguardia*, 23 April: 53.

Benavente, Jacinto (1949). 'Lope de Vega no se disgusta'. *ABC*, 28 April: 3.

Bennett, Susan (1997). *Theatre Audiences: A Theory of Production and Reception*, 2nd ed. London: Routledge.

— (2005). 'Shakespeare on vacation'. In Barbara Hodgdon and W. B. Worthen (eds), *A Companion to Shakespeare and Performance*. Chichester: Wiley-Blackwell, pp. 494–508.

Bentley, Bernard P. F. (2004). '*Fuenteovejuna* en 1947: la hipoteca del presente'. In María Luisa Lobato and Francisco Domínguez Matito (eds), *Memoria de la*

palabra: Actas del VI congreso de la Asociación Internacional Siglo de Oro. Frankfurt and Madrid: Vervuert and Iberoamericana, pp. 331–6.
Bentley, Eric, Robert Brustein and Stanley Kauffmann (2009). 'The theatre critic as thinker: a round table discussion', transcribed and ed. by Bert Cardullo. *New Theatre Quarterly*, 25.4: 310–23.
Berger, Verena (2009) 'El teatro del Siglo de Oro y el cine español: *La dama boba* de Manuel Iborra'. In Verena Berger and Mercè Saumell (eds), *Escenarios compartidos: cine y teatro en España en el umbral del siglo XXI*. Berlin: LitVerlag, pp. 61–73.
Berghaus, Günter (1996). 'Introduction'. In Günter Berghaus (ed.), *Fascism and Theatre: Comparative Studies on the Aesthetics and Politics of Performance in Europe (1925–1945)*. Providence: Berghahn Books, pp. 1–10.
Bergmann, Emilie L. (1994). 'Framing *La vengadora de las mujeres*: prophylactic introductions and postmodern performance'. *Gestos*, 17: 115–31.
Bernal, Francisca and César Oliva (1996). *El teatro público en España (1939–1978)*. Madrid: Ediciones J. García Verdugo.
Beverley, John (2008). *Essays on the Literary Baroque in Spain and Spanish America*. Woodbridge: Tamesis.
Billington, Michael (1989). 'In love's absence: a Spanish classic at Edinburgh', review of *La Celestina*. *The Guardian*, 25 August.
— (2002). 'The state of reviewing today'. In Maria M. Delgado and Caridad Svich (eds), *Theatre in Crisis? Performance Manifestos for a New Century*. Manchester: Manchester University Press, pp. 54–7.
Blakeley, Georgina (2008). 'Politics as usual? The trials and tribulations of the law of historical memory in Spain'. *Entelequia: revista interdisciplinary*, 7: 315–30.
Blue, William R. (1991). 'The politics of Lope's *Fuenteovejuna*'. *HR*, 59.3: 295–315.
Bodelón, Luis (1994). '*El pabellón número 6*: con Teatro de Cámara y Ángel Gutiérrez'. *PA*, 253: 116–20.
BOE (1986). 'Orden de 14 de enero de 1986 por la que se crea la Compañía Nacional de Teatro Clásico. . . .'. 27 January: 23, 3728–9.
— (2006). 'Resolución del 26 de diciembre de 2005 del INAEM. . . .'. 3 January: 2, 414–24.
Boniface, Priscilla and Peter J. Fowler (1993). *Heritage and Tourism in the Global Village*. London: Routledge.
Borrás, Tomas (1942). 'Movimiento teatral'. *Cuadernos de literatura contemporánea*, 1: 172–3.
Bosch, Aurora and M. Fernanda del Rincón (1998). 'Franco and Hollywood, 1939–56'. *New Left Review*, 232: 112–27.
Bourdieu, Pierre (1984). *Distinction: A Social Critique of the Judgement of Taste*, trans. Richard Nice. London: Routledge.
Boyle, Catherine (2007). 'Perspectives on loss and discovery: reading and reception'. In Catherine Boyle and David Johnston (with Janet Morris) (eds), *The Spanish Golden-Age in English: Perspectives on Performance*. London: Oberon Books, pp. 61–74.
— and David Johnston (2007). 'Introduction'. In Catherine Boyle and David Johnston (with Janet Morris) (eds), *The Spanish Golden-Age in English: Perspectives on Performance*. London: Oberon Books, pp. 11–14.
Bradby, David and Maria M. Delgado (2002). 'Introduction: piecing together the Paris jigsaw'. In David Bradby and Maria M. Delgado (eds), *The Paris Jigsaw: Internationalism and the City's Stages*. Manchester: Manchester University Press, pp. 1–33.

Bradby, David and Annie Sparks (1997). *Mise en Scène: French Theatre Now.* London: Methuen.
Brenan, Gerald (1987). *The Face of Spain.* London: Penguin.
Breward, Christopher (2003). *Fashion.* Oxford: Oxford University Press.
Brook, Peter (1990). *The Empty Space.* London: Penguin.
Brooksbank Jones, Anny (1997). *Women in Contemporary Spain.* Manchester: Manchester University Press.
Brown, M. Gordan (1942). 'Las actividades culturales en la España de la postguerra'. *Hispania*, 25.1: 61–5.
Brown, John Russell (2003). 'Shakespeare in performance, study, and criticism'. In Frank Occhiogrosso (ed.), *Shakespeare in Performance: A Collection of Essays.* Newark: University of Delaware Press, pp. 15–26.
Bryans, John (1981). 'System and structure in Calderón's *El médico de su honra*'. *Revista canadiense de estudios hispánicos*, 5.3: 271–91.
Buffery, Helena (2006). 'Theater space and cultural identity in Catalonia'. *Romance Quarterly*, 53.3: 195–206.
— (2007). *Shakespeare in Catalan: Translating Imperialism.* Cardiff: University of Wales Press.
Burmann, Conchita (2009). *La escenografía teatral de Sigfrido Burmann.* Madrid: Fundación Jorge Juan.
Burningham, Bruce R. (2006). 'Placing the *comedia* in performative context'. In Margaret R. Greer and Laura R. Bass (eds), *Approaches to Teaching Early-Modern Spanish Drama.* New York: MLA, pp. 107–14.
Buscombe, Edward (ed.) (1993). *The BFI Companion to the Western*, 2nd ed. London: André Deutsch Limited and BFI.
Byrd, Suzanne W. (1984). *La Fuente Ovejuna de Federico García Lorca.* Madrid: Editorial Pliegos.
Caba, María Y. (2008). *Isabel la Católica en la producción teatral española del siglo XVII.* Woodbridge: Tamesis.
Cabrera, Emilio and Andrés Morós (1991). *Fuenteovejuna: la violencia antiseñorial en el siglo XV.* Barcelona: Editorial Crítica.
Calderón de la Barca, Pedro (1991). *El pintor de su deshonra/The Painter of his Dishonor*, ed. and trans. A. K. G. Paterson. Warminster: Aris and Phillips.
— (1992). *La primera versión de La vida es sueño*, ed. J. M. Ruano de la Haza. Liverpool: Liverpool University Press.
— (1994). *El médico de su honra*, adaptation Rafael Pérez Sierra. Madrid: CNTC.
— (2008). *El pintor de su deshonra*, adaptation Rafael Pérez Sierra. Madrid: CNTC.
Calvo, Luis (1952). '*Fuenteovejuna*', review. *ABC*, 1 October: 37.
— (1953). 'En el teatro Lope de Vega se repuso anoche *Fuente Ovejuna* según la refundición de Enrique Rambal'. *ABC*, 20 January: 33–4.
Calvo Sastre, Ana, Lola Millás and Antonio Papell (2005). *Literatura española: una historia de cine.* Madrid: Polifemo.
Camacho, José María (2006). '*La dama boba*, el cine en verso', review. *ABC*, 24 March: 34.
Cameron, Ian and Douglas Pye (eds) (1996). *The Movie Book of the Western.* London: Studio Vista.
Camino, Mercedes (2004).'"¡Volvióse en luto la boda!": ritual, torture and the technologies of power in Lope's *Fuente Ovejuna*'. *Modern Language Review*, 99.2: 382–93.
Camporesi, Valería (1994). *Para grandes y chicos: un cine para los españoles (1940–1990).* Madrid: Ediciones Turfán.

Canning, Elaine (2005). '"Not I, my shadow": Pilar Miró's adaptation of Lope de Vega's *The Dog in the Manger* (1996)'. *Studies in European Cinema*, 2.2: 81–97.
— (2006). 'Destiny, theatricality and identity in contemporary European cinema'. *New Cinemas: Journal of Contemporary Film*, 4.3: 159–71.
Cantero, Susana (2006). *Dramaturgia y práctica escénica del verso clásico español*. Madrid: Editorial Fundamentos.
Cañadas, Ivan (2005). *Public Theater in Golden Age Madrid and Tudor-Stuart London*. Aldershot: Ashgate.
Cañas, Gabriel (1986). 'En busca de la tradición perdida: encontrar un estilo de recitación y actores idóneos han sido los primeros problemas de la Compañía Nacional de Teatro Clásico', interview with Adolfo Marsillach. *El País*, 9 March: 12.
Cañizares Bundorf, Nathalie (2000). *Memoria de un escenario: Teatro María Guerrero (1885–2000)*. Madrid: CDT.
Caparrós Lera, José María (ed.) (1992). *Memorias de dos pioneros: Francisco Elías and Fructuós Gelabert*. Barcelona: Centro de Investigaciones Literarias Españoles e Hispanoamericanos..
Caravajal, Mery (1972). 'Entrevista con Juan Guerrero Zamora'. *Pueblo*, 20 November: 35.
Carlson, Marvin (2001). *The Haunted Stage: The Theatre as Memory Machine*. Ann Arbor: University of Michigan Press.
— (2004). *Performance: A Critical Introduction*, 2nd ed. London: Routledge.
Carr, Raymond (1980). *Modern Spain: 1875–1980*. Oxford: Oxford University Press.
Carreño, Antonio (1997). 'The poetics of closure in Calderón's plays'. In Manuel Delgado Morales (ed.), *The Calderonian Stage: Body and Soul*. Lewisburg: Bucknell University Press, pp. 25–44.
Carrillo, Mary (2001). *Sobre la vida y el escenario: memorias*. Barcelona: Ediciones Martínez Roca.
Carrillo Guzmán, Mercedes del Carmen (2008). 'La música incidental en el Teatro Español de Madrid (1942–1952 y 1962–1964)'. Unpublished dissertation, Universidad de Murcia.
Carrión, María M. (2008). 'Mencía (in)visible: tragedia y violencia doméstica en *El médico de su honra*'. In Frederick A. de Armas, Luciano García Lorenzo and Enrique García Santo-Tomás (eds), *Hacia la tragedia áurea: lecturas para un nuevo milenio*. Frankfurt and Madrid: Vervuert, Universidad de Navarra and Iberoamericana, pp. 429–48.
Carter, Robin (1977). '*Fuenteovejuna* and tyranny: some problems of linking drama with political theory'. *Forum for Modern Language Studies*, 13: 313–35.
Cartmell, Deborah (1999). 'The Shakespeare on screen industry'. In Deborah Cartmell and Imelda Whelehan (eds), *Adaptations: From Text to Screen, Screen to Text*. London: Routledge, pp. 29–37.
Cascardi, Anthony J. (1997). 'The Spanish *comedia* and the resistance to historical change'. In Anthony J. Cascardi, *Ideologies of History in the Spanish Golden Age*. Pennsylvania: The Pennsylvania State University Press, pp. 17–46.
Castells, Joan (2002). 'La programación en el Teatro Nacional de Catalunya'. *ADE*, 91: 152–6.
Castilla, Alberto (1992). 'Teatro universitario: *Fuenteovejuna* 65'. In Heraclia Castellón, Agustín de la Granja and Antonio Serrano (eds), *En torno al teatro del Siglo de Oro: Actas de las Jornadas VII–VIII celebradas en Almería*. Granada: Instituto de Estudios Almerienses and Diputación de Almería, pp. 39–58.

— (chair) (2001). 'Mesa redonda: "Teatro del Siglo de Oro en la escena actual". Intervienen Alberto Castilla, César Oliva, Manuel Canseco and Roberto Alonso'. In Irene Pardo Molina and Antonio Serrano (eds), *En torno al teatro del Siglo de Oro: XV Jornadas del Siglo de Oro*. Almería: Instituto de Estudios Almerienses, pp. 245–69.
Castro, Antonio (1974). 'Mario Camus'. In Antonio Castro, *El cine español en el banquillo*. Valencia: Fernando Torres Editor, pp. 111–19.
Castro de Paz, José Luis (2002). *Un cinema herido: los turbios años cuarenta en el cine español (1939–1950)*. Barcelona: Ediciones Paídos.
— (2005). *Suevia Films Cesáreo González: treinta años de cine español*. La Coruña: Xunta de Galicia.
CAT (2004). *CAT: 15 años del Centro Andaluz de Teatro (1988–2003)*. Seville: Junta de Andalucía and Consejería de Cultura, unpaginated.
CDN (1985). 'Theatrical Programme for *No hay burlas con Calderón*'. Madrid: Ministerio de Cultura.
CDT (1995). *Cuadernos de bibliografía de las artes escénicas: catálogo de libretos de los Teatros Nacionales*. Madrid: CDT.
— (2008). *Revista digital de la escena 2007* CD-ROM. Madrid: INAEM and Ministerio de Cultura.
Cebollada, Pascual and Mary G. Santa Eulalia (2000). *Madrid y el cine: panorama filmográfico de cien años de historia*. Madrid: Consejería de Educación, Comunidad de Madrid.
Centro Cultural de la Villa de Madrid (1981). 'Theatrical Programme for *Céfiro agreste de olímpicos embates*'. Madrid: Centro Cultural de la Villa.
Checa, Julio E. (2003). 'José Tamayo y la dirección de escena en España: la etapa del Teatro Español'. *ADE*, 96: 26–33.
Chislett, William (2010). *The Way Forward for the Spanish Economy: More Internationalism (Working Paper)*. Madrid: Real Instituto Elcano.
Cifo, Antonio (1990). 'Zampanó: la otra compañía de teatro clásico'. *Actores: revista de la Unión de actores*, 10: 22–4.
Cine Asesor (1954a). *Cine Asesor*, 606: unpaginated.
— (1954b). '*La moza de cántaro*'. *Cine Asesor*, 615: unpaginated.
Cinéma (1986). 'Raoul Ruiz s'empare du baroque sentimental de Calderon'. *Cinéma*, 25 June: 8–9.
Ciurans, Enric (2009). *El teatre Viu, una resistència cultural*. Barcelona: Associació d'Investigació Experimentació Teatral.
CNTC (1986). 'Theatrical Programme for *Los locos de Valencia*'. Madrid: CNTC.
— (1991). *Boletín de la CNTC*, 20.
— (1996). *10 años de la Compañía de Teatro Clásico*. Madrid: CNTC.
— (2001). *Calderón en la Compañía Nacional de Teatro Clásico, Año 2000*, ed. José María Díez Borque. Madrid: CNTC.
— (2002). *La Compañía Nacional de Teatro Clásico (1986–2002)*, ed. Mar Zubieta. Madrid: CNTC.
— (2003). *Lope de Vega en la CNTC*, ed. Felipe B. Pedraza Jiménez. Madrid: CNTC
— (2006a). *Boletín de la CNTC*, 45.
— (2006b). *20 años en escena (1986–2006)*. Madrid: CNTC.
— (2008). *Cuaderno pedagógico: El pintor de su deshonra*. Madrid: CNTC.
Coca Hernando, Rosario (1998). 'Towards a new image of women under Franco: the role of Sección Femenina'. *International Journal of Iberian Studies*, 11.1: 5–13.
Coira, Pepe (2004). *Antonio Román: un cineasta de la posguerra*. Madrid: Editorial Complutense.

Collado, Fernando (1989). *El teatro bajo las bombas en la Guerra Civil*. Madrid: Kayeda Ediciones.
Comas, Ángel (2004). *El star system del cine español de posguerra (1939–1965)*. Madrid: T and B Editores.
Comisión de Teatro del PSOE (1983). '"Informe" de la Comisión de teatro del PSOE'. *Pipirijaina*, 24: 9–21.
Compañía Lope de Vega (director: José Tamayo) (1966). *Veinte años al servicio del teatro en España (1946–1966)*. Madrid: Compañía Lope de Vega.
Compañía Rakatá (2009). 'Theatrical programme for *Fuente Ovejuna*'. Madrid: Compañía Rakatá.
Company Ramón, Juan Miguel (1999). 'Formas y perversiones del compromiso. El cine español de los años 40'. In José Luis Castro de Paz, Pilar Couto Cantero and José María Paz (eds), *Cien años de cine: historia, teoría y análisis del texto fílmico*. Madrid: Visor Libros, pp. 175–85.
Conley, Tom (1998). 'Foreward: A land bred on movies'. In Jenaro Talens and Santos Zunzunegui (eds), *Modes of Representation in Spanish Cinema*. Mineapolis: University of Minnesota Press, pp. xi–xxvi.
Connor (Swietlicki), Catherine (2000). 'Hacia una teoría sociocultural del espectador aurisecular'. In Bárbara Mujica and Anita K. Stoll (eds), *El texto puesto en escena: estudios sobre la comedia del Siglo de Oro en honor a Everett W. Hesse*. London: Tamesis, pp. 3–13.
Cook, Pam (1993). 'Border crossings: women and film in context'. In Pam Cook and Philip Dodd (eds), *Women and Film: A Sight and Sound Reader*. London: Scarlet Press, pp. ix–xxiii.
Cornago Bernal, Óscar (1997). 'Historia del teatro en España: la escena madrileña 1969–1970'. *ALEC*, 22.3: 405–48.
— (2001). 'Relaciones estructurales entre el cine y el teatro: de la categoría del montaje al acto performativo'. *ALEC*, 26.1: 63–89.
El correo (2004). 'La Compañía de Teatro Clásico retoma a Marsillach'. *El correo*, 13 November: 60.
Costa, Jordi (1996). 'Els perills de taxidèrmia', review of *El perro del hortelano*. *Avui*, 12 December: 48
Cotarelo y Mori, Emilio (1997). *Bibliografía de las controversias sobre la licitud del teatro en España*, ed. José Luis Suárez García. Granada: Universidad de Granada.
Cowie, Elizabeth (1997). *Representing the Woman: Cinema and Psychoanalysis*. Basingstoke: Macmillan.
Crameri, Kathryn (2008). *Catalonia: National Identity and Cultural Policy (1980–2003)*. Cardiff: University of Wales Press.
Cruickshank, Don (2003). *Critical Guides to Spanish Texts (Calderón: El médico de su honra)*. London: Grant and Cutler.
Cruz, Jacqueline (2004). 'Mujer y política: la paridad inexistente'. In Jacqueline Cruz and Barbara Zecchi (eds), *La mujer en la España actual: ¿evolución o involución?* Barcelona: Icaria, pp. 73–97.
Cuesta Martínez, Paloma (1988). 'El teatro en España (1960–1969): comunicación dramática y público'. Unpublished dissertation, Universidad Complutense.
Cueva, Jorge de la (1944). '*Fuenteovejuna*', review. *Ya*, 13 October: 9.
Cuevas, David (1990). 'Compañía Nacional de Teatro Clásico: encontrar la modernidad de los clásicos'. *El público*, 78: 73–5.
Darst, David H. (1995). 'Las analogías funcionales en *Fuenteovejuna*'. *Neophilologus*, 79.2: 245–52.

Daumas, Adrián (2005). 'Otro vendrá que bueno te hará o ¿un nuevo nepotismo en la Compañía Nacional de Teatro Clásico?'. *Assaig de Teatre*, 48–9: 245–7.
DeA Planeta (2006). *DeA Planeta presenta La dama boba de Manuel Iborra* (Press book). Madrid: DeA Planeta, unpaginated.
Deia (1983). 'La musicalidad de Lope', review of *El caballero de milagro*. *Deia*, 17 November: 36.
— (1987). 'La Compañía de Teatro Clásico actúa en un festival calderoniano'. *Deia*, 4 July: 47.
Delgado, María M (2003). *'Other' Spanish Theatres: Erasure and Inscription on the Twentieth-Century Spanish Stage*. Manchester: Manchester University Press.
— (2004). '"A lot of work and a flicker of intuition": Calixto Bieito stages *Hamlet*'. *Western European Stages*, 16.1: 71–8.
— (2006). 'Journeys of cultural transference: Calixto Bieito's multilingual Shakespeares'. *Modern Language Review*, 101.1: 106–50.
— (2008). *Federico García Lorca*. London: Routledge.
— (2012). 'Directors and the Spanish stage, 1823–2010'. In David T. Gies and María M. Delgado (eds), *A History of the Theatre in Spain*. Cambridge: Cambridge University Press, in press.
Dennis, Nigel and Emilio Peral Vega (2009). 'Introducción'. In Nigel Dennis and Emilio Peral Vega (eds), *Teatro de la Guerra Civil: al bando republicano*. Madrid: Fundamentos, pp. 7–108.
Díaz Cañabate, Antonio (1952). 'Los estrenos vistos desde el gallinero. Español: *La moza de cántaro*', review. *Semana*, 14 October: 33.
Díaz del Moral, Juan (1973). *Historia de las agitaciones campesinas andaluzas: antecedentes para una reforma agraria*. Madrid: Alianza Universidad.
Díaz Díaz, Isabel María (2000). 'Continuismo convencional en la escena española'. *Acotaciones: revista de investigación teatral*, 5: 57–72.
Díaz Sande, José Ramón (1985). '*No hay burlas con Calderón*: una brillante idea fallida', review. *Reseña*, May–June: 6–7.
Díez Borque, José María (1976). *Sociología de la comedia española del siglo XVII*. Madrid: Cátedra.
— (1978). 'Introducción'. In Pedro Calderón de la Barca, *Dos tragedias*. Madrid: Editora Nacional, pp. 9–58.
— (1986). 'Relaciones de teatro y fiesta en el barroco español'. In José María Díez Borque (ed.), *Teatro y fiesta en el barroco: España e Iberoamérica*. Barcelona: Ediciones del Serbal, pp. 11–40.
— (2004). 'Teatro clásico en la escena española del siglo XX: Madrid 1985–1999'. In José María Díez Borque and José Alcalá Zamora (eds), *Proyección y significados del teatro clásico español: homenaje a Alfredo Hermenegildo y Francisco Ruiz Ramón*. Madrid: Sociedad Estatal para la Acción Cultural Exterior, pp. 205–21.
Díez Crespo, M. (1973). 'Versión "rock" de *Marta la piadosa*', review. *El alcázar*, 6 December: 28.
Díez Ménguez, Isabel (2002). 'Adaptación cinematográfica de *El perro del hortelano*, por Pilar Miró'. In José Romera Castillo (ed.), *Del teatro al cine y la televisión en la segunda mitad del siglo XX*. Madrid: Visor Libros, pp. 301–8.
Diez Puertas, Emeterio (2002). *El montaje del franquismo: la política cinematográfica de las fuerzas sublevadas*. Barcelona: Laertes.
Diplomatic Information Office (1949). *The Spanish Cinema*. Madrid: Diplomatic Information Office.

DiPuccio, Denise M. (1989). 'Deconstructing the *comedia*'. In Everett W. Hesse (ed.) with the assistance of Catherine Larson, *Approaches to Teaching Spanish Golden-Age Drama*. York: Spanish Literature Publications Company, pp. 112–29.
Dirección General de Promoción e Instituciones Culturales (2007). *Teatro Corsario: Veinticinco años*. Castilla y León: Junta de Castilla y León.
Dixon, Victor (1988). '"Su majestad habla, en fin, como quien tanto ha acertado": la conclusión ejemplar de *Fuente Ovejuna*'. *Criticón*, 42: 155–68.
— (1989). 'Introduction'. In Lope de Vega, *Fuente Ovejuna*, ed. and trans. Victor Dixon. Warminster: Aris and Phillips, pp. 1–52.
— (1995). 'Dos maneras de montar hoy *El perro del hortelano* de Lope de Vega'. *Cuadernos de teatro clásico*, 8: 121–40.
D'Lugo, Marvin (1991). *The Films of Carlos Saura: The Practice of Seeing*. Princeton: Princeton University Press.
Doane, Mary Ann (1992). 'Film and the masquerade: theorizing the female spectator'. In John Caughie and Annette Kuhn (eds), *Screen: The Sexual Subject (A Screen Reader in Sexuality)*. London: Routledge, pp. 227–43.
Documentos cinematográficos (1961). 'Carnet del empresario: los estrenos en Madrid y Barcelona del 15 de diciembre al 5 de enero'. *Documentos cinematográficos*, 9: 201–9.
Dollimore, Jonathan (2004). *Radical Tragedy: Religion, Ideology and Power in the Drama of Shakespeare and His Contemporaries*, 3rd ed. Basingstoke: Palgrave Macmillan.
Domènech, Fernando (2000). 'Entrevista con Andrés Amorós, director de la CNTC'. *ADE*, 80: 76–81.
Domènech, Ricardo (1963). 'Homenaje del T. E.U. a Lope de Vega'. *PA*, 39: 54–5.
— (2000). 'Lectura de los clásicos'. *Acotaciones: revista de investigación teatral*, 4: 9–18.
Drove Shaw, Antonio (1972). *La leyenda del alcalde de Zalamea*. Madrid: Suevia Films.
— (1995). *Tiempo de vivir, tiempo de revivir: conversaciones con Douglas Sirk*. Murcia: Filmoteca de Murcia.
Ducay, E. (1952). 'Cine histórico y *Alba de América*'. *Ínsula*, 74: 11.
— (1954). '*El alcalde de Zalamea*', review. *Objetivo: revista de cine*, 3: 39–40.
Durán, Manuel and Roberto González Echevarría (1976). 'Calderón y la crítica'. In Manuel Durán and Roberto González Echevarría (eds), *Calderón y la crítica: historia y antología*, vol. 1. Madrid: Editorial Gredos, pp. 13–123.
Dyer, Richard (2004). *Heavenly Bodies: Film Stars and Society*, 2nd ed. London: Routledge.
Edwards, Gwynne (2007). 'Theatre Workshop and the Spanish drama'. *New Theatre Quarterly*, 23.4: 304–16.
EFE (2000). 'Filme de Pilar Miró *El perro del hortelano* se estrena en Paris'. Spanish Newswire Services, 10 April.
— (2002). 'Teatro clásico: piden paralización actividad en CNTC por mal estado del edificio'. Spanish Newswire Services, 14 February.
— (2008a). 'Teresa Viejo, primera Dulcinea de las Jornadas Cervantinas El Toboso'. *ABC*, Toledo ed., 24 April.
— (2008b). 'Casi 80.000 espectadores han asistido a XXI Festival Teatro Clásico'. Spanish Newswire Services, 18 July.
— (2008c). 'Compañía Siglo de Oro conquista Volksbühne berliné con Calderón a la Matrix'. Spanish Newswire Services, 2 October.
— (2009a). 'La CNTC invita a Teatres de la Generalitat para la temporada 2009–2010'. Spanish Newswire Services, 30 June.
— (2009b). 'El director dice que éste "ha colocado a Almagro en el mapa"'. Spanish Newswire Services, 24 July.

Eines, José (1984). 'Conversación con José Estruch'. *PA*, 206: 97–114.
Elam, Keir (1980). *The Semiotics of Theatre and Drama*. London: Methuen.
Elena, Alberto (2009). '¿Quién prohibió *Rojo y negro*?'. In Laura Gómez Vaquero and Daniel Sánchez Salas (eds), *El espíritu del caos: representación y recepción de las imágenes durante el franquismo*. Madrid: Ocho y medio, pp. 143–74.
Elliott, J. H. (1989). *Spain and Its World (1500–1700)*. New Haven: Yale University Press.
Emiliozzi, Irma (2003). 'Presencia de María Teresa León en el cine argentino'. In Maya Altolaguirre (ed.), *Recuerdo de un olvido: María Teresa León en su centenario*. Madrid: Sociedad Estatal de Conmemoraciones Culturales, pp. 79–90.
Escalonilla López, Rosa Ana (2002). 'La vigencia dramática de la *comedia nueva* en la película *El perro del hortelano*, de Pilar Miró'. In José Romera Castillo (ed.), *Del teatro al cine y la televisión en la segunda mitad del siglo XX*. Madrid: Visor Libros, pp. 309–19.
Escobar, Luis (2000). *En cuerpo y alma: memorias de Luis Escobar (1908–1991)*. Madrid: Temas de hoy.
Escolme, Bridget (2005). *Talking to the Audience: Shakespeare, Performance, Self*. London: Routledge.
Escudero Baztán, Juan M. (1998). 'Introduction'. In Pedro Calderón de la Barca and Lope de Vega Carpio, *El alcalde de Zalamea: edición crítica de las dos versiones*, ed. Juan M. Escudero Baztán. Frankfurt and Madrid: Vervuert and Iberoamericana, pp. 15–228.
Espectáculo (1954). *Espectáculo*, 81: unpaginated.
Espinosa, Manolita (1997). *Corral de Comedías en el Siglo XX: aproximación a la historia*. Ciudad Real: Area de Cultura Excmo Ayuntamiento de Almagro.
Esslin, Martin (1987). *The Field of Drama: How the Signs of Drama Create Meaning on Stage and Screen*. London: Methuen.
Estivill, Josep (2009). 'El espíritu del caos. Irregularidades en la censura cinematográfica durante la inmediata postguerra'. In Laura Gómez Vaquero and Daniel Sánchez Salas (eds), *El espíritu del caos: representación y recepción de las imágenes durante el franquismo*. Madrid: Ocho y medio, pp. 63–84.
Evans, Peter William (1990a). 'In preface'. In Peter William Evans (ed.), *Conflicts of Discourse: Spanish Literature in the Golden Age*. Manchester: Manchester University Press, pp. vi–viii.
— (1990b). 'Civilisation and its discontents in *Fuenteovejuna*'. In Peter William Evans (ed.), *Conflicts of Discourse: Spanish Literature in the Golden Age*. Manchester: Manchester University Press, pp. 110–29.
— (1997). *From Golden Age to Silver Screen: The Comedia on Film*. London: Department of Hispanic Studies, Queen Mary and Westfield College.
Facio, Ángel (ed.) (2008). *Alberto González Vergel*. Madrid: Teatro Español.
Fainlight, Ruth and Allan Sillitoe (1969). *All Citizens are Soldiers*. London: Macmillan.
Falcón Osorio, Pilar (1998). *El imperio rosa: poder e influencia de la prensa de corazón*. Barcelona: Editorial CIMS.
Fanés, Félix (1982). *CIFESA, la antorcha de los éxitos*. Valencia: Institución Alfonso el Magnánimo.
Farrán Graves, Natalia (1989). 'Adrian Mitchell y su versión de *Fuenteovejuna*'. *Cuadernos de teatro clásico*, 4: 175–80.
Fassbinder, Rainer Werner (1976). *Stücke 3: Die biteren Tränen, Der Petra von Kant, Das brenne onde Dorf, Der Müll, die Stadt und der Tod*. Frankfurt: Edicion Suhrkamp.
Faulkner, Sally (2006). *A Cinema of Contradiction: Spanish Film in the 1960s*. Edinburgh: Edinburgh University Press.

Febo, Giuliana di (2003). '"Nuevo Estado", nacional-catolicismo y género'. In Gloria Nielfa Cristóbal (ed.), *Mujeres y hombres en la España franquista: sociedad, economía, política, cultura*. Madrid: Editorial Complutense, pp. 19–44.
Feito, Francisco E. (1981). '*Fuenteovejuna* o el álgebra del amor'. In Manuel Criado de Val (ed.), *Lope de Vega y los orígenes del teatro español*. Madrid: EDI, pp. 391–8.
Fernán-Gómez, Fernando (1999). *El tiempo amarillo: memorias ampliadas (1921–1997)*, 2nd ed. Madrid: Editorial Debate.
Fernández, Esther (2006). 'El coto erótico de Diana: *El perro del hortelano*, de un texto sexual a un sexo visual'. *Gestos*, 42: 57–80.
—, and Cristina Martínez-Carazo (2006). 'Mirar y desear: la construcción del personaje femenino en *El perro del hortelano* de Lope de Vega y de Pilar Miró'. *Bulletin of Spanish Studies*, 83.3: 315–28.
Fernández, Luís Miguel (2000). *Don Juan en el cine español: hacia una teoría de la recreación fílmica*. Santiago de Compostela: Universidad de Santiago de Compostela.
Fernández, Rafa (1991). 'Todos lo son y, además, un poco brujas', review of *El rey pasmado*. *El sol*, 5 November.
Fernández Blanco, Victor (2005). 'Un público para todos los cines'. *Academia: revista del cine español*, 35: 8–13.
—, Juan Prieto Rodríguez, Cristina Muñiz Artime and Rubén Gutiérrez del Castillo (2002). *Cinéfilos, videoadictos y telespectadores: los perfiles de los consumidores de productos audiovisuales en España*. Madrid: Fundación Autor.
Fernández Colorado, Luis (1997). *Antología crítica del cine español: 1906–1995*. Madrid: Cátedra, Filmoteca Española.
Fernández-Cuenca, Carlos (1972). *La guerra de España y el cine*, vol. 1. Madrid: Editora Nacional.
Fernández Montesinos, Ángel (2008). *El teatro que he vivido: memorias dialogadas de un director de escena*, ed. Ángel Martínez Roger. Madrid: Publicaciones de ADE.
Fernández Santos, Ángel (1982). 'Ayuno Calderoniano'. *Pipirijaina*, 21: 5–7.
Fernández Torres, Alberto (1983). 'La temporada 81–82, en cifras. Cambio de tercio'. *Pipirijaina*, 24: 76–83.
— (1987). '*El médico de su honra*, de Pedro Calderón de la Barca: el primer paso'. *Ínsula*, 482: 15.
Ferrer, Juan (2006). '*Alatriste*', review. *Segre*, 7 September: 66.
Ferrers, Rafael (1953). 'Festivales de Shakespeare en Stratford'. *Teatro*, 8: 17–21.
Ferrol, M. M. (1988). '*El príncipe constante*: una tragedia ejemplar', interview with Alberto González Vergel. *PA*, 224: 99–101.
Festival International de Teatro (1989). 'La formación del actor en España'. In Festival programme. Madrid: Ayuntamiento de Madrid; Comunidad de Madrid; and Ministerio de Cultura, pp. 15–16.
Fiddian, Robin (1999). '*La vida alegre* (Colomo, 1986)'. In Peter William Evans (ed.), *Spanish Cinema: the Auteurist Tradition*. Oxford: Oxford University Press, pp. 242–53.
Fiore, Robert (1966). 'Natural law in the central ideological theme of *Fuenteovejuna*'. *Hispania*, 49.1: 75–80.
Fischer, Susan L. (1986). 'Text and context: a twentieth-century view of Calderón's *La hija del aire*'. In Robert Fiore, Everett W. Hesse, John E. Keller and José A. Madrigal (eds), *Studies in Honor of William C. McCrary*. Lincoln: Society of Spanish and Spanish American Studies, pp. 137–49.
— (2000). 'Así que pasen quince años: trayectorias escénicas de la Compañía Nacional de Teatro Clásico'. *ALEC*, 25.3: 765–820.

— (2002). 'Vigencia escénica de Calderón: la *Compañía Nacional de Teatro Clásico (1986–2000)*'. In José María Ruano de la Haza and Jesús Pérez Magallón (eds), *Ayer y hoy de Calderón: Actas seleccionadas del Congreso Internacional celebrado en Ottawa del 4 al 8 de octubre del 2000*. Madrid: Editorial Castalia, pp. 303–24.
— (2003). 'La apropiación de Calderón en escena: *El médico de su honra* y *El alcalde de Zalamea*'. In Manfred Tietz (ed.), *Teatro calderoniano sobre el tablado: Calderón y su puesta en escena a través de los siglos*. Stuttgart: Franz Steiner Verlag, pp. 129–44.
— (2005). 'The Royal Shakespeare Company and the Hispanic Golden Age season'. *B. Com.*, 57.1: 195–203.
— (2009). *Reading Performance: Spanish Golden Age Theatre and Shakespeare on the Modern Stage*. Woodbridge: Tamesis.
Folguera Crespo, Pilar (1997). 'El franquismo: el retorno a la esfera privada (1939–1975)'. In Elisa Garrido, Pilar Folguera Crespo, Margarita Ortega López and Cristina Segura Graíño (eds), *Historia de las mujeres en España*. Madrid: Síntesis, pp. 527–48.
Ford Davies, Oliver (2007). *Performing Shakespeare: Preparation, Rehearsal, Performance*. London: Nick Hern Books.
Fotogramas (2006). 'Fahrenheit 451'. *Fotogramas*, April: 45.
Fouz-Hernández, Santiago and Alfredo Martínez-Expósito (2007). *Live Flesh: The Male Body in Contemporary Spanish Cinema*. London: I. B. Tauris and Co.
Fraga Iribarne, Manuel (1980). *Memoria breve de una vida pública*. Barcelona: Editorial Planeta.
Francia, Juan (1993). *Marisa Paredes*. Barcelona: Icaria.
Francisco, Itziar de (2002). 'Calixto Bieito: "Soy polémico, pero no hago terrorismo escénico"'. *El Cultural de El Mundo*, 13 July: 50.
Frugone, Juan Carlos (1984). *Oficio de gente humilde . . . Mario Camus*. Valladolid: Semana de cine de Valladolid.
Frye, Ellen C. (2003). 'Secret portraits of Serafina: portraiture in the Golden-Age *comedia* of Spain'. *Romance Studies*, 21.1: 3–10.
Frye, Northrop (1992). 'The argument of comedy'. In D. J. Palmer (ed.), *Comedy: Developments in Criticism*. Basingstoke: Palgrave, pp. 74–84.
Gagen, Derek H. (1993). *Coming to Terms with the Civil War. Modern Productions of Lope de Vega's Fuenteovejuna (University College of Swansea Inaugural Lecture)*. Swansea: University College of Swansea.
— (2008). 'Collective suicide: Rafael Alberti's updating of Cervantes's *La destrucción de Numancia*'. *Modern Language Review*, 103.1: 93–112.
Galán, Diego (2006). *Pilar Miró: nadie me enseñó a vivir*. Barcelona: Plaza y Janés.
Galán Blanco, Eduardo (1990). '*La casa de lluvia* de Antonio Román'. In Joaquim Romaguera i Ramió and Peío Aldazabal Bardají (eds), *Hora actual del cine de las autonomías del estado español*. Barcelona: Asociación Española de Historiadores del Cine, pp. 249–57.
Gallén, Enric (1985). *El teatre a la ciutat de Barcelona durant el règim franquista (1939–1954)*. Barcelona: Institut del Teatre.
Ganelin, Charles (1991). 'The art of adaptation: building the hermeneutical bridge'. In Louise and Peter Fothergill-Payne (eds), *Prologue to Performance: Spanish Classical Theater Today*. Lewisburg: Bucknell University Press, pp. 36–48.
Gantes, Pablo (2006). *Luis Lucia: director para todos los públicos*. Valencia: Fundació Municipal de Cine, Mostra de València.
García-Alegre Sánchez, Genoveva (1981). 'Representaciones de piezas teatrales del Siglo de Oro español en Madrid durante los tres primeros años de postguerra:

marzo de 1939 – diciembre de 1941'. Unpublished article, available for consultation at the Fundación Juan March.
García Barquero, Juan Antonio (1973). *Aproximaciones al teatro clásico español*. Seville: Publicaciones de la Universidad de Sevilla.
García Berrio, Antonio (2000). '¿Actualidad de Calderón? Densidad barroca y abstracción moderna de los dramas'. In José María Díez Borque and Andrés Peláez Martín (eds), *Calderón en escena: siglo XX*. Madrid: Comunidad de Madrid and Consejería de Cultura, pp. 13–27.
García de Dueñas, Jesús (2003). *José G. Maesso el número 1*. Badajoz: Diputación de Badajoz.
García Escudero, José María (1954). *La historia en cien palabras del cine español y otros escritos sobre cine*. Salamanca: Publicaciones del cine-club del S. E. Universidad de Salamanca.
— (1995). 'Las políticas del cine español'. In José María García Escudero, *El cine español desde Salamanca (1955–1995)*. Salamanca: Junta de Castilla y León and Consejería de Educación y Cultura, pp. 13–23.
García Ferrer, J. M. and Martí Rom (1998). *Ricard Salvat*. Barcelona: Enginyers Industrials de Catalunya.
García Garzón, Juan Ignacio (2008). 'Veinte años después'. *ABC*, 17 April: 88.
García de León, María Antonia (2002). *Herederas y heridas: sobre las élites profesionales femeninas*. Madrid: Cátedra.
García Lorca, Federico (1974). 'Lope de Vega en un teatro nacional'. In *Obras completas*, vol. II, ed. Arturo de Hoyo. Madrid: Aguilar, pp. 953–5.
García Lorenzo, Luciano (1981). *Documentos sobre el teatro español contemporáneo*. Madrid: Sociedad General Española de Librería.
— (1987). 'El teatro clásico en escena: 1976–1987'. *Ínsula*, 492: 21–2.
— (1997). 'Puesta en escena y recepción del teatro clásico español: *Fuente Ovejuna* de Lope de Vega'. In Robert A. Lauer and Henry W. Sullivan (eds), *Hispanic Essays in Honor of Frank P. Casa*. New York: Peter Lang, pp. 112–21.
— (ed.) (1999). *Aproximación al teatro español universitario (TEU)*. Madrid: Consejo Superior de Investigaciones Científicas and Instituto de la Lengua Española.
— (2000). 'Puesta en escena y recepción de *Fuente Ovejuna* (1940–1999)'. In M. G. Profeti (ed.), *Otro Lope no ha de haber: atti del Convegno Internazionale su Lope de Vega 10–13 febbraio*, vol. 2. Florence: Alinea, pp. 85–105.
— (2002a). 'Los autos sacramentales en la España última'. In Enrique García Santo-Tomás (ed.), *El teatro del Siglo de Oro ante los espacios de la crítica: encuentros y revisiones*. Frankfurt and Madrid: Iberoamericana and Vervuert, pp. 405–26.
— (2002b). 'Festival de Almagro: todo un clásico'. *ADE*, 93: 205–9.
— (2005). 'Texto y representación dramática: estado actual de los estudios sobre teatro del Siglo de Oro español'. In Carlos Mata and Mihuel Zugasti (eds), *Actas del Congreso 'El Siglo de Oro en el nuevo milenio'*, vol. 1. Barañáin: Ediciones Universidad de Navarra, pp. 37–52.
— (2007a). 'La presencia de los autores clásicos en la escena española y extranjera (2000–2005)'. In José Romero Castillo (ed.), *Análisis de espectáculos teatrales (2000–2006)*. Madrid: Visor Libros, pp. 91–105.
— (2007b). *Las puestas en escena de El caballero de Olmedo*. Olmedo: Ayuntamiento de Olmedo.
— and Mañuel Muñoz Carabantes (2000). 'El teatro de Calderón en la escena española (1939–1999)'. *BHS (Glasgow)* 77.1: 421–33.

— and Andrés Peláez Martín (eds) (1997). *Festival Internacional de Teatro Clásico de Almagro, 20 años 1978–1997*. Toledo: Caja Castilla la Mancha and Festival de Almagro.

García-Martín, Elena (2004). 'Negotiating the Golden Age tradition since the Spanish Second Republic'. Unpublished dissertation, University of Texas.

García May, Ignacio and Carlos Rodríguez (eds) (1990). *1978–1989 Talleres de la Real Escuela Superior de Arte Dramático de Madrid*. Madrid: Departamento de Publicaciones de la RESAD.

García-Posada, Miguel (1997). 'No es sombra lo que vi'. *El País*, 30 October: 36.

García de la Rasilla, Carmen (2006). 'Teaching Golden-Age theater through filmic adaptations'. In Margaret R. Greer and Laura R. Bass (eds), *Approaches to Teaching Early-Modern Spanish Drama*. New York: MLA, pp. 69–75.

García Ruiz, Víctor (1997a). '"La guerra ha terminado," empieza el teatro. Notas sobre el teatro madrileño y su contexto en la inmediata posguerra'. *ALEC*, 22.3: 511–33.

— (1997b). 'Un poco de ruido y no demasiadas nueces: los autos sacramentales en la España de Franco (1939–1975)'. In Ignacio Arellano *et al.* (eds), *Divinas y humanas letras. Doctrina y poesía en los autos sacramentales de Calderón: Actas del Congreso Internacional*. Pamplona: Universidad de Navarra, pp. 119–65.

— (2010). *Teatro y fascismo en España: el itinerario de Felipe Lluch*. Frankfurt and Madrid: Iberoamericana and Vervuert.

García Santo-Tomás, Enrique (2000a). *La creación del Fénix: recepción crítica y formación canónica del teatro de Lope de Vega*. Madrid: Gredos.

— (2000b). 'Diana, Lope, Pilar Miró: horizontes y resistencias de clausura en *El perro del hortelano*'. In M. G. Profeti (ed.), *Otro Lope no ha de haber. atti del Convegno Internazionale su Lope de Vega 10–13 febbraio 1999*, vol. 2. Florence: Alinea, pp. 51–61.

— (2001). '"Más allá del Fénix": de la estética receptiva a una poética cultura'. *Ínsula*, 658: 26–8.

Gaylord, Mary M. (1992). '"Las damas no desdigan de su nombre": decoro femenino y lenguaje en el *Arte nuevo* y *La dama boba*'. In Elena Gascón Vera and Joy Renjilian-Burgy (eds), *Justina: Homenaje a Justina Ruíz de Conde en su ochenta cumpleaños*. Erie: ALDEUU, pp. 71–81.

Generalitat Valenciana and Filmoteca Valenciana (1986). *Retrospectiva Luís Lucia*. Valencia: Generalitat Valenciana and Filmoteca Valenciana, unpaginated.

George, David (2002). *Theatre in Madrid and Barcelona, 1892–1936: Rivals or Collaborators*. Cardiff: University of Wales Press.

— (2004). 'Enric Borrás and Margarita Xirgu: two Catalans on the Spanish stage'. *Hispanic Research Journal*, 5.1: 43–56.

— (2006). 'Sergi Belbel's production of *El alcalde de Zalamea*'. In Sandra N. Harper and Polly J. Hodge (eds), *El próximo acto: teatro español en el siglo XX*. Delaware: Estreno, pp. 145–53.

Gil, Alberto (2009). *La censura cinematográfica en España*. Barcelona: Ediciones B.

Gil, Cristina (1993). 'Se puede jugar con los clásicos'. *Ya*, 17 November: 44.

— (1996). 'Hacer una película en verso es el mayor reto de mi carrera'. *Ya*, 26 November: 42.

Gilmore, David D. (1987). 'Introduction: the shame of dishonor'. In David D. Gilmore (ed.), *Honor and Shame and the Unity of the Mediterranean*. Washington: American Anthropological Association, pp. 2–21.

Giménez Caballero, Ernesto (1944). '¡Fuenteovejuna, todos a una'. *Cuadernos de teatro*, 1: 4–7.

Gledhill, Christine (1991). *Stardom: Industry of Desire*. London, Routledge.
Gómez, María Asunción (2000). *Del escenario a la pantalla: la adaptación cinematográfica del teatro español*. Chapel Hill: University of North Carolina Press.
Gómez Sierra, Esther (2003). '*La dama boba*, la autoridad y Stefano Arata, autore'. *Criticón*, 87–9: 359–78.
Gómez Tello (1947). '*Fuenteovejuna*', review. *Primer Plano*, 23 November: unpaginated.
— (1950). 'Cine español mereció ser premiado'. *Primer Plano*, 17 September: unpaginated.
Gómez Torres, David (1996). '*La dama boba* de Lope de Vega: un caso de subversión aparente o el proceso de formación de un discurso monólogo'. *B.Com*, 48.2: 315–28.
González, Bernardo Antonio (1993). 'Teatro nacional e ideología en España: el caso del María Guerrero'. *Gestos*, 15: 65–82.
González, Luis M. (2005). 'De Isabel y Fernando el espíritu impera: fascismo y cine histórico en España (1939–1951)'. Unpublished dissertation, University of Georgetown.
González Ballesteros, Teodoro (1981). *Aspectos jurídicos de la censura cinematográfica en España con especial referencia al período 1936–1977*. Madrid: Editorial Complutense.
González Fernández de Sevilla, José Manuel (ed.) (1993). *Shakespeare en España: crítica, traducciones y representaciones*. Alicante: Universidad de Alicante and Libros Pórtico.
Gónzalez Palencia, A. (1943). 'El arte de Calderón'. *Revista nacional de educación*, 35: 18–33.
González Ruiz, Nicolás (1943). 'Cómo representar los clásicos'. *Barcelona teatral: seminario de espectáculos*, 11 November: 3.
— (1949). *La cultura española en los últimos veinte años: el teatro*. Madrid: Instituto de Cultura Hispánica.
González Vergel, Alberto (2003). 'La puesta en escena de los autores clásicos'. In Olivia Navarro and Antonio Serrano (eds), *En torno al teatro del Siglo de Oro: XVI–XVII Jornadas de Teatro del Siglo de Oro*. Almería: Instituto de Estudios Almerienses and Diputación de Almería, pp. 153–62.
Graells, Guillem-Jordi (1990). *L'Institut del Teatre, 1913–1988: història gràfica*. Barcelona: Institut del Teatre.
— (ed.) (2007). *Teatre Lliure, 1976–2006*. Barcelona: Fundació Teatre Lliure.
Granda Marín, Juan José (2000). 'Calderón, los cómicos y el verso en el siglo XX'. In José María Díez Borque and Andrés Peláez Martín (eds), *Calderón en escena, siglo XX*. Madrid: Consejería de Cultura de la Comunidad de Madrid, pp. 79–100.
Green, Stuart (2007). 'Carry on under Franco: Edgar Neville's satire on Spanish film and national stereotype in *Producciones Mínguez, S.A.*'. *Estreno*, 33.1: 38–44.
Gregor, Keith (1998). 'Spanish "Shakespeare-mania": *Twelfth Night* in Madrid, 1996–97'. *Shakespeare Quarterly*, 49.4: 421–31.
Griffin, Nigel (1994). 'Some performance constants in Calderón's *El médico de su honra*'. In Nigel Griffin, Clive Griffin, Eric Southworth and Colin Thompson (eds), *The Discerning Eye: Studies Presented to Robert Pring-Mill on his Seventieth Birthday*. Llangrannog: The Dolphin Book Co., pp. 95–116.
Griffin, Roger (1996). 'Staging the nation's rebirth: the politics and aesthetics of performance in the context of fascist studies'. In Günter Berghaus (ed.), *Fascism and Theatre: Comparative Studies on the Aesthetics and Politics of Performance in Europe (1925–1945)*. Providence: Berghahn Books, pp. 11–29.

Gubern, Román (1981). *La censura: función política y ordenamiento jurídico bajo el franquismo (1936–1975)*. Barcelona: Ediciones Peninsulares.
— (2005). 'La censura bajo el franquismo'. In Pedro Poyato (ed.), *Historia(s), motivos y formas del cine español*. Córdoba: Plurabelle, pp. 51–64.
Gutiérrez Mandado, Fernando María (2003). 'Manuel Altolaguirre: un cineasta en la generación del 27'. In *La cultura del exilio republicano español de 1939*, vol. 2. Madrid: Universidad Nacional de Educación a Distancia, pp. 149–58.
Guerenabarrena, Juanjo (1986). 'José Estruch, nunca dar gato por liebre', interview. *El público*, 31: 26–7.
Guerrero Zamora, Juan (1962). 'Esta noche *Fuenteovejuna* en Televisión Española'. *ABC*, 30 March: 57.
Guzmán, Almudena (2004). 'Lope en libertad', review of *El perro del hortelano*. *ABC*, 16 October: 54.
Hall, J. B. (1974). 'Theme and structure in Lope's *Fuente Ovejuna*'. *Forum for Modern Language Studies*, 10: 57–66.
— (1985). *Critical Guides to Spanish Texts (Lope de Vega: Fuenteovejuna)*. London: Grant and Cutler/Tamesis.
Hall, Peter (2000). *Exposed by the Mask: Form and Language in Drama*. London: Oberon Books.
Haro Tecglen, Eduardo (1986). 'Un Calderón confundido y disperso', review of *El médico de su honra*. *El País*, 25 October: 32.
— (1988). 'Pedro Crespo sobrevive'. *El País*, 16 November: 54.
— (1999). *El refugio*. Madrid: Punto de lectura.
— (2001). 'La herencia', review of *El alcalde de Zalamea*. *El País*, 8 January: 28.
— (2005). 'La modesta revolución', review of *Fuente Ovejuna*. *El País*, 20 September: 37.
Harvie, Jen (2005). *Staging the UK*. Manchester: Manchester University Press.
Heigl, Michaela (1998). 'La representación de la mujer en *La dama boba*'. *B.Com*, 50.2: 291–306.
Hernández, Emilio (1968). 'Entrevistas con los directores de dos Teatros Nacionales: José Luis Alonso and Miguel Narros'. *Yorick*, 29: 43–5.
— (2002). 'Las villanas'. In Felipe B. Pedraza Jiménez, Rafael González Cañal and Elena Marcello (eds), *La comedia villanesca y su escenificación: Actas de las XXIV Jornadas de teatro clásico Almagro (10, 11 y 12 de julio de 2001)*. Almagro: Festival de Almagro and Universidad Castilla La Mancha, pp. 17–25.
Hernández Araico, Susana (2000). 'La popularidad de *La dama boba* y su recepción americana en el siglo veinte'. *Revista canadiense de estudios hispánicos*, 25.1: 79–93.
Hernanz Ángulo, Beatriz (1999). 'Aproximación a una teoría de la puesta en escena del teatro histórico español'. In José Romera Castillo and Francisco Gutiérrez Carbayo (eds), *Teatro histórico (1975–1998)*. Madrid: Visor Libros, pp. 93–109.
Herrera Montero, Bernal (1989). '*Fuenteovejuna* de Lope de Vega y el maquiavelismo'. *Criticón*, 45: 131–51.
Herrero, Fernando (1968). '*La dama del Olivar*', review. *PA*, 94: 71–2.
Herrero, Javier (1974). 'Lope de Vega y el barroco: la degradación por el honor'. *Sistema*, 6: 49–71.
Herrero, Vene (2011). 'José Estruch en Inglaterra'. *Acotaciones: revista de investigación teatral*, 26: 33–46.
Herzberger, David K. (1995). *Narrating the Past: Fiction and Historiography in Post-War Spain*. Durham: Duke University Press.
Hewison, Robert (1995). *Culture and Consensus: England, Art and Politics Since 1940*. London: Methuen.

Heymann, Jochen (1998). '*Kitsch as kitsch can*: estética trivial como instrumento ideológico en el teatro de la posguerra. El caso de Juan Ignacio Luca de Tena'. In Albert Mechthild (ed.), *Vencer no es convencer: literatura e ideología del fascismo español*. Frankfurt and Madrid: Vervuert and Iberoamericana, pp. 131–47.

Higginbotham, Virginia (1988). *Spanish Film under Franco*. Austin: Texas University Press.

Higuera, Felipe (1992). 'La dirección de escena en Madrid (1900–1975)'. In *Cuatro siglos de teatro en Madrid*. Madrid: Consorcio Madrid Capital de Cultural, pp. 117–43.

— (1995). 'Los títeres: teatro nacional de juventudes (1969–1972)'. In Andrés Peláez Martín (ed.), *Historia de los Teatros Nacionales (1960–1985)*. Madrid: CDT, pp. 115–25.

Higueras, Modesto (1965). 'El teatro de ensayo en España'. Unpublished article available for consultation at the Fundación Juan March, Madrid

Hindle, Maurice (2007). *Studying Shakespeare on Film*. Basingstoke: Palgrave Macmillan.

Hipólito, Carlos (1999). 'El actor de hoy frente al teatro del Siglo de Oro'. In Irena Pardo Molina, Luz Ruiz Martínez and Antonio Serrano (eds), *En torno al teatro del Siglo de Oro: Actas de las Jornadas XIV celebradas en Almería, Marzo 1997*. Almería: Instituto de Estudios Almerienses and Diputación de Almería, pp. 71–8.

Hodge, Francis (1963). '*Fuente Ovejuna* on the American stage'. *The Texas Quarterly*, 6.1: 204–13.

Holguín, Sandie (2002). *Creating Spaniards: Culture and National Identity in Republican Spain*. Madison: University of Wisconsin Press.

Holland, Peter (2000). 'Foreward'. In Mark Thornton Burnett (ed.), *Shakespeare, Film, Fin de Siècle*. Houndmills: Macmillan Press, pp. xii–xxiv.

Holloway Jr, James E. (1972). 'Lope's neoplatonism: *La dama boba*'. *BHS*, 49: 236–55.

Holub, Robert C. (1985). *Reception Theory: A Critical Introduction*. London: Routledge.

Honig, Edwin (1972). *Calderón and the Seizures of Honor*. Cambridge: Harvard University Press.

Hooper, John (1995). *The New Spaniards*, 2nd ed. London: Penguin.

Hormigón, Juan Antonio (1986). *La vengadora de las mujeres*, adaptation of play by Lope de Vega. Madrid: Publicaciones de la Compañía de Acción Teatral.

— (ed.) (1991). *Teatro de cada día: escritos sobre el teatro de José Luis Alonso*. Madrid: Publicaciones de la ADE.

— (2002a). 'La dirección de escena en España'. In Juan Antonio Hormigón, *Trabajo dramatúrgico y puesta en escena*, vol. 1, 2nd ed. Madrid: Publicaciones de la ADE, pp. 36–82.

— (2002b). *Trabajo dramatúrgico y puesta en escena*, vol. 2, 2nd ed. Madrid: Publicaciones de la ADE.

— (2002c). 'Los clásicos y el cine'. In José Romera Castillo (ed.), *Del teatro al cine y la televisión en la segunda mitad del siglo XX*. Madrid: Visor Libros, pp. 63–9.

— (ed.) (2003). *Un teatro necesario: escritos sobre el teatro de Adolfo Marsillach*. Madrid: Publicaciones de la ADE.

Hortmann, Wilhem (2002). 'Shakespeare on the political stage in the twentieth century'. In Stanley Wells and Sarah Stanton (eds), *The Cambridge Companion to Shakespeare on Stage*. Cambridge: Cambridge University Press, pp. 212–29.

Huerta, Teresa (1987). 'Tiempo de iniciativa en la *Fuenteovejuna* de García Lorca'. *Hispania* 80.3: 480–7.

Huerta Calvo, Javier (2002). 'El Calderón de Pasolini'. In Javier Huerta Calvo, Emilio Peral Vega and Héctor Urzáiz Tortajada (eds), *Calderón en Europa: Actas del seminario internacional celebrado en la Facultad de Filología en la Universidad Complutense de Madrid (23–26 octubre 2000)*. Frankfurt and Madrid: Vervuert and Iberoamericana, pp. 263–9.
— (2006). 'Análisis'. In Javier Huerta Calvo (ed.), *Clásicos entre siglos*. Madrid: CNTC, pp. 25–128.
— (ed.) (2008). *Clásicos sin fronteras*, 2 vols Madrid: CNTC.
— (2009). 'De Calderón a Pasolini (pasando por Lorca)'. *PA*, 328: 30–42.
— (2011). '"Todos a una": de la *Fuente Ovejuna* teatral de Garcia Lorca a la *Fuente Ovejuna* cinematográfica de Antonio Román'. In Clara Isabel Martínez and Pablo Alonso González (eds), *Del papel a la imagen*. Astorga: Universidad de León and Ayuntamiento de Astorga, pp. 53–63.
Iden, Peter (1976). 'Making an impact: Rainer Werner Fassbinder and the theatre'. In Tony Rayns (ed.), *Fassbinder*. London: BFI, pp. 17–23.
Iturrino, Calle (1938). *Lope de Vega y la clave de Fuenteovejuna*. Bilbao: Casa Dochao.
Ivars Baidal, Josep A. (2004). 'Tourism planning in Spain: evolution and perspectives'. *Annals of Tourism Research*, 31.2: 313–33.
J. A. (1997). 'Entrevista con Josep María Flotats. Director del Teatre Nacional de Catalunya'. *ADE*, 62–3: 44–6.
Jackson, Russell (2000). 'From play-script to screenplay'. In Russell Jackson (ed.), *The Cambridge Companion to Shakespeare on Film*. Cambridge: Cambridge University Press, pp. 15–35.
Jaime, Antoine (2000). *Literatura y cine en España (1975–1995)*. Madrid: Cátedra.
J. B. (1954). '*El alcalde de Zalemea*', review. *Cine mundo*, 16 January: unpaginated.
J. B. (2007). 'Cuando hay verdad, no cuesta hablar en verso', interview with Blanca Oteyza. *ABC*, 27 September: 81.
Jeffs (Mountjoy), Kathleen (2005a). 'Interview with Laurence Boswell'. *Comedia Performance*, 2.1: 171–92.
— (2005b). 'Golden-Age page to Stratford stage: analysis of a rehearsal process'. Unpublished M.Phil thesis, Oxford University.
— (2007). 'Literal and performance text'. In Catherine Boyle and David Johnston (with Janet Morris) (eds), *The Spanish Golden-Age in English: Perspectives on Performance*. London: Oberon Books, pp. 75–88.
— (2008). 'Golden Age page to Stratford stage: rehearsing and performing the Royal Shakespeare Company's Spanish season'. Unpublished dissertation, Oxford University.
— and Duncan Wheeler (2007). 'Modern productions of Golden Age plays in English in Great Britain', appendix to Jonathan Thacker, 'History of performance in English'. In Catherine Boyle and David Johnston (with Janet Morris) (eds), *The Spanish Golden Age in English: Perspectives on Performance*. London: Oberon Books, pp. 23–8.
Jiménez Smerdou, J. I. (1962). 'España y su cine histórico'. *Espectáculo*, 169: 12–13.
Johnston, David (2004). *The Dog in the Manger*, Lope de Vega, trans. David Johnston. London: Oberon Books.
—. (2007a). 'Historicizing the Spanish Golden Age: Lope's *El perro del hortelano* and *El caballero de Olmedo* in English'. In Catherine Boyle and David Johnston (with Janet Morris) (eds), *The Spanish Golden-Age in English: Perspectives on Performance*. London: Oberon Books, pp. 49–60.

— (2007b). 'Interview with Laurence Boswell'. In Catherine Boyle and David Johnston (with Janet Morris) (eds), *The Spanish Golden-Age in English: Perspectives on Performance*. London: Oberon Books, pp. 148–54.
Johnston, Robert M (2003). 'El movimiento escénico y las "relaciones proxémicas" en *A secreto agravio, secreta venganza* y *El pintor de su deshonra* de Calderón'. In Manfred Tietz (ed.), *Teatro calderoniano sobre el tablado: Calderón y su puesta en escena a través de los siglos*. Stuttgart: Franz Steiner Verlag, pp. 235–49.
Jones, R. O. (1971). 'Poets and peasants'. In David A. Kossoff and José Amor y Vázquez (eds), *Homenaje a William L. Fichter: estudios sobre el teatro antiguo hispánico y otros ensayos*. Madrid: Castalia, pp. 341–55.
Jongh, Nicholas de (2000). *Politics, Prudery and Perversions: The Censoring of the English Stage 1901–1968*. London: Methuen.
Jordan, Barry and Rikki Morgan-Tamosunas (1998). *Contemporary Spanish Cinema*. Manchester, Manchester University Press.
J. S. R. (1960). '*El príncipe encadenado*', review. *Primer Plano*, 25 December: unpaginated.
Kennedy, Dennis (2000). 'Shakespeare and cultural tourism'. In Edward J. Esche (ed.), *Shakespeare and his Contemporaries in Performance*. Aldershot: Ashgate, pp. 3–20.
— (2006). 'Memory, performance and the idea of the museum'. In Peter Holland (ed.), *Shakespeare, Memory and Performance*. Cambridge: Cambridge University Press, pp. 329–45.
Kercher, Dona M. (1997). 'The marketing of Cervantine magic for a new global image of Spain'. In Marsha Kinder (ed.), *Refiguring Spain: Cinema/Media/Representation*. Durham: Duke University Press, pp. 99–132.
Kidnie, Margaret Jane (2005). 'Where is *Hamlet*? Text, performance and adaptation'. In Barbara Hodgdon and W. B. Worthen (eds), *A Companion to Shakespeare and Performance*. Chichester: Wiley-Blackwell, pp. 101–20.
King, Margaret L. (1991). *Women of the Renaissance*. Chicago: University of Chicago Press.
Kirby, Carol Bingham (1981). 'Theater and history in Calderón's *El médico de su honra*'. *Journal of Hispanic Philology*, 5.1: 223–35.
Kirschner, Teresa J. (1977a). 'Sobrevivencia de una comedia: historia de la difusión de *Fuenteovejuna*'. *Revista canadiense de estudios hispánicos*, 1.3: 255–71.
— (1977b). 'Evolución de la crítica de *Fuenteovejuna* de Lope de Vega en el Siglo XX'. *Cuadernos hispanoamericanos*, 320–1: 450–65.
— (1979). *El protagonista colectivo en Fuenteovejuna de Lope de Vega*. Salamanca: Ediciones Universidad de Salamanca.
Labanyi, Jo (1989). *Myth and History in the Contemporary Spanish Novel*. Cambridge: Cambridge University Press.
— (2000). 'Feminizing the nation: women, subordination and subversion in post-Civil War Spanish cinema'. In Ulrike Sieglohr (ed.), *Heroines Without Heroes: Reconstructing Female and National Identities in European Cinema (1945–51)*. London: Cassell, pp. 163–82.
— (2003). 'Impossible love and Spanishness: *Adventures of Don Juan* (Sherman, 1949) and *Don Juan* (Sáenz de Heredia, 1950)'. In Federico Bonaddio and Xon de Ros (eds), *Crossing Fields in Modern Spanish Culture*. Oxford: European Humanities Research Centre, pp. 146–54.
Laborda, Ángel (1973). '*Marta la piadosa* en el Español', review. *ABC*, 5 December: 83.
— (1977). 'Entrevista de Ángel Laborda a Francisco Nieva'. *ABC*, 2 November: 62.

Ladra, David (1985). '*El castigo sin venganza* de Lope de Vega'. *PA*, 210–11: 58–70.
— (2000). 'A propósito de una representación de *El príncipe constante*'. *PA*, 286: 107–16.
Laín Entralgo, Pedro (1956). *La aventura de leer*. Madrid: Espasa Calpe.
Lannon, Frances (1987). *Privilege, Persecution and Prophecy: The Catholic Church in Spain (1875–1975)*. Oxford: Clarendon Press.
Lanza (2005). 'El congreso de diputados aprueba potenciar el Festival de Almagro'. *Lanza*, 11 May: 7.
Lara, Antonio (2002). 'Del libro al celuloide; algunas reflexiones sobre el fenómeno de la adaptación'. In Norberto Mínguez Arranz (ed.), *Literatura española y cine*. Madrid: Editorial Complutense, pp. 1–12.
Larson, Catherine (1991). '"Violent hierarchies": the deconstructive voice and writing undone in *Fuenteovejuna*'. In Catherine Larson, *Language and the Comedia: Theory and Practice*. London: Associated UP, pp. 109–25.
Larson, Donald R. (1973). '*La dama boba* and the comic sense of life'. *Romanische Forschungen*, 85: 41–62.
Larson, Paul E. (2001). '*Fuente Ovejuna*: history, historiography and literary history'. *B.Com.*, 53.2: 267–90.
Lauer, A. Robert (1997). 'The recovery of the repressed: a neo-historical reading of *Fuenteovejuna*'. In José A. Madrigal (ed.), *New Historicism and the Comedia: Poetics, Politics and Praxis*. Colorado: Society of Spanish and Spanish American Studies, pp. 15–28.
L. B. (2003). 'La Junta, dispuesta a gestionar al Festival de Teatro de Almagro'. *El día*, 14 February: 26.
León Sierra, P. (2004). 'La Royal Shakespeare: los instrumentos técnicos como paradigmas'. *PA*, 306: 68–71.
Lewis, Tom (1994). 'Afterword: aesthetics and politics'. In Silvia L. López, Jenaro Talens and Darío Villanueva (eds), *Critical Practices in Post-Franco Spain*. Minneapolis: University of Minnesota Press, pp. 160–82.
Lichtenfels, Peter and Lynette Hunter (2002). 'Seeing through the national and global stereotypes: British theatre in crisis'. In Maria M. Delgado and Caridad Svich (eds), *Theatre in Crisis? Performance Manifestos for a New Century*. Manchester: Manchester University Press, pp. 31–53.
Linares, Francisco (1996). 'Theatre and Falangism at the beginning of the Franco regime'. In Günter Berghaus (ed.), *Fascism and Theatre: Comparative Studies on the Aesthetics and Politics of Performance in Europe (1925–1945)*. Providence: Breghahn Books, pp. 210–28.
Lluch, Felipe (1940). 'El teatro español'. *Tajo*, 29 June: 18.
London, John (1997). *Reception and Renewal in Modern Spanish Theatre: 1939–1963*. London: W. S. Maney and Son.
— (2000). 'Non-German drama in the Third Reich'. In John London (ed.), *Theatre Under the Nazis*. Manchester: Manchester University Press, pp. 222–61.
— (2007). 'Drama in the Spanish Civil War: was there *teatro de urgencia* in the Nationalist zone?'. In John London and David George (eds), *Spanish Film, Theatre and Literature in the Twentieth Century*. Cardiff: University of Wales Press, pp. 205–36.
Lonsdale, Laura (2011). 'Don Juan in exile'. In Helena Buffery (ed.), *Stages of Exile*. Bern: Peter Lang, pp. 95–106.
López, Guillermo (2008). 'Alegato de Calderón contra la violencia machista en el Principal alicantino: *El pintor de su deshonra* retrata el amor posesivo y los crímenes por honor', review. *ABC*, Valencia ed., November 18.

López, Silvia L., Jenaro Talens and Darío Villanueva (1994). 'Introduction: the politics of theory in post-Franco Spain'. In Silvia L. López, Jenaro Talens and Dario Villanueva (eds), *Critical Practices in Post-Franco Spain*. Minneapolis: University of Minnesota Press, pp. ix–xxv.
López Antuñano, José Gabriel (2007). 'Emilio Hernández: Almagro será la capital europea del teatro clásico', interview. *ADE*, 115: 97–101.
López Estrada, Francisco (1989). 'Músicas y letras: más sobre los cantares de *Fuente Ovejuna*'. *Cuadernos de teatro clásico*, 3: 45–52.
López Rubio (1947). '*Fuenteovejuna* ovacionada'. *Primer Plano*, 23 November: unpaginated.
López Sancho, Lorenzo (1974). '*El mejor alcalde, el rey*, versión libre y sugestiva de Lope de Vega', review. *ABC*, 1 May: 77.
— (1988). 'Un "Calderón" entre Pasolini y Foucault en la sala Olimpia'. *ABC*, 17 April: 177.
— (1992). 'Calderón puesto al gusto del día de la Fiesta Barroca de la Plaza Mayor'. *ABC*, 7 July: 105.
Lorente Acosta, Miguel (2001). *Mi marido me pega lo normal: agresión a la mujer: realidades y mitos*. Barcelona: Ares & Mares.
Loureiro, Ángel. G. (2003). 'Spanish nationalism and the ghost of empire'. *Journal of Spanish Cultural Studies*, 4.1: 65–76.
Luca de Tena, Cayetano (1953a). 'Ensayo general: notas, experiencias y fracasos de un director de escena, III'. *Teatro*, 3: 45–8.
— (1953b). 'Los autos sacramentales y el director de escena'. *Teatro*, 5: 43–4.
— (1962). 'Plan de los teatros nacionales'. *PA*, 36: 3.
Machado, Manuel and Antonio Machado (1931). *El perro del hortelano*. Madrid: La Farsa.
MacKay, Angus and Geraldine McKendrick (1986). 'The crowd in theater and the crowd in history: *Fuenteovejuna*'. *Renaissance Drama*, 17: 125–47.
Madrid Diplomatic Office (1952). *Fifteen Years of Spanish Culture (1938–1952)*. Madrid: Diplomatic Office.
Madroñal, Abraham (2002). 'La representación de *Casa con dos puertas* en 1979 y notas sobre el lenguaje y la técnica dramática en las adaptaciones de los clásicos'. In José María Ruano de la Haza and Jesús Pérez Magallón (eds), *Ayer y hoy de Calderón: Actas seleccionadas del Congreso International celebrado en Ottawa del 4 al 8 de octubre del 2000*. Madrid: Editorial Castalia, pp. 291–302.
Magone, José M. (2009). *Contemporary Spanish Politics*, 2nd ed. London: Routledge.
Mainer, José Carlos (1971). *Falange y literatura*. Barcelona: Editorial Labor.
Maldonado, Luis (2008). 'Alcalde de Almagro'. *Global Castilla-La-Mancha: 31 Festival de Teatro Clásico de Almagro*, June–July: 26.
Mancing, Howard (2006). 'See the play, read the book'. In Bruce McConachie and F. Elizabeth Hurt (eds), *Performance and Cognition: Theatre Studies and the Cognitive Turn*. London: Routledge, pp. 189–206.
Mañas Martínez, María del Mar (2003). 'Reflexiones sobre *El perro del hortelano* de Pilar Miró'. *Cuadernos de filología hispánica*, 21: 139–56.
Marañon, Gregorio (1952). 'Más no el honor'. *Teatro*, 1: 4–5.
Maravall, José Antonio (1972). *Teatro y literatura en la sociedad barroca*. Madrid: Seminarios y Ediciones.
Marías, Miguel (1975). 'Entrevista: Antonio Drove'. *Dirigido por*, 20: 22–7.
Marín, Diego (1985). 'Introducción'. In Lope de Vega, *La dama boba*, ed. Diego Marín. Madrid: Cátedra, pp. 11–58.

Marín, Juan María (2001). 'Introducción'. In Lope de Vega, *Fuente Ovejuna*, ed. Juan María Marín. Madrid: Cátedra, pp. 13–78.
Mariscal, George (1990). 'An introduction to the ideology of Hispanism in the US and Britain'. In Peter William Evans (ed.), *Conflicts of Discourse: Spanish Literature in the Golden Age*. Manchester: Manchester University Press, pp. 1–25.
Maroto Camino, Mercedes (2003). '"Esta sangre quiero": secrets and discovery in Lope's *El perro del hortelano*'. *HR*, 71.1: 15–30.
Marqueríe, Alfredo (1942). *Desde la silla eléctrica*. Madrid: Editora Nacional.
— (1944a). *En la jaula de los leones: memorías y crítica teatral*. Madrid: Ediciones Españolas.
— (1944b). '*Fuenteovejuna*', review. *ABC*, 13 October: 17.
— (1956). 'Ayer murió en Valencia Enrique Rambal'. *ABC*, 11 May: 54.
— (1962). '*Fuenteovejuna* de Lope de Vega, en el Español', review. *ABC*, 1 May: 65.
— (1969). *El teatro que yo he visto*. Barcelona: Editorial Bruguera.
— (1973). '*Marta la piadosa* en el Español', review. *La hoja del lunes*, 10 December: 31.
Marsh, Steven (2006). *Popular Spanish Film under Franco: Comedy and the Weakening of the State*. Basingstoke: Palgrave Macmillan.
Marsillach, Adolfo (1986). 'Pompa y circunstancia de la Compañía Nacional de Teatro Clásico'. In *Anuario Teatral*. Madrid: CDT, pp. 35–6.
— (2002). *Tan lejos, tan cerca: mi vida*. Barcelona: Tusquets, Fábula.
— (2003). '¿Quién teme a Don Pedro Calderón?' In Juan Antonio Hormigón (ed.), *Un teatro necesario: escritos sobre el teatro de Adolfo Marsillach*. Madrid: ADE, pp. 192–4.
Martin, Vincent (2009). '2009 Festival de teatro clásico de Almagro'. *B.Com.*, 61.2: 159–73.
Martín Bermúdez, Santiago (2005). 'Encuentro con Eduardo Vasco'. *PA*, 307: 97–104.
— (2006). 'Madrid: por dónde van los tiros'. *PA*, 314: 61–8.
Martín Gaite, Carmen (1994). *Usos amorosos de la postguerra española*. Barcelona: Editorial Anagrama.
Martín-Márquez, Susan (1999). *Feminist Discourse and Spanish Cinema: Sight Unseen*. Oxford: Oxford University Press.
Martín Rodríguez, Mariano (2004). 'Compañías extranjeras y teatro español en la posguerra civil: nota sobre una visita de la *Comédie Française* al Madrid de los 50'. *ALEC*, 29.2: 51–61.
Martínez Aguinagalde, Florencio (1996). 'Cine y literatura en Mario Camus'. Unpublished dissertation, Universidad del País Vasco.
Martínez Ortiz, José and Rodolfo Sirera (1989). *Rambal, mago de la escena española, valenciano ilustre, hijo de Utiel*. Utiel: Agrupación escénica Enrique Rambal.
Martínez Roger, Ángel (2003). 'Escenografía teatral en la posguerra. El caso de Emilio Burgos'. *Acotaciones: revista de investigación teatral*, 11: 21–44.
Maso, Ángeles (1974). 'Fantástico *El mejor alcalde, el rey*', review. *La vanguardia*, 23 August.
Mateo, Nieves (2006). 'Crisol de voces canarias: un SOS a la política cultural actual'. *PA*, 313: 167–74.
— (2009). 'La propuesta de *Calderón PPP*'. *PA*, 328: 62–6.
Matyjaszczyk Grenda, Agnieska (2008). 'Los clásicos españoles en la escena polaca a fines del siglo XX'. In Javier Huerta Calvo (ed.), *Clásicos sin fronteras*, vol. 1. Madrid: CNTC, pp. 59–68.
Mayordomo, Alejandro (1993). *Vencer y convencer: educación y política, España 1936–1945*. Valencia: Universitat de València.

McCarthy, Jim (1999). *Political Theatre During the Civil War*. Cardiff: University of Wales Press.
McCrary, William C. (1961). '*Fuenteovejuna*: its platonic vision and execution'. *Studies in Philology*, 58: 179–92.
McGaha, Michael (1991). 'Bridging cultures'. In Louise and Peter Fothergill-Payne (eds), *Prologue to Performance: Spanish Classical Theater Today*. Lewisburg: Bucknell University Press, pp. 85–92.
McGrady, Donald (1993). 'Prólogo'. In Lope de Vega, *Fuente Ovejuna*, ed. Donald McGrady. Barcelona: Crítica, pp. 3–38.
McIntosh, Alison J. (2007). 'Into the tourist's mind: understanding the value of the heritage experience'. In Dallen J. Timothy (ed.), *The Heritage Tourist Experience: Critical Essays*, vol. 2. Aldershot: Ashgate, pp. 235–58.
McKendrick, Melveena (1989). *Theatre in Spain 1490–1700*. Cambridge: Cambridge University Press.
— (1993). 'Calderón and the politics of honour'. *BHS*, 70.1: 135–46.
— (2000a). *Playing the King: Lope de Vega and the Limits of Conformity*. London: Tamesis.
— (2000b). 'Anticipating Brecht: alienation and agency in Calderón's wife-murder plays'. *BHS (Glasgow)*, 77.1: 217–36.
— (2006). 'Representing their sex: actresses in seventeenth-century Spain'. In Richard J. Pym (ed.), *Rhetoric and Reality in Early Modern Spain*. London: Tamesis, pp. 72–91.
Menéndez y Pelayo, Marcelino (1881). *Calderón: conferencias dadas en el círculo de la unión católica*, vol. 6. Madrid: Librería de M. Murillo.
— (1925). *Estudios sobre el teatro de Lope de Vega*, vol. 5. Madrid: Librería General de Victoriano Suárez.
Menéndez Pidal, Ramón (1924). 'El Rey Rodrigo en la literatura'. *Boletín de la Real Academia Española*, 11: 519–85.
— (1958). *De Cervantes y Lope de Vega*. Madrid: Espasa-Calpe.
Miller, Jonathan (1986). *Subsequent Performances*. London: Faber and Faber.
Ministerio de Información y Turismo (1963). 'Programme to Festivales de España, 1963 Cuenca III Festival (2 al 11 de agosto)'. Cuenca: Ministerio de Información y Turismo.
Mira Nouselles, Alberto (1999). 'Al cine por razón de Estado: estética y política en *Alba de America*'. *BHS*, 76.1: 123–38.
Miralles, Alberto (1981). *Céfiro agreste de olímpicos embates: Premio 'Valladolid de Teatro Breve, 1980*. Valladolid: Caja de Ahorros Provincial de Valladolid.
Miró, Pilar (1997). 'Síntomas de envidia'. *El Mundo*, 25 January: 2.
Moir, Duncan and Edward M. Wilson (1971). *A Literary History of Spain: The Golden Age Drama 1492–1700*. London: Ernest Benn Ltd.
Moix, Terenci (1993). *Suspiros de España: la copla y el cine de nuestro recuerdo*. Barcelona: Plaza y Janés.
Molina, Margot (1999). 'La intifada del Siglo de Oro', review of *Fuente Ovejuna*. *El País*, 2 January.
Monleón, José (1961). '*El anzuelo de Fenisa*', review. *PA*, 20: 48.
— (1962). 'Acabando el IV centenario de Lope'. *PA*, 37: 2–4.
— (1966). 'Los siete infantes de Laura', review. *PA*, 73: 51–2.
— (1980). 'Política general. Política teatral'. In Francisco Ruiz Ramón (ed.), *II Jornadas de Teatro Clásico Español: Almagro 1979*. Madrid: Ministerio de Cultura, pp. 245–64.

— (chair) (1987). 'Debate sobre la representación actual de los clásicos'. *PA*, 217 (supplement): 2–24.
— (1992). '*Fuenteovejuna* por Fassbinder. Ginebra: talento, escándalo y herejía'. *PA*, 243: 112–15.
— (2005). 'Un proyecto emblemático y sus preguntas: *La hija del aire* en el Teatro Español'. *PA*, 307: 89–96.
— (2009). '*Fuenteovejuna* por Samarkanda: un ejemplo de investigación'. *PA*, 327: 72–6.
Monterde, José Enrique (1989). 'El cine histórico durante la transición'. In José A. Hurtado and Francisco M. Pico (eds), *Escritos sobre el cine español (1973–1987)*. Valencia: Filmoteca de la Generalitat Valenciana, pp. 45–63.
— (1995). 'El cine de la autarquia (1939–1950)'. In Román Gubern (ed.), *Historia del cine español*, 2nd ed. Madrid: Cátedra, pp. 181–238.
— (2007). 'Un modelo de reapropiación nacional: el cine histórico'. In Nancy Berthier and Jean-Claude Seguin (eds), *Cine, nación y nacionalidades en España*. Madrid: Casa de Velázquez, pp. 89–98.
Montero, Esther (2008). 'De Calderón a "*Matrix*"; *La vida es sueño* se moderniza en Alcalá de Henares'. *El Mundo*, 24 June: 10.
Montero, Manuel (1996). 'Miró: "Despreciamos nuestra cultura"'. *El periódico*, 26 November: 58.
Moral, Ignacio del (2001). 'José Luis Alonso de Santos: "El enemigo del teatro actual nunca puede ser el teatro clásico"'. *Las puertas del drama: revista de la Asociación de Autores de Teatro*, 6: 24–9.
Moral, José María del (1987). 'Con ojos de niño', interview with José Estruch. *El público*, 40: 71–2.
Morales, José Ricardo (2002). 'Ardor con ardor se apaga'. In José Ricardo Morales, *Teatro ausente*, ed. Claudia Oretego Sanmartín. La Coruña: Edicios de Castro, pp. 283–346.
Morales, Manuel (1967). 'Los títeres, teatro nacional de juventudes'. *Yorick*, 23: 13.
Morales Astola, Rafael, 2003. *La presencia del cine en el teatro*. Seville: Alfar.
Morales y Marín, Antonio (1995). 'Teatro Español 1962–1982, de teatro oficial a teatro municipal'. In Andrés Peláez Martín (ed.), *Historia de los Teatros Nacionales (1960–1985)*. Madrid: CDT, pp. 87–113.
— (2008). 'Vergel: los clásicos al día'. In Ángel Facio (ed.), *Alberto González Vergel*. Madrid: Teatro Español, pp. 105–30.
Morcillo, Aurora G. (2000). *True Catholic Womanhood: Gender Ideology in Franco's Spain*. Illinois: Northern Illinois University Press.
Muez, Mikel (2000). 'Rafael Pérez Sierra dirigirá el festival de teatro clásico de Olite'. *El País*, 19 February: 8.
Munso Cabús, Joan (1988). *Escrito en el aire: 50 años de Radio Nacional de España*. Madrid: RTVE.
Muñóz, Diego (1996). '¿Quién sabe lo que quiere el público?', review of *El perro del hortelano*. *La vanguardia*, 26 November: 23.
— and Miguel Bayón (1991). 'El sexo coronado', review of *El rey pasmado*. *El País*, Barcelona ed., 29 October.
Muñoz Carabantes, Manuel (1992). 'Puesta en escena y recepción del teatro clásico y medieval en España desde 1939 a nuestros días'. Unpublished dissertation, Universidad Complutense.
Navarrete-Galiano, Ramón (1999). 'Los clásicos en el cine español'. In Irene Pardo Molina, Luz Ruíz Martínez and Antonio Serrano (eds), *En torno al teatro del Siglo*

de Oro: Actas de las Jornadas XIV celebrados en Almería Marzo 1997. Almería: Instituto de Estudios Almerienses and Diputación de Almería, pp. 79–92.
Neuschafer, Hans-Jörg (1994). *Adiós a la España eterna: la dialéctica de la censura. Novela, teatro y cine bajo el franquismo*. Barcelona: Editorial Anthropos.
Nieva de la Paz, Pilar (2001). 'Pilar Miró ante el teatro clásico'. *ALEC*, 26.1: 255–76.
Nosferatu (1998). 'Pilar Miró', *Nosferatu*, 28.
Noval Clemente, Mercedes (1999). 'La sección femenina en Murcia: educación, cultura e ideología (1939–1977)'. Unpublished dissertation, Universidad de Murcia.
Núbila, Domingo di (1960). *Historia del cine argentino*, vol. 2. Buenos Aires: Cruz de Malta.
O'Connor, Patricia (1966). 'Government censorship in the contemporary Spanish theatre'. *Educational Theatre Journal*, 18.4: 443–9.
— (1973). '*Torquemada* in the theatre: a glance at government censorship'. *Theatre Survey*, 14.2: 33–45.
O'Connor, Thomas Austin (1997). 'Culpabilidad, expiación y reconciliación en la versión de *Fuenteovejuna* filmada por Juan Guerrero Zamora'. In A. Robert Lauer and Henry W. Sullivan (eds), *Hispanic Essays in Honor of Frank P. Casa*. New York: Peter Lang, pp. 122–31.
— (2000). *Love in the Corral: Conjugal Spirituality and Anti-Theatrical Polemic in Early Modern Spain*. New York: Peter Lang.
Oliva, César (1975). *Ocho años de teatro universitario: T. U. de Murcia, 1967–75*. Murcia: Publicaciones de la Universidad de Murcia.
— (1977). *Corral de Almagro: una propuesta sin resolver*. Madrid: Dirección General de Teatro y Espectáculos.
— (co-ord.) (1980). *Los papeles del seminario teatro y universidad*. Murcia: Centro Nacional de Documentación Teatral.
— (1994a). 'Teatro y poder en la escena española de hoy'. *Crítica Hispánica*, 16.1: 169–76.
— (1994b). 'La puesta en escena en el teatro español de los ochenta'. *Gestos*, 18: 45–60.
— (1997). 'La dama boba, hoy'. In Ysla Campbell (ed.), *El escritor y la escena V, estudios sobre teatro español y novohispano de los Siglos de Oro: homenaje a Marc Vitse*. Ciudad Juárez: Universidad Autónoma de Ciudad Juárez, pp. 39–48.
— (1998). 'Trayectoria escénica del Tenorio'. In Ana Sofía Pérez-Bustamente (ed.), *Don Juan Tenorio en la España del siglo XX: literatura y cine*. Madrid: Cátedra, pp. 27–38.
— (1999). 'La escena universitaria española'. In Luciano García Lorenzo (ed.), *Aproximación al teatro español universitario (TEU)*. Madrid: Consejo Superior de Investigaciones Científicas, Instituto de la Lengua Española, pp. 15–30.
— (2000). 'Calderón en la escena de hoy'. *Ínsula*, 644–5: 41–4.
— (2002a). *Teatro español del siglo XX*. Madrid: Síntesis.
— (2002b). 'La pantalla como documento sobre la interpretación en España durante el siglo XX: una experiencia ampliable'. In José Romera Castillo (ed.), *Del teatro al cine y la televisión en la segunda mitad del siglo XX*. Madrid: Visor Libros, pp. 41–5.
— (2005). *Adolfo Marsillach: las máscaras de su vida*. Madrid: Síntesis.
— (2008). 'García Lorca y la puesta en escena de los clásicos'. *Gestos*, 45: 31–46.
— (2009). 'Mi hermano Ricard'. *Assaig de Teatre*, 73–4: 74–8.
Olmo, Lauro (1968). 'Lo nacional y el teatro'. *Yorick*, 29: 5–6.
Ordóñez, Marcos (2003). *A pie de obra: escritos sobre teatro*. Barcelona: Alba Editorial.

Oriel, Charles (2000). '"Laughing and silence": performing friendship and honor in Calderón's *El pintor de su deshonra*'. *Caliope: Journal of the Society for Renaissance and Baroque Hispanic Poetry*, 6.1–2: 85–102.
Orizana, Gabriel (1940). 'La literatura española, como medio de formar la juventud de la nueva España: lección explicada en la VIII Semana de Educación Nacional'. *Atenas*, 100–1: 106–15.
Orozco, Lourdes (2006). 'National identity in the construction of the theater policy of the Generalitat de Catalunya'. *Romance Quarterly*, 53.3: 211–22.
Ortiz, Lourdes (1990). 'Yo a las cabañas baje'. In Virginia Marquieira and Cristina Sánchez (eds), *Violencia y sociedad patriarcal*. Madrid: Editorial Pablo Iglesias, pp. 137–50.
Ostlund, DeLys (1997). *The Re-Creation of History in the Fernando and Isabel Plays of Lope de Vega*. New York: Peter Lang.
Otto, C. (2008). 'El Festival está "mantiendo el nivel de la pasada edición"'. *El día*, 11 July: 18.
P. (1954). 'Un film clásico de moderna realización'. *Primer Plano*, 3 January: unpaginated.
PA (2005). 'Entrevista con Mario Gas: "Crear un lugar de agitación social"'. *PA*, 307: 75–83.
El País (2008). 'Más allá de Madrid'. *El País*, 19 February: 44.
Palacio, Manuel (2005). *Historia de la televisión en España*. Barcelona: Gedisa Editorial.
— (2007). 'La televisión pública española (TVE) en la era de José Luis Rodríguez Zapatero'. *Journal of Spanish Cultural Studies*, 8.1: 71–83.
Pando, Juan (1996). 'El Rey con Pilar Miró en el estreno de su última película'. *El Mundo*, 27 November: 51.
Parker, A. A. (1953). 'Reflections on a new definition of "Baroque drama"'. *BHS*, 30: 142–51.
— (1957). *The Approach to the Spanish Drama of the Golden Age*. London: Grant and Cutler.
— (1962). 'Towards a definition of Calderonian tragedy'. *BHS*, 39.4: 223–37.
Parr, James A. (1999). 'Selected evidence for Tirso's authorship of *El burlador de Sevilla*'. In A. Robert Lauer and Henry W. Sullivan (eds), *Hispanic Essays in Honor of Frank P. Casa*. New York: Peter Lang, pp. 156–64.
Parrack, John C. (2008). 'La desglosada de *La Estrella de Sevilla*: la muerte del autor y la construcción del texto'. In Frederick A. de Armas, Luciano García Lorenzo and Enrique García Santo-Tomás (eds), *Hacia la tragedia áurea: lecturas para un nuevo milenio*. Frankfurt and Madrid: Universidad de Navarra, Vervuert and Iberoamericana, pp. 301–13.
Pascual, Itziar (1992). 'Todos a una', review of *Fuente Ovejuna*. *El Mundo*, un verano europeo (supplement), 23 August: 1–2.
— (1996). 'Aquí concluye una manera de hacer teatro'. *El Mundo*, 30 November: 45.
Pasolini, Pier Paolo (2009). 'Calderón', trans. Carla Matteini. *PA*, 328: 67–111.
Paterson, Alan K. G (1969). 'The comic and tragic melancholy of Juan Roca: a study of Calderón's *El pintor de su deshonra*'. *Forum for Modern Language Studies*, 5.3: 244–61.
— (1989). 'Reflexiones sobre una traducción inglesa de *El pintor de su deshonra*'. *Cuadernos de teatro clásico*, 4: 113–32.
Paun de García, Susan (2008). 'Calderón a ritmo de Charleston. Entrevista con Francisco García Vicente'. *Comedia Performance*, 5.1: 135–53.
Pavis, Patrice (1992). *Theatre at the Crossroads of Culture*. London: Routledge.

Pavlović, Tatjana *et al.* (2009). *100 Years of Spanish Cinema*. Chichester: Wiley-Blackwell.
Payne, Stanley G. (1961). *Falange: A History of Spanish Fascism*. Stanford: Stanford University Press.
— (2008). *Franco and Hitler: Spain, Germany and World War II*. New Haven: Yale University Press.
Pedraza Jiménez, Felipe B. (2002). 'El resurgir escénico de las comedias de comendadores'. In Enrique García Santo-Tomás (ed.), *El teatro del Siglo de Oro ante los espacios de la crítica: encuentros y revisiones*. Frankfurt and Madrid: Iberoamericana and Vervuert, pp. 379–404.
— (2006). 'Adolfo Marsillach ante el repertorio clásico'. *Lectura y signo: revista de literatura*, 1: 333–47.
Peláez Martín, Andrés (ed.) (1991). *50 años de teatro José Tamayo (1941–1991)*. Almagro: Ministerio de Cultura.
— (ed.) (1993). *Historia de los Teatros Nacionales (1939–1962)*. Madrid: CDT.
— (ed.) (1995). *Historia de los Teatros Nacionales (1960–1985)*. Madrid: CDT.
— (1996). 'Lope de Vega en la programación de los teatros nacionales y en festivales de España'. In Felipe B. Pedraza Jiménez and Rafael González Cañal (eds), *Lope de Vega: comedia urbana y comedia palatina. Actas de las XVIII Jornadas de Teatro Clásico*. Almagro: Universidad de Castilla La Mancha and Festival de Almagro, pp. 83–103.
— (1997). 'El corral de comedias de Almagro: un espacio y un patrimonio dramático recuperados'. In Luciano García Lorenzo and Andrés Peláez Martín (eds), *Festival Internacional de Teatro Clásico de Almagro, 20 años 1978–1997*. Toledo: Caja Castilla la Mancha and Festival de Almagro, pp. 19–36.
Pemán, José María (1939). '*Fuenteovejuna* en la provincia'. *ABC de Sevilla*, 1 January: 1–3, 5.
Pérez Bastías, Luis and Fernando Alonso Barahona (1995). *Las mentiras sobre el cine español*. Barcelona: Royal Books.
Pérez Bowie, José Antonio (1999). 'El TEU Salmantino: treinta años de actividad teatral universitario (1940–1964)'. In Luciano García Lorenzo (ed.), *Aproximación al teatro español universitario (TEU)*. Madrid: Consejo Superior de Investigaciones Científicas, Instituto de la Lengua Española, pp. 139–71.
Pérez Cabrera, María del Carmen (1984). 'Teatro Español de Madrid: un cuarto de siglo de cartelera'. University of Paris-Sorbonne, unpublished article available for consultation at the Fundación Juan March, Madrid.
Pérez Coterillo, Moisés (1979). 'La batalla teatral I: política de recambios: *Pipirijaina* en el parlamento'. *Pipirijaina*, 10: 4–6.
— (1980). 'El día que se estrenó aquello'. *Pipirijaina*, 14: 12–13.
Pérez Millán, Juan Antonio (2007). *Pilar Miró: directora de cine*, 2nd ed. Madrid: Fundación Festival de Cine de Huesca, Ediciones Calamares.
Pérez de Olaguer, Gonzalo (1966). 'García Escudero habla para *Yorick*'. *Yorick*, 16: 15.
— (1971). 'Con Ricard Salvat: director del Teatro Nacional de Cataluña'. *Yorick*, 45: 5–13.
— (1999a). 'Teatro y universidad: del compromiso al olvido'. In Luciano García Lorenzo (ed.), *Aproximación al teatro español universitario (TEU)*. Madrid: Consejo Superior de Investigaciones Científicas, Instituto de la Lengua Española, pp. 55–61.
— (1999b). 'Las mujeres, unidas y todas a una', review of *Fuente Ovejuna*. *El periódico*, 23 May.

Pérez Fernández, Herminio (1978). 'Antonio Gala: "En el teatro del futuro no habrá individualidades"'. *ABC*, 17 November: 53.
Pérez-Magallón, Jesús (2002). 'Hacia la construcción de Calderón como icono de la "identidad nacional"'. In Enrique García Santo-Tomás (ed.), *El teatro del Siglo de Oro ante los espacios de la crítica: encuentros y revisiones*. Frankfurt and Madrid: Iberoamericana and Vervuert, pp. 275–305.
Pérez-Rasilla, Eduardo (1989). '*El perro del hortelano*: poca confianza en Lope', review. *Reseña*, October: 12.
— (1994). '*El médico de su honra*: cambio de actores', review. *Reseña*, October: 21–2.
— (1999). 'La situación del teatro universitario en España desde 1939 a 1967'. In Luciano García Lorenzo (ed.), *Aproximación al teatro español universitario (TEU)*. Madrid: Consejo Superior de Investigaciones Científicas, Instituto de la Lengua Española, pp. 31–53.
— (2006). 'El rey Basilio y la Compañía Nacional de Teatro Clásico: dos escenificaciones de *La vida es sueño*'. In Luciano García Lorenzo (ed.), *El teatro clásico español a través de sus monarcas*. Madrid: Fundamentos, pp. 379–99.
— (2008). 'La puesta en escena de los clásicos. La crítica académica'. *Acotaciones: revista de investigación teatral*, 20: 9–22.
Pérez-Reverte, Arturo and Carlota (1996). *El capitán Alatriste*. Buenos Aires: Alfaguara.
Pérez Sierra, Rafael (1994). 'Interpretación actual de la escena'. In José Antonio Gómez Rodríguez and Beatriz Martínez del Fresno (eds), *F. Bances Candamo y el teatro musical de su tiempo*. Oviedo: Universidad de Oviedo y Ayuntamiento de Avilés, pp. 257–71.
— (1996). 'Versión cinematográfica de *El perro del hortelano*'. In Felipe B. Pedraza Jiméncz and Rafael González Cañal (eds), *Lope de Vega: comedia urbana y comedia palatina. Actas de las XVII jornadas de teatro clásico, Almagro*. Almagro: Universidad de Castilla la Mancha, pp. 107–14.
— (1997). 'Almagro y sus raíces'. In Luciano García Lorenzo and Andrés Peláez Martín (eds), *Festival Internacional de Teatro Clásico de Almagro, 20 años 1978–1997*. Toledo: Caja Castilla la Mancha and Festival de Almagro, pp. 47–51.
— (1999a). *Acercar los clásicos*. Murcia: ESAD de Murcia.
— (1999b). 'Historia de una experiencia: *El perro del hortelano*'. In Irene Pardo Molina, Luz Ruíz Martínez and Antonio Serrano (eds), *En torno al teatro del Siglo de Oro: Actas de las Jornadas XIV celebradas en Almería Marzo 1997*. Almería: Instituto de Estudios Almerienses and Diputación de Almería, pp. 93–102.
Pérez Zalduondo, Gemma (2001). 'La música en el contexto del pensamiento artístico durante el franquismo (1936–1951)'. In Gemma Pérez Zalduondo, José Castillo Ruiz, Ignacio Luis Henares Cuéllar and María Isabel Cabrera García (eds), *Dos décadas de cultura artística en el franquismo (1936–1956)*, vol. 2. Granada: Universidad de Granada, pp. 83–104.
Perriam, Chris (2003). *Stars and Masculinities in Spanish Cinema*. Oxford: Oxford University Press.
Peristiany, John S. (ed.) (1966). *Honour and Shame: The Values of Mediterrancean Society*. Chicago: University of Chicago Press.
Phillippon, Alain (1987). 'Calderon dans un miroir'. *Cahiers du Cinéma*, January: 15.
Piña, Begoña (1994). '¿Las mujeres aman a los hombres por lo que tienen de hombres o de mujer?', review of *Don Gil de las calzas verdes*. *Diario 16*, 6 March: 24.
Piñar, Blas (1962). 'El *sí* de *Fuenteovejuna*'. *ABC*, 17 November: 31, 33.

Pipirijaina (1974). 'Detenidos en espera de juicio – Los Goliardos'. *Pipirijaina*, 4: 25–30.
Pitt Rivers, Julian (1977). *The Fate of Shechem or the Politics of Sex: Essays in the Anthropology of the Mediterranean*. Cambridge: Cambridge University Press.
Portalo, Ana (2002). 'Mario Camus: "No hay películas perfectas"'. *Época*, 29 March: 124.
Powell, Charles T. (1995). 'Spain's external relations 1898–1975'. In Richard Gillespie, Fernando Rodrigo and Jonathan Store (eds), *Democratic Spain: Reshaping External Relations in a Changing World*. London: Routledge, pp. 11–29.
Pozo, Santiago (1984). *La industria del cine en España. Legislación y aspectos económicos (1896–1970)*. Barcelona: Universidad de Barcelona.
Pozuelo, José María and Rosa María Aradra Sánchez (2000). *Teoría del canon y literatura española*. Madrid: Cátedra.
Pratt, Dale J. and Valerie Hegstrom (2006). 'Mentoring environments and Golden Age theater production'. In Margaret R. Greer and Laura R. Bass (eds), *Approaches to Teaching Early-Modern Spanish Drama*. New York: MLA, pp. 198–205.
Preston, Paul (1995). *Franco: a Biography*. London: Fontana.
Pring-Mill, R. D. F. (1961). 'Introduction'. In Lope de Vega, *Five Plays (Peribáñez, Justice Without Revenge, The Knight from Olmedo, Fuenteovejuna, The Dog in the Manger)*, trans. Jill Booty. New York: Hill and Wang, pp. vii–xxxvii.
— (1962). 'Sententiousness in *Fuente Ovejuna*'. *Tulane Drama Review*, 7.1: 5–37.
Pruneda, José A. (1961). 'El príncipe encadenado', review. *Film Ideal*, 63.1: 30.
Puigdomènech, Jordi (2007). *Treinta años de cine español en democracia (1977–2007)*. Madrid: Ediciones JC.
Punzano, Israel (2005). 'El TNC alza el telón con Lope como muestra de "normalidad cultural"'. *El País*, Barcelona ed., 27 September: 8.
Pym, Richard J. (1998). 'Tragedy and the construct self: considering the subject in Spain's seventeenth-century *comedia*'. *BHS*, 75.3: 273–92.
Quaknine, Serge (1968). 'Alrededor de *El príncipe constante*'. *PA*, 95: 28–43.
Quintana, Juan Antonio (1999). 'Aportación de las aulas de teatro universitarias al hecho teatral'. In Jesús Rubio Jiménez (ed.), *Teatro universitario en Zaragoza (1939–1999)*. Zaragoza: Prensa Universitaria de Zaragoza, pp. 319–23.
Quinto, José María de (1965). 'Crónica de teatro'. *Ínsula*, 222: 15.
— (1997). *Crítica teatral de los sesenta*, ed. Manuel Aznar Soler. Murcia: Universidad de Murcia.
Ragué-Arias, María-José (1996). *El teatro de fin de milenio en España: de 1975 hasta hoy*. Barcelona: Editorial Ariel.
Ramírez de Arellano, Rafael (1901). 'Rebelión de Fuente Obejuna contra el Comendador mayor de Calatrava, Fernán Gómez de Guzmán'. *Boletín de la Real Academia de la Historia*, 39: 446–512.
Ramón Diaz-Sande, José (1985). '*No hay burlas con Calderón*: una brillante idea fallida', review. *Reseña*, May–June: 6–7.
Ramón Fernández, José (2003). 'El hombre que amaba a las mujeres'. In Lope de Vega, *Es de Lope*, ed. Emilio Hernández. Madrid: Centro Cultural de la Villa, pp. 15–34
Regalado, Antonio (1995). *Calderón: los orígenes de la modernidad en la España del Siglo de Oro*, 2 vols. Barcelona: Ediciones Destino.
Reina Ruiz, María (2010). 'El teatro español sin fronteras: Rafael Rodríguez y 2RC Teatro Compañía de Repertorio'. *Gestos*, 49: 177–82.
Revista internacional del cine (1961). 'Premios al cine de 1960'. *Revista internacional del cine*, 39: 12–13.

Resina, Joan Ramón (2000). 'Introduction'. In Joan Ramón Resina (ed.), *Disremembering the Dictatorship: The Politics of Memory in the Spanish Transition to Democracy*. Amsterdam: Editions Rodopi B.V., pp. 1–15.
— (2005). 'Whose hispanism? Cultural trauma, disciplined memory, and symbolic dominance'. In Mabel Moraña (ed.), *Ideologies of Hispanism*. Nashville: Vanderbilt University Press, pp. 160–86.
Richards, Michael (1996). 'Constructing the nationalist state: self-sufficiency and regeneration in the early Franco years'. In Clare Mar-Molinero and Ángel Smith (eds), *Nationalism and the Nation in the Iberian Peninsula: Competing and Conflicting Identities*. Oxford: Berg, pp. 149–67.
Robinson, M. (1996). 'Sustainable tourism for Spain: principles, prospects and problems'. In M. Barke, J. Towner and M. T. Newton (eds), *Tourism in Spain: Critical Issues*. Wallingford: CAB International, pp. 401–25.
Rodenas, Miguel (1942). 'Informaciones teatrales', review of *Peribáñez. . . . ABC*, 18 October: 27.
Rodríguez, Carlos (2002). 'Adolfo Marsillach: "estoy un poco cansado de dirigir"', interview. *ADE*, 90: 147–56.
Rodríguez Cuadros, Evangelina (1998). *La técnica del actor español en el barroco: hipótesis y documentos*. Madrid: Editorial Castalia.
— (2002). *Calderón*. Madrid: Síntesis.
Rodríguez Fuentes, Carmen (2002). *Las actrices en el cine español de los cuarenta*. Málaga: Caligrama Ediciones.
Rodríguez López-Vázquez, Alfredo (1996). 'The analysis of authorship: a methodology'. In Frederick A. de Armas (ed.), *Heavenly Bodies: the Realms of La Estrella de Sevilla*. Lewisburg: Bucknell University Press, pp. 195–205.
— (2000). 'Introducción'. In Tirso de Molina, *El burlador de Sevilla*, ed. Alfredo Rodríguez López-Vázquez. Madrid: Cátedra, pp. 9–143.
Rodríguez Méndez, José María (1972). *Comentarios impertinentes sobre el teatro español*. Barcelona: Península.
— (1990). 'Spanish theater in the eighties: a decade of conflict', trans. Alma Amell. In Samuel Amell (ed.), *Literature, the Arts and Democracy: Spain in the Eighties*. London: Associated UPs, pp. 102–11.
— (1993). *Los despojos del teatro*. Madrid: J. García Verdugo.
Rodríguez Puértolas, Julio (1987). *Literatura fascista española: segunda antología*. Madrid: Akal.
Rodríguez Zapatero, José Luis (2004). '"El compromiso con la cultura" (del discurso de investidura de José Luis Rodríguez Zapatero)'. *PA*, 303: 7–8.
Rojo, J. A. (1987). "Estruch". *Teatra: revista de teatro*, 6: unpaginated.
Román, Manuel (1995). *Los cómicos*, vol. 1. Barcelona: Royal Books.
Romero Castillo, José (1993). '*El alcalde de Zalamea* de Calderón y Francisco Brines'. In José Romero Castillo (ed.), *Frutos del mejor árbol: estudios sobre teatro español del Siglo de Oro*. Madrid: UNED, pp. 220–3.
Romero Salvadó, Francisco J. (1999). *Twentieth-Century Spain: Politics and Society in Spain, 1898–1998*. New York: St Martin's Press.
Rooney, David (1996). '*The Dog in the Manger*', review. *Variety*, 14 October: 60.
Rozas, José Manuel (1981). 'Fuente Ovejuna desde la segunda acción'. In Alberto Navarro González (ed.), *Actas del I Simposio de Literatura Española*. Salamanca: Universidad de Salamanca, pp. 173–92.
RSC (2004). 'Theatrical Programme for *The Dog in the Manger*'. London: RSC.

Ruano de la Haza, José María (1996). 'Tirso's stagecraft'. In Henry W. Sullivan and Raúl Galoppe (eds), *Tirso de Molina: His Originality Then and Now*. Ottawa: Dovehouse Editions, pp. 15–39.
Rubio Gil, Luis and Rafael Gil (eds) (1998). *Rafael Gil: director de cine*. Madrid: Ibercaja, Comunidad de Madrid, Ayuntamiento de Madrid, Universidad de Zaragoza.
Rubio Jiménez, Jesús (1995). 'José Luis Alonso, su presencia en los teatros nacionales'. In Andrés Peláez Martín (ed.), *Historia de los Teatros Nacionales (1960–1985)*. Madrid: CDT, pp. 10–85.
— and Patricia Almárcegui (1999). 'El teatro universitario en Zaragoza (1955–1965)'. In Jesús Rubio Jiménez (ed.), *Teatro universitario en Zaragoza (1939–1999)*. Zaragoza: Prensa Universitaria de Zaragoza, pp. 43–123.
Ruiz, N. de la (1971). 'Miscelanea teatral 1945–1960'. *Yorick*, 49–50: 18–24.
Ruiz Carnicer, Miguel (1996). *El sindicato español universitario (SEU) 1939–1965: la socialización política de la juventud universitaria en el franquismo*. Madrid: Siglo Veintiuno.
Ruiz-Fornells, Enrique (1963). 'El IV centenario del nacimiento de Lope de Vega en España'. *Hispania*, 46.3: 563–6.
Ruiz García, Enrique (1971). *25 años de teatro en España: José Tamayo director*. Barcelona: Planeta.
Ruiz Ramón, Francisco (1968). 'Introducción'. In Pedro Calderón de la Barca, *Tragedias (2): A secreto agravio, secreta venganza, El médico de su honra, El pintor de su deshonra*, ed. Francisco Ruiz Ramón. Madrid: Alianza Editorial, pp. 7–28.
— (1988). *Celebración y catarsis: leer al teatro español*. Murcia: Cuadernos de Teatro de la Universidad de Murcia.
— (1997). *Paradigmas del teatro clásico español*. Madrid: Cátedra.
Sáenz de la Calzada, Luis (1976). *'La Barraca': Teatro Universitario*. Madrid: Biblioteca de la Revista de Occidente.
Saffar, Ruth El (1989). 'Anxiety of identity: Gutierre's case in *El médico de su honra*'. In Dian Fox, Harry Sieber and Robert Ter Horst (eds), *Studies in Honor of Bruce W. Wardropper*. Newark: Juan de la Cuesta, pp. 105–24.
Sagarra, Joan de. (1993). 'Lope tebeo', review of *Fuente Ovejuna*. *El País*, Barcelona ed., 5 April: 32.
Salaverria, José María (1938). 'Movilización de sombras insignes'. *ABC de Sevilla*, 22 October: 11.
Salvador, Lola (2008). 'Un director nuevo para el más viejo teatro de Madrid'. In Ángel Facio (ed.), *Alberto González Vergel*. Madrid: Teatro Español, pp. 171–6.
Salvat, Ricard (1974). *El teatro de los años 70: diccionario de urgencia*. Barcelona: Península.
— (1984). *El teatro como texto, como espectáculo*. Barcelona: Montesinos.
— (1999). 'El problema de la creación de un repertorio en los teatros subvencionados españoles'. In Irene Pardo Molina, Luz Ruíz Martínez and Antonio Serrano (eds), *En torno al teatro del Siglo de Oro: Actas de las Jornadas XIV celebradas en Almería Marzo 1997*. Almería: Instituto de Estudios Almerienses and Diputación de Almería, pp. 103–21.
— and August Coll (2001). 'Entrevista a Alberto González Vergel'. *Assaig de Teatre*, 26–27: 275–86.
Sánchez, Alfonso (1972). '*Fuenteovejuna*', review. *Informaciones*, 30 November: 31.
— (1974). '*El mejor alcalde, el rey*', review *Informaciones*, 30 April: 37.
Sánchez, Robert G. (1957). 'La obra clásica y el escenario'. *Ínsula*, 123: 10.
Sánchez Díaz, Andrés (2000). *Prensa rosa, voto azul*. San Sebastian: Arakatzen.

Sánchez Jiménez, Antonio (2006). 'Entrevista a Eduardo Vasco'. *B. Com.*, 58.2: 501–9.
Sánchez Noriega, José Luis (1998). *Mario Camus*. Madrid: Cátedra.
Sánchez Vidal, Agustín (1991). *El cine de Florián Rey*. Zaragoza: Caja de Ahorros de la Inmaculada Aragón.
— (2003). 'Manuel Altolaguirre: de *Cartas a los muertos* a *El cantar de los cantares*'. *Litoral: revista de poesía, arte y pensamiento*, 235: 221–31.
Santa-Cruz, Lola (1991). 'Pensé que ya estaba fuera de circulación', interview with Cayetano Luca de Tena. *El público*, 84: 34–35.
— (1993). 'Cayetano Luca de Tena. Director del Teatro Español de 1942 a 1952'. In Andrés Peláez Martín (ed.), *Historia de los Teatros Nacionales (1939–1962)*. Madrid: CDT, pp. 69–79.
— (1995). 'Festivales de España: una mancha de color en la España gris'. In Andrés Peláez Martín (ed.), *Historia de los Teatros Nacionales (1960–1985)*. Madrid: CDT, pp. 189–208.
Santolaria Solano, Cristina (1998). 'José Luis Alonso de Santos y el teatro independiente: veinte años de vinculación (1960–1980)'. *ALEC*, 23.3: 791–810.
Santos, Jesús María (1973). 'Entrevista con Mario Camus, director cinematográfico'. *El adelanto*, 3 August: 12.
Santoveña Setién, Antonio (1994). *Menéndez Pelayo y las derechas en España*. Santander: Ayuntamiento de Santander y Ediciones de Librería Estudio.
Schauer, Frederick (1998). 'The ontology of censorship'. In Robert C. Post (ed.), *Censorship and Silencing: Practices of Cultural Regulation*. Los Angeles: The Getty Research Institute for the History of Art and the Humanities, pp. 147–68.
Schechner, Richard (2002). *Performance Studies: An Introduction*. Abingdon: Routledge.
Schneider, Jane (1971). 'Of vigilance and virgins: honor, shame and access to resources in Mediterranean societies'. *Ethnology*, 10.1: 1–24.
Schwartz, Kessel (1969). *The Meaning of Existence in Contemporary Hispanic Literature (Hispanic-American Studies, no. 23)*. Miami: University of Miami Press.
Seliger, H. W. (1984). '*Fuenteovejuna* en Alemania: de la traducción a la falsificacción'. *Revista canadiense de estudios hispánicos*, 8.3: 381–403.
Sen, Purna (2005). '"Crimes of honour", value and meaning'. In Lynn Welchman and Sara Hossain (eds), *Honour: Crimes, Paradigms and Violence Against Women*. London: Zed Books, pp. 42–63.
Serrano, Antonio (2003). 'La recepción escénica de los clásicos'. In Javier Huerta Calvo (ed.), *Historia del teatro español*, vol. I. Madrid: Gredos, pp. 1321–49.
— (2009). 'Ricard Salvat, en las jornadas de Almería'. *Assaig de Teatre*, 73–4: 104–7.
Shalhoub-Kevorkian, Nadera (2003). 'Re-examining femicide: breaking the silence and crossing "scientific" borders'. *Signs*, 28.2: 581–608.
Shepherd, Simon and Mick Wallis (2004). *Drama/Theatre/Performance*. London: Routledge.
Showalter, Elaine (2003). *Teaching Literature*. Oxford: Blackwell Publishers.
Sieber, Diane E. (2006). 'The digital *comedia*: teaching Golden Age theater with new and emerging technologies'. In Margaret R. Greer and Laura R. Bass (eds), *Approaches to Teaching Early-Modern Spanish Drama*. New York: MLA, pp. 206–13.
Simón, Adolfo (2003). 'Ricard Salvat: cinco décadas de memorial teatral', interview. *PA*, 301: 148–57.
Sinfield, Alan (1994). 'Royal Shakespeare: theatre and the making of ideology'. In Jonathan Dollimore and Alan Sinfield (eds), *Political Shakespeare: New Essays in Cultural Materialism*, 2nd ed. Manchester: Manchester University Press, pp. 182–205.

Singer, Armand E. (1993). *The Don Juan Theme: An Annotated Bibliography of Versions, Analogues, Uses and Adaptations.* Morgantown: West Virginia University Press.
SIPE (1946). 'El médico de su honra'. *Servicio informativo de publicaciones y espectáculos,* 211: 7.
Skrine, Peter N. (1978). *The Baroque: Literature and Culture in Seventeenth-Century Europe.* London: Methuen.
Smith, Alan E. (1993). 'Ritual y mito en *Fuenteovejuna* de Lope de Vega y los casos de la honra'. *Sociocriticism,* 9.2: 141–66.
Smith, Melanie K. (2003). *Issues in Cultural Tourism Studies.* London: Routledge.
Smith, Paul Julian (1988). *Writing in the Margin: Spanish Literature of the Golden Age.* Oxford: Clarendon Press.
— (1996). *Vision Machines: Cinema, Literature and Sexuality in Spain and Cuba (1983–1993).* London: Verso.
— (1998). *The Theatre of García Lorca: Text, Performance, Psychoanalysis.* Cambridge: Cambridge University Press.
— (1999). 'Towards a cultural studies of the Spanish state'. *Paragraph,* 22.1: 6–13.
— (2006). *Spanish Visual Culture: Cinema, Television, Internet.* Manchester: Manchester University Press.
Soria, Florentino (1974). '*El mejor alcalde, el rey*', review. *Arriba,* 6 May: 22.
Sorlin, Pierre (2001). 'How to look at an "historical film"'. In Marcia Landy (ed.), *The Historical Film: History and Memory in Media.* New Brunswick: Rutgers University Press, pp. 25–49.
Soufas, Teresa Scott (1981). 'Beyond justice and cruelty: Calderón's King Pedro'. *Journal of Hispanic Philology,* 6.1: 57–65.
— (1984). 'Calderón's melancholy wife-murderers'. *HR,* 52.2: 181–203.
— (1997). 'Writing wives out of Golden Age drama: gender ideology and Lope's *La dama boba*'. In José A. Madrigal (ed.), *New Historicism and the Comedia: Poetics, Politics and Praxis.* Boulder: Society of Spanish and Spanish-American Studies, pp. 129–48.
Spitzer, Leo (1955). 'A central theme and its structural equivalent in Lope's *Fuenteovejuna*'. *HR,* 23.4: 274–92.
Stacey, Jackie (1994). *Star Gazing: Hollywood Cinema and Female Spectatorship.* London: Routledge.
Stack, Oswald (1969). *Pasolini on Pasolini.* London: Thames and Hudson in association with the BFI.
Stainton, Leslie (1998). *Lorca: A Dream of Life.* London: Bloomsbury.
Stam, Robert (2005). 'Introduction: the theory and practice of adaptation'. In Robert Stam and Alessandra Raengo (eds), *Literature and Film: A Guide to the Theory and Practice of Film Adaptation.* Oxford: Blackwell Publishers, pp. 1–52.
Stewart, T. A. (1992). 'Spain outbound'. *EU Travel and Tourism Analyst,* 2: 53–71.
Stone, Rob (2002). *Spanish Cinema.* Harlow: Pearson Education Limited.
Strother, Darci L. (1999). *Family Matters: A Study of On- and Off-Stage Marriage and Family Relations in Seventeenth-Century Spain.* New York: Peter Lang.
Stroud, Matthew D. (1990). *Fatal Union: A Pluralistic Approach to the Spanish Wife-Murder Comedias.* Lewisburg: Bucknell University Press.
— (2006). 'Defining the *comedia*: on generalizations once widely accepted that are no longer accepted so widely'. *B.Com.,* 58.2: 285–305.
— (2008). 'The play of means and ends: justice in Lope's *Fuenteovejuna*'. *Neophilologus,* 92.2: 247–62.
Suárez Fernández, Luís (1993). *Crónica de la Sección Femenina y su tiempo.* Madrid: Asociación Nueva Andadura.

Suárez Miramón, Ana (2002). 'Las producciones televisivas de teatro clásico'. In José Romera Castillo (ed.), *Del teatro al cine y la televisión en la segunda mitad del siglo XX*. Madrid: Visor Libros, pp. 571–95.

Suelto de Sáenz, Pilar G. (1964). 'El teatro universitario español en los últimos treinta años'. *Thesaurus: boletín del Instituto Caro y Cuervo*, 19.3: 543–57.

Sullivan, Henry W. (1983). *Calderón in the German Lands and the Low Countries: His Reception and Influence, 1654–1980*. Cambridge: Cambridge University Press.

Swietlicki, Catherine (1992). 'Close cultural encounters: speech and writing in *Fuenteovejuna*'. *HR*, 60.1: 33–53.

Taibo I, Paco Ignacio (2000). *Un cine para un imperio*. Mexico: Lecturas Mexicanas.

Takahashi Nagasaki, Hiroyuki (2000). 'Una hipótesis sobre la escenificación de *Fuente Ovejuna*'. *La palabra y el hombre: revista de la Universidad Veracruzana*, 114: 37–47.

Tamayo, José (1953). 'El teatro español visto por un director'. *Teatro*, 5: 33–8.

Tamayo, Nuria (1998). 'El CAT muestra su grito contra el poder'. *Diario de Andalucía*, 30 December: 29.

Tamayo, Victoriano (1935). 'Información teatral. Ante el tricentenario de Lope'. *La voz*, 2 February: 3.

Taylor, Scott K. (2008). *Honor and Violence in Golden Age Spain*. New Haven: Yale University Press.

Teatro (1953). 'La Compañía Lope de Vega presenta en Roma *La cena del rey Baltasar* de Calderón de la Barca'. *Teatro*, 8: 27–32.

Teatro Español (1941). 'Theatrical Programme for *La dama duende*'. Madrid: Teatro Español.

— (1944). 'Theatrical Programme for *Fuente Ovejuna*'. Madrid: Teatro Español.

— (1971). 'Theatrical Programme for *La Estrella de Sevilla*'. Madrid: Teatro Español.

— (1973). 'Theatrical Programme for *Marta la piadosa*'. Madrid: Teatro Español.

Thacker, Jonathan (1999). 'Rethinking Golden-Age drama: the *comedia* and its contexts'. *Paragraph*, 22.1: 14–34.

— (2004). '"Puedo yo con sola la vista oír leyendo", reading, seeing and hearing the *comedia*'. *Comedia Performance*, 1.1: 143–73.

— (2007). *A Companion to Golden Age Theatre*. Woodbridge: Tamesis.

— (2008). 'Lope, the comedian'. In Alexander Samson, and Jonathan Thacker (eds), *A Companion to Lope de Vega*. Woodbridge: Tamesis, pp. 159–70.

Theatre Record (1995). '*The Painter of Dishonour*', selection of reviews. *Theatre Record*, 2–15 July: 920–3.

Thiem, Annegret (2009). 'Formas de la teatralidad en *El perro del hortelano* (1995) de Pilar Miró'. In Verena Berger and Mercè Saumell (eds), *Escenarios compartidos: cine y teatro en España en el umbral del siglo XXI*. Berlin: LitVerlag, pp. 49–60.

Thiher, Roberta J. (1970). 'The final ambiguity of *El médico de su honra*'. *Studies in Philology*, 67.2: 237–44.

Thompson, Michael (2007). *Performing Spanishness: History, Cultural Identity and Censorship in the Theatre of José María Rodríguez Méndez*. Bristol: Intellect Books.

Threlfall, Monica (1996). 'Feminist politics and social change in Spain'. In Monica Threlfall (ed.), *Mapping the Women's Movement: Feminist Politics and Social Transformation in the North*. London: Verso, pp. 115–51.

Torralba, Mariano (1982). '*La prudencia en la mujer*', review. *Diario 16*, 25 August: 21.

Torreiro, Casimiro (1995). 'Del tardo franquismo a la democracia (1969–1982)'. In Román Gubern (ed.), *Historia del cine español*, 2nd ed. Madrid: Cátedra, pp. 341–97.

Torreiro, M. (2006). 'A vueltas con el amor', review of *La dama boba*. *El País*, 24 March: 37.
Torrente (1956). '*Fuenteovejuna* de Lope en Fuente Obejuna', review. *Arriba*, 8 July: 29.
Torrente Ballester, Gonzalo (1941). *El casamiento engañoso*. Madrid: Ediciones Escorial.
Torres, Carmen (1991). 'José Estruch: el arte de vivir por caminos cortados'. *Canelobre*, 20–1: 209–18.
Torres, Isabel (2004). '"Pues no entiendo tus palabras,/y tus bofetones siento": linguistic subversion in Lope de Vega's *El perro del horetalano*'. *Hispanic Research Journal*, 5.3: 197–212.
Torres, Rosana (1996). 'Pérez Sierra y García Lorenzo sustituyen a Marsillach y De Miguel'. *El País*, 18 September: 44.
— (1999a). 'Amorós sustituye a Pérez Sierra en la Compañía Nacional de Teatro Clásico'. *El País*, 17 November: 51.
— (1999b). 'Grandes directores de escena denuncian injerencias políticas en los teatros públicos. Los últimos vetos a Jorge Lavelli y a José Carlos Plaza desatan las protestas del sector'. *El País*, 10 December: 51.
— (2005). 'El "Quijote" compite con Shakespeare en Almagro'. *El País*, 16 May: 47.
— (2006a). 'El Festival de Almagro se abre a toda creación'. *El País*, 23 June: 64.
— (2006b). 'El Festival de Almagro recuerda la estrecha relación entre el teatro y la II República'. *El País*, 3 July: 50.
— (2007). 'Lope y los menores de 30'. *El País*, 3 July: 43.
— (2008). 'Vuelve Calderón'. *El País*, 29 March.
Torres Monreal, Francisco (1974). 'El teatro español en Francia (1935–1973): análisis de la penetración y de sus mediaciones'. Unpublished dissertation, 2 vols. Universidad de Murcia.
Torres Nebrera, Gregorio (2004). 'La revista *Teatro*: una crónica del teatro español de los años cincuenta'. *ALEC*, 19.3: 383–440.
Trancón, Santiago (1990). 'Con Pepe Estruch: El teatro es un arte colectivo'. *PA*, 233: 121–8.
Triana-Toribio, Nuria (1998). 'In memoriam: Pilar Miró (1940–1997)'. *Film History*, 10.2: 231–40.
— (2003). *Spanish National Cinema*. London: Routledge.
Trías, Carlos (1968). 'Lope de Vega y Cervantes: el teatro oficial frente al loco marginado'. *Yorick*, 29: 12–16.
Umbral, Francisco (1982). *Spleen de Madrid/2*. Barcelona: Ediciones Destino.
Unamuno, Miguel de (1964). *En torno al casticismo*. Madrid: Espasa Calpe.
Urzáiz Tortajada, Héctor (2006). '*Fuente Ovejuna* CAT, 1999'. In Javier Huerta Calvo (ed.), *Clásicos entre siglos*. Madrid: CNTC, pp. 243–47.
Utrera Macías, Rafael (2002). 'El teatro clásico español transformado en género cinematográfico popular: dos ejemplos'. In José Romera Castillo (ed.), *Del teatro al cine y la televisión en la segunda mitad del siglo XX*. Madrid: Visor Libros, pp. 71–89.
Valbuena Prat, Ángel (1941). *Calderón: su personalidad, su arte dramático, su estilo y sus obras*. Barcelona: Editorial Juventud.
— (1956). *Historia del teatro español*. Madrid: Editorial Noguer.
Valls, Fernando (1983). *La enseñanza de la literatura en el franquismo (1936–1951)*. Madrid: Antonio Bosch.
Valverde, Fernando (2006). 'Un maestro del teatro'. *El País*, 8 February: 11.

Van Watson, William (1989). *Pier Paolo Pasolini and the Theatre of the World*. Ann Arbor: UMI Research Press.
Vara, Javi (2006). '*La dama boba*', review. *Cinemania*, April: 119.
Varey, J. E. (1976). *La inversión de valores en 'Fuenteovejuna'*. Santander: Universidad Internacional Menéndez Pelayo.
— (1990). 'La edición de textos dramáticos del Siglo de Oro'. In Dolores Noguera Guirao, Pablo Jauralde Pou and Alfonso Reyes (eds), *La edición de textos: Actas del I Congreso Internacional de Hispanistas del Siglo de Oro*. London: Tamesis, pp. 99–109.
Vargas Llosa, Mario (2007). 'El viaje de Odisea'. *Letras libres*, 66: 32–9.
Vasco, Eduardo, 2006. 'José Estruch'. *Boletín de la CNTC*, 50: unpaginated.
Vega Carpio, Lope de. (1860). 'Prólogo dialogístico a la parte XVI'. In *Comedias escogidas de Frey Lope Félix de Vega Carpio (Vol IV)*, ed. Don Juan Eugenio Hartzenbusch. Biblioteca de Autores Españoles, pp. xxv–xxvi.
— (2001). *Fuente Ovejuna*, ed. Juan María Marín. Madrid: Cátedra.
— (2006). *La dama boba*, ed. Alonso Zamora Vicente. Madrid: Espasa-Calpe.
Vega García-Luengos, German, Don W. Cruickshank and J. M. Ruano de la Haza (2000). 'Introducción'. In Calderón de la Barca, *La segunda version de La vida es sueño*, ed. German Vega García-Luengos, Don W. Cruickshank and J. M. Ruano de la Haza. Liverpool: Liverpool University Press, pp. 37–232.
Vernon, Kathleen M. (1999). 'Culture and cinema to 1975'. In David T. Gies (ed.), *The Cambridge Companion to Modern Spanish Culture*. Cambridge: Cambridge University Press, pp. 248–66.
Vicente Hernando, César de (1999). 'José Estruch: un camino para los "clásicos" durante el destierro'. In Manuel Aznar Soler (ed.), *El exilio teatral republicano de 1939*. Barcelona: Gexel, pp. 181–8.
Vieites, Manuel F. (2009). 'Varapolo a las enseñanzas teatrales'. *ADE*, 127: 7–8.
Vila San-Juan, Press. (1956). *Memorias de Enrique Borrás*. Barcelona: Editorial AHR.
Vilches de Frutos, María Francisca (1999). 'Teatro histórico: la elección del género como clave de la escena española contemporánea'. In José Romera Castillo and Francisco Gutiérrez Carbayo (eds), *Teatro histórico (1975–1998)*. Madrid: Visor Libros, pp. 73–92.
— (2008). 'La temporada teatral española (1986–1987)'. *ALEC*, 13.3: 331–69.
Villán, Javier (2004). 'Royal Shakespeare Company: fascinante y ejemplar', review of *The Dog in the Manger*. *El Mundo*, 29 October: 56.
— (2006). 'Amor a bofetadas', obituary of Glenn Ford. *El Mundo*, 2 August: 11.
Villegas Ruiz, Manuel (1990). *Fuenteovejuna: el drama y la historia*. Córdoba: Adisur.
Villena, Miguel Ángel (2002). *Ana Belén, biografía de un mito: retrato de una generación*. Barcelona: Random House.
— (2008a). 'Calderón o la mujer como víctima'. *El País*, Andalucía ed., 19 February: 44.
— (2008b). 'Después de un rato, ya te enrollas'. *El País*, 4 July: 9.
Víllora, Pedro (2009). 'Con Lope de Vega a capa y espada'. *Acotaciones: investigación y creación teatral*, 23: 146–50.
Vincendeau, Ginette (ed.) (1995). *Encyclopedia of European Cinema*. London: Cassell, BFI.
Vitse, Marc (2007). 'Del canon calderoniano: el singular caso de *El médico de su honra* o prolegómenos para la historia de una catonización'. In Enrique García Santo-Tomás (ed.), *El teatro del Siglo de Oro ante los espacios de la crítica: encuentros y revisiones*. Frankfurt and Madrid: Iberoamericana and Vervuert, pp. 307–34.
Vossler, Karl (1940). *Lope de Vega y su tiempo*. Madrid: Revista de Occidente.

Wahnón, Sultana (1996). 'The theatre aesthetics of the Falange', trans. R. I. MacCandless. In Günter Berghaus (ed.), *Fascism and Theatre: Comparative Studies on the Aesthetics and Politics of Performance in Europe (1925–1945)*. Providence: Berghahn Books, pp. 191–209.
Wardropper, Bruce W. (1956). '*Fuente Ovejuna*: el gusto and lo justo'. *Studies in Philology*, 53: 159–71.
— (1978). 'La comedia española del Siglo de Oro'. Appendix to Elder Olson, *Teoría de la comedia*. Barcelona: Ariel, pp. 181–242.
— (1981). 'The wife-murder plays in retrospect'. *Revista canadiense de estudios hispánicos*, 5.3: 385–95.
— (1982). 'The standing of Calderón in the twentieth century'. In Michael D. McGaha (ed.), *Approaches to the Theater of Calderón*. Washington: University Press of America, pp. 1–16.
Watson, A. Irvine (1963). '*El pintor de su deshonra* and the neo-Aristotelian theory of tragedy'. *BHS*, 40.1: 17–34.
Weimer, Christopher B. (1996). 'Desire, crisis and violence in *Fuenteovejuna*: a Girardian perspective'. In Barbara Simerka (ed.), *El arte nuevo de estudiar comedias: Literary Theory and Golden Age Drama*. Cranbury: Bucknell and Associated UPs, pp. 162–86.
— (2000a). 'El arte de la refundición y (de) la protesta política: la comedia española en el Chile de Pinochet'. In Bárbara Mújica and Anita K. Stoll (eds), *El texto puesto en escena: estudios sobre la comedia del Siglo de Oro en honor a Everett W. Hesse*. Woodbridge: Tamesis, pp. 193–204.
— (2000b). 'The politics of adaptation: *Fuenteovejuna* in Pinochet's Chile'. In Barbara Simerka and Christopher B. Weimer (eds), *Echoes and Inscriptions: Comparative Approaches to Early Modern Spanish Literatures*. Lewisburg: Bucknell University Press, pp. 234–49.
Weiner, Jack (1982). 'Lope de Vega's *Fuenteovejuna* under the tsars, commisars and the second Spanish Republic (1931–39)'. *Annali Istituto Universitario Orientale Sezióne Romanza*, 24.1: 167–223.
Welles, Marcia L (2000). *Persephone's Girdle: Narratives of Rape in Seventeenth-Century Spanish Literature*. Nashville: Vanderbilt University Press.
Wheeler, Duncan (2006). '*Don Quixote rides again*', review. *Comedia Performance*, 3.1: 217–22.
— (2007). '*We are living in a material world and I am a material girl*: Diana, Countess of Belflor materialised on the page, stage and screen'. *BHS*, 84.3: 267–86.
— (2008a). 'The performance history of Golden-Age drama in Spain (1939–2006)'. *B.Com*, 60.2: 119–55.
— (2008b). 'Intimate partner abuse in Spain (1975–2006)'. *Cuestiones de género*, 3: 173–204.
— (2009). 'La presencia del teatro español en la cartelera inglesa durante el siglo XXI'. *Contraviento*, 8: 18–21.
— (2010). 'All about Almodóvar? *All About My Mother* on the London stage'. *BHS*, 87.7: 821–41.
— (2011a). '¿*La película duende?*; María Teresa León, Rafael Alberti and alternative traditions of resurrecting Golden Age drama'. In Helena Buffery (ed.), *Stages of Exile*. Bern: Peter Lang, pp. 71–93.
— (2011b). 'From the town with more theaters than taxis: Calderón, Lope and Tirso at the 2008 Almagro Festival (part one)'. *Comedia Performance*, 8.1: 151–200.

— (2011c). 'Beyond the black legend of Calderón's wife-murder plays: amorous strife, violence and the *comedia*'. In Aaron Kahn (ed.), *On Wolves and Sheep: Exploring the Expression of Political Thought in Golden Age Spain*. Newcastle: Cambridge Scholars Publishing, pp. 113–46.

— (2012a). 'Contextualising and contesting José Antonio Maravall's theories of baroque culture from the perspective of modern-day performance', *B.Com.*, 64.1: in press.

— (2012b). 'From the town with more theaters than taxis: Calderón, Lope and Tirso at the 2008 Almagro Festival (part two)'. *Comedia Performance*, 9.1: in press.

— (2012c). 'The representation of domestic violence in Spanish cinema'. *Modern Language Review*, 107.2: 454–515.

Willem, Linda M. (2003). *Carlos Saura Interviews*. Jackson: University of Mississipi Press.

Williams, Raymond (2002). 'Argument: text and performance'. In Michael Huxley and Noel Witts (eds), *The Twentieth-Century Performance Reader*, 2nd ed. London: Routledge, pp. 407–19.

Wischnewski, Klaus (1956). 'Verfilmte klassik und mangelnde voraussetzungen', review of *Der Richter von Zalamea*. *Deutsche Film Kunst*, 168: 72.

Worley Jr, Robert D. (2003). 'La inversión de funciones en *Fuente Ovejuna*'. In Aurelio González *et al.* (eds), *Estudios del teatro áureo: texto, espacio y representación*. Mexico: Universidad Autónoma Metropolitana y Aiteuso, pp. 199–209.

Worthen, W. B. (2004). 'Disciplines of the text'. In Henry Bial (ed.), *The Performance Studies Reader*. New York: Routledge, pp. 10–25.

— (2010). *Drama: Between Poetry and Performance*. Chichester: Wiley-Blackwell.

Wright, Sarah (2005). 'Dropping the mask: theatricality and absorption in Sáenz de Heredia's *Don Juan*'. *Screen*, 46.4: 415–31.

— (2007). *Tales of Seduction: The Figure of Don Juan in Spanish Culture*. London: Tauris Academic Studies.

Ya (1939). 'Teatro Nacional'. *Ya*, 21 July: 3.

Yarza, Alejandro (2004). 'The petrified tears of General Franco: kitsch and fascism in José Luis Sáenz de Heredia's *Raza*'. *Journal of Spanish Cultural Studies*, 5.1: 49–66.

Yorick (1965). 'Tras el triunfo del T.N.Universidad en Nancy'. *Yorick*, 5–6: 26–7.

Zamora Vicente, Alonso (2006). 'Introducción' in Lope de Vega, *La dama boba*, ed. Alonso Zamora Vicente. Madrid: Espasa-Calpe, pp. 9–37.

Zapatero Vicente, Antonio (1999). 'Teatro herido'. In Jesús Rubio Jiménez (ed.), *Teatro universitario en Zaragoza (1939–1999)*. Zaragoza: Prensa Universitaria de Zaragoza, pp. 197–214

Zatlin, Phylis (2005). *Theatrical Translation and Film Adapatation: A Practitioner's View*. Clevedon, Multilingual Matters.

Zeta, León (1966). 'Teatro en T.V.'. *Yorick*, 13: 19.

Index

2Rc Producciones 205–6

A secreto agravio, secreta venganza 106–7, 129
Abascal, Silvia 179 n. 74, 180, 182–3, 185
Abre el ojo 48 n. 60
Absalón 51
El acero de Madrid 27, 34–5, 58, 128 n. 29
Achiperre Coop. Teatro 99
actors and acting
    stardom and celebrity 28, 33, 139 n. 7, 141–3, 146–7, 149, 151, 171–2, 179 n. 73 182–6
    training and theatre schools 31, 112–13, 116–17, 120–1, 180, 194–7, 199
    verse declamation 30–1, 38, 51, 53, 62, 89, 99–100, 103, 112, 115, 117–19, 126, 130, 132, 149–51, 159, 169, 171, 185, 193, 196–7, 201–3
    see also specific actors by name
adaptation *see* textual fidelity, and film adaptation
Aguilera, Paco 93
Aguirre, Esperanza 63
Aguirresarobe, Javier 171
Alarcón, Juan Ruiz de 37, 171, 205
Alatriste 178, 186–7
Alberti, Rafael 17, 20 n. 7, 21, 47, 79 n. 3.
El alcalde de Zalamea 19, 22, 26–7, 29 n. 28, 48, 57–8, 65–6, 102, 114 n. 14, 136, 146, 148–52, 158–64, 166, 188, 198–200, 209
Almagro,
    Centro para la Interpretación de los Clásicos 70
    and cultural tourism 59, 190, 207–15
    Festival de Teatro Clásico 4, 14, 48, 51, 59, 61–2, 67–8, 70, 72, 190, 205, 207–15, 218
    Jornadas 4, 46, 48, 207
    Museo de teatro 4
    Town 30, 41, 207, 211–12
Almeria, *Jornadas* 4, 113
Almodóvar, Pedro 207, 211 n. 27
Alonso, José Luis 32–3, 37, 41, 48, 57–8, 64, 116
Alonso, Roberto 117
Alonso de Santos, José Luis 65–6, 68, 120
Amar después de la muerte 68, 70 n. 112, 94, 123
Amestoy, Ainhoa 72
Amestoy, Ignacio 191, 205
Amorós, Andrés 65, 122, 124, 198
Anderson, Benedict 83
Antes que todo es mi dama 57, 116
El anzuelo de Fenisa 32 n. 34, 33, 64, 174
Arano, Iñaki 73
Archivo General de la Administración (Alcalá de Henares) 26 n. 21
Ardor con ardor se apaga 52
Ardovia, Eusebio F. 152
Arévalo, Carlos 138, 151

El arrogante español 70
Arte nuevo de hacer comedias 72
Asalto a una ciudad 61
El astrólogo fingido 40
Aub, Max 152
audiences
  composition of 1, 14, 26, 29, 35, 37–8, 54–6, 65, 67, 70, 73, 87–88, 90, 140–1, 208–9, 212
  models of spectatorship 6, 12, 30, 56, 87–8, 96–8, 103, 140–3, 202–3, 213
  ticket prices 29, 38, 70, 141, 214
  see also reception theory
autonomous regions 14, 61, 72, 89, 189, 197–8, 204–7, 216–17
  see also Catalonia
autos sacramentales 18–20, 22, 24, 30, 49–50, 52 n. 72, 58–9, 61, 65, 106, 109, 207
Aventura 137–8
Avignon Festival *see* French theatre
Aznar, José María 170
Azorín (José Martínez Ruiz) 108, 164

Bajarse al moro 65
Los balcones de Madrid 70–1, 113
Ballesteros, Carlos 49 n. 65, 114
Ballesteros, María Paz 92
Barbican *see* British theatre
Bardem, Javier 176
Bardem, Juan Antonio 146, 148
La Barraca 17 n. 1, 19, 21, 52, 79–81, 86, 90, 101, 103, 112–13, 138, 152 n. 30
Bate, Jonathan 14, 75–6, 103–4
Bautista, Aurora 48, 88
Belbel, Sergi 66, 198, 200, 204
Belén, Ana 49
La bella aurora 62
La bella malmaridada 34–5
Benavente, Jacinto 27
Bermúdez, Rafael 92
Bermúdez de Castro, Major General Luis 138
Biblioteca Nacional 26, 73, 88 n. 23
La Bicicleta 65

Bieito, Calixto 63, 66, 123, 200–3, 207, 216
Las bizarrías de Belisa 58, 69
Blume, Ricardo 31–2
Bollaín, Iciar 175
Bonnín, Hermann 3 n. 3
Borrás, Enrique (Enric Borràs) 21, 27, 80–1, 152, 198–9, 204
Boswell, Laurence 102–3, 129, 190–1, 194–7
Botella, Ana 170
Bourdieu, Pierre 209
Brecht, Bertolt 38, 42, 99, 131, 203
British theatre,
  Barbican 200
  Cheek By Jowl 212
  Edinburgh Festival 200, 201 n. 22, 208, 213
  image in Spain 30, 39, 67, 118, 189, 191–2, 205
  performance and reception of Golden Age drama 67, 76, 107, 111, 189, 190–7, 200–1
  RSC 5, 14, 67, 102, 129, 133, 189–97, 205–6, 211 n. 27, 216
  Theatre Workshop 81 n. 7
Brook, Peter 54, 79
Buch, René 107
Bueno, Ana María 93
Buñuel, Luís 160
Burgos 139, 202
Burgos, Emilio 20
El burlador de Sevilla 32, 42, 66–7, 70 n. 112, 145, 152, 176 n. 66, 214–15,
Burmann, Sigfrido 20, 85–7, 154

Caballero, Ernesto 122
Caballero, José 19, 20, 91
El caballero de milagro 34, 25 n. 18, 53, 99
El caballero de Olmedo 41, 58, 66, 70 n. 112, 112, 117, 171, 174, 199, 216
Calderón 72
Calderón de la Barca, Pedro
  biographical depictions 65

fourth centenary of birth (2000) 61,
    64–6, 119
third centenary of death (1981)
    48–9, 65
Calderón enamorado 65
Calvo, Rafael 27, 152
Calvo, Ricardo 21
Campany, Jaime 43–4
Campany, Maria Aurèlia 199
Campos, José Antonio 119–20
Camus, Mario 90, 158, 160–4, 188
Canseco, Manuel 48, 73, 111, 117
Caprile, Lorenzo 69, 121, 181–2, 185 n. 77
Caride, José 53
Carmona, Ángel 90
Carrillo, Mary 28
Casa con dos puertas mala es de guardar 48, 73, 101 n. 42
El casamiento engañoso 18
Casanova, Vicente 139
Castelvines y Monteses 38, 70, 151 n. 26
El castigo sin venganza 29, 38, 50, 69, 100, 123–4, 128, 174–5, 211
Castile, equation of Spain with 26, 83, 89, 141
Castilla, Alberto 40–1, 90
Castillo, Pilar del 67
Castro, Juan Antonio 48
Catalonia
    during Franco dictatorship 90, 198–99
    international relations 198–201, 207, 216
    language and theatre 21, 90, 198–201, 203–4, 216
    post-1975 199–200, 203–4, 216
    relationship with Madrid 21, 66, 100–1, 190, 198–200, 203–4
    Teatro Nacional de Barcelona 41, 199
    Teatre Nacional de Catalunya 66, 99, 198–200, 203–4
Catholic Church 18, 24, 30 n. 29, 50–1, 83, 101, 108, 138, 140, 142, 153, 163

Catholic Monarchs *see* Ferdinand and Isabella
Céfiro agreste de olímpicos embates 50–1, 61, 109
La Celestina 105, 170, 201 n. 22
La cena del rey Baltasar 19, 28, 30, 48, 113 n. 12
censorship 20, 26, 32, 35, 45, 87, 89 n. 24, 108, 136–7, 139, 147, 149, 151–4, 158–9, 165, 216
Centro Andaluz de Teatro 93–8, 103
Centro de Documentación Teatral 26 n. 22, 50 n. 68, 53 n. 75, 60 n. 85, 85
Centro Dramático Nacional 48–49, 52
Centro Nacional de Nuevas Tendencias Escénicas 52, 72
Cerezo, Enrique 169–70
Cervantes, Miguel de 17–18, 22, 35, 39, 70, 80–1, 90, 143, 190, 219
Chapalo films 144
Charles V, King 17–18, 45
Cheek By Jowl *see* British theatre
Christie, Agatha 108
CIFESA 139, 144, 148–9, 151–2, 168 n. 51
Cinema
    attendance and cinema-going habits in Spain 14, 140–1, 143, 146, 156, 168, 170, 173, 177, 185–6
    international festivals and distribution 137–9, 141, 143–5, 147, 156, 166, 170, 173, 187–8
    co-productions 138, 160, 164, 166, 187–8
    comparisons with the *comedia* 14, 72, 135
    intertextual references to the *comedia* 135, 137–8, 160, 167, 171, 174–6, 186
    see also film adaptations, and television
La cisma de Inglaterra 48
Ciudad de la Luz 178
Civil War *see* Spanish Civil War
Colomé, Héctor 118
Columbus, Christopher 146, 168

Coma, Roger 203
Comédie Française *see* French theatre
Los comendadores de Córdoba 123 n. 125
Compañía Nacional de Teatro Clásico
    4, 13–14, 49–50, 54–70, 73–4,
    92–3, 100, 105–34, 168, 170–1,
    174, 181, 183, 185, 189, 193,
    196–8, 200–7, 218
Compañía Noviembre 62, 68, 120, 133
Compañía Rakatá 102–3, 196–7
Compañía del Siglo de Oro de la
    Comunidad de Madrid 72
Con quien vengo, vengo 62
El condenado por desconfiado 22, 38, 145,
    152
Constantin, David 136
Convergència i Unió 199
Coronado, José 179–80, 183–4
Cortezo, Víctor 20
costume and wardrobe 20, 32, 69, 127,
    146, 169, 171–2, 181–2, 184–5
critics
    role and function 26, 41, 132
    in Spain 25–6, 29–30, 39, 48, 67, 81,
        114–16, 132–3, 140, 163–4, 175,
        187, 190–3, 195, 209
Cruz, Penélope 170
Cruz, Ramón de la 68
Cruz, Sor Juana Inés de la 190
Cuesta, Vicente 115
Cueva, Juan de la 62
La cueva de Salamanca 22
Cytrynowksi, Carlos 54–5, 92

La dama de Alejandría 48
La dama boba 22, 29, 31, 48, 136,
    176–88, 210, 211 n. 27
La dama duende 21, 24–5, 27, 29, 65–6,
    136, 152, 158, 175
La dama del Olivar 40
Dar tiempo al tiempo 68
Daumas, Adrián 211–12
¿De cuándo acá nos vino? 68–9,
    205–6
Desde Toledo a Madrid 70 n. 112
El desdén con el desdén 174–5
La desdichada Estefanía 219

El despertar a quien duerme 47
destape 45, 167
La devoción de la cruz 145, 160
Díaz-Plaja, Guillem 23
Dicenta, Manuel 88
Dido Teatro 32, 40, 112
Díez Borque, José María 10–13, 66,
    108 n. 5, 217, 219
direction and directing 20, 24–5, 28–9,
    63, 96 n. 35, 102–3, 139 n. 7,
    173, 175, 194, 196–7, 200–1
    see also specific directors by name
La discreta enamorada 21, 27, 29–30, 33,
    87 n. 19, 147, 176
domestic violence 121–4, 129–32, 219
Don Gil de las calzas verdes 22, 27, 30,
    34, 57, 61, 70 n. 112, 157
Don Juan (character), 42, 52, 144–6,
    176, 18
    see also El burlador de Sevilla and *Don
        Juan Tenorio*
Don Juan Tenorio 42, 135, 144–6, 176,
    180
Don Quijote 70, 135, 178, 187, 143 n.
    12, 211 n. 27
dramatic closure 52, 86, 90, 92, 96–9,
    110, 130–2, 151, 164
Drove, Antonio 160–4
Duato, Ana 171, 174

Edinburgh Festival
    see British theatre
education
    Spanish universities and academics
        3–5, 34, 49, 55, 65, 106, 199
    Golden Age drama and pedagogy
        8–9, 22–3, 34, 69–70, 81, 83,
        106, 129, 168–9, 217
    productions by and/or for children
        and adolescents 22, 34, 65,
        88–9, 99, 113
Elías, Francisco 138
Ello dirá 219
Los embustes de Celauro 219
Los encantos de la culpa 22
entremés 17, 20, 39, 58, 80, 90
Escobar, Luis 19–20

Escola d'Art Dramàtic Adrià Güal 199
El Escorial 48, 72, 168, 202
Escrivá, Javier 154–5
Escuela de Teatro Clásico 57, 62, 117
Espert, Núria 84, 176
La Estrella de Sevilla 43, 128 n. 29, 153–4
Estruch, José (Pepe) 46–7, 70, 111–13, 120
European integration and normalisation 31, 49–50, 109, 122–23, 167, 208, 212, 214–15
Exile
  see Spanish Civil War, and Spanish American theatre

Facio, Ángel 52
Fainlight, Ruth 81 n. 7
Falange; *see* fascism
Farsa del triunfo del Sacramental 52 n. 72
fascism,
  and aesthetics 83, 85, 136–8, 202–3
    see also Germany.
  as an ideology 82–3, 85, 136–7, 202–3
  in Spain 22 n. 16, 36 n. 43, 81–5, 136–8, 153, 202–3
    see also Germany
Fassbinder, Rainer Werner 92
Ferdinand and Isabella 78–9, 83–4, 86, 88, 90–4, 96, 99–100, 103, 139, 140–2, 159, 168 n. 50
Las ferias de Madrid 123 n. 125
Fernán-Gómez, Fernando 48, 160, 162, 178
Fernández Montesinos, Ángel 32, 213
Festival de teatro clásico de Olmedo 72
Festivales de España 29, 35, 47, 208
La fianza satisfecha 39
La fiera, el rayo y la piedra 48 n. 60
Fiesta barroca 58–9, 171
Figora, Father Antonio 138
Film adaptations
  El alcalde de Zalamea 136, 146, 148–52, 158–64, 188
  La Celestina 170

cine histórico (in relation to) 137, 139, 140, 143, 146, 150–1, 166, 178, 186–7
La dama boba 136, 176–88, 210
La dama duende 136, 152, 175
El desdén con el desdén 174–5
Don Juan 135, 144–6, 152, 180, 183, 185
La Estrella de Sevilla 153–4
Fuente Ovejuna 138–43, 158–9
genre (in relation to) 137–9, 146, 154, 160–63, 171, 174, 177, 183
El mejor alcalde, el rey 164–66
La moza de cántaro 136, 146–8
never completed 72 n. 114, 138, 151–4, 174–5
El perro del hortelano 62, 64, 168–75, 188, 190, 194 n. 9, 198 n. 17
Shakespeare 65, 165, 168, 173, 179, 188, 238 n. 26
Spanish literary adaptations (in relation to) 135, 139, 160–1, 164–70
theory of 159–60, 180–81, 186
La vida es sueño 152, 154–7, 187–8
La viuda valenciana 155
see also cinema, and television
Flotats, Josep Maria 199–200, 204
Fórmica, Mercedes 22
Forqué, Verónica 179–81
Fraga, Manuel 38, 123, 157–8, 199
Franco, Francisco 1, 3, 17–20, 22, 45, 82, 90, 138, 144, 149, 152–3, 208
French theatre
  Avignon Festival 208
  Comédie Française 30, 54, 205
  Nancy Theatre Festival 41, 90
  performance and reception of Golden Age drama 41, 90, 107, 164, 173, 190 n. 4, 216
Fuente Ovejuna (town) 35, 77, 88–9, 95, 209–10, 214
Fuente Ovejuna 14, 17, 23, 26–7, 35–6, 38, 40–1, 57–8, 70, 75–104, 209–10, 214
La fuerza lastimosa 62, 123

Gades, Antonio 98 n. 39
Gala, Antonio 47, 200
Galán, Carmen 101
Galán, Eduardo 63
El galán fantasma 48, 65
García Berlanga, Luis 146, 148, 210
García Escudero, José María 113 n. 12, 146, 153
García Espina, Gabriel 153–4
García Lorca, Federico 19, 21, 36, 60–1, 79, 80–1, 90, 99, 112–13, 133 n. 34, 176, 216, 219
García Lorenzo, Luciano 63, 210, 212
García Valdés, Ariel 64, 201
Garcilaso de la Vega 17–18
Garrido, José Manuel 53
Gas, Mario 191
Gascón, Ricardo 152
Generalitat de València 72, 138, 206
Genovés, Vicente 206
German theatre
  Nazism and the *comedia* 22, 85, 146
  performance and reception of Golden Age drama 22, 29, 72, 85, 92, 152, 212
Gil, Edmundo 177–8
Giménez Caballero, Ernesto 84–7
Gómez, Carmelo 117, 170–1, 174
Gómez, José Luis 48–9
Gómez, Macarena 185 n. 77
Góngora, Luis de 35, 181
González, Césareo 152
González, Manuel 19, 81
González Ruiz, Nicolás 26, 88
González Vergel, Alberto 41–4, 62, 66 n. 102, 113–14, 177
El gran mercado del mundo 179
El gran teatro del mundo 21–2, 49, 61, 158, 167
Grau, Jorge 42
Grotowski, Jerzy 112
Grupo de Teatro 'Lope de Vega' 28–9, 31, 35, 45, 88
Los guanches de Tenerife y conquista de Canarias 35
Guerrero Zamora, Juan 157–60
Gutiérrez, Ángel 70–1, 113

Hall, Peter 5
Haro Tecglen, Eduardo 58, 114–15, 132, 218
Herans, Carlos 99
Heras, Guillermo 72
Hermida, Alicia 112–13, 171, 174, 180, 202
Hernández, Emilio 70, 72, 93–8, 101, 103, 193–4, 196, 211–12, 215
La hidalga del valle 207
Higueras, Modesto 21, 53, 84
La hija del aire 49, 64, 68
El hijo pródigo 33
Hipólito, Carlos 118
honour code(s) 55, 58, 62, 87, 90, 106–10, 119–32, 142, 147, 149, 162–3, 193, 219
El honroso atrevimiento 219
Hormigón, Juan Antonio 40, 51–2
El hospital de los locos 19, 113 n. 12

Iborra, Manuel 136, 176–88
INAEM 57, 63, 65, 116, 119–20, 204
Institut del Teatre 3 n. 3, 23
Instituto de Investigaciones y Experiencias Cinematográficas 148
Instituto del Teatro 3 n. 3
Italy 19, 29–30, 41, 69, 144–5, 147, 164, 166, 173, 208

El jardín de Falerina 117
Jato, David 87
Jerónima de Burgos 182
Johnson, Rebecca 195
Johnston, David 193–6
El José de las mujeres 48
Joven Compañía Nacional de Teatro Clásico 69–70, 121

Khilly, Bishara 93
kingship 78–9, 83–4, 86–88, 90, 93, 100, 110–11, 115, 118, 140–1, 147–8, 151, 203, 217

Landa, Alfredo 34
Lavelli, Jorge 64, 68

Law of Historical Memory 98
Layton, William 61, 112, 118, 176
León, Paco 186
La leyenda del alcalde de Zalamea
  see film adaptation, El alcalde de Zalamea
El lindo don Diego 35
Littlewood, Joan 81 n. 7
Llosa, Vicente 158
Lluch, Felipe 20, 24, 26 n. 20
Los locos de Valencia 32, 36, 38, 54, 57, 113 n. 11
Lope 175
Lope de Vega a capa y espada 73
Losada, Jaime 112–13
Luca de Tena, Cayetano 24–6, 30 n. 32, 34–5, 37, 42, 47, 85–7, 90, 103, 138
Lucia, Luis 154–7
Luna, Manuel 149, 151

Machado, Antonio and Manuel 42, 192
Madrid
  centralism 14, 21, 29, 49 n. 65, 60–1, 68, 100–1, 140, 190, 197–9, 204–7, 216
  City of Culture 58–9, 92
  Festival de Otoño 58, 92, 190
  town council 48, 73, 114, 191, 206
  Veranos de la villa 73
  see also Castile, equation of Spain with
El maestro de danzar 113
El mágico prodigioso 49 n. 65, 64, 70 n. 112
La malcasada 34, 62
Mañanas de abril y mayo 65
Las manos blancas no ofenden 68, 133, 213
Maravall, José Antonio 10–13, 140, 217–18
Marcos, Tomás 42, 63
Marqueríe, Alfredo 26, 132, 137–8
Marsillach, Adolfo 4, 32, 36, 38, 41, 48, 53–9, 63–4, 76, 94, 99 n. 41, 105–7, 110–11, 113–21, 125, 128, 130, 132–3, 171, 193, 196–8
Marta la piadosa 43–5, 55, 113
Martín, Agustín 214
Martín Gaite, Carmen 33 n. 35, 116
Marxism 25, 40, 78, 81, 83, 99
Mayo, Alfredo 149, 168 n. 50
El mayor hechizo, amor 61
Mayorga, Juan 204
El médico de su honra 9, 14, 54–5, 57, 105–8, 110–11, 114, 116–9, 121–2, 123 n. 25, 125, 128 n. 29, 129, 132–33
El mejor alcalde, el rey 35, 92 n. 29, 164–6
Mejor está que estaba 49 n. 65
El mejor mozo de España 35
Mémoire des apparences 135
Mencía, Nuria 126
Menéndez Pidal, Ramón 135
Menéndez y Pelayo, Marcelino 25, 78, 80, 82, 107, 153
Menos es más 174–5
Merino, Pepe 126
Micomicón 62
Millson, Joseph 195
Ministry of Culture (and Welfare) 45, 48–50, 63–4, 67, 169, 208
Ministry of Information and Tourism 27, 34, 38, 45
Ministry of Interior 18
Ministry of National Education 20, 23, 27, 144, 207
Ministry of Propaganda 20
Mira, Magüi 186, 192–3, 215
Miralles, Alberto 50–1, 109
Miró, Pilar 62, 64, 116, 161, 167–75, 177–9, 186, 188, 190, 194 n. 9, 198 n. 17
Misiones Pedagógicas 21, 76 n. 1
Molière 6, 59–61, 105, 133 n. 34, 216
Molina, Josefina 116, 158
El monstruo de los jardines 65
Morales, José Ricardo 52
Moreno, Pedro 64, 121, 171
Moreto, Agustín 29–30, 35, 174–5
La moza de cántaro 136, 146–8

La mujer por fuerza 21
Mumby, Jonathan 197
Muñoz Seca, Pedro 19
Murcia 3, 4, 40, 42, 70, 90, 101, 176
La musa y el Fénix 136
music 5, 26, 32–3, 40, 43–4, 62, 69, 86, 90, 118, 147, 161

Nancy Theatre Festival *see* French theatre
Narros, Miguel 38, 41–2, 48, 50, 58, 61, 65–7, 112, 116–18, 176, 179
national theatre
   origin of concept in Spain, 20, 26 n. 20, 82
   administration and financing 21, 34, 41, 49, 53, 63–4, 68–9, 70, 113 n. 12, 133, 197–8
   see also individual theatres by name
nepotism and politicisation of cultural appointments 20 n. 7, 56 n. 78, 63–4, 74, 154, 167–8, 178–9, 199, 214–16,
New York 98, 188, 201 n. 21
Nieva, Francisco 46
Nieves de Conde, José Antonio 153
NO-DO 89
No hay burlas con el amor 64, 70, 73, 173
No hay burlas con Calderón 52
No son todos ruiseñores 62
La noche de San Juan 68–9
La noche toledana 35, 117
El nuevo mundo 35
Numancia 17

Osborne, John 39
Osuna, José 38, 89, 92
Oteyza, Blanca 196–7
Othello 107–8, 124, 130, 219
Ozores, Adriana 118

Palestine 93–8
Pallín, Yolanda 62, 69, 121
Parada de la Puente, Manuel 26, 86
Paredes, Marisa 43
Partido Popular 63, 67 n. 105, 98, 206, 210, 214

Partido Socialista Obrero Español 3, 46 n. 56, 49–50, 52–3, 56, 61 n. 87, 67, 98, 100–1, 122, 167–8, 170 n. 49, 172 n. 60, 177, 207, 210–11, 214, 217
Paso, Alfonso 35
Pasolini, Pier Paolo 72
Pasqual, Lluís 49, 216
Pastores de Belén 34
Pellicena, José Luis 47, 115, 130
Pemán, José María 50, 82, 89 n. 24, 102, 138
Pérez, Isabel 214
Pérez de la Fuente, Juan Carlos 72
Pérez de la Ossa, Huberto 37
Pérez Puig, Gustavo 191, 207
Pérez Sierra, Rafael 23, 46, 54, 57, 63–6, 68, 116–17, 121, 123, 125, 169, 171, 173–4, 190, 213
performance studies 2–15, 75–6, 103, 184, 192–3, 201
performance tradition 13–15, 31, 41, 47–8, 54–5, 62, 73–4, 99, 102–3, 105–7, 111–13, 116–17, 119–20, 125, 133, 169–71, 186–8, 202–3, 210, 213, 218–20
Peribáñez y el Comendador de Ocaña 23, 26–8, 66–7, 85, 88, 90, 113 n. 12, 128 n. 29, 138, 157
Perón, Eva 87
El perro del hortelano 34–5, 62, 64, 117, 168–75, 177–8, 181, 186, 188–97, 205, 219
Pesca Films 152
Pimenta, Helena 69, 121, 134, 183
El pintor de su deshonra 14, 68, 106–8, 121, 123–33, 192
Piñar, Blas 36
La Pipironda 90
Philip IV, King 25, 147–8, 168, 187
Plaza, José Carlos 64, 99
El pleito matrimonial del cuerpo y el alma 34
Por la puente, Juana 34
Porfiar hasta morir 36, 62
Portes, Francisco 117
Portillo, Blanca 68

Primer Acto 30, 39, 55
El príncipe constante 22, 62, 112
El príncipe encadenad see film adaptations, *La vida es sueño*
propaganda,
   and the *comedia* in contemporary Spain 18–20, 23, 36, 40, 46–7, 77–83, 87–8, 101–3, 217, 218
   and the *comedia* in the Golden Age 10–13, 40, 46, 87–8, 103, 140, 192, 217–19
   during the Franco regime 18–20, 23–4, 36, 40, 46–7, 82–3, 89, 103, 136–7, 140. 145, 217–18
La prudencia en la mujer 53
La prudente venganza 158
Pujol, Carlos 202
Pujol, Jordi 199–200, 204

Quevedo, Francisco de 35, 186
Querejeta, Arturo 126, 128, 130

Rabal, Francisco 28, 160, 162–3
radio 19, 101, 217
Rafter, Denis 64, 112
Rambal, Enrique 21, 27
Ramírez, José A. 101
Ramón, Carlos 169
rape 57–8, 64, 86, 92, 94, 142, 149, 151, 158, 160–61, 163–6, 219
reception theory 1–2, 6, 12, 14, 75–7, 87, 102, 218–20
Reixach, Domènech 204
Renoir, Jean 138
RESAD 46–8, 65, 70, 73, 112–13, 117, 120
Resines, Antonio 186
El retablo de las maravillas 81, 90
Rey, Fernando 139
Rey, Florián 146–8
El rey pasmado 168
Rico, Francisco 116
Rico, Paquita 147
Ridruejo, Dionisio 18
Rivas Cherif, Cipriano 20 n. 7, 21
Rivelles, Amparo 139, 141–2, 146
Rodríguez, Rafael 205–6

Rodríguez Gallardo, Isidro 123 n. 125, 214
Rodríguez Méndez, José María 39 n. 45, 53, 56 n. 78, 61 n. 87, 90
Román, Antonio 138–43, 158–9
Rossetti, Ana 93–5
Royal family in democratic Spain, 48, 67, 170, 174, 182
RSC *see* British theatre
Ruano de la Haza, José María 65
Rubio, José López 164
Rueda, Lope de 47, 48 n. 60
El rufián castrucho 158
Rufo, Eva 69
Ruíz, Raul 135
Ruíz Gallardón, Alberto 191
Ruiz Ramón, Francisco 4, 49
Russia 77–9, 90, 112–13, 141, 168 n. 52.

Sáenz de la Calzada, Luis 80–1
Sainetes 68
Sainz de la Peña, Vicente 92
Saiz, Jesús 148
Salvat, Ricard 41, 114, 199–200
Samarkanda Teatro 99
San Martín, Roberto 180, 184, 185 n. 77
Sánchez, Alicia 4 n. 4, 58
Sanchís Sinisterra, José 51
Santa Teresa de Ávila 143, 178
Saura, Carlos 160, 167
scenery and staging technology *see* theatre buildings and spaces
Schroeder, Juan Germán 113 n. 11
Sección Femenina 22, 32 n. 33, 33–5, 88–9
Second Republic 34, 78–9, 85, 89–90, 101
El secreto a voces 61
Sendino, Fernando 127
Sentido del deber 122
Shakespeare, William 1–2, 6, 23, 29–30, 38, 58–61, 65, 67, 75, 79, 96, 108, 118, 123, 133 n. 34, 168–9, 178–80, 185, 188, 193, 211 n. 27, 216, 218

Los siete infantes de Lara 38
Sillitoe, Alan 81 n. 7
Simó, Ramón 204
Sindicato Español Universitario 21, 35, 37, 82
Sindicato Nacional Español 143
Sirk, Douglas 160–1
Sociedad Estatal de Conmemoraciones Culturales 101
Solana, Javier 208
Spanish American theatre
  and Republican exiles 52, 111–12, 152
  tours by Spanish actors and acting companies 28, 114
  treated in context of peninsular Spain 31–2, 36, 64, 68, 107, 112
Spanish Civil War
  and the international community 18, 72, 81, 138
  Nationalist theatre 17–19, 82
  Republican exiles 46–7, 52, 111–12, 152
  Republican theatre 17, 19–20, 39, 76, 78–9, 81
Stefanelli, Simonetta 164
Strasberg, John 58
student drama 21–3, 27, 29, 31–2, 34–5, 37, 40–1, 70, 73, 82, 96, 98, 101
see also education
Suárez, Emma 171, 174
subsidies 21, 28–9, 31, 36, 48, 50, 59 n. 84, 62, 101, 137–8, 143–4, 168–9, 176, 209–10, 212, 216
Suevia Films 151–2

Tamayo, José 28–31, 35–7, 45, 48, 58, 88–90, 115, 146, 160, 213
Tamayo, Manuel 149
Teatres de la Generalitat de Valéncia 72, 206
Teatre Lliure 198
Teatre Nacional de Catalunya *see* Catalonia
Teatro (periodical) 30
Teatro de la Abadía 3 n. 3, 214

Teatro Albéniz 197
Teatro Alcázar 35
Teatro Al-Kasaba 93–8
Teatro de Arte de Marta Grau y Arturo Carbonell 21
Teatro de las Bellas Artes 45, 176
Teatro de Cámara Chejov 70–1
Teatro Cervantes, Alcalá de Henares 68
Teatro de la Comedia 65, 205–7
Teatro Corsario 61
Teatro Español 19–21, 24–9, 31, 34–8, 41–5, 47–8, 54, 62 n. 93, 67–8, 73, 84–9, 107–8, 113 n. 12, 114, 117, 190–1
Teatro Español de Cámara 32, 40, 61, 70–1, 113
Teatro Español Independiente 3, 37, 45–6, 50, 61, 65, 90, 112, 118, 121, 176
Teatro Español Universitario *see* student theatre
Teatro de Hoy 62
Teatro Lara 32, 51, 81 n. 7
Teatro María Guerrero, 20–1, 27–9, 31, 32 n. 33, 33, 35, 37–8, 47, 49 n. 64, 64, 73, 112, 117
Teatro Nacional de Barcelona *see* Catalonia
Teatro Pavón 70, 73, 126, 205–6
Teatro Principal (Zaragoza) 35
Teatro Reina Victoria 32
Teatro Rialto 72
Teatro de la Zarzuela 90
television
  collaboration with European networks 160, 164, 187
  Estudio 1 41, 47, 157–8, 178, 198 n. 17
  investment in cinema 158–60, 164, 169, 177, 187
  Teatro de siempre 41, 157–8
  TVE 43, 47, 62, 90, 107, 157–8, 160, 164, 168, 177, 187, 217
textual fidelity 5, 6, 20, 24–5, 44–5, 55, 79–80, 83, 85–6, 93–4, 102–3, 116, 125–6, 129, 145, 163–5, 171, 179–80, 192–7, 201

theatre buildings and spaces
   corrales 4, 30, 41, 114, 157–8, 208
   alternatives to traditional
      proscenium stage 68, 90, 92–4, 206–7
   scenery and staging technology 18–20, 24–6, 29–31, 35–6, 43–5, 54–5, 58, 68–9, 85–6, 88–9, 92–4, 116, 194–5, 201–3,
Theatre Workshop *see* British theatre
Los Títeres, Teatro Nacional de Juventudes 34
Torrente Ballester, Gonzalo 18, 153–4
Torres Naharro, Bartolomé de, 48
Tragicomedia de don Duardos 68, 124
Trancón, Eva 126
translation, plays in 6–7, 76–7, 93, 152, 187–8, 193–5, 198, 200
Trinder, Simon 195

Ugarte, Eduardo 79
Unamuno, Miguel de 107–8, 164
Unión de Centro Democrático 48, 53 n. 24
Urdiales, Fernando 61
Uruguay 36, 111–12

Vajda, Ladislao 146
Valle-Inclán, Ramón María del 38, 60–1, 72, 133 n. 34, 216, 219
Van Loo, Michel 99
Vargas Llosa, Mario 31–2
Vasco, Eduardo 62, 68–9, 106, 119–23, 125–34, 196, 204–6, 214–15
Vega Carpio, Lope de
   biographical treatments 35, 136, 175
   third centenary of death (1935) 34, 85
   fourth centenary of birth (1962) 33–7, 65, 89, 112
   house as museum 209
Velázquez, Diego 24–5, 143

La vengadora de las mujeres 51–2
La venganza de Tamar 64, 190
La verdad sospechosa 38, 171, 205
El vergonzoso en palacio 58–9, 126
La vida es sueño 21–2, 27, 29 n. 28, 38, 45, 48–9, 62, 65–6, 68, 72, 101 n. 42, 102, 113, 128 n. 29, 135, 152, 154–7, 167, 176, 187–8, 200–3, 207
La villana de Getafe 158, 219
El villano en su rincón 26, 34, 90
Villena, Luís Antonio de 116
La viuda celosa see film adaptations, *La viuda valenciana*
La viuda valenciana 32, 40, 72, 112, 152, 206, 213, 215
Viudes, Vicente 21
verse *see* actors and acting

Waddington, Andrucha 175
Wilder, Thornton 21
women
   in the *comedia* 11, 14, 23, 33–5, 52, 78, 86, 94, 108–9, 119, 123–4, 129, 172–3, 176, 179 n. 73, 190, 193
   in the democratic period 52, 92, 106, 121–4, 172–3, 177–8, 179 n. 73, 193
   on the stage and screen 80, 90, 92
   under Franco 23, 33–4, 86, 89, 122
   see also actors and acting, domestic violence, and rape

Xirgu, Margarita 80, 111–12, 182

Zalamea (town) 209
Zampanò teatro: 61–2, 65
La zapatera prodigiosa 36
Zorrilla, Francisco de Rojas 48 n. 60
Zorrilla, José 42, 135, 144–6, 176, 178, 180